D1507206

The Illicit Joyce
of Postmodernism

The Illicit Joyce
of Postmodernism

Reading against the Grain

KEVIN J. H. DETTMAR

The University of Wisconsin Press

The University of Wisconsin Press
114 North Murray Street
Madison, Wisconsin 53715

3 Henrietta Street
London WC2E 8LU, England

Printed in the United States of America

Library of Congress Cataloging-in-Publication Data

Dettmar, Kevin J. H., 1958–
    The illicit Joyce of postmodernism: reading against the grain /
Kevin J. H. Dettmar.
        292 pp.   cm.
        Includes bibliographical references and index.
        ISBN 0-299-15060-7 (cloth: alk. paper)   ISBN 0-299-15064-X (pbk.: alk. paper)
        1. Joyce, James, 1882–1941—Criticism and interpretation.
    2. Postmodernism (Literature) I. Title.
    PR6019.09Z5296   1996
823'.912—dc20   96-1194

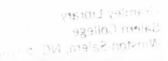

For my wife, Robyn, constant source of inspiration, strength, and encouragement; and for our children, Emily Susan, Audrey Elizabeth, Esther Katherine, and Colin Adam, whose love bears all things, believes all things, hopes all things, endures all things. Few other scholars can count so many tangible blessings on the fingers of one hand.

The work of commentary, once it is separated from any ideology of totality, consists precisely in *manhandling* the text, *interrupting* it.

—Roland Barthes, *S/Z*

My ideal, when I write about an author, would be to write nothing that could cause him sadness, or if he is dead, that might make him weep in his grave. Think of the author you are writing about. Think of him so hard that he can no longer be an object, and equally so that you cannot identify with him. Avoid the double shame of the scholar and the familiar. Give back to an author a little of the joy, the energy, the life of love and politics that he knew how to give and invent.

—Gilles Deleuze, *Dialogues*

The works of Joyce, Duchamp, and Satie in different ways have resisted the march of understanding and so are as fresh now as when they were first made. I don't know how many books on *Hamlet* there are that set out to elucidate its mysteries, but there is beginning to be a very large number in relation to the work of Joyce and the work of Duchamp. I prefer the ones that pay attention but stop short of explanation.

—John Cage, "James Joyce, Marcel Duchamp, Erik Satie: An Alphabet"

Contents

Preface

In his provocative essay "Against *Ulysses*," Leo Bersani muses on what a naive reading of *Ulysses* might be like.[1] Well, it's been twenty years now, but I still remember mine: something of that first experience is, I suppose, what I'd like *The Illicit Joyce of Postmodernism* to capture, or recapture. I first read *Ulysses*—my first encounter with any of Joyce's writing—during the summer between my sophomore and junior years of high school; I was a tender fifteen at the time. I had no idea that the novel was based on correspondences with the *Odyssey*; indeed, I did not know, even after I'd finished it, that the book recounted one day in the life of Stephen Dedalus and Leopold Bloom. I read the book because I was gaining a reputation amongst my teachers as something of a "literary critic," interested in modernist literature (I'd done a term paper on *The Waste Land*); *Ulysses* was suggested, by some perverse soul, as a logical next step. And that first reading gave me, like Eliot, "all the surprise, delight, and terror" I required.

I couldn't make heads or tails of the narrative, but I was bowled over by the style—the styles. The abundant, joyous, excessive, rambunctious, irresponsible carnival of styles. And I decided that one day, I'd have to read it again—with help.

Fortunately for me, that help came in the person of Sandra Gilbert, who taught *Ulysses* as part of an undergraduate course on the modern British novel at UC Davis. Professor Gilbert's approach to the text was, if I remember it correctly, to emphasize the intuitive rather than the allusive; I remember, for instance, her likening the Sirens of chapter 11 to the two women who ran the bakery near her home in Berkeley. After the course was finished, I still didn't know precisely what the "ineluctable modality of the visible" was, but I did feel that *Ulysses* was a book I could handle.

My earliest attempts to write about Joyce—again, if my memories are clear, and not simply dictated by the desire to tell a good story—were essentially attempts to figure out what Hugh Kenner and Richard Ellmann would have written about passages that they had, for some inexplicable reason, passed over. But then a funny thing began to happen. In attempting to out-Kenner Kenner, to out-Ellmann Ellmann, I began to grow weary of the conclusions to which I was, by the force of my (unarticulated) critical premises, driven. In my analyses, Joyce's texts came to look as ordered and regular as the "clipped privet" Thomas Kinsella writes about in "Nightwalker"; and my essays had all the excitement and unpredictability of a Danielle Steel novel. My experience of Joyce's texts, though—what first piqued my interest, and what after twenty years has kept me coming back—was their luxuriant wildness. It was this wildness, I decided, that I should like to celebrate.

The party favors for that celebration I found in postmodernism. Not postmodern theory—though that has often been helpful—but primarily postmodern fiction. Again, though, you will not find many postmodern novels cited in the analysis that follows; for postmodern fiction—to which I was, effectively, introduced in graduate school—has shaped the way that I read Joyce in a global, rather than any specific, way. Returning to Joyce by way of Beckett's trilogy, for instance, caused a critical paradigm shift for me—without any conscious effort on my part, I began some time ago to read Joyce through postmodern glasses. What I saw thrilled me: not the staid, imperturbable, omniscient, omnipotent Joyce of modernist criticism, but rather a playful, rambunctious, anarchic—and considerably less godlike—writer. This is the Joyce I will hope to highlight in the pages that follow: the illicit Joyce of postmodernism.

This book, like *Ulysses,* works (in Joyce's description) "by different means in different places." There's no single sustained argument, no single sustained mode of attack, but various incursions. In other words, the approach here is postmodern, as I attempt to define it in chapter 2: grounded in local rather than global strategies, and less interested in philosophical consistency than in discovery and delight. I hope that it will provide you with both in good supply.

Acknowledgments

Surely the most enjoyable aspect of finishing a long-term project like this one is the opportunity now to thank those friends and colleagues without whose help it could not have been done. My heartfelt thanks go out to:

Cal Bedient, whose passion for intelligent and sensitive criticism has set a standard of critical and artistic integrity that continues to inspire me;

Jennifer Wicke, the most generous Joycean of them all, for her unstinting help and her rich, rich laugh;

Michael Seidel, myriadminded man, who gives and gives and doesn't count the cost;

Bill and Esther Richey, for hospitality, love, encouragement, and patient indulgence;

Michael North, mentor and now friend, the most knowledgeable student of modernism I know;

Tom Burkdall, whose concern and gentle criticism often helped get my writing back on track;

John Alberti, for helping me keep it all in perspective;

Steve Watt, for believing in me when I needed it;

Pat McGee, for liking what I'd done and wanting it to be better;

Eloise Knowlton, for teaching me how politely to disagree with one's elders and smarters and betters;

Derek Attridge, for discovering the direction in which Joyce criticism must go, and then leading the way;

Jack Kolb, erse solid man;

Chris Mott, for teaching me about postmodernism while humiliating me on the racquetball court;

Susan Friedman, for support above and beyond the call;

Michael Andrew Jackson, far more challenging and demanding than any high-school English teacher had a right to be;

my anonymous press readers, without whose keen criticism this
   would all make less sense;

Kerri Hamberg and Ross Wagner, for their eagle eyes and diligent
   good cheer;

Susan Tarcov, gracious and intelligent editor;

Allen Fitchen, for his infectious belief in and unwavering commitment to this project;

and my students over the past ten years at UCLA, Loyola Mary-
   mount University, and Clemson University, whose fresh and un-
   embarrassed responses to Joyce's texts acted as a corrective to
   my own conditioned, jaded, "scholarly" readings.

My most considerable debt—indeed, one I am literally incapable of re-
paying—is reflected in the dedication.

Portions of chapters 3 and 6 have previously been published. I am grate-
ful to Western Illinois University for permission to reprint " 'From In-
terpretation to 'Intrepidation': Joyce's 'The Sisters' as a Precursor of the
Postmodern Mystery," which appeared in *The Cunning Craft: Original
Essays on Detective Fiction and Literary Theory*, ed. Ronald G. Walker and
June M. Anderson, University of Western Illinois Essays in Literature
Book Series, 1990; and to the University of Michigan Press for permis-
sion to reprint "'Working in Accord with Obstacles': A Postmodern
Perspective on Joyce's 'Mythical Method,'" from *Rereading the New: A
Backward Glance at Modernism*, University of Michigan Press, 1992.

Abbreviations

The following abbreviations for frequently cited texts have been employed in parenthetical notes in the reading text. When reproducing passages from *Ulysses* quoted in other works, I have when necessary silently amended the text and citation to agree with the 1986 Random House edition. Full bibliographic information can be found in the bibliography.

CJJ	Arthur Power, *Conversations with James Joyce*
CW	James Joyce, *Critical Writings*
D	James Joyce, *Dubliners*
Deming	Robert H. Deming, ed., *James Joyce: The Critical Heritage*
DI	Mikhail Bakhtin, *The Dialogic Imagination*
Eliot	T. S. Eliot, *Selected Prose of T. S. Eliot*
FW	James Joyce, *Finnegans Wake*
Hassan	Ihab Hassan, *The Postmodern Turn*
IMT	Roland Barthes, *Image, Music, Text*
JG	Jean-François Lyotard and Jean-Loup Thébaud, *Just Gaming*
JJ	Richard Ellmann, *James Joyce*
L	James Joyce, *Letters*
Lawrence	Karen Lawrence, *The Odyssey of Style in "Ulysses"*
P	James Joyce, *A Portrait of the Artist as a Young Man*
PC	Jean-François Lyotard, *The Postmodern Condition*
PDP	Mikhail Bakhtin, *Problems of Dostoevsky's Poetics*
PT	Roland Barthes, *The Pleasure of the Text*
R	Mikhail Bakhtin, *Rabelais and His World*
RL	Roland Barthes, *The Rustle of Language*
SH	James Joyce, *Stephen Hero*
S/Z	Roland Barthes, *S/Z*
U	James Joyce, *Ulysses*
WDZ	Roland Barthes, *Writing Degree Zero*

The Illicit Joyce
of Postmodernism

1

The Illicit Joyce of Postmodernism

Every language and every well-knit technical sublanguage incorporates certain points of view and certain patterned resistances to widely divergent points of view. This is especially so if language is not surveyed as a planetary phenomenon, but is as usual taken for granted, and the local, parochial species of it used by the individual thinker is taken to be its full sum.

—Benjamin Lee Whorf

Almost as soon as I began to study philosophy, I was impressed by the way in which philosophical problems appeared, disappeared, or changed shape, as a result of new assumptions or vocabularies.

—Richard Rorty

My own hunch . . . is that in any field of study which, like history, has not yet become disciplinized to the point of constructing a formal terminological system for describing its objects, in the way that physics and chemistry have, it is the types of figurative discourse that dictate the fundamental forms of the data to be studied. This means that the *shape* of the *relationships* which will appear to be inherent in the objects inhabiting the field will in reality have been imposed on the field by the investigator in the very *act of identifying and describing* the objects that he finds there.

—Hayden White

The threshold between Classicism and modernity (though the terms themselves have no importance—let us say our prehistory and what is still contemporary) had been definitively crossed when words ceased to intersect with representations and to provide a spontaneous grid for the knowledge of things.

—Michel Foucault

At a crucial moment—arguably *the* crucial moment—of her story, Miss Eveline Hill, standing "among the swaying crowd in the station at the North Wall," stops to ask her God for direction: "She felt her cheek pale and cold and, out of a maze of distress, she prayed to God to direct her, to show her what was her duty" (*D* 40). As I will explore in more detail

3

in chapter 4, the subtly nuanced rhetoric of the *Dubliners* characters—
the linguistic formulations and narrative schemata through which they
understand, and consequently tell, their stories—is of the utmost importance in understanding these tales, and to date proper attention has
by and large not been paid to it. The most striking rhetorical feature of
Eveline's prayer, as it is reported in the narrative, is its repetition—repetition with a difference. Eveline first asks God to direct her, a reasonable gesture under the circumstances. And to ask God for direction is
to ask a relatively open-ended question; He might respond in any number of ways. In the present situation, He might instruct Eveline to go off
with Frank, or to stay behind and care for her family; He might even, if
Hugh Kenner's research is correct, warn Eveline that ships for Buenos
Aires don't leave from the North Wall.[1] But Eveline doesn't, hasn't the
courage, to ask this open question; she quickly revises it, under the guise
of restating it, and asks God "to show her what was her duty."

Duty. In the context of "Eveline," this is anything but an open question; asking about duty prematurely answers the question before it is
fully articulated. Certain kinds of answers immediately become more,
certain others considerably less, likely. What are the odds, for instance,
that Eveline will learn it is her duty to quit her job, abandon her family,
run off with a young, exciting sailor, and begin living life for herself?
The language in which she has framed her question presupposes an entire moral system; *duty* ties her into the patriarchal language of Roman
Catholicism, as exemplified (in its extreme form) by Sister Mary Margaret Alacoque, a figure of some interest to Eveline, who at the age of
four took a vow of chastity (and, some time later, carved the name
"Jesus" on her breast with a penknife [*D* 470]).[2] After restating her
question in the form that she does, Eveline is no longer an autonomous
agent. The duty of this young woman—woman of the house, oldest
daughter of her widower father—as defined in the lexicon of early-
twentieth-century lower-middle-class Irish Catholicism, can only be to
her family. One has no duty to a lover. And here the plot gets even
thicker, for Eveline asks God about her duty, we begin to suspect, precisely because she wishes to stay: as for so many other characters in
Dubliners, the banality of the known is for Eveline far preferable to the
terror of the unknown.[3]

The moral of Eveline's story—one of them, at any rate—is that we
must be very careful what questions we ask; questions to some degree
always constrain their answers. One proverbial version of this insight—
one applicable to Eveline's situation—is the saying, "Be careful what
you pray for: you might get it." Let's for the moment read Eveline's

story as an allegory of the critical process. For we too, as readers, as critics, to some extent presuppose certain kinds of answers when we ask certain kinds of interpretive questions. Asking, for instance, about the development of Joyce's writing over the course of his career presumes progression; it assumes both continuity and artistic growth between one text and the next, and would tend to suggest that his crowning achievement is his ultimate text, *Finnegans Wake*—a view that I myself cannot accept. It would also suggest that *A Portrait of the Artist as a Young Man* (1916) is a more sophisticated, more challenging, unsettling text than *Dubliners* (1914); this conclusion is also, I will argue in chapter 5, problematic. Asking about the meaning of Father Flynn's chalice, or Stephen's riddle, or Bloom's potato; or who the man in the Macintosh is, or why Stephen picks his nose, or why Molly Bloom menstruates[4]— all these questions assume a specifically symbolic (more specifically, I would say *modernist*) relationship between the text's signifiers and signifieds in the real world, a relationship which frequently does not obtain in postmodern fiction and which may, if not interrogated, prematurely foreclose our reading of Joyce's texts, as well.[5] There are nearly as many different Joyces as there are Joyce readers; what I've attempted to do here is to describe as best I can a Joyce I'll call the postmodern Joyce, the collective creation of a group of readers who, for better or worse, I'll describe as postmodern in their approach to texts.

In the introduction to *Rereading the New,* I maintained that modernism was not just a way of writing, but equally a way of reading.[6] I'd like here to add a further refinement to that claim: that modernism is not just a style of creative writing, but equally a style of critical writing, even critical thinking. Modernism comprises a sort of specialist, coterie language; and language, as William S. Burroughs (and, more recently, Laurie Anderson) have been at pains to remind us, is a virus, always contaminating the ostensible object of its descriptions, blithely replicating itself without the cooperation or even the knowledge of its host and sustainer.[7] In the nineteen teens and twenties, modernism was a new way to talk about aesthetic phenomena—new in both its vocabulary and its concepts; some of those concepts—the ideological "baggage" that comes along with modernist discourse—are discussed in chapter 6. Well, one measure of modernism's ascendancy in the academy is precisely that once it had been forged as a discourse in the arts, critics learned to speak modernism very quickly—in part through the examples of "crossover" artist/critics like Ezra Pound, T. S. Eliot, and Virginia Woolf. Donald Marshall has written about this mimetic desire on the part of the critics of modernism: "The fascination must be a fascination of style:

how could anyone learn to talk this way? The glimpsed prospect, the promised land is the possibility that . . . I too may learn to talk like this."[8] Having learned to talk in a certain way about modernism, however, we may be inclined to ask only certain narrowly circumscribed questions about it, and therefore to come to certain fairly predictable conclusions about it.

What is the way out of this impasse? Benjamin Lee Whorf suggests that the only way out would be a kind of linguistic relativity: the difference in perspective that speaking another, a minority, language would provide. "No individual is free," Whorf writes, "to describe nature with absolute impartiality but is constrained to certain modes of interpretation even while he thinks himself most free. The person most nearly free in such respects would be a linguist familiar with very many widely different linguistic systems. As yet no linguist is in any such position."[9] If the official language of Joyce criticism is, has always been, modernism, then postmodernism provides one alternative avenue of inquiry, one somewhat different language in which we might attempt to (re)articulate Joyce's texts. We need, perhaps, more bilingual critics of Joyce: those, like Fritz Senn, who speak German and English, but also those who speak both modernism and postmodernism, both Marxism and feminism, both New Criticism and new historicism. The results will inevitably be a different Joyce.

One might reasonably ask, Why change? Why do we need to construct another Joyce, after all? One reason, I believe, is that when we speak of Joyce today we speak not just of a writer, nor even of his texts, but rather of an entire discourse that has grown up around—and barred our access to—Joyce's texts. Ulysses, for instance, has quickly become the most densely explicated and minutely analyzed text in all of English literature—and largely because Joyce wanted it that way.[10] Joyce scholarship, like any discourse that centers on a "great man," is profoundly conservative, tending to tame the radically subversive spirit of Joyce's style(s), and thereby to recoup Ulysses (and sometimes even Finnegans Wake) for a modernist canon; but as Joyce and his milieu recede further into the past, the Joyce the academy has built sounds less and less satisfactory. As Derek Attridge and Daniel Ferrer put it, "one would have thought that the need to make Joyce readable and reputable had long since passed, and that the time had come to take the full measure of his literary revolution—to produce Joyce's texts in ways designed to challenge rather than comfort, to antagonize instead of assimilate."[11]

Another, no less important, reason for attempting to reconfigure our discourse about Joyce is the intellectual activity that Richard Rorty calls "keeping the conversation going." This, he writes, is the goal of "edifying philosophy"; it is equally, I would submit, the goal of edifying criticism: "The point of edifying philosophy is to keep the conversation going rather than to find objective truth. Such truth, in the view I am advocating, is the normal result of normal discourse. Edifying philosophy is not only abnormal but reactive, having sense only as a protest against attempts to close off conversation by proposals for universal commensuration through the hypostatization of some privileged set of descriptions. The danger which edifying discourse tries to avert is that some given vocabulary, some way in which people might come to think of themselves, will deceive them into thinking that from now on all discourse could be, or should be, normal discourse."[12] In a review of Albert Wachtel's *The Cracked Lookingglass: James Joyce and the Nightmare of History*, I took issue with Wachtel on precisely this point: the relative importance of what Thomas Kuhn calls normal discourse and what Rorty calls "abnormal discourse." Here's what I said in that review:

> He [Wachtel] takes the opportunity in a short epilogue . . . to upbraid an unnamed Venice symposiast who justified new theoretical approaches to Joyce on the grounds that they "keep the conversation going." "Having more things to say," Wachtel rejoins, "is less important than finding true things to say." I suppose, after reading *The Cracked Lookingglass*, that if I must choose, I will side with the anonymous Venetian; criticism—especially of Joyce, especially at this late date when such a prodigious body of careful scholarly work already exists—must do more than simply string together "true things to say." Though Wachtel dismisses Stephen [Dedalus]'s advocacy of the Beautiful out of hand, perhaps we ought not. Beauty without Truth is mere aestheticism, as Wachtel rightly maintains; but Truth without Beauty is equally unsatisfactory in the long run.[13]

It's important to point out, I think, that this shift in interpretive paradigm is not, cannot be made in the hope of reaching a "better," more judicious, more veridical assessment of Joyce's texts. If Kuhn's work has taught literary critics anything—and I think it has—it's that the structure of literary-critical revolutions is more capricious than progressive; new does not necessarily mean NEW & IMPROVED. Stephen Daedalus, in *Stephen Hero*, has not yet grasped this idea, and hence makes naively hyperbolic claims for the genius of his own generation: "The modern spirit is vivisective. Vivisection itself is the most modern process one can conceive. The ancient spirit accepted phenomena with a bad grace. The ancient method investigated law with the lantern of justice, morality with the lantern of revelation, art with the lantern of tradition. But all these lanterns have magical properties: they transform and disfigure. The modern method examines its territory by the light of day" (*SH* 190). Stephen here contends that earlier paradigms imposed distortion, while the modern does not: it makes its inquiries "by the light of day," without prejudice, value-free. In this, of course, he's wrong, and Joyce knows it; Stephen himself, in the passage quoted, is still working in clearly metaphorical rather than "literal" language, and his new "vivisective," "modern" method is as much in thrall to a cultural mythology as were those older forms of inquiry that he mocks. Joyce, I believe, early on understood this linguistic relativity principle; the eighteen prisms that make up *Ulysses* are but the most sensational result.

Jean-François Lyotard, in his most famous formulation, characterizes postmodernism as an incredulity toward metanarratives; by metanarratives he means those big stories that societies and cultures tell themselves in order to make sense of their world (*PC* xxiv). *Ulysses* is, of course, a narrative (or perhaps already a metanarrative, built as it is around Homer's *Odyssey*); around that central narrative have been built metanarratives, such as Stuart Gilbert's *James Joyce's "Ulysses,"* or even critical narratives of Joyce's own, like the "mythical method" (for modernist texts very often come with their own instructions). A postmodern reading of *Ulysses*, then, might begin by looking at the incommensurability of these two narratives—approaching *Ulysses* with a skepticism regarding those critical narratives which have grown up around it, the most persistent and powerful of which were in fact authored by the modernists themselves in order to contain and promote their ungainly products. The postmodern moment of those texts is the point at which we see these narratives of containment breaking down, failing to account for the wildness we feel in our reading experience. In this sense, postmodern criticism's motivation is similar to that Richard Eder attributes to deconstruction: "It [deconstruction] sounds like fun, and originally, in France, it was a playful-serious way of turning meanings on their head and seeing what fell out of the pockets."[14]

Let me try yet one more metaphor before moving on. In his conversations with Claire Parnet, Gilles Deleuze uses the image of the kaleidoscope to talk about the supple, protean quality of the mind of his late friend and colleague, Félix Guattari: "Few people have given me the impression as he did of moving at each moment; not changing, but moving in his entirety with the aid of a gesture he was making, of a word which he was saying, of a vocal sound, like a kaleidoscope forming a new combination every time."[15] Now let me shift the ground of the metaphor, as Dana Polan has done in his translator's introduction to Deleuze and Guattari's Kafka book: "It is as if the book before us is only one version, one twist of the kaleidoscope (to use an image from Guattari), of an infinitely permutating, connecting process in which the single event—here, the life of Kafka—is never more than one step in a larger process."[16] The same is true of my treatment of Joyce: the same elements, the same texts or bits of tissue paper, are here put into a different constellation; some elements move toward the center, some drift toward the margins. All the same shimmering, brilliant particolored bits are still there, but they've been thrown into a different constellation; both centripetal and centrifugal forces are at work, and as a result some stylistic features of Joyce's texts are brought toward the center and take on a heightened significance, while others are pushed toward the periphery. Taking the logic of Deleuze's metaphor seriously, one certainly can't argue that any one constellation is correct and others incorrect; but some will be more pleasing, more *interesting* (to use the criterion of John Cage's late texts) than some others, and maybe that's our only measure of excellence in postmodern critical writing.

I should say a brief word about the rather selective nature of the readings to be presented. I discuss only half of the *Dubliners* stories in any detail, dip in and out of *A Portrait* at whim, and ignore entire episodes of *Ulysses*; and as for *Finnegans Wake*, you'll have to read the brief afterword to appreciate just how little attention I've paid to Joyce's most widely acknowledged postmodern text; in some chapters, I have spent as much time reading Joyce criticism as I have reading Joyce "proper" (my argument, in part, being that we can't any longer separate the two). I hope to have demonstrated a number of pervasive patterns in Joyce's texts, and to have suggested, and outlined, a way of reading them; I certainly have not exhausted it.

The Illicit Joyce of Postmodernism positions itself within both Joyce criticism and the ongoing debate over modernism and postmodernism by looking closely at three of Joyce's four major prose texts, tracing briefly their critical histories, exploring the blindnesses and insights of the modernist analyses, and articulating a postmodern reading of two of them—*Dubliners* and *Ulysses*. *A Portrait of the Artist* I treat more skeptically, for I am convinced that it really cannot be fruitfully discussed in terms of its postmodernism in the way *Dubliners* and *Ulysses* can. The afterword on *Finnegans Wake* argues that, in spite of its obvious postmodern stylistic features—indeed, *because* of the explicitness and insistence of its textual strategies—the *Wake* is in fact less daring in its procedures than is its predecessor, *Ulysses*.

Chapter 2 steps back from the literary-critical paradigm I've suggested in this first chapter and derives a working definition of post-modernism, particularly as the description of a stylistics, using primarily the work of Mikhail Bakhtin, Jean-François Lyotard, and Roland Barthes, as well as the synthetic work of Ihab Hassan. Postmodern stylistics, I argue, values textual play over high artistic purpose, respects mystery over the writer's desire for mastery, and renounces global narrative structures in favor of small, local, often capricious textual strategies, celebrating the ineluctably heterogeneous, participatory, and excessive character of all texts. Freeing the term "postmodernism" from notions of temporality and literary history, as these theorists try to do, helps remove some of the barriers to a reading of Joyce that would reveal his untimely postmodernity.

Chapter 3, the first in which I look closely at Joyce's fiction, is devoted to an extended reading of Joyce's first published text, "The Sisters," in which I tease out what I believe to be Joyce's fundamental attitude toward literary interpretation—what he, in *Finnegans Wake,* calls "intrepidation"—a style of analysis which is both "intrepid" and filled with "trepidation" in the presence of its object. Playing on the conventions of the classical detective story, Joyce's "mystery" in fact solves few, if any, of the troubling questions it raises about the nature of perception and our yearning for narrative closure, in life as in art. Chapter 4 continues the examination of *Dubliners*—in my opinion the Joycean text least well served by the imposition of a modernist paradigm. Looking at the critical history of *Dubliners,* as well as reexamining some of the textual cruxes discussed time and again by critics (such as the baffling endings of many of the stories, or the problematic moment of "epiphany"), I read the *Dubliners* stories in a spirit counter to that of the modernist analyses—emphasizing their incompletion, their dogged resistance to interpretation, and the insidious strategies by which they implicate the reader in their text of paralysis.

My fifth chapter examines Joyce's "Stephen Dedalus" texts—the short essay "A Portrait of the Artist," the draft novel *Stephen Hero,* the modernist masterpiece *A Portrait of the Artist as a Young Man,* and the first three episodes of *Ulysses.* I believe *A Portrait* to be the Joycean text that fares least well in a postmodern age. Because the novel is the spiritual autobiography of a would-be Byronic artist/hero, and Joyce doggedly adheres to the tenets of an imitative stylistics, the subject and subject matter are inherently serious and self-important, in a way that postmodernism does not allow itself to be. There are signs, especially if we consider *Stephen Hero* in conjunction with its later incarnation *A Portrait* and the first three chapters of *Ulysses,* that Joyce was aware of Stephen's limitations and tried to some extent to distance himself from them; but Joyce's irony was too little, too late.

My two chapters on *Ulysses* return to some of those features of the novel that have most often been discussed in the criticism, most notably the notion of "expressive form" and Joyce's Homeric framework—what Eliot famously called his "mythical method"—and argue that while the novel is obviously one of the pillars of Anglo-American literary modernism, its postmodernism is at the same time busting out all over. The willful narrative consistently overflows its ostensible mythic framework; the language is increasingly ludic as the narrative progresses; the rapid shifts in style and language, in fact, seem almost the stylistic correlative of the Irish wake, which Joyce was to make the "objective correlative" of his last novel. I argue that Joyce's use of Homer, rather than the modernist structuring device that Eliot argued, was primarily a means of setting himself a new structural puzzle to solve—that Joyce's "imagination" was stymied otherwise. Like the postmodern American composer John Cage, who attempts to "work in accord with obstacles," Joyce was happiest and most productive when some compositional "problem" was plaguing him. *Ulysses* is certainly a modernist classic; but in its playful unwillingness to take itself or its modernist devices too seriously, it is at the same time pregnant with a nascent postmodernism. And finally, I close with an afterword, "On Ignoring *Finnegans Wake*," in which I'll quickly explain why I think you should stop wasting your time on that nightmare production and get back to *Dubliners* and *Ulysses*.

Richard Ellmann opens his monumental Joyce biography with the assertion that "We are still learning to be James Joyce's contemporaries, to understand our interpreter" (*JJ* 3). For a critic like Ellmann, the ne plus ultra of literary criticism would be to replicate within oneself the mind of Joyce, or as one of his titles has it the consciousness of Joyce; Joyce's characteristic posture, on the other hand, was to remain apart, to wage guerrilla war, both on those things that he hated and on those he loved. Surely the time has come for his critics to do the same.

2

Theorizing Postmodern Stylistics

"The important thing is not what we write, but how we write, and in my opinion the modern writer must be an adventurer above all, willing to take every risk, and be prepared to founder in his effort if need be. In other words, we must write dangerously."

—James Joyce

Postmodernism is surely one of the most contested of all categories in current literary and cultural studies; in *The Signs of Our Time*, Jack Solomon nominated the term for "the fastest-rising yet least well-defined semiotic adjective of the 1980s."[1] Indeed, it has proven more potent an irritant to the literary establishment than even the term *modernism* did for an earlier generation.[2] Even its most ardent apologists (like Ihab Hassan and Jean-François Lyotard) feel compelled to apologize for it; Lyotard, for instance, concedes that " 'postmodern' is probably a very bad term, because it conveys the idea of a historical 'periodization.' "[3] But it does, potentially, serve to describe the motive spirit behind an enormously wide range of phenomena; for as Hassan points out, we now speak (more or less comfortably) of postmodern film, theater, dance, music, art, architecture, literature and literary criticism, philosophy, theology, psychoanalysis, historiography, cybernetics, and cultural lifestyles. More recently Thomas Docherty, focusing on the academic disciplines, has written that postmodernism "leaves its traces in every cultural discipline from architecture to zoology, taking in on the way biology, forestry, geography, history, law, literature and the arts in general, medicine, politics, philosophy, sexuality, and so on."[4]

Polemics about the existence or nonexistence of postmodernism have been raging for something over two decades now, and show no signs of dying down; I have no desire to enter into that debate here myself. It will suffice for my purposes simply to assume that something like post-

12

modernism does indeed exist *as a stylistic feature* of some number of literary texts; I will take it as my task to elucidate wherein that postmodernism might reside chez Joyce. I will therefore neither rehearse nor enter into the numerous and lively debates over the idea of postmodernism (most notably, in the case of Lyotard's version of postmodernism, his triangular debate with Jürgen Habermas and Richard Rorty), many of which are ongoing; neither will I be concerned with those characteristics of postmodernism that might be called its "philosophical" traits—for instance Brian McHale's concept of a modernist "epistemological dominant" and postmodern "ontological dominant"[5]—but solely with the stylistics of postmodernism, as it manifests itself in literary texts. In this chapter I will attempt to discover just what a postmodern stylistics—what Roland Barthes calls an "unquantifiable germ" (*RL* 73)—looks like when it "infects" literary texts; throughout the remainder of the book I will look for the postmodern spirit when it rears its unruly head unpredictably throughout Joyce's oeuvre.

In order to adumbrate a postmodern stylistics, we must begin with either a canon of postmodern writing or a definition of postmodern stylistics: either a well-defined object of study or a clearly articulated paradigm of postmodern writing. Thus critics who seek to discuss postmodernism in literature typically employ one of two different approaches. The one most commonly used (witness influential recent books by McHale and Linda Hutcheon, for example) is what we might call an "inductive" approach: texts that are taken to be postmodern are analyzed, and the rules of their construction teased out by the critic; the commonalities between these texts then add up to a de facto description of postmodern stylistics. McHale's *Postmodernist Fiction* is perhaps the clearest example of this approach;[6] his book is an exhaustive catalogue of postmodernist stylistic devices. But *Postmodernist Fiction* also, I think, points up quite clearly the limitations of this approach; for while McHale's scope and reading are prodigious, his writing often seems more taxonomic than critical—an inventory, rather than a rigorous analysis, of what he considers "postmodernist fiction."

If we call McHale's method "inductive"—asking, as it does, what stylistic features a preestablished canon of texts has in common—the alternative method should then be called "deductive," seeking to discover which texts might conform in some measure to a preestablished description or definition of "the postmodern." Beginning with a theory or description of a generalized impulse called "postmodernism," the deductive critic interrogates various texts in order to discover their philosophical and stylistic alliances.

I find this second method—the deductive—to be, for my purposes, the more suggestive of the two. Of course, I'm biased; the author whose texts I want to discuss is not usually considered a postmodern writer. McHale's *Postmodern Fiction* treats the Joyce of *Dubliners, A Portrait,* and *Ulysses* as strictly a modernist precursor of postmodern writing; *Finnegans Wake* is the only Joyce text to pass his litmus test for postmodernity.[7] Likewise, Joyce is present in Hutcheon's *Poetics of Postmodernism* merely as a modernist reference point; she declares him, at one point, one of "the great modernists, not postmodernists."[8] And in her sequel, *The Politics of Postmodernism,* Joyce doesn't even make the index. The most serious limitation of the inductive method, then, is that in deploying it one would never question the workings of a text were it not beforehand considered a postmodern text; no one would consider, for instance, looking at the workings of *Ulysses,* never mind *Dubliners,* in order to learn something about the will to postmodernism in general, or Joyce's will to postmodernism more particularly. The inductive method is certainly the more conservative of the two as concerns the shape of the literary canon; it includes no mechanism by which the chronological boundaries of "the postmodern" can be opened up, for by starting out with texts defined before the fact as postmodern, the critic can do no more than confirm and catalog the hallmarks of their presumptive postmodernity. Not coincidentally, then, McHale's and Hutcheon's versions of postmodernism are to a great extent historically bounded; postmodernism is seen in their texts to be as much a literary-historical category as a philosophical, stylistic, or methodological one.

The deductive method, on the other hand, starting with rather different assumptions, produces noticeably different results. It too is unavoidably the victim of critical bias: for while the range of texts it may interrogate is in theory unbounded, its definition of postmodernism cannot be—one of the unknowns in this equation must be fixed before a solution can be attempted. The inductive method makes assumptions about a group of texts, hoping by examining them to learn more about the nature of postmodernism; the deductive critic, on the other hand, assumes that she knows what postmodernism is—declares, in effect, that "I know it when I see it"—and sets out to search texts where she suspects the postmodern might be hiding. The inherent limitation in this deductive approach, obviously, is that while discovering postmodernism in unexpected places, it is unlikely to turn up anything new about the nature of postmodern stylistics itself.

The results produced by this deductive method can therefore only be as good as the theoretical base from which it starts (just as the results of the inductive method are limited by the postmodern syllabus that's employed); my study of Joyce's postmodernism rests on a description of postmodern stylistics culled primarily from the writing of Roland Barthes, Mikhail Bakhtin, and Jean-François Lyotard, with grace notes supplied by Ihab Hassan and Julia Kristeva. My choice of "theorists" is, of necessity, to some extent idiosyncratic and personal; the criterion for their selection, besides the obvious importance of their ideas for contemporary narrative theory, is quite simply that I believe that together they provide a compelling and *productive* description (if not a definition) of postmodern stylistics: one that provides avenues for new research, allows for exciting new discoveries in apparently stodgy old—or aging—texts. One thing that these writers have in common is that their work has been productive of new research and new knowledge; the ideas of these theorists have "made something happen" in research in the human sciences in general, and in literary studies in particular. I believe that when read together, and against one another, their meditations on postmodern stylistics provide a solid basis for an investigation of Joyce's illicit postmodernity. Most readers will notice that a few important names are missing from my survey—most noticeably, I suppose, those of Fredric Jameson and Jean Baudrillard. As important as both have been to recent discussions of postmodernism, I do not find in their work anything like a coherent description of postmodern stylistics; indeed, when reading Jameson's work, I sometimes wonder whether we're looking at the same Andy Warhol, listening to the same John Cage. Which suggests one further point upon which Barthes, Bakhtin, and Lyotard, Hassan and Kristeva (and, for that matter, Baudrillard) agree: they're all shameless promoters of postmodernism.

In the discussions of these theorists that follow, I will tease out their stylistics of postmodernism—the stylistic features that each identifies with the larger impulse of postmodernism. At the close of the chapter, I will attempt to do some synthesizing, or at least some *bricolage*—constructing, out of more or less disparate materials, a working description of the postmodern impulse in literary stylistics. In the chapters that follow, I will use that paradigm to read Joyce's prose texts—pursuing a somewhat perverse examination of those modernist texts through postmodern glosses.

Roland Barthes

Of the critics I will look at here in some detail, Roland Barthes was the first to have a notable impact on the development of a postmodern stylistics—although only recently have we been able to see his work in that light, since in his writings Barthes refers often to "modern texts" and "limit texts," but never postmodern texts.[9] From the very beginning— in *Writing Degree Zero* (*Le degré zéro de l'écriture*, 1953)—Barthes was writing about postmodern stylistics; but due to his untimely death in 1980, he never "learned its name," or the name Lyotard brought into the French language for it. Lyotard's *La Condition postmoderne* was published in late 1979; Barthes was hit by a laundry truck in February 1980. During his lifetime Barthes had tried out at least five pairs of terms that he associated with what he enjoyed in *les nouveaux romanciers*—what is now conventionally called their "postmodernism." Those pairs, listed chronologically, are: *écrivain* (author)/*écrivant* (writer), 1960; *Écrivain* (Writer)/écriture (writing), 1968; *lisible* ("readerly")/*scriptible* ("writerly"), 1970; *oeuvre* (work)/*Texte* (Text), 1971; and finally—perhaps most notoriously—*texte de plaisir* (text of pleasure)/*texte de jouissance* (text of "bliss"), in *Le Plaisir du texte*, 1973 (trans. *The Pleasure of the Text*, 1975).[10] All his career Barthes was fascinated with postmodernism, but he died before it had been definitively christened—hence, I believe, the relative infrequency with which his name is invoked in current discussions of postmodernism.[11]

But would Barthes have adopted, and then stuck with, the label postmodernism if he had lived long enough to adopt it? Considering the above list of his "name changes," it seems unlikely; more probably, Barthes would have used "postmodernism" for a time, and then thrown it off once it began to hypostatize for him or his readers; as he says of another of his coinages, *semiology*, he was inclined "to shift its definition (almost as soon as I found it to be formed)."[12] Barthes enjoyed the inherent, ineluctable slipperiness of his nomenclature; just one year after setting out the pair "work/Text," for instance, he took the opportunity in 1972, introducing a special issue of the journal *Communications*, to upbraid his audience for their "misuse" of the terms: "The Text: let us make no mistake about either this singular or this capital letter; when we say *the Text*, it is not in order to divinize it, to make it the deity of a new mystique, but to denote a mass, a field requiring a partitive and not a numerative expression" (*RL* 73). For all his protest, of course, Barthes was largely responsible for the abuse about which he complains; his enthusiasm for Text in "From Work to Text" (1971) is palpable—indeed he seems in that essay guilty of the very "divinizing" that he locates in his readers.

From work/Text, Barthes moved on in short order to "pleasure/bliss," and made quite explicit from the start that those terms, too, were happily vague: "*Pleasure/Bliss:* terminologically, there is always a vacillation—I stumble, I err. In any case, there will always be a margin of indecision; the distinction will not be the source of absolute classifications, the paradigm will falter, the meaning will be precarious, revocable, reversible, the discourse incomplete" (*PT* 4). Barthes's last phrase here—while ostensibly confessing his own terminological imprecision—evokes as well his dream of postmodern writing: a writing which is constantly, to invoke Kristeva's trope from *Revolution in Poetic Language, en procès* (in process/on trial). Thus Barthes not only describes postmodern stylistics, he incarnates it in his writing.

Terminological imprecision aside, however, Barthes took the description of what we now call postmodern style a long way. One advantage of his avoidance of the term "postmodern" is that his stylistic categories are never confused with literary-historical categories—so that while "postmodernism" is regularly used in criticism as the description of both a stylistics and a literary period, Barthes's idiosyncratic nomenclature manages to fly by those nets. In calling the postmodern text a "text of bliss," for instance, Barthes runs no danger of bringing to mind a literary-historical era; there is no "Bliss Period," but merely bliss *(jouissance)*—period. Bliss is what Barthes calls "the formidable underside of writing": "bliss which can erupt, across the centuries, out of certain texts that were nonetheless written to the glory of the dreariest, of the most sinister philosophy" (*PT* 39). Thus postmodern stylistics is not time-bound, and cannot be contained by any historical or literary period, but can crop up anywhere, anytime.

Similarly, using the nomenclature work/Text in his introduction to a special issue of the journal *Communications,* Barthes insists that "there is no necessity that the Text be exclusively modern: there can be Text in ancient works; and it is precisely the presence of this unquantifiable germ that makes it necessary to disturb, to transcend the old divisions of Literary History; one of the immediate, obvious tasks of new research is to proceed to such *accounts of writing,* to explore what Text there can be in Diderot, in Chateaubriand, in Flaubert, in Gide: this is what many of the authors gathered here are doing; as one of them says, speaking implicitly in the name of several of his comrades: 'Perhaps our work merely consists in identifying fragments of writing caught up in a discourse still guaranteed by the Father.' No better definition of what, in previous work, is Literature, and what is Text. In other words: how can this past work *still* be read?" (*RL* 73). Barthes here would seem, not surprisingly, to endorse the deductive method for the study of postmodernism. Besides enlisting yet another term in opposition to postmodernism ("Literature")[13]—and through the words of his unnamed "young researcher" indirectly intoning still another (discourse "guaranteed by the Father," which is opposed to "writing")—Barthes here also acknowledges the fluid, permeable boundaries between the periods of literary history. Furthermore, Barthes suggests, the "discovery" of postmodern writing in our own time—its prevalence in the artistic writing done since the Second World War—has accustomed our eyes to rather different constellations of stylistic characteristics, which we can now see when we turn back to "classic" texts. Postmodernism, or Text, or the *scriptible,* or the text of bliss, etc., is not only not constrained to a particular phase of literary history; it is a timeless literary phenomenon which, once our perceptual apparatuses have adjusted themselves to its workings, we can see animating the quirky textual antics of texts through the ages—afterimages of postmodernity cast over the range of modern texts.[14] This is a notion, as we shall see, that is central to both Lyotard's and Hassan's understanding of the postmodern spirit, and implicit in Bakhtin's texts as well. And it is obviously critical for us if we wish to examine Joyce's texts for their postmodernity since, as Hassan and many others posit, the postmodern "period" began about 1939, the year Joyce's last text was published.

In Barthes's discussion of the transhistorical, diachronic aspect of postmodern writing, we have a glimpse as well of what that stylistics consists of. Two characteristics, according to Barthes, are paramount: postmodern stylistics champions heterogeneity over homogeneity, plurality over "authority"; and postmodern texts are inherently participatory: they encourage, perhaps even demand, their co-creation, rather than passive consumption, by the reader. Comparing postmodern writing to postserial music, Barthes writes that "The Text is very much a score of this new kind: it asks of the reader a practical collaboration" (*IMT* 163). Hence, Barthes's writing suggests, postmodernism can be constructed either by writers or by readers—or both, working in concert. As Mary Bittner Wiseman puts it, "Any text, no matter its birth date and the sign of literature under which it was born, can be read in a writerly way."[15]

The text of bliss, Barthes writes—the postmodern text—is a heterogeneous Babel of languages, in stark contrast to the tight, polished cadences of the "classic" text: "Imagine someone (a kind of Monsieur Teste in reverse) who abolishes within himself all barriers, all classes, all exclusions, not by syncretism but by simple discard of that old specter: *logical contradiction;* who mixes every language, even those said to be incompatible; who silently accepts every charge of illogicality, of incongruity. . . . Now this anti-hero exists: he is the reader of the text at the moment he takes his pleasure. Thus the Biblical myth is reversed, the confusion of tongues is no longer a punishment, the subject gains access to bliss by the cohabitation of languages *working side by side:* the text of pleasure is a sanctioned Babel" (*PT* 3–4). Again, the postmodernity of Barthes's writing is striking here. As the passage begins, it sounds as if Barthes is talking about the postmodern author ("a kind of Monsieur Teste in reverse") who, like Stephen Dedalus (quoting Whitman), declares, "Do I contradict myself? Very well then, I contradict myself" (*U* 14).[16] But at the close of the passage, Barthes identifies this "anti-hero" *not* as the author, but as the reader. Thus the passage is predicated on precisely the active reader it describes; you must be sucked in, allow Barthes's writing to have its way with you, before you can appreciate its insights. In chapter 4 I will examine in greater detail Joyce's strategy of enforced reader participation which I call, after Clive Hart (though with a different meaning than his), the "reader trap." The postmodern text's "confusion of tongues" that Barthes describes here is quite similar to Bakhtin's notions of polyphony and heteroglossia, the language of carnival, and one of the techniques of carnivalesque stylistics; we will have an opportunity to explore these similarities when we consider Bakhtin's texts in greater detail. Barthes here describes the production of a postmodern reading text by a postmodern reader, working with modernist inputs; he "takes his pleasure" with the text of pleasure, willfully, perversely transforming it into a postmodern text of bliss. "What I enjoy in a narrative is not directly its content or even its structure," Barthes writes in *The Pleasure of the Text*, "but rather the abrasions I impose upon the fine surface: I read on, I skip, I look up, I dip in again. Which has nothing to do with the deep laceration the text of bliss inflicts upon language itself, and not upon the simple temporality of its reading" (*PT* 11–12). Barthes thus suggests a text postmodern not by birth, but by reading.

In *The Pleasure of the Text*, Barthes elaborates on the plural nature of postmodern texts: they are heterogeneous not by choice, as it were, but rather by circumstance; they do not choose their heterogeneity but, unlike modern texts, do choose to acknowledge rather than try to elide it. To put it another way: all writing, both modern and postmodern, is Writing (*écriture*), is Text; the postmodern text of bliss differs from the modernist text of pleasure ("Text" differs from "work") only in that it accepts this limitation of its means, and rather than mourning an imaginary past in which the writer was in control of his language and wrote with an authentic "voice," the postmodern text both celebrates and thematizes its confusion of tongues—its "Babelization"—in ways that would have been unthinkable to a classical author. The postmodern writer mixes styles without nostalgia for a time when he imagines things might have been different:

> With Flaubert, for the first time, discontinuity is no longer exceptional, sporadic, brilliant, set in the base matter of common utterance: there is no longer a language *on the other side* of these figures (which means, in another sense: there is no longer anything but language); a generalized asyndeton seizes the entire utterance, so that this very readable discourse is *underhandedly* one of the craziest imaginable: all the logical small change is in the interstices.
>
> This is a very subtle and nearly untenable status for discourse: narrativity is dismantled yet the story is still readable: never have the two edges of the seam been clearer and more tenuous, never has pleasure been better offered to the reader—if at least he appreciates controlled discontinuities, faked conformities, and indirect destructions. In addition to the success which can here be attributed to an author, there is also, here, a pleasure of performance: the feat is to sustain the *mimesis* of language (language imitating itself), the source of immense pleasures, in a fashion so *radically* ambiguous (ambiguous to the root) that the text never succumbs to the good conscience (and bad faith) of parody (of castrating laughter, of "the comical that makes us laugh"). (*PT* 9)

Paradoxically enough, given his tireless promotion of the *scriptible*, Barthes here appears very suspicious of the postmodern author: Is it all, he asks, a confidence game? Is the only true postmodernism in the hands and eyes and brains of the reader? Barthes's anti-"author"-itarian bias is palpable in this passage. Thus the danger of Barthes's stylistics is that it levels all texts to the status of raw material, equally available for the anarchy of postmodern readings. The text itself disappears behind the spectacle of its consumption.

Barthes's seeming praise of Flaubert is thus undercut by criticism: for while Flaubert had recognized, *"for the first time,"* that language "has a will of its own," he was not wholly able to surrender himself—and his text—to that will. Flaubert, it would seem, remains too much an Author for Barthes, with his "controlled discontinuities, faked conformities, and indirect destructions": on the brink of a postmodern understanding of the unmasterable nature of all language, Flaubert wrests his texts back from the brink—or attempts to. In the last analysis, as strongly as the postmodern pulse beat within him, Flaubert remains a product of the nineteenth century, the classical mind-set.

For the postmodern text acknowledges no master. "The *brio* of the text (without which, after all, there is no text) is its *will to bliss:* just where it exceeds demand, transcends prattle, and whereby it attempts to overflow, to break through the constraints of adjectives—which are those doors of language through which the ideological and the imaginary come flowing in" (*PT* 13–14). The postmodern text is a text of excess (what Stephen Dedalus calls "the art of surfeit" [*U* 165])—excess defined, of course, relative to the "flat," "neutral," "transparent," "white" language of the classical norm. In *Roland Barthes,* he puts it this way: "Addendum to *The Pleasure of the Text:* Bliss is not what *corresponds to* desire (what satisfies it) but what surprises, exceeds, disturbs, deflects it. One must turn to the mystics for a good formulation of what can cause the subject to deviate in this way: Ruysbroek: 'I call intoxication of the mind that state in which pleasure exceeds the possibilities which desire had entertained.' "[17] Barthes is careful to distinguish this pleasure of excess—revealed in an excess of the text, represented on or through the surface of the text—from a mere representation of pleasure which does not itself disrupt the field of representation. That, after all, happens frequently enough in the classic text: "Of course, it very often happens that representation takes desire itself as an object of imitation; but then, such desire never leaves the frame, the picture; it circulates among the characters; if it has a recipient, that recipient remains interior to the fiction (consequently, we can say that any semiotics that keeps desire within the configuration of those upon whom it acts, however new it may be, is a semiotics of representation. That is what representation is: when nothing emerges, when nothing leaps out of the frame: of the picture, the book, the screen)" (*PT* 56–57). As he writes elsewhere, "Desire is stronger than its interpretation."[18] Lyotard will develop this theme— the postmodern text and the limitations of representation—in greater detail in *The Postmodern Condition,* under the rubric of the sublime, which we will examine in some detail below. Suffice it to say for now that a stylistics that contents itself with a representation of desire, but that does not allow desire to disrupt its representational strategies, is deemed a modern rather than postmodern stylistics by both Barthes and Lyotard.[19] Modernism remains wedded to the project of ever more faithfully representing the signified; but the pleasure of the text, Barthes claims, derives from "value shifted to the sumptuous rank of the signifier" (*PT* 65). As he writes in "From Work to Text," "The Text . . . practises the infinite deferment of the signified, is dilatory; its field is that of the signifier. . . . The logic regulating the Text is not comprehensive (define 'what the work means') but metonymic; the activity of associations, contiguities, carryings-over coincides with a liberation of symbolic energy (lacking it, man would die); the work—in the best of cases—is *moderately* symbolic (its symbolic runs out, comes to a halt); the Text is *radically* symbolic: *a work conceived, perceived and received in its integrally symbolic nature is a text"* (*IMT* 158–59).

The linguistic awareness that engenders postmodern writing—the writer's acknowledgment that he possesses no solid ground upon which to make his stand—necessarily puts postmodern writing at odds with its predecessors. The convention that we call "realism," Barthes argues, is a fiction, and a dangerous one—dangerous in its steadfast refusal to admit its status as fiction, to acknowledge that it is merely one stylistic choice among many.[20] As Barthes says of the school descended from Flaubert, for instance, "The writing of Realism is far from being neutral, it is on the contrary loaded with the most spectacular signs of fabrication" (*WDZ* 67–68). The classical style sets itself up as a "natural," "intuitive" norm; but the function of writing in our time, according to Barthes, is "to make ridiculous, to annul the power (the intimidation) of one language over another, to dissolve any metalanguage as soon as it is constituted" (*S/Z* 98). An incredulity toward metanarratives—of which Barthes's "metalanguage" would be one of the most prevalent— has of course become the rallying cry associated with Lyotard's version of postmodernism, and we will return to it later in this chapter. We might at this point, however, venture a tentative distinction: for while the grand narratives that concern Lyotard are largely metalinguistic structures (religious, philosophical, political creeds), Barthes always ends up back at the level of language itself—the language we use to create those larger narratives is always itself employed uncritically in their construction, and is *of itself* a comforting fiction—the lie of a common (and cooperative) language that would be our servant. Instead, Barthes argues, it is always us who, knowingly or unknowingly—joyfully or morosely—serve language. Let it, says Barthes, be joyfully.

This is a theme that, as we will see, Bakhtin takes up in a good bit more detail, and in a more explicitly political context. But even for Barthes, there is a politics of style—politics in the sense of the expression and use of power:

> Encratic language (the language produced and spread under the protection of power) is statutorily a language of repetition; all official institutions of language are repeating machines: school, sports, advertising, popular songs, news, all continually repeat the same structure, the same meaning, often the same words: the stereotype is a political fact, the major figure of ideology. Confronting it, the New is bliss (Freud: "In the adult, novelty always constitutes the condition for orgasm"). Whence the

present configuration of forces: on the one hand, a mass banalization (linked to the repetition of language)—a banalization outside bliss but not necessarily outside pleasure—and on the other, a (marginal, eccentric) impulse toward the New—a desperate impulse that can reach the point of destroying discourse: an attempt to reproduce in historical terms the bliss repressed beneath the stereotype. (*PT* 40–41)

Citing Kristeva's observation that "every ideological activity is presented in the form of compositionally completed utterances," Barthes maintains that the converse is true as well: "Any completed utterance runs the risk of being ideological" (*PT* 50). Kristeva's remark comes in the course of her early (1966) essay "Word, Dialogue, and Novel," devoted to Mikhail Bakhtin's translinguistics; this notion of the completed as ideologically oppressive is one of the many points of agreement between Bakhtin's and Barthes's stylistics of postmodernism. "The forces of freedom which are in literature," Barthes declared in his inaugural lecture at the Collège de France, "depend not on the writer's civil person, nor on his political commitment—for he is, after all, only a man among others—nor do they even depend on the doctrinal content of his work, but rather on the labor of displacement he brings to bear upon the language."[21]

The postmodern text—the text of bliss—is furthermore a text which to some degree thwarts the author's creative ego. The text of bliss is excessive, eccentric, willful, headstrong; rather than obediently carrying out the tasks assigned it by its Creator, it rebels against its Creator/Father—like a Frankenstein's monster—and the writer can glory only in what the text is, not in what she has done, what she has made. In the text of bliss it is language, and not an Author, that speaks: "Here it is impossible to attribute an origin, a point of view, to the statement. Now, this impossibility is one of the ways in which the plural nature of a text can be appreciated. The more indeterminate the origin of the statement, the more plural the text. In modern[22] texts, the voices are so treated that any reference is impossible: the discourse, or better, the language, speaks: nothing more" (*S/Z* 41). This statement is of course rife with the characteristic Barthesean hyperbole; Barthes's critical texts are themselves frequently, delightfully given to the excess which he finds characteristic of the text of bliss. To judge by his account, there would be no way to distinguish the way that Balzac's language speaks from the way that, for instance, Robbe-Grillet's language speaks. This weakness—a focus on the reader and his reading process so complete that it nearly denies any constructive role for the author—is not uncommon in reader-oriented theories of the text; but in his more lucid (less rapturous, less mystical) moments, Barthes does of course recognize that the text that I as reader co-create with the writer of the *lisible* (readerly) work will be very different from what I am able to make in collaboration with the scriptor of the *scriptible* (writerly) Text. For while he rarely bothers to make it explicit, Barthes does realize that different writers have very different attitudes toward the willfulness of language; the difference between Balzac and Robbe-Grillet, for instance, isn't so much in the language that they use as in the way that they use it—the authority they attempt to arrogate for it, their understanding of their own relationship to it. Barthes's stylistics, however, doesn't really provide the tools for such a distinction.

The Text, then—the postmodern Text—is, Barthes says, "above all (or after all) that long operation through which an author (a discoursing author) discovers (or makes the reader discover) the *irreparability* of his speech and manages to substitute *it speaks* for *I speak*" (*RL* 75). This is, he says elsewhere, the process wherein the Author extinguishes himself; as we will examine in greater detail in chapter 5, turning the text over to the headstrong autonomy of language necessarily results in a diminished role for the Author—it implies, finally, what Barthes calls for in his best-known essay: "the birth of the reader must be at the cost of the death of the Author" (*IMT* 148).

The movement from modern work to postmodern Text is also signaled in the shift of focus from the ends of narrative to its means—from the plane of the signified to what Barthes calls "the sumptuous rank of the signifier." In *S/Z*, Barthes gives his clearest account of the assumptions implicit in the classic (modernist) text: "A classic narrative always gives this impression: the author first conceives the signified (or the generality) and then finds for it, according to the chance of his imagination, 'good' signifiers, probative examples; the classic author is like an artisan bent over the workbench of meaning and selecting the best *expressions* for the concept he has already formed. . . . The *mastery of meaning*, a veritable semiurgism, a divine attribute, once this meaning is defined as the discharge, the emanation, the spiritual effluvium overflowing from the signified toward the signifier: the *author* is a god (his place of origin is the signified); as for the critic, he is the priest whose task is to decipher the Writing of the god" (*S/Z* 173–74). The notion that an author has a message, an idea, or a plot to express is one of the first conventions to be abandoned in postmodern writing; we will examine the way Joyce jettisons the "baggage" of expression—specifically the modernist stylistic credo of "expressive form"—in chapter 6. As Samuel Beckett remarked to an interviewer in 1956, "There seems to be a kind of esthetic axiom that expression is achievement—must be an achievement. My little exploration is that whole zone of being that has always been set aside by artists as something unusable—as something by definition incompatible with art."[23] The discussion cited above—the distinction Barthes attempts to draw between those who focus on the signifier and those who focus on the signified—finds its echo (or rather its anticipation) in a 1960 essay that has been translated "Authors and Writers" (in the French the equally slippery *"Écrivants et Écrivains"*). In this pair, the "author"—the *écrivant*—is Barthes's preference; because he later denigrates the title "Author," however, in "The Death of the Author" (where, as we have just seen, "Authorship" is something to be outgrown), I will supply the French terms here in brackets.

In "Authors and Writers" (included in translation in *Critical Essays*), Barthes announces his intention "to sketch a comparative typology of the author and the writer with reference to the substance they share: language":

> The author [*écrivant*] performs a function, the writer [*écrivain*] an activity. Not that the author [*écrivant*] is a pure essence: he acts, but his action is immanent in its object, it is performed paradoxically on its own instrument: language; the author [*écrivant*] is the man who *labors*, who works up his utterance (even if he is inspired) and functionally absorbs himself in this labor, this work. . . . In short, it is precisely when the author's work becomes its own end that it regains a mediating character: the author [*écrivant*] conceives of literature as an end, the world restores it to him as a means: and it is in this perpetual inconclusiveness that the author [*écrivant*] rediscovers the world, an alien world moreover, since literature represents it as a question—never, finally, as an answer. . . .
>
> The *writer* [*écrivain*], on the other hand, is a "transitive" man, he posits a goal (to give evidence, to explain, to instruct), of which language is merely a means; for him language supports a *praxis*, it does not constitute one. Thus language is restored to the nature of an instrument of communication, a vehicle for "thought." Even if the writer [*écrivain*] pays some attention to style, this concern is never ontological. . . . For what defines the writer [*écrivain*] is the fact that his project of communication is *naïve:* he does not admit that his message is reflexive, that it closes over itself, and that we can read in it, diacritically, anything else but what he means: what writer [*écrivain*] would tolerate a psychoanalysis of his language? He considers that his work resolves an ambiguity, institutes an irreversible explanation (even if he regards himself as a modest instructor); whereas for the author [*écrivant*], as we have seen, it is just the other way around: he knows that his language, intransitive by choice and by labor, inaugurates an ambiguity, even if it appears to be peremptory, that it of-

fers itself, paradoxically, as a monumental silence to be deciphered, that it can have no other motto but Jacques Rigaut's profound remark: *and even when I affirm, I am still questioning*.[24]

The writer [*écrivain*] vainly resists the deconstruction (what Barthes here calls the diacritical reading) of his work; the author [*écrivant*], on the other hand, anticipates the deconstruction of his text—indeed, he attempts to carry it out himself. To paraphrase the title of another of his essays, for Barthes *écrire*—to write—is an intransitive verb. Bakhtin, in his writing on Rabelais and elsewhere, celebrates what he calls the "gay relativity" of the carnival tradition—an ability to see the fallible nature of all things, including oneself and one's every attempt at transcendence. This awareness informs the author's project, as well: she recognizes the limitations inherent in her "calling," and yet does feel herself called—not in order to change the world perhaps, but in order to celebrate it as she finds it. "Writing," according to Barthes, "makes knowledge festive."[25]

Clearly, Roland Barthes was just such an author; his writing does not so much "describe" or "set out" an aesthetics of postmodernism as *perform* it—enact it on the very stage of his writing. Speaking of the goals of interpretation in *S/Z*, Barthes insists that "it would be wrong to say that if we undertake to reread the text we do so for some intellectual advantage (to understand better, to analyze on good grounds): it is actually and invariably for a ludic advantage: to multiply the signifiers, not to reach some ultimate signified" (*S/Z* 165). Hence, the chameleonlike changes in his nomenclature and thought can be seen not as the byproduct of methodological sloppiness—though there is perhaps an element of that as well—but rather as a symptom, or better the sign, of a joyously postmodern celebration of the possibilities inherent in language.

Mikhail Bakhtin

Though written in the Soviet Union in the 1930s through the 1960s, Mikhail Bakhtin's work in linguistics and poetics did not become known to Western readers until the late 1960s—and then through the writing, in part, of Barthes's student, friend, and colleague (fellow semiotician and *Tel Quel* member) Julia Kristeva who, happily, reads Russian. Bakhtin's first work to be translated, *Rabelais and His World*, did not appear in English until 1968, two years after Kristeva wrote her first essay on his work. Kristeva's first book, Σημειωτιχὴ: *Récherches pour une sémanalyse* (1969), thus "introduced" Bakhtin's work to a Western audience: her essay "Word, Dialogue, and Novel" (dated 1966, the year after the Russian publication of the Rabelais book) set out most of the major categories of Bakhtin's thought, describing "carnival," for instance, as "a homology between the body, dream, linguistic structure, and structures of desire."[26]

There is indeed textual evidence, if any be deemed necessary, for Bakhtin's influence on Barthes's late writing; besides the many incidental echoes of Bakhtin's terms and concepts, this entry from his last work, *Roland Barthes*, introduces Bakhtin's favorite trope—the carnivalesque—under the heading *"Le monstre de la totalité ~ The monster of totality"*: " 'Let us imagine (if we can) a woman covered with an endless garment, itself woven of everything said in the fashion magazine . . .' *(Système de la Mode)*. This imagination, apparently methodical since it merely sets up an operative notion of semantic analysis ('the endless text'), actually (secretly) aims at denouncing the monster of Totality (Totality as monster). Totality at one and the same time inspires laughter and fear: like violence, is it not always *grotesque* (and then recuperable only in an aesthetics of Carnival)?"[27] And it is this "aesthetics of carnival" of which Barthes speaks that constitutes Bakhtin's most important contribution to the emerging aesthetics of postmodernism.

Like Barthes, Bakhtin never used the word "postmodernism" or any of its cognates in his writings. As is the case with Barthes, "it seems history is to blame" (*U* 17): there was simply no Russian-language equivalent for the English "postmodernism" at the time he was writing; indeed, it didn't even come into English until Toynbee coined it in 1947, when most of Bakhtin's work had already been written (if not published), and didn't gain any real currency until the publication of Hassan's *The Dismemberment of Orpheus: Toward a Postmodern Literature* (1971). And yet reread in the context of later discussions of the postmodern, Bakhtin's remarks on the poetics of Dostoyevsky, or even further back,[28] in his description of the carnivalesque impulse of Rabelais's texts, sound like the evocation of an as yet unnamed postmodernism. As Katerina Clark and Michael Holquist point out in their critical biography, it was for political reasons difficult for Bakhtin to write about modernist writers: "One of the many enigmas about Bakhtin is that he makes no mention in *Rabelais* of James Joyce's *Ulysses*, a book that might be described as a celebration of heteroglossia and of the body as well. This is especially surprising since Joyce was known to several of Bakhtin's associates. Pumpiansky was at work on a book on Joyce in 1932, and V. O. Stenich, who was close to members of the Bakhtin circle in Leningrad . . . translated Joyce. Once again, Bakhtin's choosing not to include Joyce could have been motivated politically. As of at least the First Writers' Congress in 1934, *Ulysses* could no longer be praised in print, and this was still true in 1965 when the dissertation was published as a book [*Rabelais and His World*]. Thus, Bakhtin effectively had two choices as regards Joyce, to attack him or not to mention him."[29] Since the modernists were still personae non grata in the Soviet Union during the period Bakhtin was writing the bulk of his work, his argument was necessarily couched in a celebration of the proletariat spirit in Rabelais and Dostoyevsky—the anarchic principle of the carnival which, when it came in contact with literary texts, created a new genre: the carnivalized novel.

For Bakhtin, the novel and the carnivalesque are almost synonymous. Just as the carnivalesque celebrates the gay relativity of all life, so the novel proclaims the relativity of all "truth," and the inherent fallibility of all discourse. Again, Clark and Holquist: "The novel is for him not just another literary genre but a special kind of force, which he calls 'novelness.' . . . Bakhtin assigns the term 'novel' to whatever form of expression within a given literary system reveals the limits of that system as inadequate, imposed, or arbitrary."[30] While Bakhtin calls this dethroning force "novelness," Barthes, as we have seen, calls it simply "writing"; despite their seeming disagreement over the ubiquity of this textual force, however, both men sought to identify it with what they thought best—most exciting, most revolutionary, most exhilarating—in literature.

In the years since the introduction of his work to English-speaking readers, Bakhtin's writings (like Barthes's) have become associated with, and to some extent stigmatized by, a number of neologisms. Among the most important of these, the terms which have most quickly been assimilated into current critical discourse, are "heteroglossia," "dialogism," "polyphony," "grotesque realism," and "the carnivalesque." Holquist, in his introduction to *The Dialogic Imagination*, argues that of these, only heteroglossia is absolutely central to Bakhtin's conception of language: " 'Heteroglossia' is a master trope at the heart of all his other projects, one more fundamental than such other categories associated with his thought as 'polyphony' or 'carnivalization.' These are but two specific ways in which the primary condition of heteroglossia manifests itself" (*DI* xix). Holquist is surely wrong to call "heteroglossia" a trope; as he himself says, Bakhtin's heteroglossia is a "primary condition" of language, which manifests itself in the "real world" and in texts in a number of diverse forms—textual polyphony, intercharacter dialogism, the unofficial carnival life of the common people, and the "grotesque realism" of a writer like Rabelais—a sort of carnivalesque stylistics. In any case it would seem that heteroglossia is prior to and subsumes most of the other important concepts in Bakhtin's thought. Yet Holquist and Clark say in *Mikhail Bakhtin* that "the act of authorship . . . is the master trope of all Bakhtin's work,"[31] somewhat complicating the situation, and Krystyna Pomorska, in the introduction to the American edition of *Rabelais and His World*, argues persuasively that "just as dialogization is the *sine qua non* for the novel structure, so carnivalization is the condition for the ultimate 'structure of life' that is formed by 'behavior and cognition' "(R x), thereby putting carnival in the privileged position in Bakhtin's thought. In the overall structure of Bakhtin's work, however, there can be no serious doubt that the concepts of heteroglossia and the carnivalesque are at the very heart of Bakhtin's theory of the novel, of that unique impulse he calls novelness. And the notion of "novelness" is the closest Bakhtin ever got to describing postmodernism.

In "Discourse in the Novel," Bakhtin defines heteroglossia this way: "The internal stratification of any single national language into social dialects, characteristic group behavior, professional jargons, generic languages, languages of generations and age groups, tendentious languages, languages of the authorities, of various circles and of passing fashions, languages that serve the specific sociopolitical purposes of the day, even of the hour (each day has its own slogan, its own vocabulary, its own emphases)—this internal stratification present in every language at any given moment of its historical existence is the indispensable prerequisite for the novel as a genre. The novel orchestrates all its themes [polyphony], the totality of the world of objects and ideas depicted and expressed in it, by means of the social diversity of speech types [heteroglossia] and by the differing individual voices that flourish under such conditions [dialogism]." (*DI* 262–63). This orchestration of sociolects, Bakhtin goes on to say, "is the basic distinguishing feature of the stylistics of the novel"; "the novel can be defined as a diversity of social speech types (sometimes even diversity of languages) and a diversity of individual voices, artistically organized" (*DI* 263, 262).

As Bakhtin's discussion makes evident, the boundaries between the terms "heteroglossia" (sometimes "polyglossia"), "polyphony," and "dialogism" are somewhat fluid; his thought is characterized—as is Barthes's, and to a lesser extent Lyotard's—by its terminological fuzziness. "Heteroglossia" is used by Bakhtin to describe the stylistics of the novel, but it originates in the real social interaction of people. When heteroglossia, the "social diversity of speech types," is incorporated into the structure of a text, in Bakhtin's terms that text has become "dialogized," or "polyphonic." To confuse matters even further, Bakhtin at times calls the process of dialogization "novelization," sometimes even "carnivalization." What these processes have in common, however, is their ability to open up the text to a multiplicity of autonomous voices which, via the author's artistic orchestration, interact dialogically within the text—the "Babelization" that Barthes celebrates in *The Pleasure of the Text*.

In Bakhtin's polemical history of the novel, heteroglossia's archenemy, the linguistic condition out of which heteroglossia arises (in Roman literary consciousness), is termed "monoglossia." As would be expected, while heteroglossia revels in the diversity of speech types that exist within a given society, monoglossia opposes this diversity with a monolithic "official" language, sealed off from the language of the people, effectively silencing the voice of the "other." The monoglotic author—like Barthes's *écrivain*—writes in the full confidence of the sufficiency of his language: "One who creates a direct word—whether epic, tragic or lyric—deals only with the subject whose praises he sings, or represents, or expresses, and he does so in his own language that is perceived as the sole and fully adequate tool for realizing the word's direct, objectivized meaning. This meaning and the objects and themes that compose it are inseparable from the straightforward language of the person who creates it: the objects and themes are born and grow to maturity in this language, and in the national myth and national tradition that permeate this language" (*DI* 61). Monoglossia, according to Bakhtin, has reigned in literary texts only sporadically since the Roman Empire, when "the creative literary consciousness of the Romans functioned against the background of the Greek language" and the pure Latin genres, "conceived under monoglotic conditions, fell into decay" (*DI* 61). Bakhtin claims that the bilingual consciousness of Roman literature is reflected in its "word 'with a sideways glance,'" its constant awareness of the Greek word and literary tradition. Thus with the flowering of the Roman tradition, says Bakhtin, "Two myths perish simultaneously: the myth of a language that presumes to be the only language, and the myth of a language that presumes to be completely unified" (*DI* 68). Heteroglossia dances her jig on the grave of the monoglot, the *écrivain*, the Author.

Monoglossia, when it rears its ugly head in the modern world, is often used in the service of the desires of the ruling class, and rigidifies into what Bakhtin calls "authoritative discourse." Authoritative discourse is for Bakhtin a term of opprobrium, to be distinguished from the "ambivalent," or "novelistic," word, which acknowledges within itself the unfinalized quality of its statement, and the possibility of rejoinder. Authoritative discourse, on the other hand, seeks not to converse, but to put its hearers on notice: "The authoritative word demands that we acknowledge it, that we make it our own; it binds us, quite independent of any power it might have to persuade us internally; we encounter it with its authority already fused to it" (*DI* 342). Authoritative discourse does not allow for dialogue; it presents itself as indisputable truth, and has the muscle behind it to enforce a reverent silence—it is the word, to paraphrase Teddy Roosevelt, that "speaks softly and carries a big stick." For Bakhtin, such a conception was no merely theoretical construct; "Discourse in the Novel," the essay in which he develops the notion of "authoritative discourse," was written in 1934–35, while Bakhtin was in Kustanai in exile from his beloved Moscow, as a result of his underground Christian activities. The Soviet Union under Stalin was a living example of the reign of authoritative discourse, and Bakhtin himself knew only too well the power of that discourse to marginalize its opponents.

In Bakhtin's poetics, the ambivalent word becomes the minimal unit of discourse in the novel. Julia Kristeva writes of Bakhtin's "conception of the 'literary word' as an *intersection of textual surfaces* rather than a *point* (a fixed meaning), as a dialogue among several writings"; this conception opens the individual text into history, thus rescuing it from the self-imposed blindness of a purely structural analysis—Kristeva says that it "allows a dynamic dimension to structuralism."[32]

Authoritative discourse, the silencing of all discord, is the logical outcome of a monoglotic society; thus in its very constitution it cannot serve as the language of the novel, because "its role in the novel is insignificant. It is by its very nature incapable of being double-voiced; it cannot enter into hybrid constructions" (*DI* 344). The novelistic word, on the other hand, arises from and is always involved in an ongoing dialogue; the temporal world of the novel is a world "where there is no first word (no ideal word), and the final word has not yet been spoken" (*DI* 30). For Bakhtin, a radical skepticism toward any unmediated discourse is characteristic of the novel: "The novel is the expression of a Galilean perception of language, one that denies the absolutism of a single and unitary language—that is, that refuses to acknowledge its own language as the sole verbal and semantic center of the ideological world" (*DI* 366).

When the Dostoyevsky book was first published in 1929, Bakhtin was arguing that Dostoyevsky had invented a fundamentally new literary form, which he called the polyphonic novel: "We consider Dostoyevsky one of the greatest innovators in the realm of artistic form. He created, in our opinion, a completely new type of artistic thinking, which we have provisionally called polyphonic. . . . Dostoyevsky is the creator of the polyphonic novel. He created a fundamentally new novelistic genre" (*PDP* 3, 7). A few years later, in "Discourse in the Novel," Bakhtin backed off from this claim for Dostoyevsky's radical (post)-modernity, stating instead that Dostoyevsky's novels did not represent a rupture in the history of the novel, but rather were the logical outcome of the great march of novelness. But fifty years later, one suspects that while he overplayed his hand in the Dostoyevsky study, Bakhtin was onto something. There *is* something radically different about Dostoyevsky's use of heteroglossia—something inherently postmodern. While Dostoyevsky is usually considered the first Russian modernist novelist, his heteroglossia is, from another perspective, part and parcel of the postmodernism seething beneath the surface of his texts.

In a purely stylistic sense we can speak of Dostoyevsky's fiction as postmodern precisely in its orchestration of a number of independent voices—in Dostoyevsky's eschewal of a privileged position of authority for himself, his own voice, a turning loose of his book to his characters. In *Problems of Dostoyevsky's Poetics*, Bakhtin claims that Dostoyevsky created the polyphonic novel; polyphony, he says, consists of *"a plurality of independent and unmerged voices and consciousnesses"* (*PDP* 6). Dostoyevsky gives his characters their own voices:

> Dostoyevsky's major heroes are, by the very nature of his creative design, *not only objects of authorial discourse but also subjects of their own directly signifying discourse.* In no way, then, can a character's discourse be exhausted by the usual functions of characterization and plot development, nor does it serve as a vehicle for the author's own ideological position (as with Byron, for instance).[33] The consciousness of a character is given as *someone else's* consciousness, another consciousness, yet at the same time it is not turned into an object, is not closed, does not become a simple object of the author's consciousness. In this sense the image of a character in Dostoevsky is not the usual objectified image of a hero in the traditional novel. . . . A character's word about himself and his world is just as fully weighted as the author's word usually is; it is not subordinated to the character's objectified image as merely one of his characteristics, nor does it serve as a mouthpiece for the author's voice. (*PDP* 6–7)

Since polyphony is for Bakhtin the hallmark of the novel as a genre, it is meaningless in Bakhtinian poetics to talk about the style of an authentically polyphonic novel—just as it is nonsensical to talk of the style of a Barthesean "text of bliss." One can speak only of the orchestration of styles: "The novel as a whole is a phenomenon multiform in style and variform in speech and voice" (*DI* 261). Though he approaches the text with a very different set of preconceptions, Bakhtin would be in full agreement with T. S. Eliot's famous pronouncement that *Ulysses* is without style;[34] the difference between Bakhtin's discussion of the "style" of the novel, and Eliot's, however, is one of emphasis, for in a Bakhtinian reading, Joyce's novel differs from other novels in degree perhaps, but not in kind. The stylistic variety that Joyce flaunts in *Ulysses* is in Bakhtin's view the very essence of the novel as a genre.

Eliot's remark on the styles of *Ulysses* holds true for all authentic novels, which are characterized not by their "style," conceived as a monolithic, monotonous authorial voice, but by their orchestration of styles—what Bakhtin, in "Discourse in the Novel," calls their polyphony. Clearly the "style(s)" of a novel are much richer than, and not coincident with, the voice of its author. As Bakhtin describes it, the artist's task, compared for instance with that granted the artist in Romantic poetics, sounds a great deal impoverished, as it does in Barthes's description. The novel is composed of "a diversity of individual voices"; "the style of a novel," Bakhtin observes, "is to be found in the combination of its styles; the language of a novel is the system of its 'languages' " (*DI* 262). The task of the novelist, then, is "merely" to organize them artistically: "The prose artist elevates the social heteroglossia surrounding objects into an image that has finished contours, an image completely shot through with dialogized overtones, he creates artistically calculated nuances on all the fundamental voices and tones of this heteroglossia" (*DI* 278–79). The novelist's job, although obviously a crucial one, unfortunately remains shrouded in mystery in Bakhtin's writings. What are the principles of this "artistic organization"? How does the critic differentiate "artistic" from "inartistic" organization of materials in the novel? We are made to understand the importance of the artist's function, but as to the actual process involved, Bakhtin unfortunately has little to say.

The author in Bakhtin's system resembles Claude Lévi-Strauss's bricoleur, who creates nothing *ab nihilo*, but rather orchestrates preexisting units into new formal structures: "The 'bricoleur' is adept at performing a large number of diverse tasks . . . the rules of his game are always to make do with 'whatever is at hand'. . . . The elements which the 'bricoleur' collects and uses are 'pre-constrained' like the constitutive units of myth, the possible combinations of which are restricted by the fact that they are drawn from the language where they already possess a sense which sets a limit on their freedom of manoeuvre."[35] Ultimately, the effect of Bakhtin's (and Lévi-Strauss's) conception of the artist is to

emphasize the role of the artist's social and cultural context in the production of his art. "The novel must represent all the social and ideological voices of its era, that is, all the era's languages that have any
claim to being significant; the novel must be a microcosm of heteroglossia," Bakhtin claims at the close of "Discourse in the Novel"; the
consequence for literary theory is that "any stylistics capable of dealing
with the distinctiveness of the novel as a genre must be a sociological
stylistics" (*DI* 411, 300).

Heteroglossia is, to use Saussure's terminology, essentially a synchronic phenomenon; but when it enters the novel in the guise of the
ambivalent word, it takes on a diachronic aspect as well, interacting dialogically with works of the literary canon. Kristeva describes the synchronic and diachronic axes of the ambivalent word this way: "We
must first define the three dimensions of textual space where various
semic sets and poetic sequences function. These three dimensions or
coordinates of dialogue are writing subject, addressee, and exterior
texts. The word's status is thus defined *horizontally* (the word in the text
belongs to both writing subject and addressee) as well as *vertically* (the
word in the text is oriented toward an anterior or synchronic literary
corpus)."[36] The horizontal, synchronic axis is familiar enough to us all;
in their attempt to wrench literature from history, the Formalists sought
to examine the horizontal axis in isolation, and such an approach is at
the heart of the New Critical enterprise as well. The vertical, diachronic
axis is the aspect of the work which Bakhtin calls "intertextuality." The
ambivalent word is the minimal unit of intertextuality; it retains the
memory of its prior uses, its earlier social, historical, and literary contexts, and echoes them in its new text; "each word tastes of the context
and contexts in which it has lived its socially charged life" (*DI* 293).[37] It
is precisely this diachronic reconstitution of literary history that
Bakhtin calls "intertextuality," that element of the work which the Formalists always wanted to admit to their analyses, and as a practical
matter often did admit, but which their theory forbade.

While Holquist is probably right to argue that heteroglossia is more
fundamental to Bakhtin's poetics than is carnival, carnival certainly occupies a unique place in Bakhtin's thought. Carnival approaches the
status of a symbol for him, though it too is *not* merely a trope but a
(once-) living, breathing, participatory example of the stylistics with
which he is concerned. With a certain amount of justice, one could say
that if heteroglossia is the central concept of Bakhtin's work, carnival is
his most vigorous symbol, the flesh-and-blood embodiment of what
might otherwise remain a rather bloodless concept. Bakhtin develops

his notion of the carnivalesque primarily in two places—throughout his study *Rabelais and His World* and in the fourth chapter of *Problems of Dostoevsky's Poetics* ("Characteristics of Genre and Plot Composition in Dostoevsky's Work"); passing reference is made as well in the essay "Forms of Time and Chronotope in the Novel," in which he describes the "Rabelaisian chronotope." Rabelais and Dostoevsky, the only two writers to whom Bakhtin devoted entire books, are separated by 350 years of literary history; and yet one of the things that unites them is the popular-festive image system, born of the medieval and early Renaissance carnival. Pomorska speaks of the integral connection between the novel and carnival: "Bakhtin's ideas concerning folk culture, with carnival as its indispensable component, are integral to his theory of art. The inherent features of carnival that he underscores are its emphatic and purposeful 'heteroglossia' *(raznogolosost')* and its multiplicity of styles *(mnogostil'nost')*. Thus, the carnival principle corresponds to and is indeed a part of the novelistic principle itself. . . . Since the novel represents the very essence of life, it includes the carnivalesque in its properly transformed shape" (*R* x).

Bakhtin begins *Rabelais* by claiming that Rabelais is "the least popular, the least understood and appreciated" of all great writers of world literature (*R* 1). The single most important element of Rabelais's culture that we have lost—the knowledge of which, Bakhtin argues, we must recover in order to understand Rabelais in the way his contemporaries would have understood him—is the medieval/Renaissance tradition of carnival. The license of carnival is the stylistic impulse behind Rabelais's greatest novels: "The suspension of all hierarchical precedence during carnival time was of particular significance. . . . This led to the creation of special forms of marketplace speech and gesture, frank and free, permitting no distance between those who came in contact with each other and liberating [them] from norms of etiquette and decency imposed at other times" (*R* 10). As a result, Bakhtin says, "Rabelais' images have a certain undestroyable nonofficial nature. No dogma, no authoritarianism, no narrow-minded seriousness can coexist with Rabelaisian images; these images are opposed to all that is finished and polished, to all pomposity, to every ready-made solution in the sphere of thought and world outlook" (*R* 3).

Bakhtin writes in "Forms of Time and Chronotope in the Novel" that in the novel, "Time, as it were, thickens, takes on flesh, becomes artistically visible" (*DI* 84); and when the festive spirit that animates the polyphonic novel "thickens," it issues forth in a weave of popular-festive images that bear witness to the carnivalesque spirit which informs the novel. Metaphors of the Eucharist, images of the word being made flesh and dwelling among us, were very powerful for Bakhtin, as they were for Joyce; in Joyce's famous description in *A Portrait*, the artist is "a priest of eternal imagination, transmuting the daily bread of experience into the radiant body of everliving life" (*P* 221). When heteroglossia and polyphony take on flesh, however, they look like carnival.[38]

Bakhtin's conception of carnival, as he himself points out, is a rather loose interpretation of that festive institution; he calls carnival and similar marketplace festivals "the second life of the people, who for a time entered the utopian realm of community, freedom, equality, and abundance" (*R* 9). Carnival always celebrates the return of the repressed; for a time, even if only a very short time, slaves master their masters, and the dispossessed can be kings. Carnival laughter "builds its own world versus the official world, its own church versus the official church, its own state versus the official state. Laughter celebrates its masses, professes its faith, celebrates marriages and funerals, writes its epitaphs, elects kings and bishops" (*R* 88). When modern literature is infused with this festive laughter, it becomes "carnivalized." Nietzsche, in his own terms, describes the carnivalization of art in *The Birth of Tragedy;* he declares that the significance of "festivals of world redemption and days of transfiguration" is that with them "nature for the first time attains her artistic jubilee; it is with them that the destruction of the principium individuationis for the first time becomes an artistic phenomenon."[39]

Bakhtin's description of the dynamic between literary history and the individual talent is worked out most completely in the Dostoyevsky book. The existence of carnival images and motifs in Dostoyevsky's work, to judge by Bakhtin's comments in *Rabelais*, would seem an anachronism; but those elements exist, he argues in *Dostoevsky's Poetics*, because they are transmitted to the artist indirectly, through the wisdom of forms: "To say that carnival and its later derivatives (the masquerade line of development, the farcical street comedy, and so on) exercised a direct and vital influence on Dostoevsky is difficult (although real experiences of a carnival type did certainly exist in his life). Carnivalization acted on him, as on the majority of other eighteenth- and nineteenth-century writers, primarily as a literary and generic tradition whose extraliterary source, that is, carnival proper, was perhaps not even perceived by him in any clearly precise way" (*PDP* 156–57). In a manner that sounds almost unconscious, the author is ventriloquized by the generic tradition in which he is working; in chapter 5, we will consider a practical example of this phenomenon in Joyce's writing—the ways in which the conventions of the Romantic autobiography undermine Joyce's deconstructive project in *A Portrait of the Artist as a Young Man.*

The literary genres which most interest Bakhtin are what he calls "the genres of the seriocomical"; in *Problems in Dostoevsky's Poetics,* he delineates three distinguishing characteristics of such texts. The first is what he calls "a carnival sense of the world": "For all their motley external diversity, they are united by their deep bond with *carnivalistic folklore.* They are all—to a greater or lesser degree—saturated with a specific *carnival sense of the world,* and several of them are direct literary variants of oral carnival-folkloric genres. . . . Literature that was influenced—directly and without mediation, or indirectly, through a series of intermediate links—by one or another variant of carnivalistic folklore (ancient or medieval) we shall call *carnivalized literature*" (*PDP* 107). "The second characteristic," Bakhtin writes, "is inseparably bound up with the first: the genres of the serio-comical do not rely on *legend* and do not sanctify themselves through it, they *consciously* rely on *experience* (to be sure, as yet insufficiently mature) and on *free invention;* their relationship to legend is in most cases deeply critical, and at times even resembles a cynical exposé. Here, consequently, there appears for the first time an image almost completely liberated from legend, one which relies instead on experience and free invention" (*PDP* 108). And the third characteristic is "the deliberate multi-styled and hetero-voiced nature of all these genres. They reject the stylistic unity (or better, the single-styled nature) of the epic, the tragedy, high rhetoric, the lyric. Characteristic of these genres are a multi-toned narration, the mixing of high and low, serious and comic; they make wide use of inserted genres—letters, found manuscripts, retold dialogues, parodies on the high genres, parodically reinterpreted citations; in some of them we observe a mixing of prosaic and poetic speech, living dialects and jargons (and in the Roman stage, direct bilingualism as well) are introduced, and various authorial masks make their appearance. Alongside the representing word there appears the *represented* word; in certain genres a leading role is played by the double-voiced word. And what appears here, as a result, is a radically new relationship to the word as the material of literature" (*PDP* 108). These three characteristics should sound familiar, for we have already seen them in Barthes (and will see them again in Lyotard's writings on postmodernism); for like Barthes, Bakhtin spent the most productive years of his life writing about a stylistics—an aesthetics, a philosophy, an ontology—that would be widely recognized only after his death. Bakhtin as much as Barthes was a voice crying out in the wilderness, announcing the arrival of an anonymous postmodernism.

Jean-François Lyotard

More than any other thinker, Jean-François Lyotard has set out the terms in which subsequent critics must discuss postmodern aesthetics. In 1979 he declared postmodernism to be our "condition," and that diagnosis stuck; in aesthetics generally and literary studies specifically, as well as philosophy and the human sciences broadly conceived, Lyotard has been one of the people in the past decade most responsible for setting out the terms of the debate—and thereby, of course, helping to shape its course. For, as Hassan has observed, there's more than just convenience involved in the nomenclature theorists adopt: "the history of literary terms serves only to confirm the irrational genius of language," Hassan writes in "Toward a Concept of Postmodernism." "We come closer to the question of postmodernism itself by acknowledging the psychopolitics, if not the psychopathology, of academic life. Let us admit it: there is a will to power in nomenclature, as well as in people or texts. A new term opens for its proponents a space in language" (Hassan 86).

In Lyotard's way of thinking, the postmodern is something like an artistic form of critique. The postmodern, he says, continues the venerable tradition of the avant-garde, the function of which has always been to destroy the latest illusion, the most recent solid ground upon which the modern artist would build. "The avant-gardes," Lyotard writes in "Answering the Question: What Is Postmodernism? [*le postmoderne:* "the Postmodern"]," "are perpetually flushing out artifices of presentation which make it possible to subordinate thought to the gaze and to turn it away from the unpresentable" (*PC* 79). Lyotard's use of the term "avant-garde," however, is (as one learns after reading more of his writing) somewhat idiosyncratic: by "avant-garde" he means not a specific artistic movement, or even a constellation of related movements, but rather the very essence of "the artistic." Indeed, "avant-garde artist" is almost an oxymoron in Lyotard's thought, for to be an artist is to be in the avant-garde: "an 'artist,'" he writes elsewhere, "is someone who presents problems of forms."[40] The notion that the role of art is to make the bourgeoisie feel uncomfortable is of course not unique to Lyotard; but he sees this critical function as specifically characteristic of the arts since the "crisis in the arts" that he locates in the past century: "I would say it started at the end of the 19th century, when, between 1880 and 1920, a whole series of things which signified a complete mutation of the 'specialist's' relation to form began to appear. The function of the artist, from then on, is no longer to produce *good* forms, new good forms, but on the contrary to *deconstruct* them systematically and to accelerate their obsolescence. . . . You cannot consider what has been happening in painting, music or sculpture for almost a century without having the feeling that the function of art has overturned. Art no longer plays the role it used to, for it once had a religious function, it created good forms, some sort of a myth, of a ritual, of a rhythm, a medium other than language through which the members of a society would communicate by participating in a same music, in a common substratum of meaning."[41] The function of art has become to discomfort rather than comfort its audience; this is a theme we have seen already in Barthes's writing, especially *The Pleasure of the Text*, where he describes the text of bliss as the text that causes a certain discomfort, that breaks with a comfortable practice of reading and the culture that would promote such a reading. Kristeva has been one of the most forceful spokespersons for this viewpoint; in *Revolution in Poetic Language*, for instance, she writes, "Poetry—more precisely, poetic language—reminds us of its eternal function: to introduce through the symbolic that which works on, moves through, and threatens it. The theory of the unconscious seeks the very thing that poetic language practices within and against the social order: the ultimate means of its transformation or subversion, the precondition for its survival and revolution."[42]

Appropriately enough, in Lyotard's account, the development that he describes as a "crisis in the arts" has resulted in the artist's taking on the role of critic: "Instead of continuing to produce unifying, reconciling forms, his activity has become a deconstructing one which is necessarily critical. . . . This deconstructing activity is a truly radical critical activity for it does not deal with the *signifieds* of things, but with their plastic organization, their signifying organization. It shows that the problem is not so much that of knowing what a given discourse says, but rather how it is disposed."[43] Again, as in Barthes's writing, we see an emphasis on the signifier, rather than on its signified, as a marker of the postmodern spirit. Language, instead of being the neutral and transparent medium of communication that the "writer" *(écrivain)* would like to believe it is, is instead a discursive space, heavy with the odor of previous usages, and incapable, unwilling to serve as the instrument for the search for Truth. Under the influence of postmodern stylistics, language has become a self-conscious critic of its own ability to transcend its inherent materiality—and the more useful paradigm becomes Wittgenstein's notion of the language game, which Lyotard brings over into his criticism in his 1979 publications *La Condition postmoderne* and *Au Juste*.

Lyotard brought the term "postmodernism" into French suddenly and forcefully in 1979, with the publication of his best-known (though certainly not most representative) work to date—*The Postmodern Condition*. On the first page of that "report on knowledge," Lyotard explains briefly his decision to import the term "postmodern": "The object of this study is the condition of knowledge in the most highly developed societies. I have decided to use the word *postmodern* to describe that condition. The word is in current use on the American continent among sociologists and critics; it designates the state of our culture following the transformations which, since the end of the nineteenth century, have altered the game rules for science, literature, and the arts. The present study will place these transformations in the context of the crisis of narratives" (*PC* xxiii). The American critic most likely responsible for Lyotard's adoption of the term is Ihab Hassan, with whom Lyotard must have worked during his residence at the Center for Twentieth-Century Studies at the University of Wisconsin, Milwaukee (where Hassan was the reigning spirit).

But like Barthes, Lyotard had been writing about postmodernism long before he settled on a name for it—a fact that one of the footnotes to *Just Gaming* (*Au Juste*, 1979) captures. In his dialogue with Jean-Loup Thébaud, Lyotard has been trying to make a distinction between two different attitudes or spirits, the "classical" and the "modern." This opposition is allowed to stand in the body of the text; indeed, the term "postmodern" occurs only in a single note, but has the effect of putting the nomenclature of the entire book under suspicion: "JFL [Lyotard] believes that he can dissipate today (October 1979) some of the confusion that prevails in this conversation on modernity by introducing a distinction between the modern and postmodern within that which is confused here under the first term. . . . Romanticism would be modern as would the project, even if it turns out to be impossible, of elaborating a taste, even a 'bad' one, that permits an evaluation of works. Postmodern (or pagan) would be the condition of the literatures and arts that have no assigned addressee and no regulating ideal, yet in which value is regularly measured on the stick of experimentation. Or, to put it dramatically, in which it is measured by the distortion that is inflicted upon the materials, the forms and structures of sensibility and thought. Postmodern is not to be taken in a periodizing sense" (*JG* 16n). The seven dialogues that make up *Just Gaming* took place between November 1977 and June 1978; Lyotard is careful in his note/commentary to date the revision October 1979, more than a year after the dialogues were completed, and, more important, when his *Postmodern Condition* had been completed. Thus in Lyotard's writings we find two different sets of oppositions—classicism/modernism and piety/paganism—which will ultimately be subsumed into the categories of modern and postmodern. For obvious reasons, once Lyotard had written *The Postmodern Condition* he no longer used the classic/modern opposition, but the "pagan" remains one of the categories of his thought. In those pre-1979 texts in which Lyotard uses "modern" in the unreconstructed sense—i.e., when he's using the term "modern" to describe what he would today call the postmodern—I have amended the translation to read "[post]modern" to minimize confusion.

As Lyotard develops the notion in *Just Gaming*, to be postmodern is to be in the realm of the "pagan." The pagan is a space outside received law; to be pagan is to accept the fact that there is no universal language game, and that the best that one can do is to play one's game well, with imagination, with ruse. As a result, Lyotard claims that "humor is an essential tone" of the postmodern (*JG* 12); the artistic language game played by a writer like Joyce is, he says, "a matter of treatments, I would almost say 'tortures,' inflicted upon language" (*JG* 50). In postmodernity, "one 'hams' it up, because one invents, because one inserts novel episodes that stand out as motifs against the narrative plot line, which, for its part, remains stable" (*JG* 33).

In allying the postmodern with humor, Lyotard echoes the more radical equation that Kristeva makes in *Revolution in Poetic Language;* in a section devoted to Lautréamont, she says that he "makes laughter a *symptom of rupture* and of the heterogeneous contradiction within signifying practice when he requires that poetry *bring about an explosion of laughter within metalanguage* at the same time he *refuses the laughter* that is a phenomenon of psychological decompression (or compensation) or narcissistic compromise."[44] This textual laughter is the laughter of the late Joycean comic texts; it is what I have called "carnivalesque stylistics"—the gay relativity that Bakhtin says characterizes the medieval institution of carnival, turned into a textual impulse.[45] Indeed, Kristeva may have derived her notion of textual laughter—what I would call, after the individually wrapped cubes of Gruyère cheese, *le texte qui rit*—from Bakhtin. In the Dostoyevsky book, he writes of carnival laughter as an entire perceptual/literary paradigm: "Laughter is a specific aesthetic relationship to reality, but not one that can be translated into logical language; that is, it is a specific means for artistically visualizing and comprehending reality and, consequently, a specific means for structuring an artistic image, plot, or genre. Enormous creative, and therefore genre-shaping, power was possessed by ambivalent carnivalistic laughter. This laughter could grasp and comprehend a phenome-

non in the process of change and transition, it could fix in a phenomenon both poles of its evolution in their uninterrupted and creative re-
newing changeability: in death birth is foreseen and in birth death, in
victory defeat and in defeat victory, in crowning a decrowning. Carnival laughter does not permit a single one of these aspects of change to
be absolutized or to congeal in one-sided seriousness" (*PDP* 164). Kristeva goes on to say that "the practice of the text is a kind of laughter
whose only explosions are those of language"; "the novelty of a practice . . . indicates the jouissance invested therein and this quality of new-
ness is the equivalent of the laughter it conceals": "He [the artist] replaces the effect of laughter with the production of new devices (new
texts, a new art) . . . and, conversely, the new devices contain the rupture from which laughter bursts forth."[46]

Another distinguishing feature of paganism (or the postmodern) lies
in the situation of the writer: the writer, Lyotard says, launches his texts
as one tosses a bottle into the sea, with no clear idea who one's audience
might be. For a clear understanding of one's audience is, Lyotard believes, one of the preconditions for modernism: "This is what I would
call classicism [modernism]: a situation in which an author can write
while putting himself at the same time in the position of a reader, being
able to substitute himself for his own reader, and to judge and sort out
what he has accomplished from the point of view of the reader that he
also is. . . . Whereas in what we call [post]modernity, he no longer
knows for whom he writes, since there no longer is any taste; there no
longer is any internalized system of rules that would permit a sorting
out, the dropping of some things and the introduction of some others,
all of this before the fact, in the act of writing" (*JG* 9). Thus the postmodern condition is characterized, in one of its aspects, by what Lyotard calls "the evanescence of the addressee" (*JG* 12); the postmodern
writer has lost her audience—or at any rate has no idea who that audience might be—and in this situation, Lyotard believes, she wins a certain degree of freedom: "today the majority of people who write interesting things, write without knowing to whom they are speaking. That
is part of the workings of this society, and it is very good. There is no
need to cry about it" (*JG* 9). Barthes makes reference in *The Pleasure of
the Text* to this same situation: "Does writing in pleasure guarantee—
guarantee me, the writer—my reader's pleasure? Not at all. I must seek
out this reader (must 'cruise' him) *without knowing where he is*. A site of
bliss is then created. It is not the reader's 'person' that is necessary to me,
it is this site: the possibility of a dialectics of desire, of an *unpredictability* of bliss: the bets are not placed, there can still be a game" (*PT* 4).

This situation—in which writers write without a conception of their potential readers—frees the writer to experiment: after all, why hold back, if you have no idea of "audience," of the taste to which you are supposed to appeal? "What is at stake in artistic language today is experimentation. And to experiment means, in a way, to be alone, to be celibate. But, on the other hand, it also means that if the artifact produced is really strong, it will wind up producing its own readers, its own viewers, its own listeners. . . . If the work is strong (and we don't really know what we are saying by this) it will produce people to whom it is destined. It will elicit its own addressees. These are things that Barthes had seen. I think that such is [post]modernity. It does not lend itself at all to the legitimation of the jeremiads of the misunderstood artist or of the haughtiness of the genius ahead of his time. Communication simply does not obtain because the value system is not sufficiently stable for a work to be able to find its appointed place and to be assured of a hearing" (*JG* 10–11). In a sense, then, the "evanescence of the addressee" frees the writer to indulge the critical function of her writing, for in the postmodern condition there is no possible consensus of taste, no possibility of writing for an audience of one's peers—and no nostalgia, if Lyotard is right, for a situation like the one Habermas evokes in his own criticism of the postmodern breakdown of community and communication. Instead of plunging him into despondency, the lack of an audience, according to Lyotard, frees the artist to pursue the "proper" aim of all art—interrogation of the received. "As for the artists and writers who question the rules of plastic and narrative arts and possibly share their suspicions by circulating their work," he writes, "they are destined to have little credibility in the eyes of those concerned with 'reality' and 'identity'; they have no guarantee of an audience" (*PC* 75).

Instead of conforming to the rules of the language game that "describes" him, therefore, the postmodern artist sets out to change the rules of that game, criticizing, in the process, the game as it has been played in the past, by a transgression of the "good forms" of the tradition. Creation, under these conditions, becomes the pure manifestation of the will to power. Lyotard sometimes calls this powerful, willful stylistics "ruse": "Ruse is not just a technique or a device for the purpose of overcoming one's opponents; it is much more than that. Ruse is an activity bound up with the will to power, because the will to power, if the word is to have a meaning, is carried out without criteria. Ruse is used on grounds and in fields, in both the topological and in the chronological sense, precisely where there are no criteria. That's what I mean by 'pagan.' I believe that [post]modernity is pagan" (*JG* 16).

This will to power in the realm of creation, upon closer examination, turns out to be a special case of the larger distinction between the modern and the postmodern: for if postmodernity, in its briefest Lyotardian formulation, is an "incredulity toward metanarratives,"[47] then ruse and paganism result from an incredulity on the part of the artist toward the rules that have traditionally proscribed the game which he wishes to play. "A [post]modern will," Lyotard writes, "is a will (or an imagination) that does not occult itself, that does not attribute its power to a conceivable model that must be respected"; for central to the postmodern spirit is a radical skepticism toward "conceivable models," to any system that would circumscribe its possibilities before the start of play. Instead, the postmodern imagination attempts "to elaborate actions and discourses, works in general, without going through a conceptual system that could serve as a criterion for practice" (*JG* 18).

Another distinction between the modern and postmodern in Lyotard's account is their differing responses to the sublime. "Modern aesthetics," Lyotard asserts, "is an aesthetics of the sublime, though a nostalgic one. It allows the unpresentable to be put forward only as the missing contents; but the form, because of its recognizable consistency, continues to offer to the reader or viewer matter for solace and pleasure" (*PC* 81).[48] The modern, according to Lyotard, uses all the equipment at its disposal to insist that "the unpresentable exists" (*PC* 78)—to present the unpresentable, make visible the invisible. Both modern and postmodern art are poignantly aware of the sublime sentiment—"the conceivable which cannot be presented" (*PC* 81). They adopt, however, slightly different means of accommodating their art to the fact that the unpresentable exists. "Modernity, in whatever age it appears, cannot exist without a shattering of belief and without discovery of the 'lack of reality' of reality, *together with the invention of other realities*" (*PC* 77). The discovery that Lyotard describes here is thus common to both the modern and postmodern artist. The difference is in their reaction to that insight: the modernist reaction, which I have italicized, is to turn from that insight and immediately begin the construction of another, a better, world. Hence the modernist reaction is a nostalgic one; but, as Lyotard insists, "there is no nostalgia in the [post]modern" (*JG* 14). For Lyotard, this is one of the hallmarks of "piety" (a.k.a. modernity): "it implies the representation of something that of course is absent, a lost origin, something that must be restored to a society in which it is lacking" (*JG* 20).

The modern in art, then, is that "which devotes its 'little technical expertise' *(son 'petit technique')*, as Diderot used to say, to present the fact that the unpresentable exists. . . . they [modern artists] devote themselves to making an allusion to the unpresentable by means of visible presentation" (*PC* 78). Not so the postmodern: "The postmodern would be that which, in the modern, puts forward the unpresentable in presentation itself; that which denies itself the solace of good forms, the consensus of a taste which would make it possible to share collectively the nostalgia for the unattainable; that which searches for new presentations, not in order to enjoy them but in order to impart a stronger sense of the unpresentable" (*PC* 81). The postmodern, while sharing the conviction that the unpresentable exists, no longer believes that the unpresentable can be made perceptible in writing without the shattering of "good forms."[49] Rather than writing about the incommensurability of words and things, the postmodern text performs that incommensurability; hence, the postmodern text always has the character of an event (*PC* 81).

The Postmodern Condition—and particularly the appendix to the American edition called "Answering the Question: What Is Postmodernism?"—were written in part as rebuttals of the work of Habermas, whom the phrases "the consensus of a taste" and "to share collectively" in the preceding quotation, for instance, are meant to evoke. For Habermas, the loss of this consensus has resulted in a "legitimation crisis"; Lyotard's response is that this delegitimation need not be seen as a crisis, if one can look at it without nostalgia. In his nostalgia for consensus, Lyotard implies, Habermas is atypical of his age: "Most people have lost the nostalgia for the lost narrative. It in no way follows that they are reduced to barbarity. What saves them from it is their knowledge that legitimation can only spring from their own linguistic practice and communicational interaction. Science 'smiling into its beard' at every other belief has taught them the harsh austerity of realism" (*PC* 41).

Lyotard's distinction of the modern from the postmodern artistic product—a distinction which rests, as he himself admits, on very little—is somewhat abstract, and only made more so in translation. But in "Answering the Question," Lyotard does spend some of his analysis working more or less concretely with two of the premiere writers of the twentieth century—Proust and Joyce—who he feels illustrate the small but profoundly significant difference between the modern and postmodern temper. For Lyotard, the pair Proust/Joyce becomes something of a paradigm for the difference between modernist and postmodern stylistics:

> The work of Proust and that of Joyce both allude to something which does not allow itself to be made present. . . . In Proust, what is being eluded as

the price to pay for this allusion is the identity of consciousness, a victim
to the excess of time *(au trop de temps)*. But in Joyce, it is the identity of
writing which is the victim of an excess of the book *(au trop de livre)* or of
literature.

Proust calls forth the unpresentable by means of a language unaltered
in its syntax and vocabulary and of a writing which in many of its operators still belongs to the genre of novelistic narration. . . . the unity of the
book, the odyssey of that consciousness, even if it is deferred from chapter to chapter, is not seriously challenged: the identity of writing with itself throughout the labyrinth of the interminable narration is enough to
connote such unity. *(PC 80)*

Joyce's procedure, however, is marked by a small but significant devia-
tion: "Joyce allows the unpresentable to become perceptible in his writing itself, in the signifier. The whole range of available narrative and
even stylistic operators is put into play without concern for the unity of
the whole, and new operators are tried. The grammar and vocabulary
of literary language are no longer accepted as given; rather, they appear
as academic forms, as rituals originating in piety (as Nietzsche said)
which prevent the unpresentable from being put forward" *(PC* 80–81).
For Lyotard as for Barthes, one of the significant modulations of postmodern stylistics is an emphasis on the signifier, on the dance and play
and excess—the carnival—of signs, rather than on a (naïve, nostalgic)
attempt to use the signifier as a means to communicate something about
the changed status of the signified. For Proust, an intuition of the unpresentable—the sublime—has changed the very nature of his vision,
but not the means of its expression; for Joyce, however, the awareness
that the unpresentable exists has an effect not just on his message, but
much more profoundly on his medium—indeed, such facile distinc-
tions as message/medium and signified/signifier begin to break down
in the wake of a postmodern conception of language. But rather than
preventing him from "saying what he wants," this Einsteinian awareness of language instead allows the postmodern writer to "write whatever he wants"—and to want, to desire what he writes. Hence Lyotard
sees it as "a sign that people are not pagan as they should be" that "they
believe in the signified of what they are saying, that they stick to this
signified, and that they think that they are in the true. This is where paganism stops and where something like doctrine, let us say, gets back
in" *(JG* 62).

Hence a significant difference between Yeats and Joyce; for with
Yeats, doctrine most certainly gets back in—with a vengeance—whereas
the spirit of the postmodern is, according to Lyotard, always anarchic,

antiform, antitotalitarian in its orientation.[50] "The system, as it exists, absorbs every consistent discourse," Lyotard writes in "Notes on the Critical Function of the Work of Art"; "the important thing is not to produce a consistent discourse but rather to produce 'figures' within reality. The problem is to endure the anguish of maintaining reality in a state of suspicion through direct practices; just like, for example, a poet is a man in a position to hold language—even if he uses it—under suspicion, i.e. to bring about figures which would never have been produced, that language might not tolerate, and which may never be audible, perceptible, for us."[51] This assertion—that postmodernism in fact promotes a politics of plurality, of respect for difference—is one of the major bones of contention in the Lyotard-Habermas debate. "Postmodern knowledge," Lyotard insists, "is not simply a tool of the authorities; it refines our sensitivity to differences and reinforces our ability to tolerate the incommensurable. Its principle is not the expert's homology, but the inventor's parology" (PC xxv). Lyotard's belief that postmodern knowledge can lead to a more egalitarian form of political life is made most explicit in the last paragraph of "Answering the Question":

> Finally, it must be clear that it is our business not to supply reality but to invent allusions to the conceivable which cannot be presented. And it is not to be expected that this task will effect the last reconciliation between language games (which, under the name of faculties, Kant knew to be separated by a chasm), and that only the transcendental illusion (that of Hegel) can hope to totalize them into a real unity. But Kant also knew that the price to pay for such an illusion is terror. The nineteenth and twentieth centuries have given us as much terror as we can take. We have paid a high enough price for the nostalgia of the whole and the one, for the reconciliation of the concept and the sensible, of the transparent and the communicable experience. Under the general demand for slackening and for appeasement, we can hear the mutterings of the desire for a return of terror, for the realization of the fantasy to seize reality. The answer is: Let us wage a war on totality; let us be witnesses to the unpresentable; let us activate the differences and save the honor of the name. (PC 81–82)

To sum up, then. The theorizing of Barthes, Bakhtin, and Lyotard shares a number of salient characteristics. To begin with a trait for which they are frequently assailed, all three are markedly idealistic, even utopian, about the nature of postmodernism. All celebrate postmodernism; all three are utopian; two of the three are essentially mystics. Bakhtin's conception of the carnivalesque, for instance, has been criticized on the grounds that he idealizes the very "folk" in whom he finds such a strong deidealizing impulse; Bakhtin's folk, it must be admitted, never existed.

Furthermore, all three see postmodernism as a transhistorical phenomenon. One of the most valuable results of Jean-François Lyotard's work has been a highlighting of the fact that postmodernism is not a literary period, but rather "a mood," "a state of mind";[52] in fact, modernism and postmodernism often "coexist in the same piece" (*PC* 80). Lyotard points out that the very notion of historical periodization is itself a modernist notion: "Historical periodization belongs to an obsession that is characteristic of modernity. Periodization is a way of placing events in a diachrony, and diachrony is ruled by the principle of revolution."[53] Thus we cannot say that modernism precedes postmodernism, or that postmodernism engulfs and devours modernism as it finds it; for as Lyotard puts it in one of his most memorable phrases, "Modernity is constitutionally and ceaselessly pregnant with its postmodernity."[54] As a result, I believe the most "untimely" modernist texts, *Ulysses* foremost among them, always contain the germ of their own postmodernity, and effectively outline the critique of their own fictive enterprise. Hassan puts it rather nicely in *The Dismemberment of Orpheus:* "the postmodern spirit lies coiled within the great corpus of modernism."[55] "Postmodernism," Hassan writes elsewhere, "may be a response, direct or oblique, to the Unimaginable that modernism glimpsed only in its most prophetic moments" (Hassan 39); and for Hassan, as for Barthes and Lyotard, one of the benefits of such an atemporal conception of postmodernism is that it opens up old texts to new readings, and allows us to discover hitherto unexpected features of those texts: hence "we perceive now—but did not perceive thirty years ago—postmodern features in *Tristram Shandy* precisely because our eyes have learned to recognize postmodern features. And so we propose *Tristram Shandy*, but not *Tom Jones*, as a 'postmodern book'" (Hassan xvi).

For these four writers—Barthes, Bakhtin, Lyotard, and Hassan—the "shock of recognition" is all the justification necessary for the project of postmodern rereading. Quoting Deleuze, these four believe that a theory "is exactly like a box of tools. . . . It must be useful. It must function";[56] and part of that function—besides the ludic possibilities opened on the surface of otherwise nearly sacred texts—may be a kind of symbolic uncrowning of the authority of modernist literature. Again Hassan: "it is already possible to note that whereas Modernism—excepting Dada and Surrealism—created its own forms of artistic Authority precisely because the center no longer held, Postmodernism has tended toward artistic Anarchy in deeper complicity with things falling apart" (Hassan 44–45). As Bakhtin insists, "pleasure is caused by degrading high literature. All that is high wearies in the long run. The more powerful and prolonged the domination of the high, the greater the pleasure caused by its uncrowning. Hence the great success of parodies and travesties, when they appear at the right time, that is, when the reader wearies of high matters" (*R* 305).

Next, in the writings of these thinkers, postmodern texts are marked out by their provisional character. They are, as Kristeva writes, *en procès* (in process and on trial); summing up what he had learned from her during her State Doctorate exam in 1973, Barthes told Kristeva, "Several times you have helped me to change, particularly in shifting away from a semiology of products to a semiotics of production."[57] Part and parcel of this provisional nature of postmodern texts is their participatory quality. Through various techniques, such as "reader traps," postmodern writing enforces a close attention to, an intimate involvement with, the process taking place on the page. Postmodern texts are what Bakhtin calls dialogic—not in their composition alone, but also, perhaps more important, in their consumption. Thus postmodern texts are what Barthes calls *scriptible* (writerly), demanding that, rather than passive consumers, we become active co-creators of the text.

Perhaps the most immediately apparent characteristic of postmodern writing is its stylistic heterogeneity. Postmodern stylistics champions plurality over authority; it is based on an anarchic, antihierarchical notion of writing. The postmodern text is *le texte qui rit*, a text which makes textual the semiotic drives of the human subject; and it not only laughs at all writing that has come before, but reserves its heartiest guffaws for itself. As Lyotard emphasizes, postmodernism is suspicious of all "fine" writing, good forms—any assumption of a natural, neutral, transparent style that pretends to no political dimension. Every style entails, enacts a politics; given such a situation, the postmodern writer's only viable option, according to Lyotard, is the multiplication of small narratives. Hence postmodernism's preference for local stylistics, local strategies, over "fine" writing; the postmodern writer strives to dissolve any metalanguage as soon as it is constituted, as part of his generalized incredulity toward metanarratives.

Closely related to this stylistic heterogeneity is postmodernism's stylistic prodigality. Postmodern stylistics is a stylistics of excess; the text is *too* rich, the surface *too* lush, the prose *too* joyous. Postmodern stylistics is altogether too too.[58] As a result, it forces our attention away from the thing signified and back onto the plane of the signifier itself—in some of its manifestations, this is the now familiar postmodern self-conscious gesture of metafiction. Postmodern prose is not nonrepresentational, but antirepresentational; its signifiers do indeed point outside themselves to one or more signifieds, but they insist on being appreciated for themselves before communicating any information about the "real" world. Hence the tendency, in some postmodern writing, to treat with distrust all obviously metaphorical language, which would allow the reader to escape too quickly the plane of the real.[59] Postmodern writing forces us to stop and smell the phonemes, to appreciate what Barthes calls "the sumptuous rank of the signifier."

Finally, it is important that we acknowledge that postmodernism is not purely a textual phenomenon; it is also a product of, and a procedure for, our reading. There are limit texts like Artaud's, which perhaps cannot be read as anything but postmodern; on the other end of the spectrum, we have texts like a mathematical proof, which would manifest none of the stylistic features we've identified as postmodern.[60] But most of our time—and, I would maintain, our most pleasurable reading time—is spent reading between these two poles. Texts like *Dubliners*, *A Portrait*, and *Ulysses* are piquant admixtures of both the modernist and postmodernist spirits; and if *Finnegans Wake* approaches something like pure postmodernism, I believe it is proportionally less interesting as a text for that very reason. *Ulysses*, as a text, "contains" postmodernism; and I, as a reader of *Ulysses*, can choose to make much or to make little of that nascent postmodernism. As Joyce remarked to Arthur Power, "What do we know about what we put into anything? Though people may read more into *Ulysses* than I ever intended, who is to say that they are wrong: do any of us know what we are creating?" (*CJJ* 89). The critical tradition, taking its lead from the modernists themselves, have made little of—have downplayed—the stylistic anarchy of Joyce's texts; for the remainder of this book, let's try to make the most of it.

3

From Interpretation to "Intrepidation"

"The Sisters"

> I'm on the side of keeping things mysterious, and I have never enjoyed understanding things. If I understand something, I have no further use for it. So I try to make a music which I don't understand and which will be difficult for other people to understand, too.
>
> —John Cage

> There isn't much point in having the arts at all unless we have them with all their interrogative power. They are not cozy or ornamental. Critics have collaborated in making them seem cozy, assuring us that they won't hurt a bit. If the arts don't hurt, why have them? It's only modern vanity which supposes that everything can be known or that only what is knowable has a claim upon our interest. The artist and the priest know that there are mysteries beyond anything that can be done with words, sounds or forms. If we want to live without this sense of mystery, we can of course, but we should be very suspicious of the feeling that everything coheres and that the arts, like everything else, fit comfortably into our lives.
>
> —Denis Donoghue

It all began innocently enough, in June or July 1904, with a letter from George Russell (Æ): "Dear Joyce: Look at the story in this paper The Irish Homestead. Could you write anything simple, rural?, livemaking?, pathos?, which could be inserted so as not to shock the readers. If you could furnish a short story about 1800 words suitable for insertion the editor will pay £1.[1] It is easily earned money if you can write fluently and don't mind playing to the common understanding and liking for once in a way. You can sign it any name you like as a pseudonym" (*L* 2:43). Russell, an editor of the *Irish Homestead,* had been impressed with the manuscript chapters of *Stephen Hero,* and knowing Joyce to be desperate for money tried to send some work his way. Joyce would surely have welcomed the "right" kind of assignment; a few months earlier he had offered to translate Maeterlinck's *La vie des abeilles* for another trade paper, the *Irish Bee-Keeper,* but his proposal had been turned down.

Russell's offer, however, while presumably well-intentioned, imposed constraints at which Joyce balked. Russell's query, solicitous to the point of condescension, must have irritated the young poet; indeed, Magalaner and Kain hyperbolically call it "an almost rude letter."[2] The suggestion that he write something "suitable for insertion" into a paper like the *Homestead*—that he produce at Russell's request a story that would blend seamlessly with the surrounding text—doubtless offended Joyce's sense of propriety, as well as his own estimation of his gifts. The chances are he would not have been averse to Russell's putting the paper at his disposal; but the invitation was, emphatically, for Joyce to produce something to *fit into* Russell's paper—to put himself at the *Homestead*'s disposal and produce its brand of fiction. Preparing a translation of Maeterlinck for the *Bee-Keeper* was one thing; but writing fiction *for* the *Homestead* was clearly more than Joyce could bear.

Even if he had chosen to accept the commission on Russell's terms, though, it is difficult to imagine what Joyce could have written that would tastefully follow verse like this, which appeared just ahead of "The Sisters" in the 13 August 1904 edition of the *Homestead:*

> The blackbird and the thrush were in the small nut wood,
>   Making sweet music like the songs of the bards,
> And the sprightly lark with a song in her little mouth
>   Poising herself in the air aloft.
> The beautiful thrush was on top of the branch,
>   His throat stretched out in melodious song.
> And, O, God of Grace, it was fine to be
>   In beauteous Ireland at that time![3]

These lines are only slightly more maudlin and conventionalized than the poem from which Joyce silently distances himself at the conclusion of "Ivy Day in the Committee Room" *("O, Erin, mourn with grief and woe");* but while in "Ivy Day" Joyce would control the narrative environment into which the poetry is recited, and would allow himself an ironically flat comment at the end—"Mr. Crofton said that it was a very fine piece of writing" (*D* 135)—in the *Homestead*'s columns he was at his editor's mercy.

But in spite of these unfavorable conditions, Joyce accepted the assignment. Joyce's first fiction, then, was destined to be born into rather

humble surroundings. The first half of "The Sisters" is sandwiched between sprightly larks poising themselves in the air aloft and an ad for "Cantrell & Cochrane's Mineral Waters," touting club soda, ginger ale, and "Sparkling Montserrat, The Drink for the Gouty & Rheumatic" (hence, perhaps, Eliza's recollection of Father Flynn's desire to take a trip to Irishtown in a carriage with "rheumatic wheels," a passage Joyce added between periodical and book publication);[4] the second page of the story appears above a half-page ad for "Dairy Supply Co., Ltd., 'Creamery Supplies of all kinds at Lowest Rates'" that features a sketch of their sculptured "double effektive milk pump for auxiliary dairies."[5] The comic result is that by virtue of its surroundings "The Sisters" is, despite Joyce's best efforts to the contrary, a "rural" tale—and, forced between ads for minerals and dairy pumps, it becomes a tale told in the folk marketplace: the textual version of Bakhtin's carnival tale.

Russell's suggestion that Joyce use a pseudonym was also doubtless taken in a different spirit than it was offered. Russell, apparently believing that Joyce would produce a text to the *Homestead*'s specifications, suggested that he use a nom de plume as a way of distancing himself from the work, much as academics today write detective novels under assumed names (as Carolyn Heilbrun, for instance, under the name "Amanda Cross," wrote *The James Joyce Murders*). Joyce did choose to use a pseudonym—Stephen Dædalus, with an "Æ" at the heart that he would later anglicize—*not* because he was ashamed of his text, however, but rather because he was ashamed of the pages in which it appeared: in *Ulysses*, Stephen refers to the *Homestead* as "the pigs' paper" (*U* 158).

Russell's further offense was to ask for a story that would not shock the *Homestead*'s readers. By the summer of 1904 Joyce had already written several times of his disdain for what Russell delicately calls "playing to the common understanding and liking." Joyce's broadside "The Day of the Rabblement" (1901), for instance, opens on a defiant note: "No man, said the Nolan, can be a lover of the true or the good unless he abhors the multitude; and the artist, though he may employ the crowd,

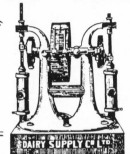
is very careful to isolate himself" (*CW* 69). Just six months before receiving Russell's offer Joyce had rendered this same antipopulist sentiment somewhat more poetically, in his essay "A Portrait of the Artist": "Let the pack of enmities come tumbling and sniffing to the highlands after their game—there was his ground: and he flung them disdain from flashing antlers" (*P* 259). At this stage in his career Joyce not only thought the "reading public" beneath his concern, but indeed seems to have believed their annoyance proof positive of his gifts. To be an artist, according to Joyce's youthful credo, was to be misunderstood; and no matter how little of *Stephen Hero* Russell had read, nor how infrequent their conversations together had been, he must surely have been aware of Joyce's disdain for the Irish reading public.[6]

So whether offended by the tone of Russell's invitation or simply unable to master what he called "the perverse devil of my literary conscience" (*L* 2:166), Joyce responded to his request in short order with "The Sisters"—a story neither simple, rural, "livemaking," nor pathetic, but rather complex, urban, morbid, chilling—and seemingly calculated to disturb Russell's readers. Incredibly, Russell accepted the story—incredible especially given what was to be the tortuous publishing history of *Dubliners* over the next ten years. The *Homestead*, after all, was not a publication that aimed to shake up its readers; and while it seems poetically just that *A Portrait* should appear serially in a small magazine called, of all things, the *Egoist*, Joyce's publishing "The Sisters" in the *Irish Homestead*, "the official organ of Irish Agricultural and Industrial Development," is roughly analogous to installments of *Naked Lunch* appearing weekly in the pages of the *Saturday Evening Post*, or *Good Housekeeping* snapping up the serial rights to *American Psycho*.

In a letter to his brother, Joyce wrote of the war that raged, during the writing of *Dubliners*, between "what you call the Holy Ghost sitting in the ink-bottle and the perverse devil of my literary conscience sitting on the hump of my pen" (*L* 2:166). In the opening act of the *Homestead* drama—Russell's commissioning a "story" and Joyce's response, "The Sisters"—we get our first glimpse of the engendering spirit of *Dubliners*, a willful and unruly spirit which would not hold its tongue. This, if we discount the abortive project to publish the essay "A Portrait of the Artist," is the inaugural gesture of Joyce's fiction, one which firmly established the oeuvre on a foundation of perversity.[7]

"At times the spirit directing my pen seems to me so plainly mischievous that I am almost prepared to let the Dublin critics have their way" (*L* 2:99), Joyce wrote his brother Stanislaus on another occasion; but of course, in the end Joyce could not let the critics have their way. The war between the Holy Ghost and Joyce's perverse devil was to rage throughout his life's writing; and in this, the first battle of *Dubliners*'s ten-year war of independence, the spirit of perversity triumphed. Not surprisingly, "The Sisters" did shock the *Irish Homestead* readers; Joyce was somehow able to publish two subsequent stories, "Eveline" and "After the Race," in the *Homestead*, but according to Florence Walzl, after these three "the editor refused to accept any more of Joyce's stories because he had had so many letters of complaint about them from readers."[8] By January 1905, when Joyce (from Pola) commissioned Stanislaus to sell the *Homestead* a fourth, "Hallow Eve" (later "Clay"), the publisher, H. F. Norman, decided that both he and his readers had had enough.[9]

It would no doubt prove delightful and instructive to see the readers' letters written to the editor of the *Homestead* in response to Joyce's stories, but none, apparently, have been preserved. We can get some idea of the public's reaction, though, from the reviews of *Dubliners* in the London press. The most appreciative reviews complained that Joyce was wasting his considerable talents; an unsigned review in the *Athenæum*, for instance, essentially suggested that if Joyce didn't have anything nice to say, he needn't say anything at all: "The fifteen stories here given under the collective title of *Dubliners* are nothing if not naturalistic. In some ways, indeed, they are unduly so: at least three would have been better buried in oblivion. Life has so much that is beautiful, interesting, educative, amusing, that we do not readily pardon those who insist upon its more sordid and baser aspects. The condemnation is the greater if their skill is of any high degree, since in that case they might use it to better purpose" (Deming 1:61). A far more appreciative review by Gerald Gould appeared in the *New Statesman;* but after quoting liberally from the conclusion of "The Dead" and praising its "mere melancholy beauty" (the phrase sounds like one of those Little Chandler concocts to praise his own imaginary verse), Gould can no longer withhold judgement: "Frankly, we think it is a pity (perhaps we betray a narrow puritanism in so thinking) that a man who can write like this should insist as constantly as Mr. Joyce insists upon aspects of life which are ordinarily not mentioned. To do him justice, we do not think it is a pose with him: he simply includes the 'unmentionable' in his persistent regard" (Deming 1:63). Such criticism did not come as a surprise to Joyce; he had encountered it from the very beginning, when his prospective publisher, Grant Richards, alarmed by the stories' frankness, suggested that he rewrite *Dubliners* "in another sense" ("Where the hell does he get the meaningless phrases he uses," Joyce wrote Stanislaus in some exasperation [L 2:166]).

But Joyce never intended to flatter his readers, to tell them what they wanted to hear; after all, the "perverse devil" that superintended the writing of *Dubliners* was no mere aesthetic anarchist but rather the emissary of Joyce's "literary conscience," and Joyce, in one of his more grandiose moments, declared that *Dubliners* was to be "a chapter of the moral history of my country" (L 2:134). "The Sisters" is an unsettling piece, Joyce's solicitous response to Russell's solicitous letter (to solicit, according to Derrida's etymology from *solicitare,* "to shake, a shaking of the whole"), calling into question the hermeneutics of reading that we bring to the text, and those structures of desire with which we control what that text will be allowed to say to us. Hence *Dubliners* is a catalogue of stylistic techniques calculated not to comfort, or console, but to disrupt: "The Sisters" is but the first of Joyce's "chronicles of disorder."

Entering *Dubliners* by way of "The Sisters" we instinctively tread softly, for we feel ourselves in the presence of the ineffable. In this his first published fiction Joyce casts a cold eye on life and on death, in his celebrated "style of scrupulous meanness" (*L* 2:134); the final version of the story, as critics have pointed out, is a self-conscious program piece, carefully setting out both the mood and the method of *Dubliners*. If "The Sisters" is *Dubliners*'s program piece, what is the program? What is this enigmatic text meant to teach us? The story's sensitive young protagonist comes to experience firsthand the reality of death: he scrutinizes both the physical death of his old friend Father Flynn and the more subtle spiritual rigor mortis of all those around him—Nannie and Eliza Flynn, his aunt and Uncle Jack, and Mr. Cotter. Father Flynn's gradual decline and final demise make up the bulk of the story; and yet time and again in *Dubliners* Joyce focuses our attention on the storytellers, rather than on the tales they tell. In the boy's eyes, and surely in Joyce's, the death-in-life of these still-breathing Dubliners, rather than the long-expected death of an old paralytic priest, supplies the story's most bitter pathos.

Traditionally "The Sisters" is read as introducing the note of paralysis that is whispered throughout the volume: "Every night as I gazed up at the window," our young narrator tells us, "I said softly to myself the word *paralysis*" (*D* 9). Thus, the story has most often been treated as a cautionary tale in which the young narrator catches a glimpse of the "deadly work" of paralysis and is given an opportunity to mend his ways, although readers have disagreed about whether or not the boy is finally changed by his experience. But of course Joyce tells us almost nothing about the final effect of Father Flynn's death on the boy. This, no doubt, is in part what Joyce meant by calling *Dubliners*'s style a "style of scrupulous meanness": puzzles remain unsolved, tensions unresolved, conclusions undrawn. William Gass, looking back on the composition of his first story, "The Pedersen Kid," described the process of revision as "covering the moral layer with a frost of epistemological doubt," and something like this seems to have been Joyce's process as well.[10] "The Sisters," especially, is a story full of unanswered questions—even the most elementary information is obscured or withheld. We cannot decide with any certainty, for instance, what exactly the priest died of; we are told in the story's first sentence that he had suffered his third stroke, but later that he had "died of paralysis." The first explanation sounds more magical than real ("There was no hope for him this time: it was the third stroke"),[11] and the second patently illogical, paralysis being a chronic rather than an acute condition. Writing about "The Sisters" William York Tindall says that "all we can be sure of is that the father's gone,"[12] and this is of course an overstatement; and yet it does get at something fundamentally true—and unsettling—about the story.

By the story's close the boy has learned, as others (like old Cotter) will never learn, that mystery is not opposed to life, but is at its very heart; it is, as well, one of the motive forces behind postmodern art. Samuel Beckett makes this point quite succinctly: "Art, an arrangement of the inexplicable, never explains. Nor, intent on mystery, does the artist."[13] Joyce knew this well; in response to Arthur Power's contention that "the classical style" is the best form of writing, Joyce replied: "Perhaps, but to my mind it is a form of writing which contains little or no mystery . . . and since we are surrounded by mystery it has always seemed to me inadequate. It can deal with facts very well, but when it has to deal with motives, the secret currents of life which govern everything, it has not the orchestra, for life is a complicated problem" (*CJJ* 73–74). In "The Sisters" Joyce begins to rehearse that orchestra, that he might adequately celebrate life's mystery; in the story our narrator moves from the interrogation of experience with the private detective's hand lens to the ecstatic worship of a devotee of the mysteries—a priest, perhaps, of eternal imagination.

Yet for all its strangeness, "The Sisters" has an oddly familiar ring. And no wonder: for from the start Joyce's first story is set out according to the narrative conventions of the detective story.[14] As we move from the boy's outcast meditations on paralysis and death in the opening paragraph to the first narrative section of the story, set in his home, we find old Cotter sitting at the fire, smoking his pipe. He is a guest—seemingly a too-frequent guest—in the boy's home, to whom the aunt makes the socially proper responses, graciously asking all the questions that Cotter hopes someone will ask in response to his teasing, elliptical statements about Father Flynn. In the dynamics of this opening scene, she plays the role of Cotter's "straight (wo)man"; or perhaps more accurately, she plays Dr. Watson to Cotter's Sherlock Holmes, for his manner, his mannerisms, betray his frustrated Holmesian aspirations.

Cotter is depicted, however, as an ironically deflated Holmes; and even if we do not initially pick up the "clews," they are scattered throughout the opening pages: "Old Cotter was sitting at the fire, smoking, when I came downstairs to supper. . . . He began to puff at his pipe, no doubt arranging his opinion in his mind. . . . I have my own theory about it, he said. I think it was one of those . . . peculiar cases. . . . But it's hard to say . . ." (*D* 9–11). Sitting in front of the fire, puffing at his pipe, speaking of the "peculiar case"[15] of Father Flynn, Cotter has Holmes's gestures down just right; the first scene of "The Sisters" is a mocking version of the fireside tableau that opens so many of the Conan Doyle stories. As John Cawelti notes, that stock scene has an important narrative function in the traditional story of detection: "The peaceful beginning in the detective's retreat establishes a point of departure and return for the story. The crime symbolizes not only an infraction of the law but a disruption of the normal order of society. It is something extraordinary that must be solved in order to restore the harmonious mood of that charming scene by the blazing fireplace."[16] But of course Joyce's scene by the fireplace is anything but "charming" and "harmonious"; readers are instead reminded of the agonistic Christmas dinner recounted in the first chapter of *A Portrait of the Artist*. And the tensions are left unresolved, for the fireside scene fades out on the boy's sublimated resentment: "I crammed my mouth with stirabout for fear I might give utterance to my anger" (*D* 11).

The story's spare, lower-middle-class urban setting is key to its power over us. The rise of the detective story, as many commentators have pointed out, is roughly contemporaneous with the rise of the modern industrial city. At the turn of the century one of Doyle's contemporaries, G. K. Chesterton, observed that the detective story is the "only form of popular literature in which is expressed some sense of the poetry of modern life."[17] The detective story fulfilled—and fulfills—an important psychic function for city dwellers increasingly alienated from meaningful control over their lives. Cawelti writes: "The special drama of crime in the classical detective story lies in the way it threatens the serene domestic circles of bourgeois life with anarchy and chaos. . . . The ordered rationality of society momentarily seems a flimsy surface over a seething pit of guilt and disorder. Then the detective intervenes and proves that the general suspicion is false. He proves the social order is not responsible for the crime because it was the act of a particular individual with his own private motives."[18] The traditional detective story exists to comfort and reassure its readers; "works in the genre," writes Dennis Porter, "provide a form of reassurance to the extent that they represent the victory of a recognizable national cultural hero over an adversary."[19] Again, however, "The Sisters" is the ironic shadow side of the traditional detective story; for far from tying up the "loose ends" and reassuring us that the menace has been contained, "The Sisters" ends on a discordant note, leaving us in almost unbearable suspense.

And too, Cotter's tired "wisdom" is ironically inadequate to the uncanny sleuthing of Holmes; like Mr. Deasy in *Ulysses*, Cotter is a parodic Nestor. Doyle frequently used the fireside chats between Holmes and Watson to establish his detective hero's credentials as a detective-philosopher—almost a detective-artist—as in the opening scene of "A Case of Identity": "'My dear fellow,' said Sherlock Holmes, as we sat on either side of the fire in his lodgings in Baker Street, 'life is infinitely stranger than anything which the mind of man could invent. We would not dare to conceive the things which are really mere commonplaces of existence. If we could fly out of that window hand in hand, hover over this great city, gently remove the roofs, and peep in at the queer things which are going on, the strange coincidences, the plannings, the cross-purposes, the wonderful chains of events, working through generations, and leading to the most *outré* results, it would make all fiction with its conventionalities and foreseen conclusions most stale and unprofitable.'"[20] We are shown that Holmes is more than a "mere" detective, for with his magnifying glass he is somehow able to read the signs, and thereby to see into the secret hearts of men. As his opening monologue here illustrates, the celebrated Holmesian "deduction" is in fact a combination of deduction and inference based on the detective's past experience of "human nature"—previous mysteries always suggesting ways of seeing the "facts," interpreting the "clews," in subsequent cases.

In old Cotter, however, Holmes's working hypotheses have hardened into prejudice; when, for instance, Cotter is described by the boy as "arranging his opinion in his mind" (*D* 10), the singular "opinion" immediately catches our eye. Seemingly, Cotter's one opinion is sufficient to explain any set of phenomena, and needs only to be adjusted to accommodate the "facts" of the case in question. But the "peculiar case" of Father Flynn is different; there was, as Cotter himself says, "something uncanny about him"—something elusive, something mysterious, something. . . .

For all his posturing, then, we quickly realize that old Cotter is only mock Sherlock. But the story presents us with *two* Holmesian pretenders—old Cotter and our narrator, the lively intelligence who shapes the story we read. Cotter, we soon discover, has cultivated the Holmesian façade but not the Holmesian intellect—the trained, disciplined, logical mind. But if we have read carefully, we will have noticed in the very first paragraph of "The Sisters," our narrator's "Preface" to *The Rev. James Flynn Murder Mystery,* that he and not Cotter is the story's real sleuth. That first paragraph, like the opening of "A Case of Identity," was conceived (in part) to convince us of the quality and sensitivity of our hero's (and narrator's) mind.

The boy begins the story by bumping up against riddles and trying to solve them: when Cotter speaks in ellipses, for instance, our narrator tries to decipher them ("I puzzled my head to extract meaning from his unfinished sentences" [*D* 11]). The story's opening paragraph is a tour de force of the boy's detective skills, in which he details his process of Holmesian "deduction" based on close observation of limited details: "There was no hope for him this time: it was the third stroke. Night after night I had passed the house (it was vacation time) and studied the lighted square of window: and night after night I had found it lighted the same way, faintly and evenly. If he was dead, I thought, I would see the reflection of candles on the darkened blind for I knew that two candles must be set at the head of a corpse" (*D* 9). The physical evidence is presented and interpreted with an economy that "Sherlock" Cotter would not wish to emulate; and in contrast to the narrative convention of the Holmes stories, the protagonist of "The Sisters" combines within himself the roles of both Holmes and Watson, acting as sleuth and author.

The story's opening displays an enthusiastic confidence in the ability of the rational mind to "make sense" of its world. The worldview that underlies these opening sections has been articulated by Michael Holquist in an essay on postwar detective fiction: "The detective, the instrument of pure logic, is able to triumph because he alone in a world of credulous men, holds to the Scholastic principle of *adequatio rei et intellectus,* the adequation of mind to things, the belief that the mind, given enough time, can understand everything. There are no mysteries, there is only incorrect reasoning."[21] Our narrator begins his quest having just this faith. Asked what he had learned from the Jesuits, Joyce told August Suter "I have learnt to arrange things in such a way that they become easy to survey and to judge" (*JJ* 27); and the boy in "The Sisters"— whether under the care of the Jesuits or no—studies the signs and follows a line of deductive reasoning, concluding that Father Flynn has not yet died; indeed, he even explains to us how he, a schoolboy, was at liberty to pass by the priest's house night after night ("it was vacation time").[22]

The controlled, poised self-presentation of those opening sentences, however, has completely evaporated when we see the boy next, sitting on the sidelines of the adults' conversation. In very short order the narrator leaves off trying to complete Cotter's fill-in-the-blank innuendos; in fact, by the midpoint of the story he has renounced the detective's quest altogether, and when we reach the story's queer ending, we can see that the narrator has traced a trajectory from Detection to Mystery. Early on the boy is eager to test his mettle against the obstinate facts of "the Flynn Case," to triumph over the seemingly incoherent constellation of fact, opinion, and rumor that confronts and confounds him. And yet even by the close of that opening paragraph we sense that he is undergoing an important change in attitude: "Every night as I gazed up at the window I said softly to myself the word *paralysis*. It had always sounded strangely in my ears, like the word *gnomon* in the Euclid and the word *simony* in the Catechism. But now it sounded to me like the name of some maleficent and sinful being. It filled me with fear, and yet I longed to be nearer to it and to look upon its deadly work" (*D* 9). Early in the paragraph the narrator had placed emphasis on his action ("I had passed," "I had . . . studied," "I had found") and knowledge ("I knew. . . . I knew"); but these last sentences emphasize instead the boy's passivity in the face of Father Flynn's death. In the first part of the paragraph the boy is playing a role, one that he has no doubt come across in his reading—that of the detective who has been called to the scene and asked to reinstate order. But in "The Sisters," our would-be detective encounters not a problem, but a mystery; and as Denis Donoghue distinguishes them, "a problem is something to be solved, a mystery is something to be witnessed and attested."[23] The narrator closes that first paragraph in awed recognition of the completely Other and unmasterable nature of Father Flynn's life and death.

Hence "The Sisters" as a detective story collapses under its own weight, no doubt because Joyce felt the whole notion of "detection" to be only a comforting fiction. Whereas the young protagonists of the "stories of childhood" live out the texts of culture they have absorbed (*The Union Jack, Pluck,* and *The Halfpenny Marvel*),[24] in "The Sisters" Joyce does Doyle with a difference—an important difference. The story opens, as we have seen, as a self-conscious imitation of the Sherlock Holmes tale of ratiocination; but the story's most striking feature is finally not its initial similarity to a classical detective story, but how very different it has become by its close. William Stowe has written that Holmes's technique of "deduction" is "a practical semiotics": "his goal is to consider data of all kinds as potential signifiers and to link them, however disparate and incoherent they seem, to a coherent set of signifieds, that is, to turn them into signs of the hidden *order* behind the manifest confusion, of the *solution* to the mystery, of the *truth*."[25] The terms that Stowe italicizes were of course extremely problematic for Joyce; in all of his subsequent work, those concepts are treated with suspicion—interrogated, indicted. We should not then be surprised that they come in for close scrutiny here.

"Order," "solution," and "truth"—or better, Truth—have been increasingly problematic terms for postwar detective fiction, as well. We might state, as a corollary to Lyotard's decree that the *meta-récit* is dead and to Adorno's dictum regarding postwar poetry, that after Auschwitz there can no longer be Detection. William Spanos puts it this way in his essay "The Detective and the Boundary":

> It was the recognition of the ultimately "totalitarian" implications of the Western structure of consciousness—of the expanding analogy that encompasses metaphysics, art, and politics in the name of the reassuring logos of empirical reason—that compelled the postmodern imagination to undertake the deliberate and systematic destruction of plot—the beginning, middle, and end structure of representational narrative—which has enjoyed virtually unchallenged privileged status in the Western literary imagination ever since Aristotle or, at any rate, since the Renaissance interpreters of Aristotle, claimed it to be the most important of the constitutive elements of literature. In the familiar language of Aristotle's *Poetics*, then, the postmodern strategy of decomposition exists to activate rather than to purge pity and terror, to disintegrate, to atomize, rather than to create a community.[26]

Thus while Sherlock Holmes, the Victorian-Edwardian-Georgian rational sleuth, is the representative man of letters for the first half of the century, Samuel Beckett's Moran, that "sensible man, cold as crystal and as free from spurious depth," is a more fitting patron for the avant-garde detective fiction written in the postwar period.[27] Moran is the archetype of the defective detective; he launches his quest for Molloy in deadly earnest—"I was so scrupulous," he tells us[28]—but in the end must renounce the project, reduced to repeating the opening of his tale with a difference ("It was not midnight. It was not raining").[29] In his art Beckett set himself the task of finding "a form to accommodate the chaos"; and in the explicitly antidetective second section of *Molloy*, he chronicles one man's reluctant surrender to the mysterious, rather than triumphant conquest of it.

A detective story—or better, a mystery—that proceeds in this manner can no longer fruitfully be called a detective story. Different critics, discussing this phenomenon, have coined various names for this bastard subgenre, among them "metaphysical detective stories" (Holquist) and "antidetective fiction" (Tani). Since according to all commentators this perverted detective tale is a postmodern genre, I will call this form the postmodern mystery—but also credit Joyce, a decade before World War I, as being one of its unheralded progenitors.

The postmodern mystery is the dark side of the Holmesian dream of interpretive infallibility; writers like Borges, Nabokov, Beckett, Eco, and others have perversely written up the stories that the ever-discreet Dr. Watson chose to suppress. For as Watson divulges at the beginning of "The Five Orange Pips," not all of Holmes's cases were successes—not all of the mysteries were eradicated: "When I glance over my notes and records of the Sherlock Holmes cases between the years '82 and '90, I am faced by so many which present strange and interesting features, that it is no easy matter to know which to choose and which to leave. Some, however, have already gained publicity through the papers, and others have not offered a field for those peculiar qualities which my friend possessed in so high a degree, and which qualities it is the object of these papers to illustrate. Some, too, have baffled his analytical skill, and would be, as narratives, beginnings without an ending, while others have been but partially cleared up, and have their explanations founded rather upon conjecture and surmise than on that absolute logical proof which was so dear to him."[30] Joyce early on recognized that the traditional detective story—indeed, any conventionalized narrative structure, when inhabited subconsciously by the writer and consumed uncritically by the reader—is a species of wish fulfillment, and one in which he did not wish to participate. His fictions are filled with characters who rehearse the traditional narratives, repeat the traditional clichés, feel the traditional emotions, and suffer the traditional delusions (cf. Hynes's poem on the death of Parnell), all as a means to escape the life that confronts them. By subtly perverting the conventions of the detective story in "The Sisters," Joyce exposes the values inherent in that form:

> Formula stories may well be one important way in which the individuals in a culture act out unconscious or repressed needs, or express latent motives that they must give expression to but cannot face openly. Possibly one important difference between the mimetic and escapist impulses in literature is that escapist literature tends to construct new disguises or to confirm existing defenses against the confrontation of latent desires. Such a view might be substantiated by the contrast between Sophocles' play *Oedipus the King* and a detective story. In the play detection leads to a revelation of hidden guilts in the life of the protagonist, while in the detective story the inquirer-protagonist and the hidden guilt are conveniently split into two separate characters—the detective and the criminal—thereby enabling us to imagine terrible crimes without also having to recognize our own impulses toward them.[31]

The result of twisting the formula in this manner is a detective story written in conscious defiance of the detective story—the postmodern mystery story. As such, it subverts many of the ideological underpinnings of the traditional detective story. Spanos, adopting for a moment the hortatory, declares that "Our time . . . calls for an existence-art, one that, by refusing to resolve discords . . . into the satisfying concordances of an inclusive *télos* (or Identity), constitutes an assault against an *art-*

ificialized nature in behalf of the recovery of its primordial terrors—
and possibilities. The most immediate task, therefore, in which the contemporary writer must engage himself—it is, to borrow a phrase ungratefully from Yeats, the most difficult of tasks not impossible—is that
of undermining the detectivelike expectations of the positivistic mind,
of unhoming Western Man, by evoking rather than purging pity and
terror—anxiety."[32] Not only does the postmodern mystery story reach—
and teach—very different answers about the nature of experience, but
by disguising itself in the detective's overcoat and deerstalker, it lures
the reader into a specially designed trap: the reader reads like a detective a tale that cautions against reading like a detective.

Living on this side of *Molloy* & Co., I think we must read "The Sisters" as a postmodern mystery story à la Pynchon's *The Crying of Lot 49*,
Nabokov's *Pale Fire*, DeLillo's *Running Dog*, and Gass's "The Pedersen
Kid"—a mystery story in which the mystery is not solved, indeed is not
soluble, a mystery story faithful to the character of real mystery. The
postmodern mystery story's puzzles are meant not to be solved—like
Stephen's riddle in the "Nestor" episode of *Ulysses*, in Hélène Cixous's
reading—but rather to stand as silent witnesses to the ineluctable mystery of life. Rather than challenging our habitual ways of seeing and
understanding, riddles, especially those that can easily be worked out,
confirm our tacit understanding of the world. The asking and answering of riddles has traditionally been a way to confer or usurp power: an
exercise in mastery rather than mystery. Our word "riddle" is derived
from the old English *rædan*, "to interpret" (also the source of our verb
"to read"); riddles assume that the world is a text open for us to read,
and he who can piece together the signs, or prevent his opponent from
construing them, secures power for himself. The classic example is the
riddle of the Sphinx; before Oedipus answered it, the Sphinx had killed
all who had come before her; after answering it, Oedipus became King
of Thebes, and the Sphinx, vanquished, dashed herself on the rocks below.

But there also exists another kind of riddle which we might call an
"antiriddle"—a riddle that perversely resists all attempts at a solution—
an unanswered question, an unsolved mystery. Were it not for their titles, the prose poems of *Tender Buttons* would be riddles, albeit insolu-
ble ones. In *Alice's Adventures in Wonderland*, the Mad Hatter challenges
Alice, "Why is a raven like a writing desk?" His question apparently
takes the form of a riddle, and Alice jumps eagerly at the chance to answer it: "'Come, we shall have some fun now!' thought Alice. 'I'm glad
they've begun asking riddles—I believe I can guess that,' she added
out loud." But Alice cannot guess the riddle; and when she gives up

and asks the Hatter the answer, he replies, "I haven't the slightest idea."[33] The Hatter's riddle, it turns out, is only a riddle posed by a madman, signifying nothing.

Because neither Alice nor the Hatter produces an answer for the riddle, it became, as Martin Gardner observes, "the object of much parlour speculation in Carroll's time."[34] Even Carroll suggested some possible solutions; but they were, as he pointed out, purely an afterthought, prompted by the reading public's desire for closure. In *Ulysses*, Joyce goes Carroll one better. In the "Nestor" episode, Stephen closes his history class by asking the students a riddle.

> –This is the riddle, Stephen said:
>   The cock crew,
>   The sky was blue:
>   The bells in heaven
>   Were striking eleven.
>   'Tis time for this poor soul
>   To go to heaven. (*U* 22)

None can answer, and Stephen, "his throat itching," proceeds to frustrate their curiosity with an apparent non sequitur: "The fox burying his grandmother under a hollybush." P. W. Joyce, whose *English As We Speak It* served James Joyce as a source for the riddle, believes the answer is a nonsense solution; certainly the students could not be expected to answer it. A riddle with a nonsense answer violates the unwritten rules of the genre, and we might legitimately question whether it is in fact a riddle after all. The students, for their part, are rescued from this uncomfortable scene by a voice in the corridor calling them to hockey, and they presumably dismiss the episode as a lark.

For Cixous, however, Stephen's riddle is much more than just a lark. She points out that we as readers share the students' confusion; "everything combines to make you 'take seriously' the existence of an answer: the very genre of the riddle, a literary and detective-story genre, which assumes as a fundamental convention that there should be a solution somewhere."[35] The absolute noncoincidence of question and answer makes for a tense moment for the students, Stephen, and the reader. Something has gone wrong here, we think; riddles have answers, and teachers bring light, not confusion. Stephen's riddle is symptomatic of a larger aporia in the book; his answer, Cixous writes, "reveals not a positive knowledge, but the gap in knowledge, the knowledge of nonknowledge, the author abandoning his rights over language, and thus the desacralization of reading in the sense that reading is implicitly the rite of passage into culture."[36] In the school office, Mr. Deasy tells Stephen, "You were not born to be a teacher, I think"; Stephen, poignantly aware of the gaps in his own knowledge, replies, "a learner rather" (*U* 29).

Stephen's riddle, along with its "answer," insists that one "stop demanding meaning"—that, as the Talking Heads insist, we "stop making sense"; Cixous says that with this scene Joyce "breaks . . . the circle of the 'readable.'"[37] Though she prefers different terminology, what Cixous describes is the postmodern moment in Joyce. Porter observes that "The formal detective story in particular is constructed on a principle similar to that of the riddle. In the same way that the latter depends on a form of punning, a detective novel presents the reader with a set of data that either appear to be meaningless or suggest an obvious but wrong interpretation at the same time that they conceal the true one. . . . As Viktor Shklovsky pointed out, the title of the Doyle story 'The Speckled Band' is in itself a riddle suggesting the false solution of the involvement of a 'gang,' when in reality a 'ribbon' is meant."[38] Indeed, the misleading riddle is one of Joyce's primary means of shaking us out of our complacent habits of reading in "The Sisters." Yet how many more articles will be written "solving" Stephen's riddle, or identifying the man in the M'Intosh, or completing Bloom's sentence in the sand "I AM A . . . ," or translating Dennis Breen's libelous postcard (U.p: up), or explaining the secret relationship between "simony," "paralysis," and "gnomon"? Thirty years ago, Tindall recognized this aspect of the story: "One of the most complex and disturbing in the sequence, this story is a riddle. Nothing comes quite clear. The nameless boy who tells the story is 'puzzled' by hints and 'intricate questions,' and so are we. Raising such questions, teasing us with possibilities, the story provides no answers."[39] In *Dubliners* riddles abound, not least in the stories' puzzling titles.[40] While some are perplexing only before one has read the story in question ("An Encounter," say, or "Grace"), others remain so after repeated readings: "A Little Cloud," for instance, and of course "The Sisters."

In both the opening and closing scenes of "The Sisters," the silent boy is engulfed by talk. The narratives that grow up around Father Flynn in order to explain what has happened to him finally tell us very little; they represent a fruitless hermeneutic practice—a dead end. Strangely enough, however, the critical history of "The Sisters" has followed not the narrator's example, but the Dubliners': much of the commentary on "The Sisters"—on *Dubliners*, on *Ulysses*, on *Finnegans Wake*—is an attempt to answer questions to which the text does not provide answers, and which the narrator of "The Sisters," by story's close, has become wise enough no longer to pursue.

For we readers and critics, of course, are the most persistent of all the detectives involved in the Flynn Case.[41] The hermeneutics that undergirds the detective's quest informs the literary critic's, as well; as Porter puts it, "A novel, like a corpse, is approached by professionals as an enigma requiring a solution. It, too, is assumed to be in need of a mediating intelligence if its true story is to be told. The activities of both literary critic and detective involve a process of selecting from a multiplicity of soliciting signs those that may be organized into an interpretation."[42] To approach the text—indeed, to approach *life*—in this way, as a text in need of interpretation, a wildness that needs to be contained, is to rob experience of its mystery, its potential to surprise and change us. Spanos, at the conclusion of his piece on the postmodern detective, quotes from *All's Well That Ends Well* to good effect: "They say that miracles are past, and we have our philosophical persons to make modern and familiar things supernatural and causeless. Hence is it that we make trifles of terrors, ensconcing ourselves into seeming knowledge when we should submit ourselves to an unknown fear."[43]

To date, Frank O'Connor is one of the few critics to respond to "The Sisters" by suspending analysis, as the story would seem to demand; he writes, refreshingly unashamed, that "the point of it still eludes me."[44] Yet this sort of response is still largely unacceptable in a critic; for while we may tacitly acknowledge that our life experience is closer to that of Beckett's Moran than to that of the legend of Baker Street, we—readers and critics—still take Holmes rather than Moran as our patron saint. "What Doyle's fictional model celebrates," Porter writes, "is the heroism inherent in the scholar/researcher's work. If Holmes is heroic, it is chiefly because he possesses the intellectual's power to produce coherence. Like the scholar/researcher, Holmes takes the fragments and finds the hidden pattern; he establishes relationships where none had previously appeared."[45] We've been trained, as readers and critics, to take control of a text; "when a thing resists me," Moran boasts, "even if it is for my own good, it does not resist me long."[46] But the Molloy affair *does* resist him to the bitter end. Joyce in "The Sisters" warns us of the dangers of jumping to conclusions, of seeking to master that which should master us, of seeking to foreclose the sense of mystery that is inseparable from experience. "The Sisters" stands as a cautionary tale, an allegory of reading: one does not solve a mystery, it says; one solves a puzzle, but is initiated into a mystery. While taking hold of fragments and finding a hidden pattern—or better, imposing a pattern, as in Eliot's "mythical method"—is characteristic of the aesthetics of modernism, this "saying yes to mystery" is one of the hallmarks of postmodernism, and "The Sisters," perched on the brink of the Joycean oeuvre, stands as a (typo)graphic manifestation of Joyce's untimely postmodernity.

Read on one level, then, "The Sisters" presents an allegory of "reading," setting out two competing models of the interpretive act. The first, represented most cogently by Eliza, is the way of mastery: Father Flynn's breakdown must be explained, and the story she tells begins the process of (posthumously) pulling the Father back into the fold. The dead man is read as a social text badly in need of interpretation; his life, his end are too extravagant, and threaten to rend the social fabric. The better part of Eliza's conversation in "the little room downstairs" is genteel and decorous; and while the wake formulae that she recites sound ironic in our ears—"He had a beautiful death, God be praised. . . . No one would think he'd make such a beautiful corpse" (*D* 15)—this is the socially acceptable script for such an occasion.[47] In stark contrast to these traditional platitudes, however, Eliza's attempt to impose a reading on the dead man sounds quite cunning:

> She stopped, as if she were communing with the past and then said shrewdly:
> –Mind you, I noticed there was something queer coming over him latterly.
> (*D* 16)

Father Flynn's final insanity doesn't catch Eliza off guard, or so she would have us believe; the signs were there for all to read, as she is careful to tell us, only she was too fond of "poor James" to admit to herself what they meant. But of course this diagnosis—insanity—is itself a profoundly social interpretation and, as the past (ab)use of mental hospitals as prisons in the former Soviet Union has taught us, one of a society's most treacherous.[48]

Significantly, this scene of domination through interpretation takes place during the Father's wake—a rite originally instituted to keep an eye on the dead until they were safely buried.[49] While for the most part cast as a detective story, "The Sisters" here flirts with the ghost story; immediately following her "shrewd" remarks regarding her brother's decline, Eliza "stopped suddenly as if to listen. I too listened; but there was no sound in the house: and I knew that the old priest was lying still in his coffin as we had seen him, solemn and truculent in death, an idle chalice on his breast" (*D* 18). Earlier, while still upstairs, the boy had hesitated to enter the "dead room," and had imagined that he would find the Father smiling in his coffin; this conviction is no doubt conditioned by his earlier vision of the Father's "heavy grey face" which pursued him even as he hid beneath his covers and "tried to think of Christmas" (D 11). This is a corpse which, for the boy at least (and seemingly for Eliza as well), won't stay dead. It is as if the Father, not yet in his grave, is turning over in his coffin in response to the defamatory tale being woven about him during the postmortem taking place in the parlor below.

Eliza is clearly aware of the impropriety of her gossip about her brother; and it is this guilt over one's ambivalence at the death of a loved one, according to Freud, that is the psychic genesis of all ghosts:

> In my view, primaeval man must have triumphed beside the body of his slain enemy, without being led to rack his brains about the enigma of life and death. What released the spirit of enquiry in man was not the intellectual enigma, and not every death, but the conflict of feeling at the death of loved yet alien and hated persons. Of this conflict of feeling psychology was the first offspring. Man could no longer keep death at a distance, for he had tasted it in his pain about the dead; but he was nevertheless unwilling to acknowledge it, for he could not conceive of himself as dead. So he devised a compromise: he conceded the fact of his own death as well, but denied it the significance of annihilation—a significance which he had had no motive for denying where the death of his enemy was concerned. It was beside the dead body of someone he loved that he invented spirits, and his sense of guilt at the satisfaction mingled with his sorrow turned these new-born spirits into evil demons that had to be dreaded.[50]

The narrator, of course, is also deeply ambivalent at the death of Father Flynn. While he knows that he *should* miss his companion ("Well, so your old friend is gone, you'll be sorry to hear," his uncle informs him), he reports instead a feeling of liberation upon learning of the Father's death: "The reading of the card persuaded me that he was dead and I was disturbed to find myself at check. . . . I found it strange that neither I nor the day seemed in a mourning mood and I felt even annoyed at discovering in myself a sensation of freedom as if I had been freed from something by his death" (D 12). His gaiety at his "friend's" death, however, creates guilt—a guilt shared by Eliza—and that guilt, in turn, makes the Father a ghost. This seems altogether appropriate in a volume so dominated by ghosts: Father Flynn, Eveline's mother, Emily Sinico, Charles Stuart Parnell, Michael Furey. . . . In weaving their tale, the sisters weave a net as well, which the priest—with his "uncanny" life and death—will fly by. As a detective story, "The Sisters" attempts to piece together the clues and demonstrate the guilt of Father Flynn; but as it blurs the distinction between crooks and spooks, Father Flynn, as ghost, threatens to float free, frustrating all their attempts to restrain him. Father Flynn's ghost traces the flight of the sign from interpretation, the slipping away of the mysterious.

Old Cotter, in the story's first reported speech, hints elliptically at the priest's insanity: "No, I wouldn't say he was exactly . . . but there was something queer . . . there was something uncanny about him" (D 9–10). Cotter's periphrasis is a method of controlling the dialogue; but it is also, more profoundly, a way of avoiding speaking the name of corruption. Nor can Eliza bring herself to pronounce the dread diagnosis, but says only that his breaking the chalice "affected his mind," and finally that "there was something gone wrong with him . . ." (D 17, 18). The lacunae and periphrases occur in two strategic areas of the text: places where the words "insane" (or "crazy") or "dead" should presumably be pronounced. Significantly, it is only the young narrator who can bring himself to use the word "dead," to utter it in this Land of the Dead. "Insanity" and "death"—or rather their absence, their elision—literally rupture the text of "The Sisters."

Insanity is a judgment pronounced on the dead man upstairs who threatens to disrupt life as they know it. With no one to contradict it, the sisters' accusation becomes a performative—Father Flynn has been declared insane by unspoken consensus. But what if he wasn't "really" demented? R. D. Laing contends that "there is no such 'condition' as 'schizophrenia,' but the label is a social fact and the social fact a *political event*. This political event, occurring in the civic order of society, imposes definitions and consequences on the labeled person. It is a social prescription that rationalizes a set of social actions whereby the labeled person is annexed by others, who are legally sanctioned, medically empowered and morally obliged, to become responsible for the person labeled."[51] Eliza claims to have realized that poor James had gone off the deep end when Father O'Rourke found him in the chapel one night "sitting up by himself in the dark in his confession-box, wide-awake and laughing-like softly to himself" (D 18). Rather than a breakdown, however, this incident could instead signal an epiphany for Father Flynn; he himself having been paralyzed spiritually by the "complex and mysterious" institutions of the Church, and the grave responsibility of the priest's duty "towards the secrecy of the confessional" (D 13), his gentle laughter might indicate a realization of the mockery of it all. Charles Peake captures the absurdity of this state of affairs quite nicely: "The corpse lies solemn, grey and truculent, but [Eliza] declares that 'He had a beautiful death,' and made 'a beautiful corpse': on the other hand, it was when the priest was found 'wide-awake and laughing-like softly to himself' that some wrong was suspected. . . . The spiritual life offered to the boy seems to be one in which grimness and death are beautiful, and laughter indicative of 'something gone wrong.'"[52] Flynn's reflective, golden Nietzschean laughter may indeed be read as a sign not of breakdown, but of breakthrough. Hayden White, paraphrasing Foucault, suggests that "the history of the treatment of the insane revealed a consistent tendency to project very general social preconceptions and anxieties into theoretical systems which justified the confinement of whatever social group or personality type appeared to threaten society during a particular period."[53]

Joyce was well aware that, as Mr. Fogarty misquotes it in "Grace," "Great minds are very near to madness" (D 168); in response to Arthur Power's complaint that "Dostoevski's characters were unreal . . . they are mad, all of them," Joyce replied: "Madness you may call it . . . but therein may be the secret of his genius. Hamlet was mad, hence the great drama; some of the characters in the Greek plays were mad; Gogol was mad; Van Gogh was mad; but I prefer the word exaltation, exaltation which can merge into madness, perhaps. In fact all great men have had that vein in them; it was the source of their greatness; the reasonable man achieves nothing" (CJJ 59-60). Father Flynn's insanity, if insanity we choose to call it, may indeed be the result of a strategic decision—as Laing describes in The Politics of Experience: "Without exception the experience and behavior that gets labeled schizophrenic is a special strategy that a person invents in order to live in an unlivable situation."[54]

Father Flynn is made a scapegoat; paralysis is located in the aberrant individual rather than in the system itself, and that deviant is then gently driven from the fold. As a result, the guilt of the community is assuaged without their having to look at themselves: "'Schizophrenia' is a diagnosis, a label applied by some people to others. This does not prove that the labeled person is subject to an essentially pathological process, of unknown nature and origin, going on in his or her body. It does not mean that the process is, primarily or secondarily, a psycho-pathological one, going on in the psyche of the person. But it does establish as a social fact that the person labeled is one of Them."[55] This scapegoating projection, in which we as readers are encouraged to participate, is the very opposite of Joyce's concept of the epiphany, which we will explore in more detail in the next chapter; rather than looking at themselves, as Joyce hoped his Dublin readers would, in his nicely polished looking glass, the sisters make their own brother Other and thereby safely locate guilt and corruption outside the community.

This, not coincidentally, is the traditional final effect of all detective stories: the reader is absolved of any responsibility for the awful state of affairs detailed in the work. Cawelti aptly describes this aspect of the classical detective formula: "The final source of pleasure in the detective's explanation [is] the sense of relief that accompanies the detective's precise definition and externalization of guilt. . . . The relief that accompanies the explanation reflects the reader's pleasure at seeing his favorites and projections clearly and finally exonerated and the guilt thrust beyond question onto a person who has remained largely outside his sphere of interest."[56] In the "case" of "The Sisters," the location of guilt is complicated by the fact that the narrative locates the guilt in a way different from that of its characters. For the sisters, and seemingly for the rest of the characters (save the boy), the corrupt figure is that of Father Flynn. But read differently, the story suggests that Father Flynn may be only a patsy—perhaps the real criminals of the story are his sisters, who try to blame him for paralysis and "its deadly work." In reality the deadly work is done by the sisters themselves; they impose deadening interpretation on the priest who, through "madness," tried to break free.[57]

At the end of "The Sisters," precisely where Holmes would elaborate in delicious detail his solution of the crime, our young narrator allows the story to trail off in ellipses. . . . While the narrative proper began in front of a warming fire, in the last scene the fire has gone out ("No one spoke: we all gazed at the empty fireplace" [D 15]). The story's conclusion resembles not so much that of a Conan Doyle story as the final scene of *The Crying of Lot 49*, where Oedipa Maas, weary finally of trying to unravel the complex web of relationships that comprise Tristero, accedes instead to the ineluctable mystery her quest has revealed to her. Therein lies her triumph; and the triumph of the narrator of "The Sisters" is the same. Stefano Tani, in his book *The Doomed Detective*, identifies the "deconstructive antidetective story" as one of the subgenres of antidetective fiction, and sees the ending of *Lot 49* as representative of that subsubgenre: "Reality is so tentacular and full of clues that the detective risks his sanity as he tries to find a solution (Oedipa Maas in *The Crying of Lot 49*). At the end he (or she) quits sizing up clues and admits the mystery: he discovers that in the meanwhile, even if he has not found an objective solution, he has at least grown and understood something about his own identity."[58] We would be hard-pressed to articulate exactly what the boy has learned at the end of "The Sisters"—indeed, he himself does not even try to articulate it, but merely listens: and this posture is a direct result of his experience of the strange case of Father Flynn. Because the story fizzles out in medias res, we are not shown precisely how the boy "interprets" the Father's death. But according to the narrative convention of the story, years have passed and that mystified young boy is now the author of the story we read. If he knows what "killed" Father Flynn, he's certainly not telling; but he has instead crafted a deferential narrative account of the experience, which preserves, to the extent possible, the sense of awe and mystery that were so palpably a part of the Father's life and death.

Susan Sontag, in her essay "Against Interpretation," points out that interpretation can be a two-edged sword: "In some cultural contexts, interpretation is a liberating act. It is a means of revising, of transvaluing, of escaping the dead past. In other cultural contexts, it is reactionary, impertinent, cowardly, stifling."[59] In a similar vein Derrida, in his early essay "Structure, Sign, and Play in the Discourse of the Human Sciences," delineates what he calls two different interpretations of "interpretation"—one that seeks to sum up, arrive at conclusions, the other that explores while preserving a text's pristine goal-less-ness: "There are thus two interpretations of interpretation, of structure, of sign, of play. The one seeks to decipher, dreams of deciphering a truth or an origin which escapes play and the order of the sign, and which lives the necessity of interpretation as an exile. The other, which is no longer turned toward the origin, affirms play and tries to pass beyond man and humanism, the name of man being the name of that being who, throughout the history of metaphysics or of ontotheology—in other words, throughout his entire history—has dreamed of full presence, the reassuring foundation, the origin and the end of play."[60] Derrida uses as an epigraph a line from Montaigne: "We need to interpret interpretations more than to interpret things"; we would do well to keep this advice in mind while reading "The Sisters," for what innocently poses as objective narrative is often cunning interpretation. It is this first style of interpretation that the text of "The Sisters" evinces, what Derrida calls "the saddened, *negative,* nostalgic, guilty, Rousseauistic side of the thinking of play whose other side would be the Nietzschean *affirmation,* that is the joyous affirmation of the play of the world . . . of signs without fault, without truth, and without origin which is offered to an active interpretation."[61] This second path, the way of joyous Nietzschean affirmation, is the path the boy ultimately takes: the way of mystery. This style of interpretation emphasizes not the solution of mysteries, but rather an acceptance of and openness to the essentially mysterious nature of existence. This is what Joyce in *Finnegans Wake* calls "intrepidation" (FW 338): a style of interpretation that is both "intrepid" and filled with "trepidation" in the presence of its object. "The Sisters," which opens as a detective story, fades to black in mystery; the story traces a trajectory from active interpretation to passive witness. This movement can be seen even within the short compass of the story's first paragraph, the "general prologue" that Joyce added to make the story a "program piece."

This acceptance of the uncanny is not, of course, the message of traditional detective fiction. David I. Grossvogel crystallizes the difference between stories of detection and stories of true mystery by contrasting the treatment of mystery in Agatha Christie's *The Mysterious Affair at Styles* with that in *Oedipus Rex*. The art of Agatha Christie, and that of all formulaic detective fiction, is an art not of disruption but of comfort. In stark contrast to a difficult and troubling work like *Oedipus*, Grossvogel argues, "The detective story does not propose to be 'real': it proposes only, and as a game, that the mystery is located on *this side* of the unknown. It replaces the awesomeness of limits by a false beard—a mask that is only superficially menacing and can be removed in due time. It redefines mystery by counterstating it; by assuming that mystery can be overcome, it allows the reader to play at being a god with no resonance, a little as a child might be given a plastic stethoscope to play doctor. Judging by the large number of its participants, this kind of elevation game is sufficient for the greatest part of the fiction-reading public."[62] The classic detective story is thus what Barthes calls a text of pleasure, a text "that contents, fills, grants euphoria: the text that comes from culture and does not break with it, is linked to a *comfortable* practice of reading."[63]

Barthes's postmodern text of bliss, on the other hand, a text like *Oedipus* or even a postmodern mystery story like "The Sisters," works with very different assumptions and aims: "The 'reality' of Oedipus is in its metaphysical discretion: it assumes as an inalienable given that there are dark regions that can be alluded to only, not broached. The awesomeness of the Oedipal myth is that of a remarkable mechanism intended to instance and comment upon the assertion of those limits."[64] This is the text of bliss, "the text that imposes a state of loss, the text that discomforts (perhaps to the point of a certain boredom), unsettles the reader's historical, cultural, psychological assumptions, the consistency of his tastes, values, memories, brings to crisis his relation with language" (*PT* 14). It is this dangerous realm of bliss that the traditional detective novel has always scrupulously avoided, offering instead the confirmation of the reader's preconceptions "at the price of a minor and spurious disruption";[65] it is into this uncharted territory that Joyce attempts to deform detective fiction, transforming mere detective story into a tale of true mystery.

4

The *Dubliners* Epiphony

(Mis)Reading the Book of Ourselves

One of Joyce's strategies for unsettling our reading habits in "The Sisters" is the liberal use of that detective fiction stock-in-trade, the red herring. False clues proliferate throughout the story, at least one per page, and seemingly in proportion as we look for them. As Hugh Kenner writes, "Joyce delights in leaving us . . . queer things we may misinterpret, as if to keep alive in us an awareness traditional fiction is at pains to lull, the awareness that we *are* interpreting."[1] A short list would begin with the story's puzzling title; thereafter Joyce throws out curious words, phrases, objects—signs apparently in need of interpretation, signs to which we critics have been only too willing to apply our ingenuity:

> "*paralysis, gnomon,* and *simony*";
> "faints and worms";
> "that Rosicrucian";
> "let him box his corner";
> "*Umbrellas Re-Covered*";
> "stories about the catacombs and about Napoleon Bonaparte";
> the boy's dream, the ending of which he cannot remember;
> the "heavy odour in the room—the flowers";
> "the empty fireplace";
> the breviary "fallen to the floor";
> "And then his life was, you might say, crossed";
> the "chalice that he broke";
> "they say it was the boy's fault"

Every one of these textual cruxes has elicited its own critical commentary; literary critics, when confronted with such a hoard of virgin signs, have a field day. The title, for example, has sent critics off in many different directions trying to explain the apparent discrepancy between the importance accorded the sisters in the title and their relatively minor role in the story. Edward Brandabur, for instance, resolves the problem by asserting that "the title, 'The Sisters,' refers not only to Nannie and Eliza, but to an effeminate relationship between the priest and his disciple."[2] While clever in its way, such an explanation in no way enriches our experience of the story; Brandabur constructs a story parallel to the text we're given, a story that spells out a good deal that "The Sisters" leaves unstated. In the end, we cannot help but feel that he is reading an altogether different story from the rather impoverished one Joyce wrote.

The story's most famous puzzle is no doubt the three mysteriously linked words *paralysis, gnomon,* and *simony,* that the boy intones in the first paragraph. Colin MacCabe writes that in the final version of "The Sisters," "the theme of paralysis is introduced and this word together with 'gnomon' and 'simony' provides a collection of signifiers which are not determined in their meaning by the text. . . . the reader is introduced to a set of signifiers for which there is no interpretation except strangeness and an undefined evil. The opening of the final version of the story displays a certain excess of the power of signification (the production of a surplus meaning)."[3] Many elaborate structures have been devised to explain the thread that connects these three magical words; entire readings of the story, and indeed of the volume, have subsequently been built around this hieratic trinity. And yet their relationship is stated explicitly right there on the page, and it seems strangely appropriate that a man named Herring should be the one to point it out to us: "No logic binds these three italicized words together—only the strangeness of their sounds in the boy's ear."[4] These "clews" are related to one another only as signifiers, not as signifieds; in and of themselves they provide the reader no means of escaping the flat realistic surface of the text.

Phillip Herring's is a scrupulously mean reading, an interpretation that bears in mind Joyce's conviction that "he is a very bold man who dares to alter in the presentment, still more to deform, whatever he has seen and heard" (*L* 2:134)—whatever he has seen and heard and *read.* For the red herrings in "The Sisters" are just that—what the French call *faux amis;* rather than providing us with a means of transcending the spare surface of the story, these "reader traps"[5] are instead Joyce's means of reinforcing the story's hermeneutics, and pulling us, kicking and screaming, into a text with which we would prefer to keep a purely professional relationship.

The most common response for critics when they come across a red herring unaware is of course to make a symbol of it. And "The Sisters" certainly has its share of ostensible symbols, the most glaring of which would be the chalice that Father Flynn has dropped. Over the years the "symbol" of the chalice has been understood in a number of ways, as standing for the Church, the phallus (male or female), the Grail, and so forth. And yet surely the demise of Father Flynn is meant in part as an allegory of the dangers of overinterpretation that any reader of the story must heed. The chalice itself, as Eliza remarks, was of no real importance—"they say it was all right, that it contained nothing, I mean" (*D* 17). But Eliza herself, as her locutions show, is not quite so sure ("they say . . ."); and indeed the incident of the dropped chalice is made the centerpiece of her narrative of the Father's final "insanity" ("That affected his mind, she said. After that he began to mope by himself, talking to no one and wandering around by himself" [*D* 17]). Of course, we do not know how the incident was interpreted by the priest; but we can see quite plainly that those close to him took the breaking of the chalice, in retrospect at least, as an omen, the chalice itself having been invested by them with too much symbolic importance.

Homer Brown surely has this episode in mind when he writes that "at least part of the symbolism of *Dubliners* has to do with the failure or inadequacy of the symbol";[6] the chalice in "The Sisters" is as self-evident a symbol as any reader could hope for, but when its significance is examined, it becomes an antisymbolic object, a "symbol" that alerts us to the dangers of reading symbolically. Again, Brown remarks that "in a sense, the symbolism of these stories consists in the failure of the symbolic, the emptiness of the symbol";[7] the chalice is an object so overinvested with meaning that it deconstructs as a symbol and returns to the realm of pure realistic detail, what Barthes calls "the sumptuous rank of the signifier." In the same way, the Catholic Church itself is seen in *Dubliners* as a dangerously overvalued symbol, which is liable at any time to crash. The chalice "contained nothing"; as a result, it is immediately filled with the needs and desires of the characters, and is made a receptacle for all that menaces them.

If this style of reading—the reader as detective—tends unjustifiably to turn objects into symbols, it simultaneously turns characters into the figures of allegory. Tindall sees the figure of the Irish "Poor Old Woman" (the *Shan Van Vocht*) behind Maria of "Clay," the slavey of "Two Gallants," and Mrs. and Kathleen Kearney of "A Mother"; but of "The Sisters" he complains: "Why are there two of them? I should find it easier if there were only one. A poor old woman (the traditional figure) could serve as an image of Ireland. . . ."[8] I should find it easier! We should all find Joyce's texts easier would they simply obey the call of our desires; but they resist us, and so we tailor them to the shape of our need as best we can. It's not always a good fit. As Garry Leonard writes, "Readers do not mind disagreeing on the particulars because all agree she [Maria] means something—and that is the main thing—*that she mean something*. . . . And so Maria's tiny shoulders have supported various interpretations that substitute what she 'means' for what critics lack."[9]

The sort of red herring with which Joyce taunts us in "The Sisters" is a recurring structural feature of *Dubliners*. The second paragraph of "Araby" is similarly littered with these false clues—*The Abbot, The Devout Communicant*, and *The Memoirs of Vidocq*—and again Herring has resisted the temptation to read these details "symbolically": "the titles probably have just enough relevance to encourage readers to inflate them with meaning. (After all, Joyce supplied the pump.) There is no indication that the boy has read them, especially since he views them as physical objects, preferring the one with yellow leaves."[10] Sometimes, even in Literature, objects are just objects; and for readers trained to read texts as storehouses of symbols, such a scrupulously mean reading requires extreme discipline:

> so much depends
> upon
>
> a red wheel
> barrow

After all, Freud himself is said to have remarked: "Sometimes a cigar is just a cigar."

Anyone who has taught *Dubliners* knows that students approach these texts as puzzles; in their estimation, the main task in reading is to figure out what the ending "means." Of course, this is only a slightly less sophisticated version of what Joyce's critics have done from the start. Reviewing the French translation of *Dubliners* in 1926, Jacques Chenevière was one of the first critics to praise Joyce for resisting simple conclusions: "a French novelist—a logician and always, in spite of himself, a moralist even when he considers himself unimpressionable—would begin and end the narrative precisely at the point when even the mysterious would be explicit. Joyce, however, only conducts the reader with a weak hand from which, however, one does not escape. He rarely informs us and does not conclude. . . . Sometimes this fog bothers us, accustomed as we are to life, translated literally and appearing logical. How dare art guide us so little and yet remain master of us!" (Deming 1:71). Most early critics, however, were not as sympathetic to Joyce's interest in, as John Cage expresses it, "keeping things mysterious."[11] The majority of critics have seen in the conclusion of "The Sisters," for instance, a moment of terrible, and perhaps incommunicable, insight for the young narrator. In Suzanne Ferguson's reading the story ends in an epiphany for the reader, in which she, in a flash of insight, synthesizes the various "clues" set out in the story and realizes that Father Flynn is guilty of a subtle form of simony.

If we are honest, however, for many of us the story ends not in epiphany but in utter muddle. At least part of our confusion stems from Joyce's refusal to state his moral; one contemporary reviewer complained that "his outlook is self-centred, absorbed in itself rather; he ends his sketch abruptly time after time, satisfied with what he has done, brushing aside any intention of explaining what is set down or supplementing what is omitted" (Deming 1:61–62). Joyce's refusal to "conclude" is understood by this early reader as self-absorption, and it provokes the critic's venom; but at least contemporary reviewers were in a position to see that Joyce had indeed refused to conclude. We are now so used to the institutionalized readings of these stories—"The Dead" is probably the prime example—that we can no longer even sense their wildness. William Empson's irritated remarks about the inconclusive nature of *Ulysses* are at least as appropriate as a description of *Dubliners:* "The difficulty about *Ulysses*," he writes, "as is obvious if you read the extremely various opinions of critics, is that, whereas most novels tell you what the author expects you to feel, this one not only refuses to tell you the end of the story, it also refuses to tell you what the author thinks would have been a good end to the story."[12]

If we turn to a poststructuralist critic like MacCabe, however, we can see how Joyce's refusal to conclude in these stories has recently been transvalued—what was described as arrogant convention flaunting in the contemporary reviews is now felt to be an integral component of his genius: "The text works paratactically, simply placing one event after another, with no ability to draw conclusions from this placing. . . . The movement of the text is not that of making clear a reference already defined and understood; of fixing the sense of an expression. Instead the text dissolves the simple scenes of Dublin as a city, as a context within which people live their lives, and replaces it with the very text of paralysis."[13] The close of "The Sisters" is precisely this "text of paralysis"; the narrative trails off in ellipses as Eliza begins to repeat yet again the story she has "written" to explain her brother's death, and Joyce resolutely refuses to come in at the end, even in the person of his narrator, in order to give us any guidance. A postmodern ending is a matter neither of appearance nor of grammar—it has to do, finally, with avoiding "the sense of an ending" (Kermode). Think, for instance, of the ending of the first part of *Molloy*: "Molloy could stay, where he happened to be."[14] Beckett gives us proper grammar, and even a kind of narrative closure, and yet suggests the influence of chance operation, creating an unsettling sense that nothing has been concluded. The postmodern ending is a conclusion ("termination") that reaches no conclusion ("inference").

At the close of "The Sisters" the narrator appears to us frozen—puzzled and paralyzed—and we cannot help but ape his response. Not only do we remain unenlightened; we cannot even decide who, if anyone, in the story has seen the light. But some sort of enlightenment—either for the character, or for the reader—is the traditional goal of a reading of the *Dubliners* story. That famous moment of enlightenment is what Joyce criticism, (mis)taking its clue from Joyce himself, has dubbed the epiphany. Zack Bowen points out, with reference to "The Sisters," that "the question of who is having the epiphany is a central issue of the story":

> If the epiphany belongs to the Flynn sisters, then the statement "So, then, of course, when they saw that, that made them think that there was something gone wrong with him" (*D* 18) constitutes the truth of the story. The priest's laughter is indeed madness. Few of us, however, subscribe to this. The question is really whether the priest, the boy, or both have an epiphany. . . . We are left to our own conclusions about whether the insight was about a senile and decadent way of life which the sisters merely confirmed. Even if that is the substance of the epiphany which presumably we share with the boy, we are still not sure if the priest is a seer of eternal truth or merely a disoriented and demented old man. At any rate, for the purpose of the present discussion, we have at once to ask ourselves where the eternal verities might lie in the case. The answer is that they depend upon the beholder: the sisters' perception is different from Father Flynn's, the boy's, or the readers', who may in themselves differ. Each of us fashions his own truth and sees it as the unalterable law of God.[15]

It is of course extremely difficult to maintain that "The Sisters" ends in an epiphany—as Bowen wants to do—if readers cannot agree on who has had the epiphany, or of what it might consist. Indeed, even the most cursory glance at the wide variety of readings of "The Sisters" over the years will suggest at once that we must not only question whether any of the characters have an epiphany, but even doubt that readers share any universal understanding of the mystery of "The Sisters," which Donald Torchiana calls "the most controversial piece in *Dubliners*."[16] Sherlock Holmes, at the end of his cases, relates the logical process by which he came upon his epiphany—the solution to the crime; but, as we have seen, the boy in "The Sisters" enjoys no such triumph.

Epiphany is Joyce's paleonym that just won't die. Our critical tradition has long privileged authors' pronouncements on their own works over the commentary of any rank "outsider," and the word epiphany from Joyce's pen has stuck stubbornly to *Dubliners* (even though, as we shall see, he never used the term to describe his short stories). In fact, his earliest impulse was to describe the method of *Dubliners* using the metaphor not of epiphany, but of *epiclesis;* in the oldest surviving reference to his story collection, he calls them "a series of epicleti—ten—for a paper" (*L* 1:55). The difference between the two terms, in brief—reverting to the nomenclature of chapter 3—is this: an epiphany evidences one's ultimate mastery of a situation, while epiclesis is instead the moment of submission to mystery.

In the Eastern Orthodox Church, epiclesis is the priest's invocation of the Holy Ghost to transmute the elements of the Lord's Supper, a feature of the Mass that had been dropped by the Roman Church before the medieval period. In the Divine Liturgy of Saint Chrysostom, the priest intones these words in a low voice: "Moreover we offer unto Thee this reasonable and unbloody sacrifice: and beseech thee and pray and supplicate; send down Thy HOLY GHOST upon us, and on these proposed gifts."[17] The difference between the Greek and Latin Church on this point is not without consequence. In the Eastern view, the efficacy of the sacrament depends upon God's response to the prayer of his priest; but in the Roman Catholic service, the elements are transformed as a direct result of the priest's reciting the words of institution—and the aspect of divine intervention is easily forgotten.[18] Thus when Stephen Dedalus in *A Portrait* figures himself as "a priest of eternal imagination, transmuting the daily bread of experience into the radiant body of ever-living life" (*P* 221), his words suggest that he will be able to effect that transubstantiation himself, without divine assistance. The reasons for Stephen's error are made patently clear in the text: earlier, during his interview with the director of Belvedere College—in response to whose luscious evocation of the power of the priest of God Stephen fashions his own vision of the priest of art—Stephen had heard the heretical suggestion that the priest has "the power, the authority, to make the great God of Heaven come down upon the altar and take the form of bread and wine" (*P* 158). The director has substituted pure selfish power for the moment of epiclesis—mastery for mystery; and Stephen's repetition of the gesture later suggests its attractiveness to him. But epiclesis is the tacit admission that neither the priest, nor certainly the artist, has such powers—it's a gesture of self-abnegation that neither the director of the college nor his rebellious disciple is capable of.

The method of epiclesis is the method of mystery courted and invoked, evoked. When he had been at work on *Dubliners* for about ten months, Joyce wrote in a 4 April 1905 letter to Stanislaus that "The Sisters" called to his mind the Eastern Orthodox mass: "While I was attending the Greek mass here [Trieste] last Sunday it seemed to me that my story *The Sisters* was rather remarkable." Joyce doesn't bother to spell out the connection between "The Sisters" and the Mass; the letter, however, goes on to describe the distinctive elements of the Greek service: "The Greek mass is strange. The altar is not visible but at times the priest opens the gates and shows himself. He opens and shuts them about six times. For the Gospel he comes out of a side gate and comes down into the chapel and reads out of a book. For the elevation he does the same. At the end when he has blessed the people he shuts the gates . . ." (*L* 2:86). Admittedly, the connection here is tenuous: but the act of elevation, in the Orthodox service, is accompanied by the priest's reading of the epiclesis. Thus, one of the elements of the Greek Mass that seems to have captured Joyce's imagination—and reminded him of his own short fiction—is the Eastern Church's act of invocation.[19]

In his memoir *My Brother's Keeper*, Stanislaus Joyce records a conversation in which Joyce again makes use of the metaphor of the Eucharist to talk about the method of *Dubliners*: "'Don't you think,' said he reflectively, choosing his words without haste, 'there is a certain resemblance between the mystery of the Mass and what I am trying to do? I mean that I am trying in my poems to give people some kind of intellectual pleasure or spiritual enjoyment by converting the bread of everyday life into something that has permanent artistic life of its own . . .?'"[20] If Stanislaus has been as careful in his recording as he says his brother was in his conversation, Joyce here focuses in not simply on the Eucharist itself, but on the *mystery* of the Eucharist; and once again, that particular mystery has a name: epiclesis. The method of the epiphany, however, especially the "curtain" epiphany that an entire generation of readers has found the perfect ending to these stories, is a means for dispelling mystery, for resolving unbearable tensions—providing a facile closure to that which in reality cannot be neatly tied up. The stories of *Dubliners* are, as we will explore shortly, militantly anti-epiphanic. The whole notion of manifestation or self-revelation is severely undercut in tale after tale; and even the comfortable critical commonplace that the reader, at least, is enlightened is finally an illusion difficult to maintain. No one, I am persuaded, realizes the full import of these stories upon a first reading; our illumination, if indeed we experience any, is not a sudden "Eureka!" but a soft, gradual, hard-won appreciation.

The epiphany has become one of Joyce criticism's most effective methods for mastering the discomforting, uncompromising qualities of these texts—to close them off, to impose closure where in fact none inheres; it is, in other words, a way to fight off the intense disquiet caused by Joyce's "scrupulous meanness."[21] Joyce would find no little irony in this situation, for the epiphanic method, as first practiced in his notebook of Epiphanies, was a resolutely decontextualizing, disorienting, discomforting technique. As MacCabe writes, Joyce's "earliest prose writings, the *Epiphanies*, lack any appeal to reality which would define what the writing produces. The conversations and situations which make up these brief ten- or twelve-line sketches, lack any accompanying explanation or context. In place of a discourse which attempts to place and situate everything, we have discourses which are determined in their situation by the reader."[22] Thus in spite of their original spirit, the name epiphany has become one of the Joyce industry's tactics for dealing with these willful and unruly texts—subjugating them in the name of Joyce the Father, Joyce the Creator.

More has been written about the epiphany than any other stratagem in the Joycean text; and no doubt due to the short, lyric quality of Joyce's stories, epiphany is discussed more often in connection with *Dubliners* than with any other of Joyce's writings. Morris Beja, who has written a study called *Epiphany in the Modern Novel*, writes elsewhere that "probably no other motif has so pervaded critical discussions of both the volume as a whole and its individual stories";[23] and in a note he goes on to list more than a dozen influential critical investigations of the epiphanies in *Dubliners*. As many have pointed out, Joyce himself never used the word epiphany in reference to *Dubliners*, nor are any of the forty surviving Epiphanies housed at Buffalo and Cornell made use of in the stories. But while none of Joyce's early sketches were incorporated wholesale into the text of *Dubliners*, subsequent critics have nevertheless found Joyce's term a durable one, and the moment of "manifestation or revelation" it describes central to what Stephen Dedalus would call the *quidditas* of these texts; and teachers and critics have found in Joyce's metaphor a powerful heuristic device.[24]

One primary difficulty with using epiphany as a term for criticism, however, is that it has accrued a fairly wide range of meanings, depending on the purposes of the critic. This is, after all, the process by which the term first entered the vocabulary of literary criticism, Joyce putting his own spin on a word brought from Greek into ecclesiastical English in the fourteenth century. In English, "Epiphany" originally referred to a feast day, "the festival commemorating the manifestation of Christ to the Gentiles in the person of the Magi; observed on January 6th, the 12th day after Christmas" *(OED)*. Given this heritage, it is no doubt ironic that "The Dead" takes place on Twelfth Night, the Feast of Epiphany; this is a point to which we shall have to return. But Joyce's redefinition stripped epiphany of its festive and religious, if not its mysterious, connotations. In a famous passage in *Stephen Hero*, we are told that the term as Stephen used it "meant a sudden spiritual manifestation, whether in the vulgarity of speech or of gesture or in a memorable phase of the mind itself. He believed that it was for the man of letters to record these epiphanies with extreme care, seeing that they themselves are the most delicate and evanescent of moments" *(SH* 211). It is perhaps not insignificant that Joyce's only explicit treatment of the doctrine of the epiphany is found in a text kept unpublished during his lifetime; like the Homeric titles for the chapters of *Ulysses*, which in spite of Joyce's removing them from the text critics insist on restoring to the novel, the epiphany is largely a way of writing, rather than a way of reading. Joyce, in rewriting *Stephen Hero* as *A Portrait*, omitted Stephen's now-famous disquisition on the epiphany; we might, for the novelty of it, assume for the time being that he knew what he was doing.

Joyce's brief discussion suggests two different sorts of epiphany, according to whether emphasis is placed on the object or event—the occasion—of the epiphany, or instead on an observer's emotional (or "spiritual," as Joyce has it) response to that instigating episode. Hence Joyce's epiphanies, as Scholes and Litz write, "were mainly of two kinds . . . they recorded 'memorable phases' of the young artist's own mind, or instances of 'vulgarity of speech or of gesture' in the world around him. In practice this resulted in two quite different *styles* of epiphany: prose poems in which a mental phase of the artist was narrated, and dramatic notations of vulgarity."[25] With respect to the archetypal epiphany, the appearance of Christ to the Magi, a Joycean rendering of the scene could conceivably capture two distinct epiphanies (and were the nativity a *Dubliners* story, both would likely be included): the first, an "objective," dramatic epiphany, focusing on the infant Christ, the scene in the manger; and a second, "subjective," psychological epiphany, focusing on the response of one Magus to the child. What is common to both styles of epiphany is the breaking forth of the mysterious through the dull veneer of the everyday; its emblem is the divine Christ in a Bethlehem stable, what Yeats called "the uncontrollable mystery on the bestial floor."

The concluding page of "Araby" makes a convenient testing ground for any discussion of Joycean epiphany in *Dubliners*, for there we are ostensibly presented two epiphanies, one of each type, in rather close proximity.[26] The first is a dramatic epiphany, very similar in style and content to the specimen Stephen records just previous to the passage from *Stephen Hero* cited above.[27] The snatch of conversation reported in "Araby" runs this way:

> At the door of the stall a young lady was talking and laughing with two young gentlemen. I remarked their English accents and listed vaguely to their conversation.
>
>   –O, I never said such a thing!
>   –O, but you did!
>   –O, but I didn't!
>   –Didn't she say that?
>   –Yes. I heard her.
>   –O, there's a . . . fib! (*D* 35)

If this is indeed an epiphany—and no critic seems to have argued that it's not—then we might pause for a moment to consider both its message and its audience: what does this epiphany mean, and to whom is it meant to speak?

Critics almost universally agree on the meaning of the epiphany: Bowen for instance writes that "In 'Araby' presumably the boy's epiphany of the absurdity in going to the fair and in his aggrandizement of Mangan's sister is brought home by the shallowness of the conversation in the confessional-gift stand at the fair."[28] In fact, however, we cannot be certain what the scene has meant to the boy—how he has interpreted or read it. Joyce, through his narrator, refuses to establish a position (explicitly at least) outside the boy, a still point in the text from which we might take our bearings. In this regard, Joyce's procedure is in marked contrast to Virginia Woolf's. She is nearly as famous for her focus on the "moment of being" as Joyce is for the epiphany; yet Woolf confirms Lily Briscoe's epiphany at the conclusion of *To the Lighthouse* in a way that Joyce scrupulously avoids: "With a sudden intensity, as if she saw it clear for a second, she drew a line there, in the centre. It was done; it was finished. Yes, she thought, laying down her brush in extreme fatigue, I have had my vision."[29]

Woolf's third-person narrative gives a certain objective distance on the scene narrated, and we are given no reason to doubt the narrative's assertion. Joyce however gives us no comforting voice from beyond the text; all we have is the boy's own words—in his retrospective narration of the incident. With that as the only concrete evidence, we're forced to conclude that he hasn't learned his lesson. The same problem that arises here has been the focus of intense debate in *A Portrait*; perhaps because of its deceptive simplicity, however, or perhaps because of Joyce's off-hand description of its style as "scrupulously mean," "Araby" has not been subjected to the kind of close stylistic scrutiny that *A Portrait* has come in for. It will prove worthwhile therefore to digress for just a bit, to consider what Wayne Booth has called the "problem of distance" in Joycean narration, especially as it is manifest in *A Portrait*.

Booth, in his comments on *A Portrait*, declares that as a result of Joyce's "refining himself out of existence," "we must conclude that many of the refinements he intended in his finished *Portrait* are, for most of us, permanently lost. Even if we were now to do our homework like dutiful students, even if we were to study all of Joyce's work, even if we were to spend the lifetime that Joyce playfully said his novels demanded, presumably we should never come to as rich, as refined, and as varied a conception of the quality of Stephen's last days in Ireland as Joyce had in mind."[30] According to Booth, Joyce in *A Portrait* has afforded us no firm ground for judgment; any decision as to whether Stephen's more remarkable rhetorical flights are to be taken seriously or ironically can finally be based only on a reader's personal predilection, since the text gives us no context for such a judgment (Booth himself uses material from *Stephen Hero* in an attempt to clear up this ambiguity).

Writing almost twenty years later, Hugh Kenner, although not responding to Booth by name, does implicitly challenge his conclusions about *A Portrait*. In his book *Ulysses*, Kenner argues that while the author takes no explicit moral position regarding his character, his judgments are to be found motivating the style: "Stephen's way of experiencing and judging may seem so thoroughly to pervade the *Portrait* that there is no way he can be appraised: whatever he says or does seems utterly reasonable. A written style, however: that is something to appraise, once we become aware of it; and the *Portrait* makes us highly aware of the style by the unusual device, much extended and complicated in *Ulysses,* of changing the style continually."[31] The argument here hinges on Joyce's use of free indirect discourse—what Kenner in another book needlessly dubs the "Uncle Charles Principle."[32] If we hold Joyce responsible for word choice and syntax throughout *A Portrait*—"But her long fair hair was girlish: and girlish, and touched with the wonder of mortal beauty, her face"—we call this (as Wyndham Lewis did) simply bad writing; but according to the tenets of free indirect discourse, we are to understand that the narrative has been subtly (or not so subtly) colored by the consciousness it narrates. So that when presenting Stephen's Uncle Charles, the narrative borrows some of the phrasing that Charles would no doubt use himself; and when describing the would-be artist as a young man, the prose takes on a slightly precious quality that we come to associate with Stephen. In particular, Kenner zeros in on Stephen's frequently over-done alliteration, and his penchant for the rhetorical figure of *chiasmus*, as tip-offs that we're to be suspicious of Stephen's writing, or rather of the seeming objectivity of the third-person narrative that shapes itself to the contours of his mind and spirit.

In the first three stories of *Dubliners*, the problems of narrative distance are considerably simpler than in *A Portrait*; all use the relatively common convention of the story of youth written in maturity. Since the boy protagonists in the first three stories are at most young adolescents, we cannot believe them to have written these narratives at the time the incidents occurred, as we are to believe the close of *A Portrait* to have been written by the postgraduate Stephen. In *A Portrait*, the age of the protagonist seems to approach the age of the writer almost asymptoti-cally, Tristram Shandy-like, so that by the close we are told of incidents "just as they happen." The final sentence, the final diary entry, is of course about nothing more than its own writing, and we can imagine Stephen's penning that entry as the completion of the manuscript of *A Portrait*. Conversely, while we might wish to characterize the prose style of the "stories of childhood" as immature, they are most certainly not written by adolescents; rather, we are to imagine these tales written by their protagonists grown into men who, for their own narrative pur-poses, pepper their texts with some of the verbal infelicities of their youth-ful minds (such as, for example, the confusion on the part of the narra-tor of "The Sisters" between "reflection" and "refraction" in the story's first paragraph).

The closing page of "Araby" contains a very clear "dramatic" epiph-any, one in which most critics have found the story's "moral," the les-son that our protagonist is intended to learn. As a result the boy pre-sumably experiences psychological epiphany; but his response to the conversation overheard at the gift stall is so hyperbolic as to seem al-most a non sequitur: "Gazing up into the darkness I saw myself as a creature driven and derided by vanity; and my eyes burned with an-guish and anger" (*D* 35). The boy sends his gaze into the darkness at the top of the hall, and in that darkness his mind's eye sees "reflected" "a creature driven and derided by vanity." Has he then, like Lily Briscoe, "had his vision"?

The critical consensus is that he has indeed. Clearly, the boy repre-sents himself as having been possessed of a terrible insight; and yet the form, or better the *style*, of his confession betrays its ostensible revelation. Many commentators have called the boy's self-evaluation too harsh; but it is much more than that. Like Saul of Tarsus, who goes from thinking himself God's anointed to believing himself chief among all sinners, the boy in "Araby" can conceive of himself only in melodramatic black or white—either chivalric knight in service of his lady fair or, when that illusion is forcibly wrested from him, the blackest of sinners. This is a pattern we see played out in other of the stories, most notably "The Dead"; Gabriel Conroy fluctuates wildly between expansive good humor and believing himself "a ludicrous figure, acting as pennyboy for his aunts, a nervous well-meaning sentimentalist" (*D* 220). As Yeats's Michael Robartes says in another context, "there's no human life at the full or the dark"; and yet Gabriel and the "devout communicant" of "Araby" both carefully avoid having to negotiate that perilous intermediate gray area called life.

This brings us back to the question: What possible criteria do we have for judging the efficacy of the boy's insight at Araby? His revelation might be evaluated in the same way we would a religious conversion, for the language of the closing page is the language of a young man who believes himself to have been spiritually transformed. If in fact he has been transformed, we may reasonably ask whether a new spirit dwells within him, and whether that new spirit has resulted in a new quality of life. For we may state as a working principle that there is no epiphany without efficacy; "Every good tree," the Lord declared, "bringeth forth good fruit" (Matt. 7:16–17). It makes no sense to speak of a character's having an epiphany in spite of all evidence to the contrary, just because we readers have seen what she has and believe that we have seen the light. The genuine experience of epiphany cannot remain without effect, in either life or art. Of those to whom more has been revealed, more shall be expected; as Eliot puts it in "Gerontion," "After such knowledge, what forgiveness?"

According to the argument put forward by Beja, however, all such considerations are beside the point. What we think about a given character's epiphany is irrelevant; "What matters is what a given character *feels* about an epiphany or the revelation it provides. An epiphany need not, after all, be 'objectively' accurate; as I have argued elsewhere, an epiphany is in its very conception and description a *subjective* phenomenon. So whether Mr. Duffy and the boy at the end of 'Araby' are 'correct' is much less relevant than how *they* feel about what they have learned." Following Beja's rubric, then, it is possible to experience an epiphany that is wholly delusional—so that he can say that "even Eveline" has her epiphany "before she represses all awareness."[33] Surely this distorts the term epiphany beyond all usefulness. To begin with, the text proffers absolutely no support for the idea that Eveline has reached any kind of higher self-awareness; indeed, it unrelentingly exposes her process of rationalization. Frank, for instance, who has been seen as a life preserver, is transformed into a millstone once Eveline realizes she cannot leave with him: "All the seas of the world tumbled about her heart. He was drawing her into them; he would drown her" (*D* 41). But even if Beja is right—even if Eveline does have a penultimate flash of insight—her ultimate action is to take no action, effectively nullifying any epiphany we might wish to find in her tale. An epiphany is, as Beja insists, by its very nature intensely personal—but that does not mean that it is not available to evaluation by outside criteria.

This is the argument that Bowen makes. "Epiphanies may be false," he writes, "because the meaning of experience, when transformed by either the artists' perception or the perception of less gifted characters may in fact be self-delusion."[34] It is this false epiphany that I am calling epi*phony*. Although the experience of epiphany is always ultimately subjective, the validity—the efficacy—of a character's epiphany *is* available to scrutiny. Two possible avenues for verification are available to us: confirmation from the narrative itself (as in the passage of *To the Lighthouse* discussed above) or the subsequent "life" of the character. But Joyce consistently refuses explicit narrative comment on the ostensible epiphany's efficacy; nor do the stories present any "postconversion" life by which we might judge.

The narrator of "Araby," though, is the story's protagonist at an advanced age. The text of "Araby" is a product of what *Ulysses* calls "the retrospective arrangement": "No longer is Leopold, as he sits there, ruminating, chewing the cud of reminiscence, that staid agent of publicity and holder of a modest substance in the funds. A score of years are blown away. He is young Leopold. There, as in a retrospective arrangement, a mirror within a mirror (hey, presto!), he beholdeth himself" (*U* 337). Does the text that the protagonist of "Araby" chooses to write give us any reason to believe that he's outgrown this youthful vanity? The boy's closing remark—his artfully rendered epiphany—calls attention to itself for its highly wrought, exquisite style. In his discussion of *A Portrait* mentioned above, Kenner has identified alliteration and chiasmus as two of the early warning signs that we're reading the free indirect discourse of an immature artist, and not surprisingly, perhaps, we find both symptoms here. The paired adjectives in the first clause—"driven and derided by vanity"—fabricate an urgent momentum out of all proportion to the motive event; those of the second clause, too— "my eyes burned with *anguish* and *anger*"—are chosen on the basis of sound, not sense. This is not the prose of a humbled man, a man whose vain romanticism has been painfully torn from him.

There have been foreshadowings of this decorative, slightly precious style throughout the story: "The space of sky above us was the colour of ever-changing violet and towards it the lamps of the street lifted their feeble lanterns"; "I had never spoken to her, except for a few casual words, and yet her name was like a summons to all my foolish blood"; "Through one of the broken panes I heard the rain impinge upon the earth, the fine incessant needles of water playing in the sodden beds" (*D* 30, 31). When used to transform—to elevate, to "poeticize"—a landscape, such purple (or "ever-changing violet") prose is harmless enough, if somewhat wearying in the long run. Indeed, one of the "paper-covered books" the boy finds in "the waste room behind the kitchen," Walter Scott's *The Abbot*, could serve him as a (turgid) stylistic model: "It was upon the evening of a sultry summer's day when the sun was half-sunk behind the distant western mountains of Liddesdale, that the Lady took her solitary walk on the battlements of a range of buildings, which formed the front of the castle, where a flat roof of flag-stones presented a broad and convenient promenade. The level surface of the lake, undisturbed except by the occasional dipping of a teal-duck or coot, was gilded with the beams of the setting luminary, and reflected, as if in a golden mirror, the hills amongst which it lay enbosomed."[35]

However, the truth, Ezra Pound was to insist, makes its own style.[36] While the florid scenic descriptions of a novel like *The Abbot* or a short story like "Araby"—wrought in what Pound liked to call "licherary langwidg"—transform a landscape, they can only falsify the self-presentation of a writing subject. Stripped of its lush, romantic atmosphere, we can imagine "Araby" ending with another, more economical, self-exposure: "—I suddenly realized how vain I was." To make such a spare confession, however, is clearly not to the narrator's taste. The Preacher of Ecclesiastes declared simply "Vanity of vanities—all is vanity"; but such a scrupulously mean disclosure is not enough for the boy. Like the Apostle Paul, who is not satisfied to confess himself a sinner but declares instead that "Christ Jesus came into the world to save sinners—of whom I am chief" (1 Tim. 1:15), our protagonist is not content simply to condemn his vanity, but must do it in the most self-important, most theatrical—the most *vain*—manner imaginable.

In a well-known letter to Grant Richards, Joyce said that he wanted to give the Irish people—those few who would read *Dubliners*—"one good look at themselves in my nicely polished looking-glass" (*L* 1:64). Such a project is, of course, fraught with danger; writers who set out to change their readers are more often than not ignored, and while some of Joyce's contemporaries may have come to see Dublin, and themselves, in a very different light after reading *Dubliners,* most doubtless remained unshaken. So too, most of his characters at the end of their tales seem unchanged; but then Joyce never promised that his characters would have that "one good look" he promised his readers. Indeed this is the final epiphany of the most powerful stories in *Dubliners: our* realization, as readers, that the characters have not had *their* epiphany. Believing that they have transcended, believing themselves finally to be free, characters like the narrator of "Araby" and Gabriel Conroy pathetically verify their prison—this is perhaps the most bitter paralysis in all of *Dubliners.*

It was this quality of Chekhov's plays, the carefully constructed dramatic illusion of freedom which tragically confirms the characters' slavery, that impressed Joyce. In conversation with Arthur Power he remarked that "As the play ends, for a moment you think that his characters have awakened from their illusions, but as the curtain comes down you realize that they will soon be building new ones to forget the old" (*CJJ* 58). This is precisely the situation of Joyce's Dubliners: the moment of epiphany, Stephen Dædalus warns in *Stephen Hero,* is "the most delicate and evanescent of moments," and while it comes to many in *Dubliners,* it is accepted by none. For as Stephen says, "it [is] for the man of letters to record these epiphanies with extreme care," and in *Dubliners* Joyce has done just that; the actual and would-be "men of letters" who experience these epiphanies in the stories, however—the boys in "The Sisters," "An Encounter" and "Araby," Little Chandler, James Duffy, and Gabriel Conroy—cannot restrict themselves to Joyce's "style of scrupulous meanness," and instead (mis)shape that delicate moment to their own ends. With the exception of the narrator of "The Sisters," they operate without Joyce's conviction, expressed to Grant Richards, that "he is a very bold man who dares to alter in the presentment, still more to deform, whatever he has seen and heard" (*L* 2:134).

While we have come to think it characteristic of the *Dubliners* story, the closing tableau in which the protagonist appears to experience a moment of self-realization actually occurs in fewer than half. Most of the characters self-evidently end the stories the same way they began them—blithely unaware of any serious problem. In what was originally to have been the volume's closing story, "Grace," for instance, none of the characters, least of all the exegete Father Purdon, learns a thing; in fact, his message is commended to Mr. Kernan's attention by his friends precisely because it requires nothing of its hearers.

In half a dozen of the stories, however, the endings are much more problematic, the tone more complex, the style more opaque; the characters here do seem to hover on the brink of some deeper self-awareness.[37] But the closing epiphonies in these stories, while not quite the "cracked lookingglass of a servant" that Stephen speaks of in *Ulysses*, are distorted and distorting mirrors of words, words of the characters' own choosing, in which they get back the flattering reflections they wish to see. Stephen's "reflection" on language in chapter 4 of *A Portrait* seems almost an ironic commentary on this trait: "Words. Was it their colours? He allowed them to glow and fade, hue after hue: sunrise gold, the russet and green of apple orchards, azure of waves, the grey-fringed fleece of clouds. No, it was not their colours: it was the poise and balance of the period itself. Did he then love the rhythmic rise and fall of words better than their associations of legend and colour? Or was it that, being as weak of sight as he was shy of mind, he drew less pleasure from the reflection of the glowing sensible world through the prism of a language manycoloured and richly storied than from the contemplation of an inner world of individual emotions mirrored perfectly in a lucid supple periodic prose?" (*P* 166–67). Like Stephen, the boy of "Araby" is in love with "the rhythmic rise and fall" of a "supple periodic prose"—this love, finally, being more real to him than his breathless romantic passion for Mangan's sister, or the vanity he claims to have rooted out from deep within his soul. This flattering portrait, rendered in prose from his own pen, is infinitely preferable to him—to all of the paralytic Dubliners—than having "one good look at themselves" in Joyce's "nicely polished looking-glass." Thus, there are at least two contradictory ways to read the last sentence of "Araby." It begins, "Looking up into the darkness, I saw myself. . . ." At first blush, we might think the boy is telling us that the blackness at the top of the tent forcibly brought home to him the blackness in his own soul. But instead, his language suggests the gesture of looking at oneself in a mirror, a leitmotif throughout *Dubliners*.[38] The boy pretends that the void, the darkness is a mirror; but we know that if he sees anything at all in that darkness, it can only be a figure projected from his own imagination. Thus the dramatic conclusion of his story is a foregone one, an epigram he's been carrying around for some time and trying to find an occasion to use.

Indeed, while Joyce thought of the stories as looking glasses held up to the reader, the characters in those stories look not into a mirror but into the genial illusions of their own making. Eveline in the end throws

Frank over, for "he would drown her," she convinces herself, and although hers was a hard life, "now that she was about to leave it she did not find it a wholly undesirable life"; Maria doesn't want "any ring or man either," she assures us with eyes that "sparkled with disappointed shyness," and has no desire to go live with the Donnellys, having "become accustomed to the life of the laundry"; Bob Doran overcomes his cold feet (and his embarrassment at Polly's vulgar locutions "I seen" and "If I had've known") by asking himself a hard-nosed, commonsensical question: "But what would grammar matter if he really loved her?"

We see much the same dynamic in the ending of "An Encounter." The young narrator replaces the mystery with which "The Sisters" closes with mere mystification. At least one critic of the story has seen through the false bravado of that story's closing epiphony; Herring writes, "The last line—'And I was penitent; for in my heart I had always despised him a little'—contains no ellipses [as does 'The Sisters'], but as a final statement it is certainly elliptical in meaning, and supports the general theme of deception. It is a good example of Joyce's uncertainty principle at work in closure, for readers are invited back into the story on a wild goose chase for evidence that will help them understand what masquerades as an epiphanic moment. But the closural incongruity seems downright flippant, for 'An Encounter' is not about how superior the protagonist feels to Mahoney, but about how necessary to youth is the bold spirit of adventure that the young 'Indian' personifies."[39] "An Encounter" ends not in epiphany but in rhetorical flourish; this writer, even if he has not learned anything of lasting importance about himself from his experience on the bank of the Dodder, *has* at least learned how to bully his reader into believing he's pointed his story's moral. But it's only trompe-l'oeil.

Compared to the peculiar endings of the first three stories, the closing section of "A Little Cloud"—set off by Joyce from the body of the story with a row of dots—sounds rather flat. Although this too is the tale of a would-be artist ("He tried to weigh his soul to see if it was a poet's soul" [*D* 73]), it is told not by T. Malone Chandler, but rather subtly ventriloquized by him through free indirect discourse. In all the later stories, the narrative situation is similarly complicated by Joyce's use of free indirect discourse—Flaubert's *style indirect libre,* in which "the narrator takes on the speech of the character, or, if one prefers, the character speaks through the voice of the narrator, and the two instances are then *merged.*"[40]

But the resolute flatness of the close of "A Little Cloud" by no means authenticates Little Chandler's moment of self-awareness. Nowhere in the course of the story do we witness Chandler taking responsibility for his own situation; instead he blames his dissatisfaction on fate ("He felt how useless it was to struggle against fortune"), his home town ("You could do nothing in Dublin"), his fellow man ("He would never be popular: he saw that. He could not sway the crowd but he might appeal to a little circle of kindred minds"), and finally, in the closing scene, his frustration is transferred onto his wife and child—"He was a prisoner for life" (D 71, 73, 74, 84). Yet while he obstinately kicks against the pricks that "oppress" him, the fault lies with him. Though married, Little Chandler has, like Mr. Duffy, the instincts of the celibate; and his celibacy poisons not just his marriage relation, but all his human relationships: "He turned often from his tiresome writing to gaze out of the office window. The glow of a late autumn sunset covered the grass plots and walks. It cast a shower of kindly golden dust on the untidy nurses and decrepit old men who drowsed on the benches; it flickered upon all the moving figures—on the children who ran screaming along the gravel paths and on everyone who passed through the gardens. He watched the scene and thought of life; and (as always happened when he thought of life) he became sad" (D 71). Little Chandler's self-pity is so pervasive that it is in the end a kind of paralysis, transforming all of experience into further evidence of his victimization.

Dubliners's next self-styled man of letters, Mr. James Duffy, makes a similar, though more conscious, decision to beat a retreat from life. Perhaps Mr. Duffy's case is especially "painful" precisely because a genuine realization of the true poverty of his life is so very close to the surface. But it is never allowed to break through; his repeated protest, for instance, that "he had been outcast from life's feast" takes his very real status as an outsider and translates it, via the logic of the victim, into something that's been done to him rather than something he's chosen for himself. The story begins by telling us rather pretentiously, in prose that bears the stylistic stamp we will come to recognize as Duffy's own, that "Mr. James Duffy lived in Chapelizod because he wished to live as far as possible from the city of which he was a citizen" (D 107); his isolation is a choice for which, however, in the last analysis, he refuses to take responsibility.

Throughout "A Painful Case," Mr. Duffy's eyes are fixed unwaveringly ahead of him: his gaze is never directed inward. He is not merely an outcast, but in fact a voyeur at life's feast; rather than joining in, he looks out his windows, lives "at a little distance from his body," looks down on the "venal and furtive loves" in Phoenix Park. Instead of look-

ing at himself, he sees himself—flatteringly portrayed—in his autobiographical prose: "He had an odd autobiographical habit which led him
to compose in his mind from time to time a short sentence about himself containing a subject in the third person and a predicate in the past
tense" (D 108).[41]

Duffy's egotism is such that even in his moment of most intense and
private pain, seemingly on the verge of admitting a fault in himself, he
again retreats into a rôle: "One human being had seemed to love him
and he had denied her life and happiness: he had sentenced her to ig-
nominy, a death of shame" (D 117). Yes, one human being *had* seemed
to love him; but what was the cost *for him* of having denied that love?
Neither he nor the reader can ever know what the consequences of that
rejection were for Emily Sinico; and although she's dead, Mr. Duffy is,
ostensibly at least, still alive. Bowen points out that "A close reading reveals that Mrs. Sinico did not begin to drink for a year and a half after
Duffy terminated their relationship. Duffy merely assumes that he is
the cause of her death. It may very well be the case that Duffy's ego has
erroneously prompted him to think that he had condemned Mrs. Sinico
to death."[42] Duffy thus seems to have been driven to his musings as a
result of faulty arithmetic; even pure mathematical reasoning, it would
appear, can be colored by the reckoner's needs and desires. But while
Duffy's equation is wrong, the insight it prompts is right; his is indeed
a painful case, for we see him not only in his moment of illumination,
but also as he chooses to ignore the light and continue to walk in darkness: "He turned back the way he had come, the rhythm of the engine
pounding in his ears. He began to doubt the reality of what memory
told him" (D 117). As Joyce said of Chekhov's characters, we realize that
as the curtain comes down, Mr. Duffy will soon be building new illusions to forget the old.

Finally we must consider, if only briefly, the most hotly contested of
all the epiphanies in *Dubliners*, Gabriel Conroy's final vision in "The
Dead." For many that famous final tableau has become, through repeated
exposure, almost invisible, and yet critical etiquette dictates that I quote
it here:

> A few light taps upon the pane made him turn to the window. It had
> begun to snow again. He watched sleepily the flakes, silver and dark,
> falling obliquely against the lamplight. The time had come for him to set
> out on his journey westward. Yes, the newspapers were right: snow was
> general all over Ireland. It was falling on every part of the dark central
> plain, on the treeless hills, falling softly upon the Bog of Allen and, far-
> ther westward, softly falling into the dark mutinous Shannon waves. It

was falling, too, upon every part of the lonely churchyard on the hill where Michael Furey lay buried. It lay thickly drifted on the crooked crosses and headstones, on the spears of the little gate, on the barren thorns. His soul swooned slowly as he heard the snow falling faintly through the universe and faintly falling, like the descent of their last end, upon all the living and the dead. (*D* 223–24)

The skill involved in writing a passage like this one has so far as I know never been called into question; even T. S. Eliot, ordinarily chary of his praise of his contemporaries, called "The Dead" "one of the finest short stories in the language."[43] But we may be excused a measure of skepticism about the authenticity of the transformation to which it pretends when we reach "The Dead" after reading the fourteen stories that precede it, stories in which false epiphanies—epiphonies—have repeatedly been foisted upon us as the real thing. Even before Gabriel's final "vision," we have reason to question his veracity, for he has "had" two other epiphanies—as a result of his encounters with Lily and Miss Ivors—and those rebuffs, now that he's safely in his room at the Gresham, haven't phased him a bit. After his patronizing and vulgar treatment of Lily, for instance, Gabriel's "self-awareness" is limited to a blush: "Gabriel coloured *as if* he felt he had made a mistake" (*D* 178; emphasis added). As a result of his embarrassment, Gabriel forces a coin on Lily, *as if* he could buy a clean conscience, and goes on his way.

These minor episodes, however, are merely preparation for the lush outpouring that closes the story.[44] The dangerous merging of decorative scenic description with the soul's anguished cry that we witnessed in "Araby" is again played out here, although in a more complex and treacherous way; indeed, it is difficult in this final paragraph to tell where ego ends and world begins. Many commentators, of course, have pointed to precisely this blurring of the boundaries of the self as a healthy sign of Gabriel's imminent renewal; he has come to realize his relatively small place in the larger, cosmic order, they argue, and in this renunciation of ego Gabriel has won (and demonstrated) his salvation.

"Isn't it pretty to think so?"—as Brett was overheard to say to Jake. As with the other epiphonies we've examined, our suspicions, which arise on the level of plot, are confirmed in the prose style of Gabriel's vision. Once again we must assume Gabriel responsible, courtesy of free indirect discourse, for the "supple periodic prose" in which his closing vision is presented; and once again Zack Bowen, who has so regularly seen the emptiness at the heart of these epiphanies, has registered the falsity of that presentation: "Gabriel, in order to characterize his own lack of feeling, presents a picture of beauty which belies the very char-

acterization he attempts to develop. . . . He breathes the life of his imagination into the portraits of both Furey and himself, because his dual
role as artist, the creator eternal and perishable buffoon, is reflected in
the majesty of his vision and in its slightly overripe language. The final
truth is indeed magnificent, but rather than the revelation of Gabriel
the reviewer-turned-poet, it is the far subtler vision of Joyce the writer."[45]
The "slightly overripe language" of which Bowen speaks is in fact quite
similar to some of the free indirect discourse surrounding Stephen in *A
Portrait*. Kenner's remarks on Stephen's penchant for chiasmus, for instance, provide a fitting commentary on the closing paragraph of "The
Dead," as well: "Shortly before he enters the University he has a period
of conspicuous indulgence in *chiasmus:* 'The towels with which they
smacked their bodies were heavy with cold seawater; and drenched with
cold brine was their matted hair.' Subject$_1$ was [predicate]: and [similar
predicate] was likewise Subject$_2$. In celebrating its rituals of finality, *chiasmus* leaves after-vibrations of sententiousness by which the young man
does not seem to be troubled. 'There's English for you,' part of his mind
is saying, and his fondness, at this period, for this figure . . . affects his
very perceptions with a certain staginess. . . ."[46] The closing pages of
"The Dead" are the last Joyce wrote before beginning the process of
transforming the clumsy prose of *Stephen Hero* into the cunningly styl-
ized writing of *A Portrait;* we should not be surprised to see him, then,
playing the same stops that Kenner has pointed out so clearly in *A Portrait* in this, the earlier text.

While many critics want to see Gabriel's transfiguration in his moving evocation of the snow, in fact his epiphony occurs a few pages earlier: "He saw himself as a ludicrous figure, acting as a pennyboy for his
aunts, a nervous well-meaning sentimentalist, orating to vulgarians and
idealising his own clownish lusts, the pitiable fatuous fellow he had
caught a glimpse of in the mirror. Instinctively he turned his back more
to the light lest she might see the shame that burned upon his forehead"
(*D* 220). This is the characteristic gesture of all those Dubliners (like the
boy in "An Encounter" and "Araby," Little Chandler, and James Duffy)
who have been blessed—or is it cursed?—with an extra measure of self-
awareness and sensitivity. Mirror, window, and darkness dominate the
last scene of "The Dead"; Gabriel consciously turns away from the mirror, and away from the light—eschewing that "one good look," eschewing self-awareness, eschewing enlightenment. In this moment of truth,
Gabriel covers his nakedness with a rhetoric not much better than the
sort he has used to dress up his after-dinner speech. We have already
seen him to be a man more concerned with style than with honesty;

and surely Gabriel is to be more strictly judged as a result of his greater awareness. If Mr. Farrington in "Counterparts" fails ever to see the light, there's surely no surprise in that; but for Gabriel, for James Duffy, for the boy in "Araby," there seems at least to have been a chance: "Joyce's insight," Bowen writes, "is that Gabriel is in fact forming a rationalization and at the same time a work of art about that rationalization. In short, while the epiphanies of *Dubliners* are only as accurate as the characters from whom they emanate, the process itself has an artistic integrity which goes far beyond the truth or falsity of the revelations themselves."[47]

Dubliners contains no psychological epiphanies for its protagonists—not even for Gabriel Conroy. Finally, epiphanies are equally a characteristic of Joyce's texts and an experience of their readers; we see epiphanies because we *need* to see epiphanies—the characters are enlightened because we need them to be. This is not the way the stories have traditionally been read. Harry Levin's *James Joyce: A Critical Introduction*, the first book-length study of Joyce's work (1941), early on fixed the relationship between one interpretation of the epiphany—the epiphany as the story's "punch line"[48]—and the plot dynamics of *Dubliners*. The closing epiphany, according to this reading, is roughly equivalent to the moral of the story, which the epiphany enacts rather than pronounces— and enacts in a way that the protagonists, or at least the artist protagonists, of the volume themselves recognize. By the time William York Tindall comes to discuss *Dubliners* in his *Reader's Guide* (1959), his assessment of the importance of the epiphany in *Dubliners* is a statement of critical orthodoxy: "The moral center of *Dubliners* . . . is not paralysis alone but the revelation of paralysis to its victims. Coming to awareness or self-realization marks the climax of these stories or of most at least. . . . The little boy of 'An Encounter' and 'Araby'. . . . comes to such knowledge; the coming to awareness of Little Chandler and James Duffy is far bitterer and more terrible because longer delayed; and the self-realization of Gabriel, the bitterest and most comprehensive of all, is not only the point and climax of 'The Dead' but of *Dubliners*."[49]

It is this understanding of the epiphany in *Dubliners*—the character's coming to awful self-knowledge—which constitutes the most widely disseminated understanding of the text, the reading that most college students carry away from their literature courses. Among a more recent generation of Joyceans, Morris Beja has become the most forceful spokesperson for this reading of the stories: "At the end of 'The Dead,'" he writes, "Gabriel achieves epiphany; other characters in *Dubliners* stories come to similar revelations as well (the narrator of 'An Encounter' and the narrator of 'Araby,' for example, or Little Chandler in 'A Little Cloud,' or notably Mr. Duffy in 'A Painful Case'—or even Eveline, before she represses all awareness)." Beja concludes his piece by asserting that "Gabriel Conroy and several characters within the volume, then, have had in the end that 'one good look at themselves.'"[50]

The dynamics of these texts, however, is not so easily contained. As Bowen points out regarding the epiphany at the close of "The Sisters," each of us involved in interpretation—in the case of "The Sisters," the boy, the sisters, Father Flynn, the reader—"fashions his own truth and sees it as the unalterable law of God."[51] The epiphony that closes many of the *Dubliners* stories, rather than a Grimm's fairy tale moral, is a relativity phenomenon, governed by what Herring calls "Joyce's uncertainty principle"; our interpretation is ineluctably slanted by the position from which we regard the text, and by the glasses through which we are constrained by gender, race, class, religion, and theoretical allegiances to read it. The readings of Levin, Tindall, and Beja—names that stand in here as proper-noun synecdoches for an entire critical tradition—are mediated by rose-colored glasses, the result inevitably being rose-colored glosses. In their desire for narrative closure, for the "happy ending"—a desire which burns within all of us, a desire of which Joyce was fully aware, and exploited for his own fictive purposes—critics are sometimes led into passionate misreadings, readings which mistake pseudo-epiphanies (epiphonies) for "the real thing." The fact that a text is written in a style of scrupulous meanness does not insure that it will be *read* in such a manner.

The word "misreadings," of course, grossly overstates the situation; we might instead refer to these interpretations as *misty*readings, in honor of the "generous tears" that fill our eyes, as they do the eyes of Gabriel Conroy and Joe Donnelly at crucial moments in their stories, and prevent our seeing things quite distinctly. Who among us, on a first reading, did not wish—indeed, did not passionately believe—that Eveline would run off with Frank to Buenos Aires? Ah yes, we're all too sophisticated now to be taken in by that ruse; we've read the story many times, and read the readings of the story, and now see plain as day from the first paragraph the ghostly written traces of Eveline's paralysis. But what was that first reading like?

The New Criticism, of course, has not encouraged us to look at the changing shape of our responses to these texts. As Jane Tompkins points out, Wimsatt and Beardsley's 1946 essay "The Affective Fallacy," one of the central documents of the New Criticism, rules out a reader-oriented criticism: "The Affective Fallacy is a confusion between the poem and its results. . . . It begins by trying to derive the standard of criticism from the psychological effects of a poem and ends in impressionism and relativism."[52] According to New Critical dogma, texts are verbal icons, to be apprehended in a timeless moment—taken in whole. In fact, this understanding of artistic experience is implicit in Stephen Dedalus's comments in the fifth chapter of *A Portrait:* "The first phase of apprehension is a bounding line drawn about the object to be apprehended. An esthetic image is presented to us *either* in space or in time. What is audible is presented in time, *what is visible is presented in space*" (P 212; emphasis added). Such a model effectively proscribes a reader-response analysis; yet the *Dubliners* stories are so process-oriented that any reading that does not take into account the way our experience of the stories changes over time cannot satisfactorily account for the way these texts work.

Our first readings of these texts must always be mistyreadings, for read innocently this is the response they provoke in us. But reading *Dubliners,* or any of Joyce's texts, is not a one-time act, but an ongoing process. To criticize an earlier generation of critics for falling for the "reader traps" in *Dubliners* is cheap sport; their sometimes credulous first wrestlings with these texts, which provide the foundation upon which a newer generation of readers has ungratefully built, are neither more nor less than carefully articulated records of their seductions by the text, a seduction which we too have undergone but have learned not to acknowledge.[53] Reading *Dubliners* is a dialectical process; our first reading is a product of seduction, while later rereadings employ cool intellection. But the second term of this interpretive dialectic does not obliterate the first; mistyreading, too, is a necessary stage in a fuller understanding of these stories. The reader, like the man of genius in Stephen's formulation, makes no mistakes: "His errors are volitional and are the portals of discovery" (U 156).

Mistyreadings: for Joe Donnelly's tears at the end of "Clay" provide the perfect example of the kind of distortion that can result when Joyce successfully taps into our hidden narrative agendas. Tindall like Levin before him argues that "Clay" ends with an epiphany for Joe; he believes that after Maria has finished her rendition of "I Dreamt That I Dwelt," with its significant "mistake," "Joe detects the meaning of her omission. 'Very much moved' by it, he calls for the missing corkscrew (one of many lost or misplaced things in the story) and presumably for another bottle in which to drown his understanding."[54] The corkscrew is not lost: but misty-eyed and "screwed" himself, Joe cannot see what is plainly in front of his face. Indeed, though he is about to have yet another drink, it would be a mistake to think that Joe's understanding is not already drowned.

Although Tindall reiterates just three words from the last paragraph of the story, they are the three crucial words, though not for the reason he thinks. Here they are again, recontextualized: "But no one tried to show her her mistake; and when she had ended her song Joe was *very much moved*. He said that there was no time like the long ago and no music for him like poor old Balfe, whatever other people might say; and his eyes filled up so much with tears that he could not find what he was looking for and in the end he had to ask his wife to tell him where the corkscrew was" (*D* 106; emphasis added). The prose of this last paragraph testifies against the idea of Joe's sudden awakening on at least three levels. The first is the level of plot. Joe, like the "colonel-looking gentleman" on the tram, is well into his cups at this point; we have watched him drinking throughout the story, trying at each refill to force Maria to drink with him, although she chooses other means to forget her troubles. As readers we realize—as Maria herself must—how easily a gentleman is moved to tears "when he has a drop taken," and view Joe's effusions with a certain skepticism. The second damnation is contained in Joe's encomium: readers steeped in Joyce's writing—again not necessarily first readers, but rereaders, readers who have slogged through both "The Sisters" and "The Dead"—cannot mistake the disdain with which Joyce records Joe's praise of the moribund: "He said that there was no time like the long ago and no music for him like poor old Balfe, whatever other people might say. . . ." A character who utters such sentiments in one of Joyce's texts has not had his epiphany.

The third stroke comes in the phrase that Tindall quotes—"very much moved." When read in the larger context of the story this description is meant to tip us off to what is—and is not—happening here. The word "very" occurs no fewer than sixteen times in the seven pages of "Clay," and is always associated with the prose of Maria's desire—the free indirect discourse shaped by Maria's mind. "Very" is one of "Maria's words," like "nice" and "little"; the first sentence of the text's description of Maria, for instance, reads: "Maria was a *very, very* small person indeed but she had a *very* long nose and a *very* long chin" (*D* 99; emphasis added). The locution "very much moved" suggests that something insincere, something automatic and falsifying is happening in the narrative. That something is that Maria, influencing the free indirect discourse of the closing paragraph, is misrepresenting Joe's sloppy, intoxicated sentimentality as genuine sympathy for Maria's unspoken plight. It is not.

At the end of "Clay," Joe is about as far from epiphany as one can easily imagine. Tindall's interpretation is too credulous; but that is certainly no accident, for it is a reading that Maria herself would "very much" appreciate. In Margot Norris's words, "narrative speech in 'Clay' is, for the most part, uttered in the language of Maria's desire; it is Maria's desire speaking."[55] In Joyce's hands, this free indirect discourse is even more insidious, more subversive of narrative certainty, than the use of a limited narrator by a writer like Faulkner; for in "Clay" and a handful of other stories in *Dubliners,* the narrative is colored by an unreliable *non*-narrator—one who not only has a vested interest in the outcome of the story, but additionally refuses to acknowledge her hand in it. In Tindall's reading of "Clay" Maria's discourse of desire has intersected the critic's interpretive predilections, and he has as a result been seduced; "In the end," Norris writes, "the reader of 'Clay' is read by the text."[56]

"Clay" *is* an extremely seductive story, but finally no more so than any number of others in *Dubliners.* The stories all demonstrate dramatically the connivance of interpretation with desire; the texts cooperate with their narrators' (or protagonists') desires; we then read the stories through the lenses of our desires. For it is only through the desire of Joyce's characters, subtly manifest in the texts they would have liked to have written, that our own desire—our interpretive desire—can be seduced into the light of day, or into cold print. The man who reviewed *Dubliners* for the *Times Literary Supplement,* for instance, in what is overall a perceptive and sensitive review, nevertheless proceeds within a fairly small space to mistyread significant aspects of three of the stories: "The author, Mr. James Joyce, is not concerned with all Dubliners, but almost exclusively with those of them who would be submerged if the tide of material difficulties were to rise a little higher. . . . One of them—a capable washerwoman—falls an easy prey to a rogue in a tramcar and is cozened out of the little present she was taking to her family. Another—a trusted cashier—has so ordered a blameless life that he drives to drink and suicide the only person in the world with whom he was in sympathy. A third—an amiable man of letters—learns at the moment he feels most drawn to his wife that her heart was given once and for all to a boy long dead" (Deming 1:60). My argument is that these are not "wrong" readings of these stories, or at least not stupidly incorrect readings; these are the wrong readings that Joyce—that Maria, James Duffy, and Gabriel Conroy—have set out for us. We must fall prey to the critical protocols that can account for such essential early misreadings; this is exactly as it should be.[57] Maria wants us to believe her plumcake stolen, rather than having to take responsibility for having forgotten it;

Duffy desperately needs to believe himself the cause of Mrs. Sinico's tragic death, to have meant something to someone; and Gabriel's melodramatic imagination insists that if his wife's heart was once pledged to another, it was therefore "given once and for all," and never belonged to him.

It should come as no surprise that this happens, to Tindall, or to the *TLS* reviewer, or to ourselves—for we have been set up. In the stories of *Dubliners* we read the text of narrative desire; this is the characteristic use to which Joyce puts his free indirect discourse. Norris writes that Joyce's purpose in "Clay" is "to dramatize the powerful workings of desire in human discourse and human lives";[58] and that drama is played out not only on the page, but also in the reader. Our mistyreadings, then, are not simply the product of a willfully perverse writer, nor yet the careless errors of ignorant readers, but instead the result of an intricate pas de deux in which, when we discover our "errors," we simultaneously find that Joyce has anticipated and cunningly prepared them. The stories of *Dubliners* are Rorschach inkblots wherein we read the text of our desire in the course of (mis)reading the book of ourselves.

Dubliners is a text that implicates us in the deadly work of paralysis, and reveals to us our own paralysis. A "superiority complex" is either a contributing cause or a symptom of paralysis in many characters in *Dubliners* (for instance the boy in "An Encounter"—"I was going to reply indignantly that we were not National School boys to be *whipped,* as he called it" [D 27]); and yet we think their problems do not touch us, and therein we too are paralyzed. The standard reading of the *Dubliners* stories—that the protagonists of "An Encounter," "Araby," "A Painful Case," "A Little Cloud," and "The Dead" all reach a new level of self-awareness by story's end—is powerful evidence of the narrative of desire that runs all through Joyce criticism. When examined closely, however, the texts simply do not support such a reading; these are not stories with happy endings, but stories that resist our desire for closure, for interpretation, for Meaning. *Dubliners,* beginning with "The Sisters," whispers: Give up the flattering project of interpretation; give in to the mystery which is life.

The stories of *Dubliners* turn us not toward certitude, but toward the void; and while we like to believe ourselves above Joyce's "poor fledglings," Joyce's texts reveal us to be as willfully blind, as "driven and derided by vanity," as any of his characters. Like the sisters in the opening story, we need to believe the paralysis extrinsic to our world. Who, after reading this text, can say "*I* am a Dubliner"? We are quick to point a finger from our superior position and pronounce Corley a paralytic, or Duffy a paralytic. Garry Leonard makes this point early on in his recent book on *Dubliners:* "Rarely in fiction do characters suffer as exquisitely for the benefit of readers as they do in *Dubliners,* and I propose that readers explore their kinship with the characters' moral paralysis rather than self-righteously suggest various cures for it."[59] In an interview, Kathy Acker has talked about this phenomenon as characteristic of one class of texts: "What the reader wants—what the reader's trained to want I should say—is to be at a distance and say, Look at those weird people over there!" Acker goes on to insist, though, that "I never wanted to say that 'over there'"; neither, I am arguing, did Joyce.[60] What these texts force us to confront is that *Dubliners* is *not* a dramatic tableau, but a mirror—and that we, like all of Joyce's Dubliners, steadfastly refuse that one good look *at ourselves* in his nicely polished looking glass. This response was for Jonathan Swift the defining characteristic of satire. He writes in the preface to *The Battle of the Books:* "Satyr is a sort of Glass, wherein Beholders do generally discover every body's Face but their Own; which is the chief Reason for that kind of Reception it meets with in the World, and that so very few are offended with it."[61]

5

Dedalus, ~~Dead Alas!~~ Dead at Last

If you're anxious for to shine in the high aesthetic line as a man of culture rare,
You must get up all the germs of the transcendental terms, and plant them everywhere.
You must lie upon the daisies and discourse in novel phrases of your complicated state of
    mind,
The meaning doesn't matter if it's only idle chatter of a transcendental kind
         And everyone will say,
         As you walk your mystic way,
"If this young man expresses himself in terms too deep for *me*,
Why, what a very singularly deep young man this deep young man must be!"
               —Gilbert and Sullivan, *Patience*, Act I

In his well-known essay "From Work to Text," Roland Barthes distinguishes between two antithetical forms of literary production, a distinction later critics have found useful: the distinction between work and text. The essay is, like most of Barthes's writing, a wonderfully partisan piece; the reader is never in much doubt as to which of these two modes Barthes approves. In fact, he never attempts to define "the work" with any real precision; rather, it is implicitly evoked in contradistinction to Barthes's preferred form, "the Text": "The difference is this: the work is a fragment of substance, occupying a part of the space of books (in a library for example), the Text is a methodological field. . . . the work can be seen (in bookshops, in catalogues, in exam syllabuses), the text is a process of demonstration, speaks according to certain rules (or against certain rules); the work can be held in the hand, the text is held in language, only exists in the movement of a discourse (or rather, it is Text for the very reason that it knows itself as text); the Text is not the decomposition of the work, it is the work that is the imaginary tail of the Text; or again, *the Text is experienced only in an activity of production*" (*IMT* 156–57). Some of the characteristics of Text that Barthes notes here— its self-reflexivity, its status as process, its demand for participation, its hard-nosed insistence on the primacy of the signifier—are, as I have argued in greater detail in chapter 2, some of the very hallmarks of postmodern prose. Barthes goes on to distinguish the Text as metonymically structured and prodigally symbolic, while the torpid work remains naively wedded to the signified: "The logic regulating the Text is not comprehensive (define 'what the work means') but metonymic; the activity of associations, contiguities, carryings-over coincides with a liberation of symbolic energy (lacking it, man would die); the work—in the best of cases—is *moderately* symbolic (its symbolic runs out, comes to a halt); the Text is *radically* symbolic: *a work conceived, perceived and received in its integrally symbolic nature is a text*" (*IMT* 158–59).

This early Barthesean discrimination between work and Text is paralleled in his later distinction between the "text of pleasure" and the "text of bliss." While in his early writings Barthes betrays a faith that Text can somehow be separated absolutely from non-Text—from work— he later realized that the distinction is one not of kind, but of degree; all writing, he later acknowledges, is Text, and the two poles represented in the work/Text opposition operate as general tendencies within individual texts, rather than creating absolute generic differences. All writing is Text. Some writers recognize this, and the diminished role it leaves for the writer, and fight against it; Stephen Dedalus, as we shall see, is a high priest of the work. The productions of these writers Barthes calls, in various essays, either "readerly" (*lisible* [*S/Z*, 1970]), "work" ("From Work to Text," 1971), or the "text of pleasure" (1973). On the other hand, some writers (consciously or unconsciously) both recognize and revel in the ineluctably textual nature of all writing; their texts are Texts, writerly *(scriptible)* texts—texts of bliss.[1]

Within this framework—these frameworks—that Barthes devises, *Dubliners* emerges as Joyce's first Text, while the later *A Portrait* turns out to be Joyce's first—and only—work. Or to put it differently: in *Dubliners* a postmodern stylistic dominates, while *A Portrait* celebrates a thoroughly modernist notion of textuality. That two different works by the same author should evidence such different textual strategies is not in itself surprising; if we are inclined to want an author's corpus to evidence a "unified development," that desire itself is largely a product of the modernist paradigm of the Author as Guarantor of his work. "It is not a question," Barthes writes, "of drawing up a crude honours list in the name of [post-]modernity and declaring certain literary productions 'in' and others 'out' by virtue of their chronological situation: there may be 'text' in a very ancient work, while many products of contemporary literature are in no way texts" (*IMT* 156). Lyotard confirms this opinion:

"The nuance which distinguishes these two modes (the modern and postmodern) may be infinitesimal; they often coexist in the same piece, are almost indistinguishable; and yet they testify to a difference *(un différend)* on which the fate of thought depends and will depend for a long time, between regret and assay" (*PC* 80).

And yet while they acknowledge in theory the possibility of these two modes coexisting in one text, both Barthes and Lyotard strongly suggest that in the evolution of styles, certainly during the modern era, the "natural" progression is for a writer to move "from work to Text," as Barthes's title has it—from a modernist to a postmodern stylistics. If this is the case, how can we account for Joyce's early "lapse," his fall from the postmodernism of *Dubliners* to the self-important modernism of *A Portrait?* It is almost inconceivable—surely one of the real oddities of modernist literary history—that Joyce wrote *Dubliners* and *Stephen Hero* concurrently, and that *Dubliners* was published before *A Portrait.* Granted, the publication of *A Portrait* more than two years after *Dubliners* was due largely to the vagaries of publishing history; for while the short story collection made its public appearance first, the novel is in its conception the earlier work—*A Portrait*'s "birthday" is in January, *Dubliners*'s in July, 1904. And while Joyce worked and reworked *A Portrait* over a period of ten and a half years (as compared with just over three years for *Dubliners*), the final version never quite succeeded in shaking off the evidence of its humble—or rather arrogant—birth. Joyce, all his life long, harbored within himself these two contradictory spirits: the high modernist purpose and the low postmodern play, a belief in the work as creation of the Artist as God, and an awareness of the Text as the construction of the Artist as *bricoleur*—the co-creation of a Text and its readers. All of Joyce's texts, to greater or lesser degree, bear witness to these two spirits lodged in the one bosom, the one inkwell; but while in *Dubliners* it is the postmodern spirit which holds sway, in *A Portrait* it is the modern. *Dubliners* is the text worst served, *A Portrait* best served, by the modernist paradigm; thus *A Portrait* is the work which holds up least well in an age of postmodern readers.[2]

I believe that the explanation for this seeming paradox is on the surface a very simple one—that as long as Joyce remained entangled with his fictional alter ego Stephen Dedalus, the thinly veiled autobiographical hero of *A Portrait* and the first three episodes of *Ulysses,* the text, like its protagonist, is locked in a state of arrested artistic development. As long as Stephen holds center stage, style—especially free indirect discourse, and what I'll later dub free indirect prose—takes itself too seriously: when Stephen is the subject of narration, the prose is tight-assed.

Once Malachi (Buck) Mulligan makes his entrance, however, lightheart-edly undoing all Stephen's narrow seriousness, followed quickly by Leo-pold Bloom, who eats with relish the inner organs of beasts and fowls rather than eating his own heart out, things are happily otherwise.

After the thoroughgoing critique of Romanticism to be found in the pages of *Dubliners*, the unabashedly Romantic style of much of *A Portrait* is somewhat difficult to understand. Joyce's basic distrust of Romanticism is well-known; in his later years, he called it a "fundamentally false at-titude" (*CJJ* 36), and certainly it is made to look that when it interferes with the lives of characters in *Dubliners*—the boy in "Araby," for instance, or Miss Eveline Hill. In conversation with Arthur Power, Joyce all but blamed the fall of humankind on Romanticism, seeing in it the source of all civilization's discontents: "In realism you are down to facts on which the world is based: that sudden reality which smashes romanti-cism into a pulp. What makes most people's lives unhappy is some dis-appointed romanticism, some unrealizable or misconceived ideal. In fact you may say that idealism is the ruin of man, and if we lived down to fact, as primitive man had to do, we would be better off. That is what we were made for. Nature is quite unromantic. It is we who put romance into her, which is a false attitude, an egotism, absurd like all egotisms" (*CJJ* 98). But like his contemporaries Eliot, Hulme, Pound, and Lewis, Joyce found it easier to disdain Romanticism in principle than to es-chew it in fact—to expunge it from his writing. In the writing of *A Por-trait*, Joyce explodes forever the notion of the Romantic autobiography; but *A Portrait*, while perhaps intended by Joyce as a rebellion against his Romantic inheritance, is written in a prose largely undisturbed by that rebellion. His intention, we may infer from extratextual material, was anti-Romantic, and his defenders argue that the Romanticism of *A Por-trait*'s prose is a silently ironic criticism of its protagonist; but there is in fact very little in the text itself to indicate whether Joyce endorses or condemns its lush prose. Indeed, this is the thrust of Wayne Booth's fa-mous discussion of the failure of Joyce's irony.[3] Arthur Power remarks this same split between "form" and "intent" in Joyce's early (1902) paper on James Clarence Mangan: "it was while reading this article that I had first become aware of Joyce's duality of character, for though the article was written in a romantic vein and in a prose which shows the influ-ence of Pater, he makes in it his first attacks on the very romantic mood which he himself was then expressing" (*CJJ* 42–43). In *Ulysses* J. J. O'Molloy recites John F. Taylor's oration, in which Moses is described com-ing down from Mt. Sinai "bearing in his arms the tables of the law, graven in the language of the outlaw" (*U* 117); the style of *A Portrait*, on the other hand, renders that novel the tome of the outlaw, graven in the language of the law—the language of the (poetic) Father.

A Portrait as published contains an uncomfortable admixture of endorsement and critique of Romanticism, for while Joyce came to distrust Romanticism as a philosophy, an attitude, a mood, the Romantic hero was a very attractive figure for the artist "as a young man," and *A Portrait* was conceived with Stephen as just such a hero, and really could not have been written otherwise—despite Joyce's best efforts to the contrary. We can see how the novel changed between the first draft *Stephen Hero* and the final product *A Portrait of the Artist as a Young Man;* but while Stephen is no longer *called* a hero in the 1916 novel, the one constant in the story, from the two-thousand-word "Portrait" essay written in haste on 7 January 1904 to the novel published on 29 December 1916, is the imperious figure of Stephen D(a)edalus.

T. E. Hulme's famous discussion of Romanticism describes the ethos of *A Portrait* quite well; he defines Romanticism as the belief that "man, the individual, is an infinite reservoir of possibilities; and if you can so rearrange society by the destruction of oppressive order then these possibilities will have a chance and you will get Progress."[4] Hulme goes on to claim that in situations where the appetites are suppressed, "the repressed instinct bursts out in some abnormal direction": "the instincts that find their right and proper outlet in religion must come out in some other way. You don't believe in a God, so you begin to believe that man is a god. You don't believe in Heaven, so you begin to believe in a heaven on earth. In other words, you get romanticism. The concepts that are right and proper in their own sphere are spread over, and so mess up, falsify and blur the clear outlines of human experience. It is like pouring a pot of treacle over the dinner table. Romanticism then, and this is the best definition I can give of it, is spilt religion."[5]

Hulme's is without doubt the best-known modernist indictment of Romanticism; yet in *Stephen Hero,* in a passage most likely written a full ten years before Hulme's essay, Joyce has Stephen champion the classical over what he calls the romantic temper, and in terms that anticipate Hulme's quite closely:

> "A classical style," he said, "is the syllogism of art, the only legitimate process from one world to another. Classicism is not the manner of any fixed age or of any fixed country: it is a constant state of the artistic mind. It is a temper of security and satisfaction and patience. The romantic temper, so often and so grievously misinterpreted and not more by others

than by its own, is an insecure, unsatisfied, impatient temper which sees
no fit abode here for its ideals and chooses therefore to behold them under
insensible figures. As a result of this choice it comes to disregard certain
limitations. Its figures are blown to wild adventures, lacking the gravity
of solid bodies, and the mind that has conceived them ends by disown-
ing them. The classical temper on the other hand, ever mindful of limitations, chooses rather to bend upon these present things and so to work
upon them and fashion them that the quick intelligence may go beyond
them to their meaning which is still unuttered." (*SH* 78)

But while able quite early in his career to spot the same flaws in the "romantic temper" that Hulme was later so memorably to point out, in his
early work Joyce was himself a Romantic. Arthur Power gets at this; he
remarks, "when I consider Joyce's character I have always two different
men in mind—the earlier Joyce, the Joyce of *A Portrait,* and the later
Joyce of *Ulysses*" (*CJJ* 42). He significantly omits mention of *Dubliners,*
which does not fit the neat chronological division he proposes; but surely
Power is right to insist that there exists a great difference between the
Joyce of *A Portrait* and the Joyce of the second half of *Ulysses,* and of
Finnegans Wake.

   While Joyce the writer is striving to shake off his Romantic inheritance, Stephen the character still defines himself according to the Romantic paradigm of the artist/poet; one of the ways we can tell is the
close echoes of Shelley's "A Defence of Poetry" in the text of *Stephen
Hero.* For instance, Stephen calls the poet "the intense centre of the life
of his age to which he stands in a relation than which none can be more
vital." "He alone," Stephen proclaims, "is capable of absorbing in himself the life that surrounds him and of flinging it abroad again amid
planetary music" (*SH* 80). The image—and language—here is very close
to that of Shelley: "Few poets of the highest class have chosen to exhibit
the beauty of their conceptions in its naked truth and splendour; and it
is doubtful whether the alloy of costume, habit, &c., be not necessary to
temper this planetary music for mortal ears."[6]

   What I've been arguing to this point is that Stephen Dedalus, the character, is a writer of works—a Romantic Artist with a capital *A* (or would
be, if he could in fact get any real writing done!)—while the James Joyce
who brought Stephen to life in the pages of *A Portrait* was a writer of
Texts. If early critics of *A Portrait* emphasized its autobiographical character, the trend for the past quarter century or more has been to move
away from that sort of narrow biographical reading, and to emphasize
instead Joyce's artful shaping of the raw materials of his biography. My

analysis, clearly, is indebted to this more recent style of reading *A Portrait;* but at the same time, in order to flesh out the complex dynamics between character and author that created Joyce's first novel, I think we need to examine as well Joyce's youthful flirtation with Romanticism, and his own attraction to the figure of the Romantic hero. Thus, while the Stephen in chapter 1 of *A Portrait* who imagines himself to be the Count of Monte Cristo is not Joyce, Joyce was, in years prior to the writing of the novel, not easily distinguishable (in his Romanticism, at least) from that young boy. The title that Joyce finally settled on for the novel, as he was wont to remind readers and critics, emphasizes both his closeness to the hero *(A Portrait of the Artist)* and also his eventual distance *(. . . as a Young Man).*

In fabricating his artistic pose as a young man Joyce the writer clearly took Paul Verlaine to heart, whose *Les poètes maudits* he had read by 1902 *(JJ* 75).[7] Verlaine's loving portrait of Arthur Rimbaud must have been particularly attractive to Joyce; Verlaine describes the younger poet at "seize à dix-sept ans" as "large, well built, almost athletic, with a perfectly oval face, the face of an angel in exile, with disheveled light-brown hair and disturbing pale blue eyes"; Joyce himself was just twenty-one in January 1904, when he began writing his self-portrait.[8] The picture Ellmann draws of Joyce at sixteen is strikingly similar to Verlaine's picture of Rimbaud: "His strong, brown hair, parted towards the middle when he bothered to comb it, and his stubborn jaw were the strongest features of a face that otherwise looked delicate, with its thin nose, pale blue eyes, and slightly pursed mouth" *(JJ* 64).[9]

Bearing a natural physical resemblance to the boy poet, it would seem Joyce decided to play the part as Rimbaud had written it: "The Poet makes himself a *seer* by a long, gigantic and rational *derangement* of *all the senses.* All forms of love, suffering, and madness. He searches himself. He exhausts all poisons in himself and keeps only their quintessences. Unspeakable torture where he needs all his faith, all his superhuman strength, where he becomes among all men the great patient, the great criminal, the one accursed—and the supreme Scholar!—Because he reaches the *unknown!*"[10] The story of the suffering, gifted young artist, especially as rendered by Rimbaud, is of necessity a tragedy; in concocting the name of the hero of his first novel, Joyce combined "Dædalus," the "old artificer," with "Stephen"—presumably with reference to Saint Stephen, the first Christian martyr. The compound suggests a martyred artist, along the lines lived out by Rimbaud. The accursed poet's talents separate him even from his fellows, about whom Joyce says (in "The Holy Office"):

Where they have crouched and crawled and prayed
I stand the self-doomed, unafraid,
Unfellowed, friendless and alone,
Indifferent as the herring-bone,
Firm as the mountain-ridges where
I flash my antlers on the air. (CW 152)

But Joyce did not have to turn to French literature for a model of the *poète maudit*, for he was quite familiar with the lore of a tormented Irish poet who had haunted the streets of Dublin fifty years earlier. In February 1902, about a year before his first trip to Paris, Joyce presented a paper to the Literary and Historical Society of University College on the Romantic poet James Clarence Mangan, the first Irish poet of note to write in English. Outside of "literary societies," Joyce claims in that paper, "Mangan has been a stranger in his country, a rare and unsympathetic figure in the streets, where he is seen going forward alone like one who does penance for some ancient sin. Surely life, which Novalis has called a malady of the spirit, is a heavy penance for him who has, perhaps, forgotten the sin that laid it upon him. . . . All his poetry remembers wrong and suffering and the aspiration of one who has suffered and who is moved to great cries and gestures when that sorrowful hour rushes upon the heart" (*CW* 76, 80). Less than twelve months after delivering this paper to the UCD Literary Society, Joyce himself was living "in exile" in Paris. That this was a voluntary exile Joyce often allowed himself, and others, to forget; preparatory to leaving, for instance, he could write to Lady Gregory, "I seem to have been driven out of my country here as a misbeliever" (*L* 1:53). As Ellmann comments, Joyce "was neither bidden to leave nor forbidden to return, and after this first departure he was in fact to go back five times. But, like other revolutionaries, he fattened on opposition and grew thin and pale when treated with indulgence" (*JJ* 109).[11] And besides, persecution—whether real or imagined—confirmed Joyce in his belief that he was a real artist.

One of Joyce's first gestures on reaching the Continent—and quite a regal gesture it was—was to send a picture postcard to his Dublin school friend John Byrne. Joyce, draped in a full-length black overcoat and black "Hamlet hat," adorns the left side of the card; and on what remains he copied out for Byrne the song he had written of his exile, focusing on Joyce's favorite autobiographical symbol, the seabird:[12]

Second Part—opening which tells of the
    journeyings of the soul.
All day I hear the noise of waters
    Making moan,

Sad as the sea-bird is, when going
    Forth alone
He hears the winds cry to the waters'
    Monotone.

The grey winds, the cold winds are blowing
    Where I go;
I hear the noise of many waters
    Far below;
All day, all night I hear them flowing
    To and fro. (*JJ* 115)

The symbol of the "sad sea-bird" going forth alone is carried over from
his poetry into Joyce's fictional self-portraits as well. In *A Portrait* the
bird becomes the young artificer Dedalus, who resolves to "fly by" the
nets of nationality, language, and religion into self-imposed exile.

The slightly older Stephen Dedalus of *Ulysses* has gained some measure of ironic distance on the "young man" of *A Portrait*, to be sure, but
that irony seems paralyzing rather than enabling, for he is now mired
in *ressentiment*. Those nets that Stephen in *A Portrait* was confident he
could overcome by an act of the will are found to be much more insid-
iously set than he had expected. When Haines declares that "I should
think you are able to free yourself. You are your own master, it seems
to me," Stephen replies that, quite to the contrary, he is the servant of
three masters: the imperial British state, the holy Roman Catholic and
apostolic Church, and Ireland, which he had in *A Portrait* called "the
old sow that eats her farrow" (*U* 17; *P* 203). In *A Portrait*, Stephen found
the declaration of *non serviam* easy enough—titillating, exciting; but
by the end of *A Portrait* he believes "that there is a malevolent reality
behind those things I say I fear" (*P* 243). To these three masters,
Stephen might well have added other, internalized dictators: the
"agenbite of inwit," for instance, or his deep-seated enmity toward
Buck Mulligan.

Given his early predilection for autobiography, and his unwavering
youthful sense of his own importance, the comic exuberance that would
break through years later in *Ulysses* was at this point perhaps beyond
Joyce's scope. *A Portrait* is of course, in Stanislaus Joyce's artless phrase,
"almost autobiographical" (*JJ* 147); and from the time that Joyce began
his first drama, the "Ibscenest nansense"[13] *A Brilliant Career*, in the summer of 1900, through the day he wrote "Mr. Leopold Bloom ate with relish the inner organs of beasts and fowls" sixteen years later, he was fun-

damentally an "almost autobiographical" writer, reading and *writing* "the book of himself" (*U* 153).

As best we can tell, Joyce's first sustained literary production, a drama about a town in the throes of a plague that he called *A Brilliant Career,* was written during a summer trip to Mullingar with his father in 1900. Joyce's next extended prose work, the two-thousand-word autobiographical story "A Portrait of the Artist," was written in one day, on 7 January 1904 (*JJ* 144); much of this essay was transplanted into Joyce's first autobiographical novel, *Stephen Hero,* which he abandoned in 1906. Many of the *Dubliners* stories continue this autobiographical thrust, especially those Joyce called "stories of my childhood"[14] ("The Sisters," "An Encounter," and "Araby"), but also to some extent "After the Race," "A Painful Case," and "The Dead." In *A Portrait* Joyce reworked the core of autobiographical material at the heart of "A Portrait of the Artist" and *Stephen Hero,* condensing the first novel's nine hundred manuscript pages into a five-chapter, 250-page work.[15] Between finishing *A Portrait* and beginning *Ulysses,* Joyce wrote *Exiles,* a drama in three acts; there, the protagonist Richard Rowan's situation closely mirrors Joyce's own. An early draft of the "Telemachiad" of *Ulysses* was originally prepared for incorporation in *Stephen Hero;* Joyce later decided to conclude *A Portrait* with Stephen's grandiloquent flight to Paris, saving his inglorious return for the beginning of *Ulysses.* Thus Joyce was almost thirty-four years old when the first of his protagonists who was truly "Other," Leopold Bloom, came to life in his pages.

One convenient way to trace the trajectory of Joyce's evolving postmodernism is by looking at the changing role of the hero in the Joycean text; the evolution of Joyce's heroes over the course of his writing career constitutes in small a kind of archeology of postmodern heroics. Joyce's early heroes, autobiographical all, were cast in the Dædalian mold— Romantic tragic heroes. His first writings—*A Brilliant Career* and "A Portrait of the Artist"—were notoriously self-important and autobiographical, herocentric. Though little is known of *A Brilliant Career,* the writer's father remembered quite clearly the play's dedication:

> To
> My own Soul I
> dedicate the first
> true work of my
> life. (*JJ* 78)

The autobiographical hero of the two-thousand-word story "A Portrait of the Artist" is also a lonely heroic figure, rejecting the taint of the masses and declaring, "Let the pack of enmities come tumbling and sniffing to the highlands after their game—here was his ground: and he flung them disdain from flashing antlers" (*P* 259). Joyce first reworked and greatly elaborated this material as *Stephen Hero*, then as *A Portrait of the Artist as a Young Man*. If the testimony of Joyce's brother Stanislaus is to be believed, the title *Stephen Hero* was meant subtly to mock that novel's hero, as was the suffix "as a Young Man" that Joyce added to his first published novel. But while Joyce tried to address the limitations of his artist-hero through these cosmetic changes, the basic conception of Stephen D(a)edalus was of a lonely heroic figure, one perhaps not sufficiently distanced from the writer's own experience to allow for any real undercutting of his heroic standing.

Even while Joyce lovingly labored over Stephen, however, another strain was simultaneously manifesting itself in his work. The writing and revision of the Stephen D(a)edalus material went on almost concurrently with his scrupulously mean text, *Dubliners*, in which any and all pretensions to heroism, even those (or especially those) of ostensibly "artistic" characters like Gabriel Conroy, are systematically destroyed. Opening with a triptych of stories in which the young protagonist becomes aware of the limitations of his own ego, and closing with the monumental failure of Gabriel Conroy to realize that the world does not revolve around him, *Dubliners* is littered with the shells of people who have believed in heroic conception of the self which has not stood them in good stead in their own lives. Indeed, this was his late criticism of the plays of Ibsen and Synge: "'The fact is, Ibsen is too simple,' he told Stanislaus on 16 May, 1907. 'Life is not so simple as Ibsen represents it. . . . It's all very fine and large, of course. If it had been written at the time of Moses, we'd now think it wonderful. But it has no importance at this age of the world. It is a remnant of heroics, too. Synge's play [*The Playboy*], also!'" (*JJ* 266).

Gradually, fitfully then, Joyce moved from the herocentric narrative which was, after all, his Romantic/Victorian inheritance, to a narrative which puts heroes in their "proper" place—embodying the deconstruction of the self about which Foucault, Barthes, Deleuze and Guattari, and Bakhtin (among others) have written. Joyce's heroic transformation might be described as the switch from Dædalus to Odysseus, from superman to "no man." On the second page of *Ulysses,* Stephen tells Mulligan, "You saved men from drowning. I'm not a hero, however" (*U* 4). This, from the young man who was named, in a previous incarnation,

"Stephen Hero"; he has moved from Stephen Hero to Stephen I'm-not-a-Hero. But Stephen can't quite let go; though he's given up his pretensions to heroism, he's still playing the role of the poet-martyr. On that same page, we are told that "Stephen suffered him [Mulligan] to pull out and hold up on show by its corner a dirty crumpled handkerchief," and the verb "suffered" is clinically precise.

The transition in *Ulysses* from Stephen Dedalus to Leopold Bloom is a convenient locus for the shift away from heroism; Joyce told Frank Budgen that he tired of Stephen, who has "a shape that can't be changed."[16] Although Stephen occupies center stage in the "Proteus" episode, Bloom is Joyce's first truly protean character—ego without boundaries, polymorphously perverse; fluid, he sympathizes, empathizes, melds with all he encounters—cats, dogs, lunatics, women in the throes of childbirth. Tim Finnegan of Joyce's last novel is the ultimate postmodern hero; he is Orpheus dismembered, his names, progeny, words, and limbs scattered throughout the Irish landscape. Rather than a concrete, tangible character, Finnegan is a shadowy figure of half-heard gossip, half-remembered stories, and twilight sightings. In *Finnegans Wake*, Joyce would seem to have taken the deconstruction of the self, and of the literary hero, about as far as it can go. Of course, he got no farther than this, dying only two years after *Finnegans Wake* was published; according to one story, however, Joyce planned next to write a story about the sea, seemingly taking the dissolution of Tim Finnegan and Anna Livia Plurabelle yet one step further.[17]

Joyce holds a unique position in the literature of our century for many reasons, not the least of which is his steady and relentless demolition of the heroic structure of the novel which was his inheritance. As early as 1905, Joyce wrote to his brother, "I am sure . . . that the whole structure of heroism is, and always was, a damned lie" (*L* 2:81); this said, however, it was the work of a lifetime to undo that structure, pointing the way for the generation of writers who would follow.[18]

How, then, does one write an antiheroic novel about a self-proclaimed hero? Is it possible to write a postmodern novel about a would-be modernist poet? The narrative of *A Portrait* and the first three episodes of *Ulysses* labor under a certain gravity because of Stephen's own gravity. It's sort of like the old Jane Austen paradox: must the description of a boring party be boring? Can anything but a modernist novel be written about a would-be modernist poet or novelist? A Text about a work-man? Joyce did try to gain distance from Stephen in *A Portrait;* a quick reading of *Stephen Hero* proves that he was in some measure successful. But irony alone, both Barthes and Bakhtin insist, is not sufficient to render a work a Text (or, according to Bakhtin's framework, dialogic). In *Stephen Hero* and *A Portrait*, the hero is of vast proportions. The only characters in *Dubliners* who rival Stephen's egotism—James Duffy, say, or Gabriel Conroy—are clearly marked out for our disapprobation. But *A Portrait* is, when all's said and done, the spiritual autobiography of a hero, and if all sympathy were withdrawn from him, the novel would collapse in upon itself. Joyce, I believe, did wish to distance himself from some of Stephen's more egotistical moments; but Joyce's central conception of *A Portrait*—that it would be a portrait of the artist as a proud, vain, narcissistic young man—simply did not allow for Joyce's changing intentions; it, like Stephen himself, had an essential shape that couldn't be changed. Richard Pearce makes much the same point in *The Politics of Narration*, arguing that "In *A Portrait of the Artist* an authorial voice was struggling with a rebellious voice. But Joyce was not ready to give the rebellious voice full reign, let alone discover these possibilities until he gave up on Stephen. . . . And perhaps Stephen's shape could not be changed because it was determined by the shape of his story."[19]

Two of Joyce's most important stylistic devices are what Yvor Winters calls "expressive form" (which we will examine in connection with *Ulysses* in chapter 6) and its kissing cousin "free indirect discourse," Flaubert's *style indirect libre*. The ideal artist, in Stephen's vision, stands "behind his handiwork," orchestrating, conducting, but never himself singing: never coming on stage in his own person. According to traditional narrative tenets, this leaves an author very few narrative possibilities. One is a stark classic realism: a story told in limited third-person narrative throughout, using direct reported speech, perhaps even incorporating passages of stream-of-consciousness narrative, but never passing explicit judgment on the character. This is what Joyce attempts in *Stephen Hero;* the result at times approaches satire. Apparently that satire was not to Joyce's taste; and when *Stephen Hero* was recast as *A Portrait*, Joyce eschewed the very few authorial comments he had allowed himself in *Stephen Hero* (such as the narrator, at one point, calling Stephen a "fantastic idealist" [*SH* 36]). With an amazing discipline, Joyce completely erased any such signs of narratorial approval or disapproval in *A Portrait;* but the result has been the muddle that Booth talks about, where the reader is left no ground but Stephen's own from which to judge the artist as a young man. Indeed, critics (starting with Joyce's brother Stanislaus) have been reduced to emphasizing the self-critical intent of the qualifying phrase in the title, "as a young man."

Having decided to remain behind his handiwork, Joyce had found in the writing of *Dubliners* that free indirect discourse provided a supple and subtle means for introducing another voice into his narrative. Some minor characters in *A Portrait*, such as Stephen's Uncle Charles, are interrogated and illuminated by Joyce's use of free indirect discourse;[20] when the narrative informs us, according to Uncle Charles's own idiom, that "every morning . . . uncle Charles repaired to his outhouse" (*P* 60), we learn more about him in that single word "repaired" than the objective narrative ever deigns to tell us. But concerning its heroic protagonist, *A Portrait* leaves us with only Stephen's voice (in direct speech, reported speech, and diary writing), free indirect discourse, and the impersonal "voice" of the faceless narrator—Stephen's voice, Stephen's voice, and an infrequent, almost inaudible, objective voice. We therefore have no ground from which to judge Stephen outside of Stephen himself. This is a ruthlessly monologic narrative; Stephen's is the only voice we're allowed to hear speaking about Stephen. And in key portions of the novel—the bird-girl episode, for instance—even the "objective" narrative modulates subtly, imperceptibly, into Stephen's voice. Hence not even the prose style of *A Portrait* provides reliable grounds for judging Stephen's pretensions.[21]

As we have seen, Joyce learned the use of free indirect discourse early in the writing of *Dubliners;* for as soon as he had left the first-person stories of childhood behind, he looked for an unobtrusive way *inside* his characters. Familiar as he was with Flaubert's writing, free indirect discourse was the solution that suggested itself. In "Eveline," the second *Dubliners* story Joyce wrote, we hear, unacknowledged, the cadences of Eveline's thought and speech from the second paragraph on: "Still they seemed to have been rather happy then. Her father was not so bad then; and besides, her mother was alive" (*D* 36-37). For Eveline, feelings are never quite clear and distinct, and so the narrative reports that she and her family "*seemed* to have been rather happy"; the expression "so bad" is Eveline's too, her genteel euphemism for her father's drinking. Free indirect discourse is a factor in all of the third-person narratives in *Dubliners;* in two of the stories, though, we get something just slightly different. "The Dead" and "A Painful Case" tell the tales of, respectively, a writer and a would-be writer—more generally, two men of letters.[22] Free indirect discourse, when used in the description of a writer or would-be writer, sometimes modulates under Joyce's hand into what I will call "free indirect prose"—prose which is an unacknowledged cipher of the subject's own prose style (as for example the closing paragraph of "The Dead," examined in some detail in chapter 4).

Seymour Chatman defines free indirect discourse, which he classes

as a species of "covert narration," as an imitation of the character's speech
or thoughts. The closing passage of "The Dead," however, fulfills neither of these functions; it is free indirect *prose,* an imitation of Gabriel
Conroy's *writing* (a fair sample of which we've listened to him read out
during his after-dinner speech). Gabriel looks out his window in silence:
there's no "speech" to be presented or imitated. Gabriel is certainly thinking; but very few of us think in cadenced and lambent prose poetry like
this. No, this is neither Gabriel's speech nor his thought, but precisely
his prose, plagiarized by the covert narrator; this, we sense, is how Gabriel would "write up" his final vision, if indeed the writing of it were
left up to him. This Joyce invented: prose influenced according to what
Kenner calls the "Uncle Charles Principle." Emma Bovary could not
have been narrated in this way; neither, for that matter, could Eveline,
or Maria, or Lenehan, or Lily the caretaker's daughter—characters not
sufficiently fluent in the conventions of written English prose style.
Irony—if indeed there is any implicit in the closing paragraphs of "The
Dead"—exists only in the minute gap between "Gabriel's style" and
the narrator's.

Joyce first used free indirect discourse in his first third-person narrative, "Eveline"; and he first used—indeed, *invented*—free indirect prose
in his first third-person narrative of a frustrated artist, "A Painful Case."
Free indirect discourse is clearly at work throughout *A Portrait;* Dorrit
Cohn calls it a species of "stylistic contagion,"[23] and one result in *A Portrait* is that all description of Stephen is, to a greater or lesser extent,
"contaminated"—or, at least, suspect. Just as there is no moral/ethical
standard outside of Stephen by which he might be judged, so too there
is no stylistic standard to which we can appeal—no neutral, "flat," objective, "plain style." None of the prose of *A Portrait* can be guaranteed
to be free from infection.

Free indirect prose is a logical outgrowth of the modernist notion of
"expressive form"; at the same time, however, it presents the covert narrator as plagiarist. Like Joyce, who raided his brother's diaries and used
their contents when it suited him—or like Stephen Dedalus, who steals
his "God of Creation" speech in *A Portrait* from Flaubert, and his "cracked
lookingglass" bon mot in the "Telemachus" chapter of *Ulysses* from
Wilde—the narrators of "A Painful Case" and "The Dead" steal uncon-
scionably from the writing, actual or virtual, of their subjects, and don't
acknowledge the debt. Or . . . or else Gabriel has bumped off the narrator of "The Dead" and is, by story's end, sitting at his desk penning the
end of the tale, as seems to happen at the end of *A Portrait,* when Stephen's diary writing takes over the narrative. Or finally, perhaps Ga-

briel has stolen the manuscript—"The Dead" is a purloined letter—and the story as it comes down to us is a forgery, ghostwritten (not to mention ghost-ridden). For free indirect prose is either pseudo-first-person narrative—the objective narrator as plagiarist—or pseudo-third-person narrative: "objective" narration has been subverted, the text purloined.

The entire notion of free indirect discourse, as we will consider in the next chapter, is a consequence of modernist stylistics; it's a subset or corollary of "expressive form," the idea that form should mirror content. In *Ulysses,* as we'll see, Joyce pushes expressive form to the breaking point, as he does with so many modernist devices, in order to show their ultimate poverty and to point the way to something different— the carnivalized novel. But as long as one believes that style must in some manner be wedded to content, style can never really laugh at content or at a pretentious character: a preponderance of free indirect discourse absolutely rules out the carnivalized novel. In *A Portrait* Stephen's demeanor, his self-conception, acts as a stylistic limit for the text, beyond which it can't grow, can't laugh at or be parodic toward itself— only toward others. Stephen the young Byron-wannabe is the millstone hung around *A Portrait's* neck, and try as he might, Joyce was never able to save the Text.[24]

There's a kind of irony—a cold, icy irony—that Joyce directs at Stephen in *A Portrait;* but it's very different from the laughter we discover (and participate in) at the end of *Ulysses.* Because Stephen equates art with "high" art, the text that laughs at itself—the carnivalized novel— violates Stephen's conception of what art should be; his Romantic notions of what literature should look like simply don't allow for the demolition of the work that the carnivalized novel insists upon. Therefore, through a weird kind of sympathetic magic, *A Portrait* is prevented from ever evolving into a carnivalized novel, as *Ulysses* was to do. Lyotard writes that "the work is . . . a priestly notion;"[25] and of course Stephen, though he rejects the priesthood that the Jesuits offer him, does opt to become a priest of eternal imagination. Mark well: Stephen wants to be not an artist, but a *priest,* of eternal imagination; in the same text wherein he first learned how to be a *poète maudit,* Arthur Symons's *The Symbolist Movement in Literature,* Joyce also read that "in this revolt against exteriority, against rhetoric, against a materialistic tradition; in this endeavour to disengage the ultimate essence, the soul, of whatever exists and can be realised by the consciousness; in this dutiful waiting upon every symbol by which the soul of things can be made visible; literature, bowed down by so many burdens, may at last attain liberty, and its authentic speech. In attaining this liberty, it accepts a heavier burden; for in speaking to us so intimately, so solemnly, as only religion had hitherto spoken to us, it becomes itself a kind of religion, with all the duties and responsibilities of the sacred ritual."[26] When the director of Clongowes Wood College talks to Stephen about joining the Society of Jesus Stephen refuses, but certainly he's attracted by the power the director speaks of: "the power of the keys, the power to bind and to loose from sin, the power of exorcism, the power to cast out from the creatures of God the evil spirits that have power over them, the power, the authority, to make the great God of Heaven come down upon the altar and take the form of bread and wine. What an awful power, Stephen!" (*P* 158). Stephen wants to have sway over people's souls, but chooses to achieve it differently. The novel's epigraph suggests that young Dedalus will "apply his mind to obscure arts"; the art of religious persuasion is, as Stephen's three-day religious retreat and his conversation with the director show, the art of rhetoric. To pursue the art of rhetoric as a profession, according to the terms set out in *A Portrait*, means a career in the Church, politics (Charles Stuart Parnell, Michael Davitt), or poetry. Not surprisingly, Stephen chooses poetry.

In *Ulysses*, Joyce was to discover the carnivalized novel—the text that laughs at itself, in which style is not allowed to take itself seriously, and no style nor any character is set up as the absolute standard for authenticity or truth. In the carnivalized novel—certain episodes of *Ulysses*, for example, beginning with "Aeolus"—style itself takes a stand outside of the subject of narration, and in many cases a stance explicitly critical of the characters. A quick example from the "Scylla and Charybdis" episode comes to mind: Stephen has just been gassing about the fact that the man of genius makes no mistakes, for "his errors are volitional and are the portals of discovery" (*U* 156); this is precisely the kind of situation where, in *A Portrait*, if Stephen stopped to take a breath, Lynch would chime in with some quip to deflate Stephen's somewhat inflated sense of himself. Here, in *Ulysses*, the narrative does it: the next sentence after the quotation from Stephen reads, "Portals of discovery opened to let in the quaker librarian, softcreakfooted, bald, eared and assiduous." Style takes on a life of its own; no longer dependent on the values, beliefs, shortcomings, or personalities of those it describes, style goes guerrilla. That guerrilla stylistics, as it manifests itself in *Ulysses*, is the subject of chapter 7.

Joyce chose to frame his second novel with the structure of the *Odyssey*; once he had made this foundational decision, many incidentals of the novel were effectively settled for him. Thus, for instance, in addition to a twentieth-century Irish Ulysses, his story would have to have both a Penelope and a Telemachus. These parts needed to be cast, but Joyce had free rein as to how he would fill them; and, having absolutely free choice, he created Leopold and Molly Bloom to be his Ulysses and Penelope—and chose to resurrect Stephen Dedalus from *A Portrait* for his Telemachus.

Why Stephen? Joyce's decision to make the star of his first novel a supporting actor in the next is, as far as I know, unprecedented. Balzac had, of course, used the *retour de personnages* in *La comédie humaine,* but on a mass scale that discourages focus on any individual character. D. H. Lawrence was later to reprieve Ursula and Gudrun Brangwen, protagonists of *The Rainbow,* as the women in love in *Women in Love;* but while these characters are carried over from one novel to its sequel, they suffer no real diminution in status, in the way that Stephen does. Miriam Henderson is the autobiographical protagonist of all thirteen volumes of Dorothy Richardson's *Pilgrimage,* but Richardson viewed the series as one novel, much like Proust's *A la recherche du temps perdu.* Stephen Dedalus, a.k.a. Stephen Hero, is of course the hero of *A Portrait,* and protagonist of the "Telemachiad" as well; as a number of scholars have pointed out, Joyce originally intended the scene in the Martello tower, which now opens *Ulysses,* to be included in *Stephen Hero,* and later in *A Portrait.*[27] But while Stephen continues to hold the stage through the first three episodes of *Ulysses,* he is relegated to a secondary role for the remainder of the novel; he is, after all, Telemachus, not Odysseus, and this is the *Odyssey.*[28] In this casting decision—one of the first involved in writing the new novel—Joyce shows that he has already decided to move Stephen from center stage, and to move someone else on. Stephen is quite aware of himself as an actor on a stage; he thinks, however, that the play is *Hamlet*—he of course is the boy prince—and that he can continue to hold the spotlight, at least until "the bloodboltered shambles in act five" (*U* 154). Stephen is, as Mulligan says, a "lovely mummer," but unknown to him he mums not *Hamlet,* but the *Odyssey;* he's to have a big part early on in the story, but is largely left behind as the plot thickens. This narrative strategy, once he divined it, very much upset Ezra Pound. While Dorothy (Shakespear) Pound, by the time she read the "Scylla and Charybdis" episode, confessed "a growing affection for Bloom,"[29] her usually percipient husband did not immediately share her enthusiasm: "Bloom has been disproportionately on ? ? ? or hasn't he. Where the hell is Stephen Tellemachus?" Pound inquired testily of Joyce after reading the "Sirens" episode.[30] Joyce's casting Stephen as

Telemachus meant that he would be forced from center stage, as Pound (who did know his *Odyssey*) quickly realized; by bringing him back in *Ulysses*, Joyce thus had the opportunity to criticize Stephen using new stylistic means not available to him in *A Portrait*.

Joyce could of course have drawn a new character to play Telemachus; the "Circe" episode, for instance, closes on Bloom's vision of his dead son Rudy, logically a sort of ghostly Telemachus, whom Joyce could have made more prominent in the narrative structure had he wished:

> (*Silent, thoughtful, alert he [Bloom] stands on guard, his fingers at his lips in the attitude of secret master. Against the dark wall a figure appears slowly, a fairy boy of eleven, a changeling, kidnapped, dressed in an Eton suit with glass shoes and a little bronze helmet, holding a book in his hand. He reads from right to left inaudibly, smiling, kissing the page.*)

>   BLOOM

> (*wonderstruck, calls inaudibly*) Rudy!

>   RUDY

> (*gazes, unseeing, into Bloom's eyes and goes on reading, kissing, smiling. He has a delicate mauve face. On his suit he has diamond and ruby buttons. In his free left hand he holds a slim ivory cane with a violet bowknot. A white lambkin peeps out of his waistcoat pocket.*) (*U* 497)

Putting Stephen in the part was tantamount to killing him off, slowly, softly. Thus bringing Stephen back in this diminished role is more than just a narrative convenience for Joyce—it is analogous to an editorial comment. Joyce decided, after working with him for over ten years, that Stephen was incorrigible. He had explained to Stanislaus early on that "what I want to wear away in this novel [*Stephen Hero*] cannot be worn away except by constant dropping" (*L* 2:83); but by the time *Ulysses* was in full sail, Joyce had had his fill. Complaining of Pound's comments, Joyce wrote to Frank Budgen, "I have just got a letter asking me why I don't give Bloom a rest. The writer of it wants more Stephen. But Stephen no longer interests me to the same extent. He has a shape that can't be changed."[31] In *A Portrait* Joyce had tried to let Stephen hang himself, but with mixed results; in *Ulysses* Stephen is brought into contact with characters—first Mulligan, then Bloom—who through their own words and deeds help point up the shortcomings in Stephen's character that Stephen's words alone could never do.

Ulysses opens with Stephen in mourning. His mother has died; he has been called home from his exile in Paris by the telegram "Nother dying come home father" (*U* 35).[32] But on 16 June 1904, she's been dead awhile; May Goulding Dedalus died on 26 June 1903 (*U* 570), and so has been dead just ten days short of a year. Why then the prolonged fuss? Not, of course, that one might not sincerely mourn a loved one for a full year and more; but Stephen seems not to have been especially close to his mother, and his mourning is, as Mulligan quickly sees, far too public, too showy, too theatrical. We begin to suspect that there's more remorse (agenbite of inwit) than grief, and more guilt than genuine mourning, in Stephen's display; for in spite of his conscientious denial, Stephen still questions whether his refusal to pray for his mother was the right decision. Thus Mulligan's offhand remark to his aunt ("it's only Dedalus whose mother is beastly dead" [*U* 7]) stings Stephen a good deal more than it should. Mulligan mocks Stephen and his exaggerated sense of decorum ("Etiquette is etiquette. He kills his mother but he can't wear grey trousers" [*U* 5], and he is surely right to do so. Mulligan is utterly tactless, and yet his criticisms of Stephen are for the most part just; Stephen is locked in a pathological pattern of mourning. In his essay "General Theory of the Neuroses" (1917), Freud suggests that "there are . . . neuroses which may be described as a pathological form of mourning,"[33] and into such a neurosis Stephen seems to have descended.

The episode over which Stephen is angry at Mulligan must have taken place quite some time before Bloomsday; it was during his first visit to Mulligan's after his mother's death, and she has been dead almost a full year. As Stephen himself admits, the issue is not so much his mother as himself: "I am not thinking of the offence to my mother," he tells Mulligan proudly, but rather "of the offence to me" (*U* 8). In "Telemachus" Mulligan tells Stephen to "give up the moody brooding," and the advice is good, no matter how distasteful the source. Yeats also counsels release, through the song "Who Goes with Fergus?" which Stephen sings but seems not to hear. For while his mother lies dying, Stephen makes an ironically contradictory gesture: he sings Fergus's song, as he recalls, "alone in the house, holding down the long dark chords" (*U* 8). Thus he broods over a song that counsels "no more turn aside and brood"; whether or not Stephen recognizes it, it is a tableau of delicious, vicious misery—a celebration of his sorrow, what Stephen elsewhere calls, in a phrase from Aquinas, "Morose delectation" (*U* 39).

In "Mourning and Melancholia," Freud attempts to describe the chronic condition of melancholia by analogy with the acute state of mourning. The similarities between the two conditions lead him to suggest that melancholia is in fact a pathological form of mourning; "Mourning is regularly the reaction to the loss of a loved person," Freud writes, "or to the loss of some abstraction which has taken the place of one, such as one's country, liberty, an ideal, and so on. In some people the same influences produce melancholia instead of mourning and we consequently suspect them of a pathological disposition."[34] I would submit—Mulligan, it seems to me, as much as says the same to Stephen—that Stephen has lost not a person (his mother) but, much more important (to him), an abstraction which has taken her place. Mulligan doesn't go so far as to name the real object of Stephen's mourning; he may not even know. I would suggest, however, that at the start of *Ulysses* Stephen is in mourning but not, as he claims, for his mother; rather he mourns the Artist—himself—in the age of mechanical reproduction; he mourns the death of the Author, the death of the Romantic artist/poet/hero/unacknowledged legislator. Stephen lost his mother, of course, long before she died; when he declared his apostasy he became as good as dead to her, and she to him. Cranly had tried to convince him that "Whatever else is unsure in this stinking dunghill of a world a mother's love is not" (*P* 241–42), but Stephen pointedly chooses intellectual and artistic freedom over "*amor matris:* subjective and objective genitive" (*U* 23).

"To discover the mode of life or of art whereby [his] spirit could express itself in unfettered freedom" (*P* 246): this is the principle for which Stephen explicitly forsakes his mother's love. Art thus takes his mother's place in his emotional life; and not art conceived in broad terms, but art conceived in specifically Romantic terms. At the close of *A Portrait* Stephen recalls the words of Yeats's Michael Robartes, who desires to press in his arms the loveliness which has long since faded from the world; in response, Stephen writes in his diary, "I desire to press in my arms the loveliness which has not yet come into the world" (*P* 251). Robartes's desire for "forgotten beauty" is nostalgic, and Stephen's formulation avoids such nostalgia, while slipping into breathless aestheticism; but both positions are, by both Hulme's and Stephen Daedalus's definitions, Romantic. By the start of *Ulysses,* Stephen has figured out that "Romantic Ireland"—and not just Ireland, but the entire world of Romanticism—is "dead and gone."[35] And he mourns its passing. Stephen's all dressed up—dressed up in proper Paris fashion as the aspiring artist—but he suddenly realizes he's got no place to go.

Indeed, it may be that Stephen Dedalus, at the start of *Ulysses,* wears mourning because he has just returned from memorial services held for the death of the Author. Both Barthes (in 1968) and Foucault (in 1969)[36] have written obituaries, but both were quite belated; both in fact put the time of death quite close to Nietzsche's announcement of the death of God: 1882, the birth year of James Augustine Aloysius Joyce and, presumably, Stephen Dedalus as well. "Writing," Barthes writes—and by which he means *écriture*, postmodern writing—"is the destruction of every voice, of every point of origin. Writing is that neutral, composite, oblique space where our subject slips away, the negative where all identity is lost, starting with the very identity of the body writing" (*IMT* 142). To paraphrase Yeats again, Stephen at the start of *Ulysses* realizes that Romantic poetry's dead and gone—It's with Shelley in the grave;[37] or to paraphrase Stephen himself, authority—authorship—is a legal fiction. John Cage puts the situation quite nicely in an anecdote about William de Kooning: "I was with de Kooning once in a restaurant and he said, 'If I put a frame around these bread crumbs, that isn't art.' And what I'm saying is that it is. He was saying that it wasn't because he connects art with his activity—he connects with himself as an artist whereas I would want art to slip out of us into the world in which we live."[38] As we explored in greater detail in chapter 2, the postmodern notion of text, of textuality, bequeaths a profoundly different role for the writer than did the classical or Romantic prototype. In a world in which Work has become text, the Artist, the Poet, has become a mere *bricoleur*, a "scriptor": "Having buried the Author," Barthes writes, "the modern scriptor can thus no longer believe, as according to the pathetic view of his predecessors, that this hand is too slow for his thought or passion and that consequently, making a law of necessity, he must emphasize this delay and indefinitely 'polish' his form" (*IMT* 146). The death of the Author has left Stephen Dedalus wondering what is to become of him. As Jean-Michel Rabaté points out, we must not be deceived by Stephen's rhetoric equating the artist with the absent God—for the artist in Stephen's scenario is far from dead; he's just orchestrating things from behind the scenes: "Joyce [I would want to say Stephen], it is true, does not say that the author has died. . . . The theory is hardly one entailing a diminished role: the godlike artist disappears tactically; he is not absent but just hidden."[39] Like his boyhood hero the cunning Dantès, Stephen the Artist is not dead, but hiding, planning his return and revenge.

The young artist about whom we read in *A Portrait*, and again in *Ulysses*, clings tenaciously to an outmoded vision of the poet; it has been made obsolete, to use another paradigm—this time Walter Benjamin's—precisely by the "age of mechanical reproduction." Benjamin argues:

For centuries a small number of writers were confronted by many thou-
sands of readers. This changed toward the end of the last century. With
the increasing extension of the press, which kept placing new political,
religious, scientific, professional, and local organs before the readers, an
increasing number of readers became writers—at first, occasional ones.
It began with the daily press opening to its readers space for "letters to
the editor." And today there is hardly a gainfully employed European
who could not, in principle, find an opportunity to publish somewhere
or other comments on his work, grievances, documentary reports, or that
sort of thing. Thus, the distinction between author and public is about to
lose its basic character. The difference becomes merely functional; it may
vary from case to case. At any moment the reader is ready to turn into a
writer.[40]

Nor was such a diagnosis limited to theoreticians, writing with 20/20
hindsight; in a lecture delivered at the Collège de France before the International Association of Students in May 1923 (and published in the
Little Review), just over a year after the publication of *Ulysses*, Fernand
Léger declared that "The artisan will regain his place which he should
always have kept, for he is the true creator, he it is who daily, modestly,
unconsciously, creates and invents these handsome objects, these beautiful machines which make us live. His unconsciousness saves him. The
immense majority of professional artists have become hateful because
of their pride and their self consciousness; they are a blight."[41] In an address to the Institute for the Study of Fascism in Paris in April 1934,
Benjamin observed that "As writing gains in breadth what it loses in
depth, the conventional distinction between author and public, which
is upheld by the bourgeois press, begins in the Soviet press to disap-
pear. For the reader is at all times ready to become a writer, that is, a de-
scriber, but also a prescriber. As an expert—even if not on a subject but
only on the post he occupies—he gains access to authorship." "Literary
qualification," he continues, "is founded no longer on specialized but,
rather, on polytechnic education, and is thus public property."[42] This
was good news for Benjamin; there is perhaps no need to point out that
for Stephen, it is anything but.

The breakdown in the distinction between author and reading public that Benjamin describes, while painful for Stephen, is liberating for
his employer, Mr. Deasy; in the "Nestor" episode, Stephen is reduced to
carrying Deasy's letter to "two editors he knows slightly," becoming
the errand boy for this hack—instead of Stephen the poet, he's Stephen
the post. Deasy assumes the columns of the paper to be open to him—
"I have a letter here for the press" (*U* 26), he tells Stephen, confident as

you like—and he's right. The *Irish Homestead*, where Stephen admits to knowing the editor "slightly," ran this "Notice to Correspondents, &c." during 1904 in its columns: "Correspondents, secretaries of societies, and other contributors, are reminded that letters, etc., intended for insertion in the issue of the IRISH HOMESTEAD following their despatch, must reach the Editor not later than Wednesday morning. . . . Queries on all the subjects with which the HOMESTEAD deals are invited. . . . All manuscripts should be written on one side of the paper only, and no notice can be taken of anonymous contributions; contributors having, however, the option of using a *nom-de-plume* for publication if they so desire. The Editor does not hold himself responsible for the opinions of correspondents."[43] The press would not have been open to Deasy just ten years earlier; in the United Kingdom, the crisis in author/reader boundaries to which Benjamin alludes dates from Saturday, 21 July 1894. On that day, the *London Evening News* first ran its "Letters to the Editor" column, called "Voice of the People."[44] Then too, we should notice that Deasy's letter is being "typed"; this sense of the word entered the language in 1888, while Joyce was at Clongowes Wood College. We're perhaps enough used to the word "typewriter" now that we don't much think about its implications, but the first typewriter to produce a line of writing visible as it was being typed—in the manner that Deasy's does— was marketed in 1890. Thus Deasy becomes, after a fashion, his own typesetter.

When Stephen tries to imagine the reaction of his friends when they learn of his efforts on Deasy's behalf, he dubs himself "bullock-befriending bard," and this is a great indignity; but worse surely is the fact that he's being used to have Deasy's hack writing published—he is helping Deasy become a published writer, something he himself cannot yet claim, but the role he feels only he is fit for. Deasy's matter-of-fact tone—his supreme confidence that his letter deserves "to be printed and read"— comes as a cold slap in the face to Stephen: "'That reminds me,' Mr. Deasy said. 'You can do me a favour, Mr. Dedalus, with some of your literary friends. I have a letter here for the press. Sit down a moment. I have just to copy the end'" (*U* 26). By suggesting that Stephen's "literary" friends are agents of the press, Deasy shamelessly blurs the distinction between literature and journalism, a distinction Stephen was careful to maintain.

Thus Garrett Deasy, with Stephen's help, becomes a published writer, and, apparently, publishes stuff like this (as Stephen's mind digests it): "May I trespass on your valuable space. That doctrine of *laissez faire* which so often in our history. Our cattle trade. The way of all our old industries. Liverpool ring which jockeyed the Galway harbour scheme. European conflagration. Grain supplies through the narrow waters of the channel. The pluterperfect imperturbability of the department of agriculture. Pardoned a classical allusion. Cassandra. By a woman who was no better than she should be. To come to the point at issue" (*U* 27).[45] This representation of Deasy's writing is of course a caricature, either on Stephen's part or on Joyce's, just as Deasy himself is something of a caricature; Joyce seldom allows himself to come this close to outright farce. But while Stephen's ruthless abridgment certainly does not cast Deasy's writing in the most favorable light, clearly Deasy at his typewriter has not suffered for "his art," has not paid his dues in the way Stephen has; Deasy is hardly an epistoler *maudit*. In their discussion in the physics theater in *A Portrait* Stephen and the dean of studies talk of the distinction between the "liberal" and the "useful" arts; and while Deasy's writing strives to be useful—proposing a cure for the foot and mouth disease—Stephen disdains such utility as inimical to the spirit of true art. Mr. Deasy is quite literally a "man of letters," which was for Joyce, as presumably for Stephen, a term of disparagement.

When all is said and done, Stephen is the only genuine object of his own pity; as the "Telemachus" episode opens Stephen is in mourning for a particular kind of heroic artist, the Romantic poet-hero—Lord Byron, for preference. Just as he defends Byron to his schoolmates in *A Portrait*, so Stephen imagines that the life of the Romantic poet is necessarily a lonely and misunderstood one; surely he will suffer, as he has suffered for his advocacy of Byron. But Stephen desires for himself a vocation which has disappeared from the modern world; even Yeats, one of "the last Romantics," resigned himself finally to "the foul rag-and-bone shop of the heart." The world of *Ulysses* is the modern world, as Kenner has described[46]—and Stephen has not yet worked out his feelings about the work of art, and the work of the artist, in an age of mechanical reproduction. The world has changed drastically, seemingly while Stephen has been at university, and the rôle for which he has so scrupulously prepared himself seems no longer to exist. His mourning is thus in one sense a metaphor for loss, nostalgia, and a refusal to come to terms with "the beauty which has already left the world"—the false beauty of the Romantics of which Joyce himself was so critical. Jennifer Wicke locates the collision between Stephen's view of art and Bloom's—roughly, between the Romantic and the pragmatic—in Bloom's ephemeral scheme (given voice in "Eumaeus") to manage Stephen's singing career. And, as Wicke writes, there's little question as to whose view, by the novel's close, has won out: "Bloom starts to hope he will be able to front for Stephen Dedalus, who after all has a B.A., 'a huge ad in its way,' although most commentators seem appalled or bemused at this transaction. Yet the 'pure' literature Stephen had hoped to make had already vanished in the wavelets of his own urine, as he drowned his book with a vengeance along the strand. Bloom may not have a B.A., but he knows that nothing can happen anymore without an 'opening' being cleared; advertising is the key in the lock."[47]

One possible reaction for the artist to this epistemic shift is that of the decadents—a reaction which is itself a slightly campy Romanticism, and toward which Stephen shows a dangerous predilection. Mulligan, in "Telemachus," insists to Haines that "we have grown out of Wilde and paradoxes" (*U* 15); but Mulligan quotes Swinburne, himself a decadent burnout, and the dialogue and interior monologue of the first three episodes additionally quote or allude to Rimbaud, Wilde, Laforgue, Pater, and Mallarmé.[48] If aestheticism is a dead end, the other option is to face squarely the new role of the artist—the one whom Stephen grandly describes in *A Portrait* as standing behind the work of art, paring his fingernails. Stephen has formulated but not lived that role; the time has come for him to put it into practice. As Lyotard writes in *The Postmodern Condition*, "That the mechanical and the industrial should appear as substitutes for hand or craft was not in itself a disaster—except if one believes that art is in its essence the expression of an individuality of genius assisted by an elite craftsmanship" (*PC* 74); elsewhere, he suggests that "we are no longer at the stage of deploring the 'mechanical reproduction' of works; we know that industry does not mean the end of the arts, but their mutation."[49]

By the time we are reacquainted with Stephen in the "Telemachiad," he is entrenched in a mourning gone sour. It has become a kind of mask for Stephen; it keeps him from having to deal with his real problems. His mother has been dead for almost a year, and by even the strictest Victorian codes of etiquette, his period of mourning should be just about over; but clearly, for his own reasons, he hides behind the screen that convention provides. Due perhaps to the unflattering portrait of Oliver Gogarty put forward by Richard Ellmann and Stanislaus Joyce, among others, critics have been quick to dismiss Mulligan's comments on Stephen wholesale. "Gay betrayer" and "usurper," the epithets for Mulligan most often picked up in the criticism, are of course Stephen's own judgments; we have perhaps been too quick in accepting their judgments without considering their source before. To be sure, the falsity of Mulligan's posturing is implicitly criticized throughout the novel, more and more as the day progresses. But critics have been too quick to throw out the baby with the bathwater; for Stephen has a lot to learn from Mulligan's barbs, whatever their motivation might be. Mulligan calls Stephen a "jejune jesuit"; "you have the cursed jesuit strain in you," he tells him, "only it's injected the wrong way" (*U* 4, 7). While Mulligan's use of the word "jesuit" might seem somewhat perverse, it is actually his metaphor for Stephen—the *OED* lists figurative uses of "jesuit" going back to the seventeenth century, meaning "a dissembling person, a prevaricator." And while the charge of hypocrisy coming from a hypocrite is perhaps a bit hard to swallow, it is nonetheless true for all that.

One of Joyce's characteristic plot devices through the range of Stephen texts is the use of a foil for Stephen; even in *Stephen Hero,* the protagonist was often with his brother Maurice, the "whetstone" against whom Stephen sharpens his wit and his artistic aspirations. In the aesthetic discussion in *A Portrait,* Stephen recites for his friend Lynch an aesthetic question from his notebook—an example that Stephen takes quite seriously, and presents without apparent irony: *"If a man hacking in fury at a block of wood . . . make there an image of a cow, is that image a work of art? If not, why not?"* Lynch's smart-assed comeback takes Stephen down a notch: "That's a lovely one. . . . That has the true scholastic stink" (*P* 214). Lynch is irreverent, and right; even the diction of Stephen's artful question ("make there"?) has the "true scholastic stink," and Stephen, as well as anyone, knows it. Lynch serves Stephen as something of an insincerity detector, and Stephen not only puts up with Lynch's criticisms, he pays for them with cigarettes. After Stephen's famous oration about the God of creation "paring his fingernails"—which has been taken "straight" by so many critics (with the notable exception of Joseph Buttigieg)—Lynch ironizes Stephen's picture of the Artist/God at his nails, suggesting that He is "trying to refine them also out of existence" (*P* 215). Touché.

Mulligan plays this same role in the "Telemachus" episode of *Ulysses.* Even though he is not a completely admirable or sympathetic character (neither is Lynch, for that matter), still there is something important in what both have to say to Stephen. Ironically enough, critics over the years may not have taken the criticisms voiced by these characters seriously enough because of the biographical fallacy—because the fictional Lynch was modeled on the real-life Vincent Cosgrave, for instance, or the fictional Mulligan was based on the real-life Oliver St. John Gogarty, critics have read the biographical figures into Joyce's fictional autobiography, and to some extent missed what was actually happening on the page. But only by assuming the subject position of Stephen Dedalus himself in the early pages of *Ulysses* can the reader come to the conclusion that he is the sympathetic character, and that Mulligan is out of line. Of course, for a biographically oriented critic like Richard Ellmann, there is every reason to adopt Stephen's site in the discourse of "Telemachus": Stephen is, after all, a version of Joyce himself, and Mulligan a thinly veiled rendition of that dastard Gogarty. Thus if we are possessed of this biographical background, we know from the get-go that Stephen merits our sympathy, for he is "the artist as a young man"; similarly, we know that Mulligan is up to no good, for we know Joyce's opinion of Gogarty. Then too, the text itself seems to want us to side with Stephen from the very beginning; for while the "objective" narrative refers to Stephen rather stiffly as "Stephen Dedalus" twice in two consecutive sentences on the first page, and at his first mention on the next page, it quickly switches to a first-name basis, calling him, invariably, just "Stephen" for the remainder of the first chapter (78 times). Nor is the fact that the narrative gives Stephen's name in full the first three times simply a product of some overly formal narrative protocol; rather, it is meant to remind Joyce's ideal reader—the reader who already has *A Portrait* under his belt—that this Stephen Dedalus is indeed *the* Stephen Dedalus, *our* Stephen Dedalus, thus enlisting our support for him in this new fictional context. "Stately, plump Buck Mulligan" is also initially presented in full name. But the narrative never moves to a first-name basis with Mulligan: he is full "Buck Mulligan" for 71 of his 75 narrative mentions, and plain "Mulligan" the other four.[50] The narrative background would thus seem, in a surprisingly heavy-handed fashion, to evidence and encourage sympathy for and intimacy with Stephen, while suggesting a more distant, formal relationship to Buck Mulligan.

What I am trying to suggest is that within the context of the opening pages of *Ulysses,* the narrative does not treat its two co-stars equally. We are tricked, at the start, into a too-easy identification with Stephen, a young man with whom, as we discover by the end of the novel, Joyce himself has largely lost sympathy. This is a reader trap; Joyce wants us to err by sympathizing with Stephen, for it is only by so doing that we can feel the full impact of his unthroning. Vicki Mahaffey puts it rather nicely: "An ironic reading must inevitably condemn Stephen for not knowing 'what the heart is and what it feels' (*P* 252) as he jauntily escapes to Paris, but a reader who eschews sympathy altogether becomes guilty of the same intellectual jauntiness he criticizes in Stephen: the ironist is implicated in the very ironies he perceives."[51] This is similar to the way Joyce operates in "Eveline"—careful rereading helps us to "correct" our initial identification with her, but that identification, though incorrect, was no accident. For if Romanticism is "a fundamentally false attitude," we see in Stephen an only slightly exaggerated version of our own secret Romantic aspirations; Stephen is different from us in degree but not (he would be aghast to learn) in kind. But the narrative in "Telemachus" contains another, contradictory thread. We are both encouraged to sympathize with Stephen, through the means I have suggested, and simultaneously warned not to sympathize with him; likewise, Mulligan is held at arm's length by the neutral narrative, but at the same time depicted as a far warmer, more generous—more sympathetic—character than Stephen, whom we were prepared to like, but just can't seem to warm up to. For instance, the "neutral" narrative's descriptions of Stephen, and Mulligan's own, more or less harmonize: Mulligan calls Stephen "fearful jesuit," "jejune jesuit," "dreadful bard" (*U* 3, 4, 6); the third-person narrative memorably describes him, in his first appearance in the novel, as "displeased and sleepy," and all his actions are described as pained, labored: Stephen "looked coldly," "followed wearily," "said quietly," etc. (*U* 3, 4). The neutral narrative does not belittle Mulligan in this fashion: "a pleasant smile broke quietly over his lips," "He pointed his finger in friendly jest," "Buck Mulligan's gay voice went on," "'It's not fair to tease you like that, Kinch, is it?' he said kindly," "A flush which made him seem younger and more engaging rose to Buck Mulligan's cheek," "Buck Mulligan's face smiled with delight" (*U* 3, 4, 6, 7, 11). Would a reader coming to *Ulysses* without any knowledge of *A Portrait* read Stephen sympathetically?

Mulligan's most concrete bit of advice to Stephen is good advice: "Give up the moody brooding" (*U* 8). Nietzsche is of course "in the air" in "Telemachus"; but while Mulligan mockingly refers to Stephen as the Dublin incarnation of Nietzsche's *Übermensch*, Nietzsche's critique of *ressentiment* is more to the point. Many of his works detail the destruction caused by the kind of *ressentiment* which is eating Stephen alive. In *Ecce Homo*, he declares that "Nothing burns one up quicker than the effects of *ressentiment*. Vexation, morbid susceptibility, incapacity for revenge, the desire, the thirst for revenge, poison-brewing in any sense—for one who is exhausted this is certainly the most disadvantageous kind of reaction: it causes a rapid expenditure of nervous energy, a morbid accretion of excretions, for example of gall into the stomach. *Ressentiment* is the forbidden *in itself* for the invalid—*his* evil: unfortunately also his most natural inclination."[52] Nietzsche's description, except for its false physicalism ("gall into the stomach"), is close to the Freudian notion of repression. While he assents in theory to the idea that art celebrates a "continual affirmation of the spirit,"[53] Stephen's mode is not joyous affirmation, but mordant satire. His spirit is still far from the

Dionysian freedom that Nietzsche finds in Goethe: "A spirit thus *emancipated* stands in the midst of the universe with a joyful and trusting fatalism, in the *faith* that only what is separate and individual may be rejected, that in the totality everything is redeemed and affirmed—*he no longer denies.*"[54] Just before counseling Stephen to "give up the moody brooding," Mulligan supplies the reason to do so: "I'm inconsequent" (*U* 8). Granted, Mulligan's rhetoric is somewhat at odds with his comportment; but, if it's a fair question to ask, would Stephen even be able to make such a statement?

Thus what Stephen passes off as mourning is in fact a form of Nietzschean *ressentiment*, which Max Scheler has defined this way: "*Ressentiment* is a self-poisoning of the mind which has quite definite causes and consequences. It is a lasting mental attitude, caused by the systematic repression of certain emotions and affects which, as such, are normal components of human nature. Their repression leads to the constant tendency to indulge in certain kinds of value delusions and corresponding value judgements. The emotions and affects primarily concerned are revenge, hatred, malice, envy, the impulse to detract, and spite."[55] In his book on Nietzsche, Deleuze summarizes the three characteristics of *ressentiment* as an "inability to admire, respect or love," "passivity," and "the imputation of wrongs, the distribution of responsibilities, perpetual accusation";[56] the appropriateness of such a diagnosis to Stephen's condition in "Telemachus" is, I should hope, readily apparent. The shaking off of this *ressentiment* is Stephen's unspoken (and perhaps unrecognized) project in *Ulysses*. His story, like Bloom's, is at the end of *Ulysses* left incomplete; try as we might, we cannot really know whether or not Stephen will "grow up" to become James Joyce, and write mature art on the order of *Ulysses*, as our criticism so often assumes. By the end of the novel he's "written" only the "Parable of the Plums" (assuming that we're not to take his vampire poem, plagiarized from Douglas Hyde, seriously)—a story more mordant, more bitter than anything in *Dubliners*; still mired in *ressentiment*, Stephen is hardly out of the woods by the book's end. Auden claimed that "mad Ireland" had hurt Yeats into poetry; thus far, however, she has hurt Stephen only into *ressentiment*.

But to the extent that *A Portrait* is a portrait of its author, we are given grounds for hope in *Ulysses*. For devoted though Stephen may be to a craft for which there is no longer a market, and desperately desiring "to press in [his] arms the loveliness which has not yet come into the world," his creator, by the time he finished *Ulysses*, had negotiated those perilous straits more successfully and more honestly. *Ulysses* is the proof.

To destroy Stephen's aesthetic, Joyce needed to adopt a guerrilla position. This he doesn't do in *A Portrait;* he does in *Ulysses.* Thus *A Portrait* has a difficult time laughing at Stephen. We need to distinguish here between *criticizing* Stephen, which I believe *A Portrait* does, and *laughing* at Stephen, which it doesn't. *A Portrait* never *laughs* at Stephen, because Stephen's not able to laugh at himself; but by the end of *Ulysses,* the novel, and its author, and its readers have had a good laugh. The "Telemachiad" is then the deconstruction, the carnivalization of *A Portrait,* especially embedded as it is in the context of the rest of *Ulysses.*

6

Toward a Nonmodernist *Ulysses*

The shared set of assumptions about literary form and value that we know as modernism has been partially articulated by a number of observers through the years. Most of modernism's central postulates were, in fact, first set out by the modernists themselves; between Eliot and Pound, for instance, we get the "impersonal" theory of poetry, the assertion that poetry must be difficult, the discovery of the "mythical method," the doctrine of the "image," and the insistence that the role of the poet is to "make it new." As a group, the essential tenets of modernism are not internally logically consistent; in the pages of *Blast* we see Pound, for instance, arguing for the autonomy of the work of art while his editor, Wyndham Lewis, insists that all art is inherently representational. Nor are the vaunted features of modernist texts always discrete: it makes no sense, for example, to talk about the modernists' penchant for primitivism apart from their desire to break Victorian taboos. Then too, many of these rallying cries are not unique to the modernist revolution; the idea that the job of the writer is to "make it new," for instance, goes back in its conception, if not its specific verbal formulation, at least to the Romantic poets (indeed, Pound himself traces it back to the bathtub of Ch'êng T'ang [1766–53 B.C.] in Canto LIII).

In spite of such shortcomings, the ideas about modernism that the modernists themselves promulgated—the ways of reading modernist texts that they promoted—were to prove formidably influential. As discussed in chapter 1, the first group of critics who found themselves in the position of having to generate critical discourse about the output of this new and unfamiliar literary movement readily took up the terms the modernists provided, while of course creating many more themselves. The result was an entire sublanguage/jargon/secret language that has become necessary for anyone who would write about modernist literature, and a central set of characteristics common to those works we call modernist. These "hallmarks" of modernism I will, for convenience sake, refer to as the axioms of modernism—based on the analogy, partial though it is, of Euclidean geometry.

Modernist literature, like Euclidean geometry, is to some extent a creation of the structures through which it has been scrutinized; and the gradual augmentation of Euclidean by non-Euclidean geometry may serve as an example of the kind of paradigm shift that often results when the basic premises of such a system are called into question. When inventing the system that would come to be known as Euclidean geometry more than two millennia ago, Euclid laid a foundation of which five postulates were absolute bedrock: from these postulates, he was able to derive the entire geometry that we now call after his name.[1] But something about his fifth postulate—"Euclid's Fifth," the Parallel Postulate (simply put, the idea that parallel lines never converge)—didn't quite sit right. Douglas Hofstadter explains: "Euclid gave five postulates to be used as the 'ground story' of the infinite skyscraper of geometry, of which his *Elements* constituted only the first several hundred stories. The first four postulates are rather terse and elegant. . . . The fifth, however, did not share their grace. . . .[2] Though he never explicitly said so, Euclid considered this postulate to be somehow inferior to the others, since he managed to avoid using it in the proofs of the first twenty-eight propositions. . . . Certainly Euclid would have found it far preferable to *prove* this ugly duckling, rather than to have to *assume* it. But he found no proof, and therefore adopted it."[3] It has been said that Euclid himself was the first non-Euclidean geometer, because of his trepidation over the Fifth. For centuries mathematicians tried to prove Euclid's Fifth; all failed, and by 1868 it had in fact been established that the Fifth cannot be derived from the first four axioms.[4] Meanwhile, toward the end of the seventeenth century, a Jesuit logician named Girolamo Saccheri attempted to prove it "in reverse"; he believed that if he assumed the *opposite* of Euclid's Fifth, and if the Fifth is correct, "after a while you will create a contradiction."[5] Proceeding in this manner, at some point Saccheri "decided he had reached a proposition which was 'repugnant to the nature of the straight line'"; that accomplished, he published his treatise *Euclid Freed of Every Flaw*, and, as Hofstadter puts it, "then expired."[6]

Unbeknownst to him, however, Saccheri had not freed Euclid of every flaw—quite the contrary. For the five axioms of Saccherian geometry, later mathematicians realized, constituted a system consistent within itself; Saccheri had not created a structure logically contradictory to Euclid's, as he had set out to do, but had rather created an internally logically consistent parallel geometry—the first groping steps toward what would become known, ninety years later, as non-Euclidean geometry. And while non-Euclidean geometry has had its greatest impact in the realm of "pure," rather than applied, mathematics, some of its conclusions, such as Bernhard Riemann's realization that the unboundedness of space does not necessarily imply infinitely long lines, were adopted by Einstein in the General Theory of Relativity (1915).

Joyce had begun working in earnest on *Ulysses* in March 1914. Now, more than ninety years into the modernist century, it is perhaps time that critics began experimenting with a nonmodernist poetics with which to examine the modernists' texts. Just as mathematicians currently countenance two distinct non-Euclidean geometries, Lobachevskian (or hyperbolic) geometry and Riemannian (or elliptic) geometry, which deny Euclid's Fifth in two different ways,[7] we can imagine a number of different nonmodernist poetics, which would violate various of the central tenets of modernist poetics and perhaps violate them in different ways, according to the whims of different critics, or the exigencies of particular critical projects.

Ulysses is the textbook example of modernist fiction, and by far the majority of criticism written on the novel has traced out the workings of these modernist axioms. Thus, there is a venerable body of critical work that examines Joyce's use of the "interior monologue," a line of inquiry (and a critical term) inaugurated by none other than Joyce himself: for instance Robert Humphrey's *Stream of Consciousness in the Modern Novel* (1954), Melvin Friedman's *Stream of Consciousness: A Study of Literary Method* (1955), and Erwin R. Steinberg's *The Stream of Consciousness and Beyond in "Ulysses"* (1972). Similarly, a great deal has been written about the Thomist aesthetics Stephen develops in *A Portrait;* that aesthetic philosophy, which emphasizes the impersonality of the creator and the static nature of the artwork, has subsequently been used to examine all of Joyce's texts, from *Dubliners* through *Finnegans Wake*. Joseph Buttigieg writes, "Much of what Stephen has to say [about aesthetics] coincides in large part and in the most important respects with the views propounded by the New Critics who dominated literary studies during the first half of our century. It is not surprising, then, that *A Portrait* 'should serve with scriptural authority as a primary source of New Critical doctrine.'"[8] The most important modernist axiom for the reading of *Ulysses*, of course, has been what Eliot, following Joyce's suggestion, was to call the "mythical method." The first book-length study of *Ulysses*, Stuart Gilbert's *James Joyce's "Ulysses,"* explored with admirable thoroughness the Homeric parallels and set the pattern for much of the critical inquiry that would follow over the next half century.

The axiomatic beliefs that lie at the heart of the modernist project consist of two different types of characteristics. Ideals like the "impersonality" of the text, or the modernists' desire for psychological realism, are quite different from notions like expressive or imitative form, spatial form, and the mythical method, which all refer specifically to stylistic practices. These axioms, then, consist of both modernist "ideals" and specific textual manifestations, both the modernists' ends and their means; some, like psychological realism, combine a presumed artistic goal with a stylistic means of attaining it, the stream of consciousness narrative. Of the two, the modernists' means, the idiosyncratic experiments of modernist style, are readily available for our scrutiny, while the writers' intentions remain shrouded in mystery. But what happens if we assume for argument's sake that *Ulysses* is *not* structured by myth, does *not* aspire to a spatialization of temporal relations or a kind of expressive form? What sort of beast are we left with?

The modernist prose technique Yvor Winters dubbed "expressive form" might be said to have its origin, as a term for criticism, around the time Joyce was beginning to write *Ulysses*. Clive Bell's influential 1913 book *Art* put forth the doctrine of "Significant Form" which, for all its fuzziness, proved important for critics in the early modernist decades; in his book, devoted to an exploration of the visual arts, Bell describes "Significant Form" this way: "lines and colours combined in a particular way, certain forms and relations of forms, stir our aesthetic emotions. These relations and combinations of lines and colours, these aesthetically moving forms, I call 'Significant Form'; and 'Significant Form' is the one quality common to all works of visual art."9 Bell's description of significant form in the visual arts does not, of course, map directly onto modernist literary texts; but his attention to the formal properties of art, to "forms and relations of forms," is an emphasis that modernist criticism would continue, and the term "significant form" was readily employed outside Bell's intended sphere. The modernists readily applied the notion of significant form to their writing, believing that style should follow naturally from an author's subject, rather than be taken over unthinkingly from past models. Pound talks about this in his 1918 "A Retrospect": "No good poetry is ever written in a manner twenty years old, for to write in such a manner shows conclusively that the writer thinks from books, convention and *cliché*, and not from life."10 After all, as he had put it so famously three years earlier, "energy creates pattern."11 The idea of an expressive form can also be seen as a logical outgrowth of the "unity of sensibility" that Eliot talks about in

"The Metaphysical Poets"; just as the metaphysical poets were "engaged in the task of trying to find the verbal equivalents for states of mind and feeling" (Eliot 65), so the modern prose writer must search for the proper style in which to embody his perceptions. Eliot was the first critic to bring Joyce's expressive stylistics to the public's attention, extolling Joyce's "use of appropriate styles and symbols to each division" (Eliot 175).

In the era of the New Critics, with their penchant for spotting literary fallacies, Winters referred to the notion that form should mirror content as "the *fallacy* of expressive form"; for while some modernist writers were partial to the original flavor it lent their prose texts, Winters thought this mimetic stylistics essentially a cheap trick: "Mr. Joyce endeavors to express disintegration by breaking down his form, by experiencing disintegration before our very eyes, but this destroys much of his power of expression. Of course he controls the extent to which he impairs his form, but this merely means that he is willing to sacrifice just so much power of expression—in an effort to express something— and no more. He is like Whitman trying to express a loose America by writing loose poetry. This fallacy, the fallacy of expressive, or imitative, form, recurs constantly in modern literature."[12] Winters was not alone among New Critics in his suspicion of this mimetic stylistics. John Crowe Ransom, for instance, following the lead of I. A. Richards, dismissed the idea because it was based on a wrongheaded belief that "style" and "content" are somehow separable, and that the literary text, rather than being autotelic, in fact can (and should) imitate the "outside" world: "We must take account of a belief that is all but universal among unphilosophical critics, and flourishes at its rankest with the least philosophical. It is this: the phonetic effect in a poem not only is (a) metrical and (b) euphonious, but preferably, and very often actually, is (c) 'expressive'; that is, offers a sort of sound which 'resembles' or partly 'is' or at least 'suggests' the object that it describes. It is necessary to say rather flatly that the belief is almost completely fallacious; both theoretically on the whole, and specifically in detail, for most of the cases that are cited to prove it. . . . I am content—though not all my readers may be—to say that the resemblance usually alleged turns out to be, for hardheaded judges, extremely slight and farfetched."[13] So while modernist writers were excited by the new avenues opened up to them by the notion of "expressive" form, contemporary criticism was obviously a bit skeptical. And Joyce, however fond he may initially have been of the idea of content dictating style, finally could not sustain a faith in the ability of prose style to mirror its object in any significant way and became, as work on *Ulysses* progressed, an increasingly antic apostate from the Modernist Church of Expressive Form.[14]

Even those most disposed to look indulgently on Joyce's experiments found the stylistic extravaganza of episodes like "Sirens" difficult to digest, or to naturalize under the rubric of "expressive form." Ezra Pound, receiving the chapters of *Ulysses* as Joyce readied them for serial publication in the *Little Review*, complained in a letter to Joyce, on receipt of the "Sirens" episode in June 1919, that "even the assing girouette of a postfuturo Gertrudo Steino protetopublic dont demand a new style per chapter";[15] but the fact that Joyce used "a new style per chapter" in *Ulysses* is itself certainly less remarkable than the fact that he additionally offered a series of plot-level justifications for these styles. For instance, the text of "Aeolus" is fractured with newspaper headlines, we are told, *because* the scene is the offices of the *Freeman's Journal;* "Cyclops" is rendered in gigantic prose *because* Polyphemous was a giant; "Eumaeus" takes place late in the novel, when the protagonists are fatigued, and the prose is *therefore* clichéd, worn out, tired.

Thus Joyce's real stylistic revolution in *Ulysses* was not simply the shaping of a distinct style for every episode; indeed, were it not for his descriptions of them in the Gilbert and Linati schemata, it is unlikely that anyone would now argue for distinguishing between the prose styles of the first six episodes (excepting possibly "Proteus"). No, the real revolution, according to both Joyce and his critics, is that he forged a style unique to each episode which would augment—ideally, help create— the "subject" of the episode. In a 6 August 1919 letter to Harriet Shaw Weaver, Joyce defended this stylistic decision, despite the obvious difficulty it posed for even his most sympathetic readers: "I understand that you may begin to regard the various styles of the episodes with dismay and prefer the initial style much as the wanderer did who longed for the rock of Ithaca. But in the compass of one day to compress all these wanderings and clothe them in the form of this day is for me only possible by such variation which, I beg you to believe, is not capricious" (*L* 1:129). By referring to an "initial style," of course, Joyce implicitly acknowledges that the prose of the early episodes is much more "of a piece" than his elaborate schemata were intended to suggest. Compared to these early episodes, the stylistic pyrotechnics of "Sirens," "Cyclops," "Nausicaa," and "Oxen of the Sun" serve not to "express" the episodes' events more clearly, but rather by calling attention to the writing itself to elevate style to the level of an event, and to call attention to the intrinsically artificial nature of all discourse—the "ways of seeing" that inhere in all narratives, no matter how neutral ("Telemachus," "Calypso") or expressive ("Aeolus," "Sirens") they might pretend to be. Indeed, through the various styles of *Ulysses* Joyce argues "artistically" what Roland Barthes was to argue "analytically" thirty-five years later in *L'écriture degrée zero:* that no style is naive, neutral, value-free—in fact none less so than a period's *écriture blanche,* which hides its program behind the mask of Nature. As Patrick McGee argues, "through the making of a polyphonic text, through the orchestration of a heterogeneous, historically produced set of styles, [Joyce] undermines the principle of univocal meaning on which history is customarily founded. *Ulysses* can now be seen as a stylistic carnival because it never values one style over another or says that one developed necessarily out of another but, instead, superimposes one style onto another, creating the effect of a play of surfaces whose boundaries are undecideable."[16]

The most explicit statement of the stylistic principle that Joyce so masterfully exploits in *Ulysses* comes in a 21 September 1920 letter to Carlo Linati: "My intention is to transpose the myth *sub specie temporis nostri.* Each adventure (that is, every hour, every organ, every art being interconnected and interrelated in the structural scheme of the whole) should not only condition but even create its own technique" (*L* 1:146–47). Years later, in Paris with Arthur Power, Joyce expressed it somewhat differently: "A living style should be like a river which takes the colour and texture of the different regions through which it flows. The so-called classical style has a fixed rhythm and a fixed mood which make it to my mind an almost mechanical device" (*CJJ* 79).

Stuart Gilbert, who wrote the first book-length study of *Ulysses,* was also the first critic to discuss at any length Joyce's fusion of "style" and "content"; his insight comes as no great surprise, since Joyce himself dictated the main lines of research which Gilbert was to carry out.[17] (For that matter, Joyce also suggested the lines of inquiry to be followed by the contributors to *Our Exagmination,* Beckett included). The most thorough exploration of Joyce's "expressive form" is to be found in Walton Litz's invaluable slim book *The Art of James Joyce* (1964). Litz defines Joyce's procedure this way: "The technique—to which I have given the name 'expressive form'—seeks to establish a direct correspondence between substance and style. The form 'expresses' or imitates qualities of its subject. Following this ideal, Joyce tried to endow each episode of *Ulysses* with a form which would suggest characteristics of the setting or action."[18]

This technique, which is thrust into the foreground in *Ulysses,* especially the episodes following Paddy Dignam's funeral, was present to some degree in Joyce's prose from the very start; but the spirit in which it was deployed changed considerably over the years he used it, and in *Ulysses* each expressive form is pushed to its breaking point. Joyce himself commented on this destruction of styles in a 1919 letter to Harriet Shaw Weaver: "the progress of the book is in fact like the progress of some sandblast. As soon as I mention or include any person in it I hear of his or her death or departure or misfortune: and each successive episode, dealing with some province of artistic culture (rhetoric or music or dialectic), leaves behind it a burntup field. Since I wrote *Sirens* I find it impossible to listen to music of any kind . . ." (*L* 1:129; ellipsis in original).

Joyce's 1904 essay "A Portrait of the Artist" opens with this rather stiff "statement of purpose," which contains in embryonic form the idea of an expressive stylistics: "The features of infancy are not commonly reproduced in the adolescent portrait for, so capricious are we, that we cannot or will not conceive the past in any other than its iron, memorial aspect. Yet the past assuredly implies a fluid succession of presents, the development of an entity of which our actual present is a phase only. Our world, again, recognises its acquaintance chiefly by the characters of beard and inches and is, for the most part, estranged from those of its members who seek through some art, by some process of the mind as yet untabulated, to liberate from the personalised lumps of matter that which is their individuating rhythm, the first or formal relation of their parts. But for such as these a portrait is not an identicative paper but rather the curve of an emotion" (*P* 257–58). The phrase "curve of an emotion," while certainly not spelling anything out (the editor of the *Dana*, to whom Joyce showed the piece, reportedly complained, "I can't print what I can't understand" [*JJ* 147]), seems in retrospect to be pointing toward the stylistic hobbyhorse that Joyce would later give such a good ride in *Ulysses* and *Finnegans Wake*.

We first see Joyce put expressive form into practice in the opening paragraph of the second (in order of composition) of his stories, "Eveline": "She sat at the window watching the evening invade the avenue. Her head was leaned against the window curtains and in her nostrils was the odour of dusty cretonne. She was tired" (*D* 36). Here we see syntax mirroring ethos, grammatical mood imitating (the as yet unnamed) Eveline's mood. Here is a woman who does not do things, but to whom things happen; she does not smell the cretonne, but rather "the odour of dusty cretonne" was "in her nostrils." The style of the narration, in retrospect, serves as a kind of grammatical judgment passed on her; when in the story's final tableau she freezes at the North Wall—"She set her white face to him, passive, like a helpless animal"—we can turn back and find the symptoms of this paralysis in the story's opening. We have already examined in some detail Joyce's use of free indirect discourse (and what I've called free indirect prose) in *Dubliners;* but the impulse behind expressive form is rather different from that behind either free indirect discourse or free indirect prose. For prose written in the free indirect mode reflects for us only the character's own thoughts, rendered in the character's own idiom, and forces us to make our own conclusions based on them; but expressive form, like that we find at the beginning of "Eveline," is written from a standpoint clearly outside the character's self-awareness. So while we can believe that a sentence like "One time there used to be a field there in which they used to play every evening with other people's children" (*D* 36) to be the prose of Eveline's own thoughts, written in Eveline's "style," we know that "in her nostrils was the odour of dusty cretonne" is not—it is written from a distance. This is similar to what Joyce attempts to do in "Eumaeus"; in "Eveline," a paragraph in the passive mood introduces us to a chronically passive—"paralytic"—woman; in "Eumaeus," a texture of clichéd language is used to present two worn-out characters, Bloom and Stephen.

Properly speaking, the more daring experiments in expressive form in *Ulysses* only really begin with the seventh episode, "Aeolus." In the schema for *Ulysses* that Joyce sent first to Carlo Linati, and then in the somewhat modified version he gave to Valéry Larbaud and Stuart Gilbert, Joyce gave a name to the "technic" of each episode. Clearly, by the time he made the schemata public Joyce had decided that each episode should have its own style; but unlike his use of Homeric parallels, this decision seems to have been reached after the writing of *Ulysses* had begun, rather than before. The schemata themselves were not devised before composition was begun, but rather represent an after-the-fact attempt to bring the increasingly willful novel under a rule: the Linati schema was probably not assembled until the summer of 1919, and the Larbaud/Gilbert "revised edition" was prepared in 1921.[19] In "*Ulysses*" *in Progress,* Michael Groden writes: "Joyce finished 'Scylla and Charybdis'—hence the book's original style—at the end of 1918, and he indicated this clearly on the fair copy of that episode. On the last page of 'Scylla and Charybdis' he wrote 'End of First Part of "Ulysses"' and the date, 'New Year's Eve 1918,' as if to indicate that one phase of *Ulysses* was ending and something new was about to begin."[20] New Year's Day, 1919, certainly has its attractions as a symbolic turning point; but in a 9 April 1917 letter to Pound that Groden does not discuss, Joyce writes "I wonder if you will like the book I am writing? I am doing it, as Aristotle would say, by different means in different parts" (*L* 1:101).

"Different means in different parts" certainly sounds, in retrospect, like what Pound later called "a new style per chapter." But the precise point at which Joyce decided to change the style every episode isn't finally important. What is clear, especially given the relative homogeneity of the first six episodes, is that it was not a notion he had when he started the book; and by the time he was halfway through *Ulysses*, "expressive form" was a notion he could no longer use, but only abuse.[21]

In the schemata he "leaked" to Linati, Gilbert, and Larbaud, Joyce dubbed the technique of "Telemachus" "narrative (young)"; "Nestor" is written in "catechism (personal)"; "Proteus," "monologue (male)"; "Calypso," "narrative (mature)"; "Lotus Eaters," "narcissism"; and "Hades," "incubism." Thus while in theory it should be possible to discern the styles of the first six episodes one from another, none of them does any real violence to the kind of artful "realistic" style that characterizes *A Portrait*. For all practical purposes, we have no need of a technique name for any of the first six episodes; having at some point during the writing of *Ulysses* decided that each episode would require its own uniquely appropriate style, Joyce later gives a name to each of their styles so as to maintain the illusion of "a style per episode," but in fact the prose texture of the third-person narrative in the first six episodes is not consistently distinguishable. The best stylistic description for all three episodes of the "Telemachia" would be "*A Portrait of the Artist as a Young Man* (continued)." "Proteus," perhaps, stands out from the rest of the early episodes in its heavy use of interior monologue; and yet, as Karen Lawrence points out, we get in Stephen's diary entries at the end of *A Portrait* a close analogue of the stream of consciousness narrative that overwhelms Stephen's walk on Sandymount strand.

Lawrence's "touchstone" from these early episodes is a narrative sentence from early in the "Telemachus" episode: "Woodshadows floated silently by through the morning peace from the stairhead seaward where he gazed" (*U* 8). This is the style of the "mature" Stephen Dedalus, toward the end of *A Portrait*; here in its new context Joyce, ironically, calls the style "narrative (young)." It exemplifies, for Lawrence, the "narrative norm" of *Ulysses* (Lawrence 42–43); and, as she goes on to show, it is hardly restricted to the one episode where it might legitimately be described as expressive form, for narrative sentences like it crop up throughout the text, even in episodes where Leopold Bloom is the center of narrative attention:

> The caretaker hung his thumbs in the loops of his gold watchchain and spoke in a discreet tone to their vacant smiles. ("Hades," *U* 88)

It passed statelily up the staircase, steered by an umbrella, a solemn beard-framed face. ("Aeolus," *U* 97)

The young woman abruptly bent and with slow care detached from her skirt a clinging twig. ("Wandering Rocks," *U* 184)

Miss Douce's brave eyes, unregarded, turned from the crossblind, smitten by sunlight. ("Sirens," *U* 220)

When we hit "Aeolus," though, we get those headlines—and there is no longer any way to naturalize what's going on in the style, even in terms of a mimetic theory of prose style—Winter's "expressive form." "Aeolus," however, occupies a special place in the final version of *Ulysses,* for Joyce, after finishing the last eight episodes, went back and cannibalized, *carnivalized* its sober surface. "Aeolus," in its final version, is one of the most striking examples of Joyce's maniacal "expressive form"; but after this early suggestion of the shape of things to come, the text of *Ulysses* does not pick up and implement its carnivalesque, guerrilla stylistics again until "Sirens."

Ezra Pound may have been a somewhat idiosyncratic reader, especially of avant-garde prose (Joyce said, "He makes brilliant discoveries and howling blunders: [*L* 1:249]); but he did realize that something very different was happening in the modern novel when he received the typescript of the "Sirens" episode. In a 10 June 1919 letter addressed "O gloire et decor de la langue Irso-Anglais," for instance—a letter from whose criticisms Joyce smarted for quite a while—Pound writes:

The peri-o-perip-o-periodico-parapatetico-periodopathetico—I dont-off-the markegetical structure of yr. first or peremier para-petitec graph—will cause all but your most pig-o-peripatec-headed readers to think you have gone marteau-dingo-maboule. . . .

—In face of *mss* just arrived, I think however I may adjoin personal op. that you have once again gone "down where the asparagus grows" and gone down as far as the lector most bloody benevolens can be expected to respire.

I dont arsk you to erase—But express opinion that a few sign posts. perhaps twenty words coherent in bunches of 3 to 5 wd. not only clarify but even improve the 1st. page. . . .[22]

And this from a sympathetic reader; this is the reaction that Joyce's more outrageous experiments in "expressive form"—I'm tempted to call it "excessive form"—occasioned.

Despite Joyce's claim that each of the eighteen episodes of *Ulysses* has its own appropriate style, "Sirens" and the episodes which follow are, not coincidentally, those that Joyce was moved to describe in such vivid terms in his letters to Frank Budgen and Harriet Shaw Weaver; indeed, Joyce seems to have enjoyed writing the descriptions of the late episodes' styles almost as much as—perhaps more than!—he did completing work on the novel itself. As we'll see in a moment when we look at his fussily precise evocation of "Oxen of the Sun," Joyce's descriptions of these late styles—as for instance his description of "Nausicaa" as "written in a namby-pamby jammy marmalady drawersy (alto-là!) style with effects of incense, mariolatry, masturbation, stewed cockles, painter's palette, chitchat, circumlocutions, etc etc" (*L* 1:135)—are as irreverent and playful as anything that made it into the novel. About these descriptions, Patrick Parrinder writes: "These explanations have their place in commentaries on Joyce, but we need not perhaps take them very seriously. They belong, rather, to the time-honoured category of Irish bulls."[23]

Unfortunately, Parrinder doesn't support this contention, or explore his reasons for thinking so; but to read, for instance, his description of the technique of "Oxen of the Sun" is to see evidence of Joyce, if not with his tongue in his cheek, at least concealing a giggle behind a parade of pseudo-scholarly erudition. The description is long, involved, and quite detailed: "Technique: a nineparted episode without divisions introduced by a Sallustian-Tacitean prelude (the unfertilised ovum), then by way of earliest English alliterative and monosyllabic and Anglo-Saxon . . . then by way of Mandeville . . . then Malory's *Morte d'Arthur* . . . then the Elizabethan chronicle style . . . then a passage solemn as of Milton, Taylor, Hooker, followed by a choppy Latin-gossipy bit, style of Britten-Browne, then a passage Bunyanesque . . . after a diarystyle bit Pepys-Evelyn . . . and so on through Defoe-Swift and Steele-Addison-Stern and Landor-Pater-Newman until it ends in a frightful jumble of Pidgin English, nigger English, Cockney, Irish, Bowery slang, and broken doggerel." On one level Joyce's evocation of the episode's style is quite reasonable, even veridical; subsequent research has located Joyce's sources for the pastiches in George Saintsbury's *A History of English Prose Rhythm* and other cribs. But once he has set out the literary landmarks, his description of the episode, like the novel itself, starts to get a bit giddy: "This procession is also linked back at each part subtly with some foregoing episode of the day and, besides this, with the natural stages of development in the embryo and the periods of faunal evolution in general. The double-thudding Anglo-Saxon motive recurs from time to time ("Loth to move from Horne's house") to give the sense of the hoofs of oxen. Bloom is the spermatozoon, the hospital the womb, the nurse the ovum, Stephen the embryo. How's that for high?" (*L* 1:139–40). Joyce's impish grin finally breaks through in that last line; for the same anarchic impulse which urged him to such lengths in his search for an appropriate form in the end subverted those wonderful structures themselves. Richard Aldington's infamous comment that Joyce was a "great undisciplined talent," despite the firestorm it set off and the reaction it occasioned—most notably, Eliot's "*Ulysses*, Order, and Myth"—was essentially *correct*; in fact, as we'll examine in the next section of this chapter, Joyce himself knew it was correct, and the history of his writing can be seen as a series of attempts to overcome this singular shortcoming. And no matter how hard Joyce tried to play the strict taskmaster with his "great undisciplined talent," that perverse spirit—Joyce's postmodern paraclete—seems always to have had the last word, ruining the Apollonian Joyce's best-laid plans.

Nearly eight years before Joyce's "postmodern turn," Pound had forcefully stated that "In every art I can think of we are dammed and clogged by the mimetic; dynamic acting is nearly forgotten; the painters of the moment escape through eccentricity."[24] In place of this slavish mimesis, Pound, in the *Blast* manifesto "Vortex: Pound," proposed instead a nonrepresentational art:

THE MAN.

The vorticist relies not upon similarity or analogy, not upon likeness or mimicry.

In painting he does not rely upon the likeness to a beloved grandmother or to a caressable mistress.

VORTICISM is art before it has spread itself into a state of flacidity, of elaboration, of secondary applications.[25]

In the manifesto's next section, which delineates the spiritual ancestry of Vorticism, Pound goes on to quote with approbation James Whistler's remark that "You are interested in a certain painting because it is an arrangement of lines and colours."

Meanwhile in Switzerland, almost concurrent with Joyce's "creative" demolition of the dream of an expressive form in literature, Ferdinand de Saussure was busy dismantling it more systematically. In the *Course in General Linguistics* (1915), Saussure argued that the linguistic sign is unmotivated, "that is to say arbitrary in relation to its signification, with which it has no natural connexion in reality";[26] and Joyce, as he increasingly broke up the relatively unified early style of *Ulysses*—for example in his late revisions and additions to the "Aeolus" episode—demonstrates the effect that such an awareness can have on a writer of his ability. It might well be, as Eliot suggested, that having written one novel, *A Portrait*, Joyce could never write another (Eliot 177).

As may be clear by now, I think very differently about the expressive form of the second half of *Ulysses* than does Litz. His is a modernist reading of that technique—a reading that attempts to reconcile Joyce's increasingly delirious stylistic play to a modernist conception of appropriate form; but by the time we get to the late episodes of *Ulysses*, Joyce is I believe satirizing the nostalgia inherent in modernist expressive form; by the time we hit "Sirens," we're in the realm of carnivalesque, rather than mimetic, stylistics. Bakhtin says that one of the characteristics of the carnivalesque is a willingness to mock not only others but oneself; and one of the effects of Joyce's increasingly wild use of "expressive form" is that it effectively mocks his earlier, "serious," uses of it. After all, Joyce was a writer who early on, even early in the work on *Ulysses*, did believe in that adequation of style to content. By the end though he has lost the faith, and yet chooses not to "erase his tracks"— he leaves the evidence of his early belief even while overturning it in the end. Karen Lawrence describes this impulse rather nicely: "Joyce's characteristic gesture is not to obliterate but to incorporate" (Lawrence 58).

My argument, then, is that the vital impulse behind Joyce's stylistic experiments in *Ulysses* is not, as Litz and others would have it, *mimetic*, expressive, but rather carnivalesque—imitating *not* the *Ding an sich*, the "matter" of the episode, but primarily previous literary attempts at expressive form, and subtly mocking their naiveté. Discussing the "Lotus Eaters" episode, for instance, Litz argues that Joyce had incorporated "the names of lots of flowers" into the text because, in addition to the Homeric parallel (the Lotus, "flowers of forgetfulness"), Bloom's pen name is Henry Flower. Litz cites Joyce's late revisions, including the addition of flower names, puns, and other floral wordplay, as "a measure of Joyce's preoccupation with 'expressive form,'" "just as five years later Joyce was to weave hundreds of river-names into the Anna Livia Plurabelle section of *Finnegans Wake*."[27] But there's no way that such a procedure can be recuperated for expressive form in the modernist sense. Working the names of rivers into the text is not style imitating form, especially since the names of rivers are themselves arbitrary markers, bearing no "natural" or "necessary" relation or similarity to the rivers they name. Now it is said that the passage opens out typographically on the page like the source of the River Liffey in the Wicklow hills, and that *is* one manifestation of modernist expressive form; the shape of the episode imitates (badly) the shape of the river (a technique that goes back in English literature at least as far as Herbert). But the impulse behind both these tricks—the multiplication of river (or flower) names, and the roughly figural shape of the four introductory lines of "Anna Livia Plurabelle"—is ludic rather than mimetic. The modernist notion of expressive form, by the late stages of *Ulysses*, has been transformed—or has transformed itself?—into the postmodern play of excessive form.

Joyce did, for a time, indulge in "expressive form"; as we have seen, his first, and probably "straightest," use of the technique occurs in his second short story, "Eveline." But by the time he was halfway through *Ulysses*, he could no longer take the project seriously. In order to chronicle the degeneration of Joyce's "expressive form," then, let's examine the impulse toward an "excessive form" in *Ulysses* by looking briefly at two of the episodes whose style is most often analyzed as expressive form, two of the episodes where Joyce's style mimics content without nostalgia for a language adequate to his vision: "Aeolus" and "Sirens."

The "Aeolus" episode is the first in *Ulysses* for which we could not hope to find an analogue in any pre-*Ulysses* literary text.[28] In its final form, the "Aeolus" episode grabs our attention primarily through the use of three salient stylistic "hooks": those brash headlines, the episode's many allusions to wind (ostensibly in deference to the episode's Homeric parallel, the windy cave and windswept cliffs of the floating island of Aeolus), and the plethora of rhetorical figures Joyce later wove into the text.

To begin then at the beginning, with the headlines Joyce so boldly superadded to the episode—the textual feature that jumps out, even *before* a first reading, and grabs us at first glance. Gilbert was the first critic to speak of the headlines as mimetic; "In *Aeolus* the text is split up into brief sections," he writes, "each headed with a caption composed in the journalistic manner," and in a footnote he goes on to explain: "It will be noticed that the style of the captions is gradually modified in the course of the episode; the first are comparatively dignified, or classically allusive, in the Victorian tradition; later captions reproduce, in all its vulgarity, the slickness of the modern press. This historico-literary technique, here inaugurated, is a preparation for the employment of the same method, but on the grand scale, a stylistic *tour de force*, in a later episode, the *Oxen of the Sun*."[29] Litz makes essentially this same argument more than thirty years later: "the text is divided into sections with captions that imitate newspaper headlines; viewed as a sequence, these captions reflect the historical development of journalistic style."[30]

Such a reading, I think, is the product of a sincere desire to make

Joyce's masterpiece seem appropriately serious; but if we investigate the episode using a different premise—that the evolution of Joyce's writing involved a gradual "relativization" of all earlier styles, and an insistent undermining of his own attempts at "fine writing"—we come to rather different conclusions about the function of the headlines. Hence, I'm suggesting that the progressive "logic" of the "Aeolus" headlines is the same as that Vicki Mahaffey identifies for the episodes of *Ulysses:* "Whereas St. Paul describes revelation as the process of seeing through a glass darkly and then face to face (1 Cor. 13:12), and as a rending of the veil (2 Cor 3:14–18), *Ulysses* approaches revelation through darkening the glass and multiplying the stylistic veils, presenting its close through clothes. We begin *Ulysses* with a deceptively clear vision that is gradually occluded; the book grows progressively more shadowy, along the with the day it parallels, a tendency that culminates in the deeper darkness of *Finnegans Wake*."[31] The captions in "Aeolus" imitate newspaper headlines far more in their typography than in their style or content; and the typography of the novel, as determined by his French printers, wasn't altogether under Joyce's control (Gabler, for instance, decided to "tone down" somewhat the typography of the episode for the 1984 edition).

The headlines of "Aeolus," which have been linked by so many critics with Joyce's "expressive form," could be more accurately described as a species of visual pun; for if the headlines are mimetic of a newspaper office at all, it is primarily in a visual sense. Karen Lawrence puts the point quite forcefully: "According to the conventions of the realistic novel, there is nothing at all 'logical' about the use of headings to help narrate the events in a newspaper office. There is, in fact, some whimsical pun of form and content enacted in the chapter, a mimicking or imitation that is a linguistic form of play" (Lawrence 58). And a pun, if it can be said to express anything, expresses the inherent slipperiness and unreliability of words—exposing them as far too clumsy a medium for anything like a faithful "expressive form," unless it is a sense of merging or of doubleness that the prose seeks to express; this is arguably the use to which Joyce puts his punning in *Finnegans Wake*.

But Joyce's punning has long been misdiagnosed as an impulse toward a more faithfully representational stylistics. Litz for instance opens his discussion of expressive form in *The Art of James Joyce* with an anecdote from Frank O'Connor—a story, however, that illustrates Joyce's penchant for punning, rather than for expressive form. Joyce had a picture of his father's native city, Cork, hung in his apartment:

The scene is Joyce's flat: O'Connor has just touched the frame of a picture
on the wall.
"What's this?"
"Cork."
"Yes, I see it's Cork. I was born there. But what's the frame?"
"Cork."[32]

Joyce's pun took some effort to set up, and he was no doubt pleased that
O'Connor fell for it; but logically a cork picture frame no more imitates,
or expresses, a picture of Cork city than would stainless steel; this much
should be apparent on the surface. The cork of the frame takes its name
from the Latin word for oak, *quercus;* Cork city is "Cobh," pronounced
"Kōv," in Irish; it was "normalized" to "Cork" during the work of the
British Ordinance Survey in the first half of the nineteenth century.[33]
The relationship between cork and Cork is therefore not conceptual,
but what Gregory Ulmer has called "punceptual"—based not on some
necessary, or "expressive," connection between the subject and its presentation, but rather on a happy accident of sound.[34]

Similarly, the notion that adding boldfaced headlines to the text of
"Aeolus" in some way helps the prose imitate its subject is based on a
rather fanciful association. Joyce's captioning of the episode is actually
an unusual form of synecdoche—employing newspaper headlines in
order to help the text imitate a newspaper, in order to conjure up the atmosphere of a newspaper's editorial offices. Using Derridean terminology, we might say that the headlines of "Aeolus" *solicit,* rather than
supplement, the basic narrative thrust of the episode; rather than reinforcing implicit features of the interheadline text, the headlines more
often function as a voice apart, interacting dialogically with the rather
sober discourse of the *Freeman's Journal* office and calling into question
its pretense and smug self-satisfaction. And it is not, as Gilbert and Litz
suggest, only the late headlines that contain this critical note; the sixth
of sixty-three headlines, for instance—WITH UNFEIGNED REGRET
IT IS WE ANNOUNCE THE DISSOLUTION OF A MOST RESPECTED
DUBLIN BURGESS—would seem to be having a laugh at the deceased's expense in using the word "dissolution" if, as Bloom implies,
Paddy Dignam's death was alcohol related.

Indeed, the headlines of the episode, rather than playing out an or-
derly history of journalism, come at the reader rather helter-skelter: some
serve a function very close to that of a conventional newspaper headline (no. 7, HOW A GREAT DAILY ORGAN IS TURNED OUT), while
others are so frisky that they refuse to serve the dependent text, and in-

stead take on a life of their own (no. 63, DIMINISHED DIGITS PROVE
TOO TITILLATING FOR FRISKY FRUMPS. ANNE WIMBLES, FLO
WANGLES—YET CAN YOU BLAME THEM?). Some headlines serve
to underscore important (and not so important) events in the plot
(no. 20, MEMORABLE BATTLES RECALLED; no. 50, RETURN OF
BLOOM); some, on the other hand, pick up almost negligible textual
features and promote them to all caps (no. 17, SAD; no. 60, WHAT?—
AND LIKEWISE—WHERE?). Other headlines embrace melodrama,
mock the characters' pretensions to eloquence and wit, elevate rather
ordinary conversation to the language of polished rhetorical figures or,
in the section containing J. J. O'Molloy's riddle, reduce a discourse to its
elemental import (no. 28, ? ? ?). The cumulative effect of the headlines,
then, is not to enhance the representational or "expressive" character of
the text, nor even, I think, to evoke the ethos of the newsroom, given the
extreme distance between real newspaper headlines and those in "Aeolus"; rather, the patent artifice of these late textual supplements serves
to highlight the highly conventional, artificial nature of the text they
would introduce, and to mock any notion that form can be made consonant with content. Joyce, instead of effecting a marriage of form and
content, heightens the dissonance between the two. In the passage quoted
above, John Crowe Ransom objects to "expressive form" because it
(falsely) assumes that form and content are separable, and therefore in
need of reunification; Joyce, on the other hand, objects to expressive
form on precisely the opposite grounds—it assumes that form and content can somehow be brought together.

The second of Joyce's expressive stylistic strategies in "Aeolus" is the
superabundance of terms related to wind contained in the text, most of
them added late in the composition process. As Gilbert writes, "A gale
of wind is blowing through this episode, literally [*sic*] and metaphorically. Doors are flung open violently, Myles Crawford blows violent puffs
from his cigarette, the barefoot newsboys, scampering in, create a hur-
ricane which lifts the rustling tissues into the air; swing doors draught-
ily flicker to and fro."[35] These windy references Gilbert calls "Aeolisms":
"Aeolisms abound in the course of the episode; 'big blow out,' 'the vent
of his jacket,' 'windfall when he kicks out,' 'the moving spirit,' 'if I could
raise the wind,' 'a cure for flatulence,' etc."; C. H. Peake says that there
are about forty expressions relating in some way to wind in the episode.[36]

In some instances, though, it's difficult to know whether a reference
to wind is a product of Joyce's expressive mania, or instead an accident
of the way our language works. "If I could raise the wind," added in the
last typescript, is quite obviously an attempt to incorporate another ref-

erence to wind into the episode; it comes at the end of one of Myles Crawford's short monologues, apropos of almost nothing, and is made as well the text of a headline (no. 54, RAISING THE WIND). But Gilbert also cites, for instance, "the moving spirit" as an example of an "Aeolism"; and while we know that in Hebrew the words for "wind" and "spirit" are the same ("And the earth was without form, and void; and darkness was upon the face of the deep. And the Spirit of God moved upon the face of the waters" [Gen. 1:2]), use of the word "spirit" in this context does not mean that Joyce was making an intentional reference to wind. Joyce most certainly did embellish the episode with numerous references to wind; but it is just possible that, setting out as we do to find references to the wind, we may find some that were not "planted" there. Some of the ostensible references to wind in the episode may be a product of our interpretive frame, rather than Joyce's expressive form; in "Aeolus" Bloom's phrase "a cure for flatulence" is cited as a reference to wind, but no one categorizes Bloom's booming fart at the end of "Sirens" this way. In fact—a fact conveniently overlooked by most commentators—both the "Sirens" and "Oxen of the Sun" episodes contain more occurrences of the word "wind" itself than does "Aeolus."

In his discussion of the "wind words" of "Aeolus," Litz quotes the following passage from Bloom's interior monologue as an especially windy passage: "Practice dwindling. A mighthavebeen. Losing heart. Gambling. Debts of honour. Reaping the *whirlwind*. Used to get good retainers from D. and T. Fitzgerald. Their wigs to show the grey matter. Brains on their sleeve like the statue in Glasnevin. Believe he does some literary work for the *Express* with Gabriel Conroy. Wellread fellow. Myles Crawford began on the *Independent*. Funny the way those newspaper men veer about when they get *wind* of a new opening. *Weathercocks*. Hot and cold in the same *breath*. Wouldn't know which to believe. One story good till you hear the next. Go for one another baldheaded in the papers and then all *blows* over. Hail fellow well met the next moment" (*U* 103). Commenting on this passage, Litz remarks that by and large Joyce tried to "give these reminders of his *schema* unobtrusive positions in the narrative, but he did not always succeed"; in this particular instance, "any one of the five references to wind introduced by Joyce in his revision of the following passage is appropriate to Bloom's normal speech, but taken together they seem a little forced."[37]

Litz is of course correct that the references to wind sound a bit strained; for this is once again excessive, rather than expressive, form. Making these references obtrusive was not an accident, as Litz assumes—it was instead a way of tipping his hand, a way of saying, "Check this out—

wind, get it?" Joyce didn't take this stylistic tick as seriously as some of his commentators, like Litz, have taken it; it was for him one more style which required overturning, just as all his other styles required dethroning; in *Ulysses*, Joyce is rather like a master magician who, in defiance of the code of his craft, always gives away his tricks. The fact that Myles Crawford parts the "vent," rather than the slit or flap, of his jacket (or the fact that he performs this action at all, added as it was to the page proofs), is no evidence of Joyce's desire, in Beckett's words, to make words "do the absolute maximum of work"; no, here Joyce does not try to make his words work, in the way that the characters in "Aeolus" do, but instead allows them to play.[38]

Finally, let's look for a moment at Joyce's embellishment of the "Aeolus" episode with over a hundred different rhetorical figures. The art of the episode, as Gilbert and others inform us, is rhetoric; why exactly an episode set in a newspaper office should have rhetoric as its art, in preference to Bloom's interview with the Citizen, or Stephen's solipsistic musings in "Proteus," is a question we shall have to leave to one side. Here again, I think the real issue for current criticism of Joyce's style is not whether or not those figures are in the text—Gilbert's (and Don Gifford's more recent) list can leave no real doubt. No, the real question is whether those tropes are a product of Joyce's desire for the episode—thus somehow marking the episode out as unique—or rather an after-the-fact product of the interpretive framework Joyce published for the episode. For rhetorical figures are everywhere; as Peake points out: "The list of nearly a hundred devices looks impressive. But on closer examination it is less so. It includes, for instance, chiasmus, metaphor, anacoluthon, apostrophe, irony, parenthesis, tautology, professional jargon, Hibernicism, epigram, sarcasm, *oratio recta-obliqua*, anticlimax, hyperbole, and neologism—all of which could be illustrated equally well from any chapter in the book: the same could be said of most of the other devices. Certainly, other chapters could be used to illustrate an equally formidable list of figures of speech."[39] And the question of whether Joyce "added" rhetorical figures or later discovered them is not easily answered; it seems most likely that his procedure was some combination of both. Groden, for instance, analyzes Joyce's notesheets for the episode, and concludes that "the notebook confirms the suspicion that Joyce went to rhetoric books to learn about the terms and devices."[40] But Stuart Gilbert, the ostensible discoverer of the rhetorical figures of "Aeolus," tells the story somewhat differently: "the long list of examples of rhetorical forms which concludes my commentary on the 'Aeolus' episode," he writes, "was compiled at his [Joyce's] suggestion, and we spent several industrious afternoons collaborating on it."[41] If Joyce had indeed planted those flowers of rhetoric himself—if they were all there, ready for the picking—why were "several" afternoons of "industrious collaboration" necessary to unearth them? Gilbert's description may be in part due to his natural desire to get some credit for the work he had done, but it also suggests that the list of rhetorical devices may be a product as much of critical exploration—and the discursive requirements of narrative—as of artistic intention.

This perhaps becomes clearer if we look at the opening of the "Sirens" episode, the chapter whose "technic" is, famously, *fuga per canonem*. Take an artificially delimited section of the "overture" to the episode—the first ten lines, for instance. The overture as a whole illustrates two rhetorical figures, anacephalaeosis ("summary"), and prolepsis ("applying now an attribute or epithet that will have relevancy later").[42] Interrogating these first ten lines with a rhetorical list in hand, as Gilbert and Joyce did the "Aeolus" episode, we in fact obtain rather similar results:

1. Bronze by gold heard the hoofirons, steelyringing.
   - –prosonomasia: calling by a name or nickname
   - –metonymy: substitution of quality for proper name
   - –synecdoche: substitution of part for whole
   - –arataxis: clauses or phrases arranged independently—a coordinate construction
   - –metalepsis: omission of the central term in an extended metaphor
   - –neologism: the use of, or practice of using, new words (Gifford)

2. Imperthnthn thnthnthn.
   - –mimesis: imitation of word or gesture
   - –hypocrisis: exaggerating an opponent's gestures or speech habits in order to mock him
   - –charientismus: soothing over a difficulty, or turning aside antagonism with a joke

3. Chips, picking chips off rocky thumbnail, chips.
   - –assonance: resemblance or similarity in sound between vowel sounds preceded and followed by differing consonant sounds in words in proximity
   - –epanalepsis: repetition at the end of a clause or sentence of the word with which it began

–pleonasmus: needless repetition

–tmesis: repetition of a word with one or a few words in between

–epimone: frequent repetition of a phrase or question

–anaphora: repetition of the same word at the beginning of successive clauses or verses

4. Horrid! And gold flushed more.

–ecphonesis: exclamation expressing emotion

–metonymy (see line 1)

–synecdoche (see line 1)

–prosonomasia (see line 1)

–parataxis (see line 1)

5. A husky fifenote blew.

–neologism (see line 1)

6. Blew. Blue bloom is on the.

–alliteration: recurrence of an initial consonant sound

–anadiplosis: repetition of the last word of one line or clause to begin the next

–parechesis: the repetition of the same sound in words in close or immediate succession

–paronomasia: punning

–antanaclasis: homonymic pun

–aposiopesis: stopping suddenly in midcourse—leaving a statement unfinished

–aporia: doubt

–homoioteleuton: a series of words with the same or similar endings (Gifford)

7. Goldpinnacled hair.

–neologism (see line 1)

8. A jumping rose on satiny breast of satin, rose of Castille.

–prosopopoeia: personification

–parelcon: addition of superfluous words

–pleonasmus (see line 3)

–paranomasia (see line 6)

–scesis onomaton: a sentence constructed of substantives and adjectives only

–polyptoton: repetition of words from the same root but with different endings

9. Trilling, trilling: Idolores.

–epizeuxis: emphatic repetition of a word with no other words between

10. Peep! Who's in the . . . peepofgold?
   –ecphonesis (see line 4)
   –palindrome: word, verse, or sentence that reads the same backwards as
     forwards (Gifford)
   –neologism (see line 1)

This mock-serious list neglects for convenience those rhetorical tropes involved in compressing the full passages of text into these shortened motifs for the overture; it also omits metaphor which, if Nietzsche was correct, lurks everywhere. Yet even with these exclusions, we come up with thirty-two different rhetorical figures in just the first ten lines of the "Sirens" episode, nine of them not included in either the Gilbert or Gifford inventories of "Aeolus"; and the art of this episode is ostensibly not the subtle craft of rhetoric, but the gentle art of music. How many rhetorical figures might we uncover were we to go through the entire episode? A figure close to the 112 that Gifford has found in the "Aeolus" episode begins to seem within the realm of possibility.

In fact, even the most remarkable aspect of the "Aeolus" episode, the all-caps headlines, finds a fanciful analogue in "Sirens"—again, in the short phrases Joyce used to build up his overture. The "Aeolus" episode has sixty-three headlines; the overture to "Sirens" is built up of precisely sixty-three phrases, each of which is a kind of headline announcing a portion of text that will surface later; the headlines in "Aeolus" are distributed throughout the text, while the headlines in "Sirens" are all lumped at the front of the episode, but in no other way (save typography) can they be distinguished. And yet in what possible way are newspaper headlines "expressive" of an episode that is concerned with the art of music? What part do headlines play in the classical *fuga per canonem*?

Many critics have argued that "Sirens" is about as close as English prose can get to "the condition of music"; Gilbert describes it as a chapter "which both in structure and in diction goes far beyond all previous experiments in the adaptation of musical technique and timbre to a work of literature."[43] Clearly this is the case; yet I believe the emphasis properly falls not on how close the writing comes, but on how far from music it finally is. Karen Lawrence has seen this quite clearly: "In a sense, the 'Sirens' chapter is Joyce's experimental and, I think, parodic answer to Walter Pater, the tutelary genius of the chapter, who said that all art constantly aspires to the condition of music" (Lawrence 91).

Joyce brought the notion of expressive form over from poetry; he was perhaps the first writer systematically, consciously to explore the possi-

bilities of expressive form in prose. In verse, expressive form is manifest
as simple onomatopoeia, in imitative words like *moo* and *sizzle*, or in the
more sophisticated onomatopoeia of verses like Tennyson's "The moan
of doves in immemorial elms, /And murmuring of innumerable bees"
(The Princess). These lines from Pope's *An Essay on Criticism* are both the
locus classicus, and something of an early definition, of expressive form
in poetry:

> 'Tis not enough no Harshness gives Offence,
> The *Sound* must seem an *Eccho* to the *Sense*.
> *Soft* is the Strain when *Zephyr* gently blows,
> And the *smooth stream* in *smoother Numbers* flows;
> But when loud Surges lash the sounding shore,
> The *hoarse, rough Verse* shou'd like the *Torrent* roar.
> When *Ajax* strives, some Rock's vast weight to throw,
> The Line too *labours*, and the Words move *slow.* . . .[44]

Not surprisingly, Pope's verse treatise on expressive form itself exploits
what he calls "a Style of Sound"—couplets extolling the notion of sound
as the echo of sense, which themselves echo their message in their
medium.

In the "Sirens" episode, however, Joyce, through Bloom, effectively
distances himself from any such romantic notion of the expressive music
of poetry or prose. The prose of the episode, according to nearly all
commentators, aspires to the condition of music; and yet in the midst of
the episode we read Bloom's commonsensical demolition of that notion: "Numbers it is. All music when you come to think. Two multiplied
by two divided by half is twice one. Vibrations: chords those are. One
plus two plus six is seven. Do anything you like with figures juggling.
Always find out this equal to that. . . . Musemathematics. And you think
you're listening to the etherial. But suppose you said it like: Martha,
seven times nine minus x is thirtyfive thousand. Fall quite flat. It's on
account of the sounds it is" *(U* 228). Bloom proves by algebra that musical prose can't work; the quality of poetry that Pound calls "melopoeia,"
"wherein the words are charged, over and above their plain meaning,
with some musical property," which he says "is practically impossible to transfer or translate . . . from one language to another," equally
does not translate from one genre to another—if indeed it can be realized even in poetry.[45]

Thus when we come to Simon Dedalus's performance of "M'appari"
from *Martha*, the sustained antepenultimate "chestnote" is rendered in
a prose which comically recreates the duration and vibrato of Si's tenor:
"It soared, a bird, it held its flight, a swift pure cry, soar silver orb it

leaped serene, speeding, sustained, to come, don't spin it out too long long breath he breath long life, soaring high, high resplendent, aflame, crowned, high in the effulgence symbolistic, high, of the etherial bosom, high, of the high vast irradiation everywhere all soaring all around about the all, the endlessnessnessness . . . ." (*U* 226-27). This passage quite effectively mocks prose's high-falutin' attempts at music; it calls to mind, I think, moments in the music of Handel, such as the "Forever!" in the *Halleluia* Chorus which is held nearly forever. Peake writes that "The handling of Simon Dedalus's performance is, in itself, sufficient to show how far Joyce's mind was from any naive intention to do in prose what can be done only in music. The use of sound as an echo to the sense or a contributing to it is as old as literature: Joyce's devices are adventurous extensions of traditional methods."[46] Thus in *Ulysses*, and nowhere more emphatically than in the "Sirens" episode, we discover—we are shown—that mimetic form always turns out to be conventional. Perhaps the most faithful passage of expressive musical form in the episode is that which closes it:

> Seabloom, greaseabloom viewed last words. Softly. *When my country takes her place among.*
> Prrprr.
> Must be the bur.
> Fff! Oo. Rrpr.
> *Nations of the earth.* No-one behind. She's passed. *Then and not till then.* Tram kran kran kran. Good oppor. Coming. Krandlkrankran. I'm sure it's the burgund. Yes. One, two. *Let my epitaph be.* Kraaaaaa. *Written. I have.*
> Pprrpffrrppffff.
> *Done.* (*U* 238–39)

Bloom's farts are usually described as commenting on the hollow rhetoric and narrow nationalism of Robert Emmet's last words (more rhetoric!); but Bloom's fundamental sounds perhaps act also as a summary judgment on the romantic notion of musical prose; they are Bloom's own "chamber music."[47]

Joseph Frank's announcement of the modernists' spatial form followed the Second World War; and while he finds authority for this principle in the writings of the modernists, Pound in particular, it seems not to have been an idea countenanced by Joyce.[48] Expressive form—the notion, as put into practice in *Ulysses*, that each episode should create its own style—was demonstrably not part of Joyce's original vision of the novel, but a relatively late accretion to the text. This, however, is patently not the case with the most famous stylistic feature of *Ulysses*—the Ho-

meric parallels. By 13 November 1906, Joyce had taken to calling his as yet
unwritten story about Mr. Alfred Hunter (later Leopold Bloom) "Ulysses." That story never was written, save in Amanda Cross's mystery
The James Joyce Murders (where the discovery and subsequent theft of
the MS of "Ulysses" provide the motive), but the notion of equating the
wanderings of a cuckolded Dublin Jew with the voyages of Odysseus—
which later grew to an entire substructure of Homeric parallels—occurred to Joyce nearly eight years before the novel proper was launched
(L 2:190; JJ 230). So while one might argue that Joyce's (ab)use of expressive form is a relatively late stylistic ornament, such an argument
cannot be made about the Homeric parallels, which were something
like the inaugural gesture of *Ulysses*.

From the start, there have been two schools of thought regarding Joyce's
use of the *Odyssey* as a framework for *Ulysses*; they are perhaps best represented by the early reactions of Eliot and Pound to Joyce's experiment
in the mythical method. Eliot, famously, considered the Homeric parallels something on the order of "a scientific discovery"; but in fact Valéry
Larbaud was the first critic to speak (December 1921) and then to write
(April 1922) on Joyce's use of Homer in *Ulysses*. Surely no one has more
forcefully argued the importance of the parallels to a proper understanding of the novel: "The reader who approaches this book without
the *Odyssey* clearly in mind," Larbaud warned his audience, "will be
thrown into dismay" (Deming 1:258). Larbaud's stance regarding the
specific utility of the parallels, however, is somewhat equivocal. On the
one hand, he talks about *Ulysses* as "a book which has a key"; at the same
time, he tries to maintain that the key isn't really necessary, for as we
read the novel, "all sorts of coincidences, analogies, and correspondences between these different parts come to light; just as, in looking
fixedly at the sky at night, we find that the number of stars appears to
increase. We begin to discover and to anticipate symbols, a design, a
plan, in what appeared to us at first a brilliant but confused mass of notations, phrases, data, profound thoughts, fantasticalities, splendid images, absurdities, comic or dramatic situations; and we realise that we
are before a much more complicated book than we had supposed, that
everything which appeared arbitrary and sometimes extravagant is really deliberate and premeditated" (Deming 1:259–60). The argument here
is strikingly similar to that F. R. Leavis would make about Eliot's notes
to *The Waste Land* many years later: if we readers have the key—Eliot's
notes, Joyce's schema—so much the better; but if it should somehow
happen that we're not privy to these indices of the author's intention,
the text itself has a coherence that obviates any real need for an inter-

pretive guide—careful reading will reveal the plan quite adequately itself. "If one reads *Ulysses* with attention, one cannot fail to discover this plan in time," Larbaud audaciously claims, for "although each of these eighteen parts differs from all of the others in form and language, the whole forms none the less an organism, a book" (Deming 1:261, 259).

As those remarks reveal, Larbaud, like so many others after him, was of two minds about Joyce's secret system. He emphasizes the fact, for instance, that Joyce left a big clue to the underlying structure of the novel on the cover—the title *Ulysses* (Deming 1:260); clearly, however, Larbaud is disappointed that Joyce had in nearly every other way erased his tracks. But Joyce's removal of the episode titles did allow Larbaud to make an important early contribution to the criticism of *Ulysses*, for he was the first to point out to the Paris literati assembled at the *Ulysses* séance at Adrienne Monnier's *La Maison des Amis des Livres*—almost two months before the novel was published!—that *Ulysses* was a book with a past, a book with a secret.

Eliot's is the best-known advocacy of Joyce's method; indeed, his 1923 essay "*Ulysses*, Order, and Myth" is not only one of the most familiar pieces of *Ulysses* criticism, but one of the best-known pieces in all modernist literary criticism. Subsequent critics, however, have moved from using Eliot's conception of the mythical method to examine Joyce, to using Eliot's words to interrogate his own artistic propensities—Perry Meisel, for instance, points insightfully to "Eliot's use of Homer to organize Joyce."[49] The anxiety of influence is almost palpable in both the essay's opening and close. In the first paragraph, Eliot admits quite readily that "it is a book to which we are all indebted, and from which none of us can escape"; in a 21 May 1921 letter to Joyce, Eliot had confessed, "I wish, for my own sake, that I had not read it."[50] But after the candor of the essay's opening, its closing paragraphs take on a defensive tone: "Mr. Joyce is pursuing a method which others must pursue after him. They will not be imitators, any more than the scientist who uses the discoveries of an Einstein in pursuing his own, independent, further investigations." Eliot says that Joyce's "parallel use of the *Odyssey* . . . has the importance of a scientific discovery" (Eliot 177), and the logic of his simile is quite cunning. Why not, for instance, call the mythical method Joyce's *invention*? Because, perhaps, while discoveries are a part of the public domain, inventions are protected by patent law. The *Random House Dictionary* discriminates between the two this way: "To DISCOVER may be to find something that had previously existed but had hitherto been unknown. . . . To INVENT is to make or create something new, esp. something ingeniously devised to perform mechanical operations."[51] If this distinction is at all meaningful, then the mythical method is an invention rather than a discovery, even by Eliot's own testimony.

Eliot need not, however, have been so anxious about Joyce's influence; the mythical method *was* Joyce's invention, but Eliot used that same invention (devised independently) and put it to rather a different use: for while Eliot believed that myth inheres in the substance of contemporary history, and must be uncovered and made explicit by the writer, Joyce, as I will argue, saw it rather as an artificial construct— simply one writer's way of working. Wallace Stevens speaks of these two different approaches to order in "Notes toward a Supreme Fiction"; in this excerpt he begins by describing an artist who, like Joyce, imposes form, *invents* form, and then expresses a longing, a nostalgia for the discovery of an inherent order, along the lines of Eliot's ideal:

> He imposes orders as he thinks of them,
> As the fox and snake do. It is a brave affair.
> . . . .
>   But to impose is not
> To discover. To discover an order as of
> A season, to discover summer and know it,
> To discover winter and know it well, to find
> Not to impose, not to have reasoned at all,
> Out of nothing to have come upon major weather,
>
> It is possible, possible, possible. It must
> Be possible.[52]

Larbaud's discussion of Joyce's (still unnamed) mythical method appeared first in French in the *Nouvelle Revue Française* and was quickly translated (in part) at Joyce's suggestion for the October 1922 inaugural issue of Eliot's *Criterion* (which also contained a new poem of Eliot's, *The Waste Land*). Larbaud's somewhat rambling discussion of all of Joyce's prose works through *Ulysses* never had the impact that Eliot's short essay did—due in part, perhaps, to Eliot's greater (and growing) influence in Anglo-American academic circles, his knack for turning an apt phrase (like "mythical method"; he had the good sense to reject Joyce's other suggestion, "the two plane"), and the poise and brute force of his rhetoric ("a way of controlling, of ordering, of giving a shape and a significance to the immense panorama of futility and anarchy which is contemporary history"; "a step toward making the modern world possible for art").

But Stuart Gilbert was the first to detail the workings of the mythical method in *Ulysses* in a widely read book for an audience of educated readers. For more than half a century Gilbert's *James Joyce's "Ulysses": A Study* has been required reading in college and university courses in which Joyce's work is taught; my May 1960 copy is the seventh Vintage printing subsequent to the original edition put out by Knopf in 1930. Gilbert's book insists on the serious intent and highly wrought structure of Joyce's work—without a knowledge of which the novel might appear, as John Middleton Murry had charged, "completely anarchic."[53] In his preface, Gilbert admits that one motivation for his book was precisely to rebut criticism like Murry's and Aldington's: "I have not tried to alleviate the rather pedantic tone of much of the writing in this Study. For one thing, Joyce approved of it; and, for another, we who admired *Ulysses* for its structural, enduring qualities and not for the occasional presence in it of words and descriptive passages which shocked our elders, were on the defensive, and the pedant's cloak is often a convenient protection against the cold blasts of propriety."[54] Perhaps most significantly, Gilbert's was the first study to publish a version of the infamous schemata for his readers' edification, "stimulating," as Eliot said of his notes to *The Waste Land*, "the wrong kind of interest among the seekers of sources."[55]

Not coincidentally, the one thing that these three main proponents of what we might call the Homeric reading of *Ulysses* have in common (apart from their unbridled enthusiasm for the mythical method) is that they were let in on the "secret" of *Ulysses* by none other than its creator. The first critic to downplay the Homeric parallels in *Ulysses*, Ezra Pound, was also a personal friend of Joyce's. Pound, while acknowledging the existence of the parallels, represents the opposing school of thought regarding their purpose, and ultimate importance, for both Joyce and his readers. In his "Paris Letter" of June 1922, written upon the publication in book form of *Ulysses*, Pound, in spite of his reservations about some of the stylistically wilder episodes, returned to stumping for Joyce, but wanted to soft-peddle the parallels: "Telemachus, Circe, the rest of the Odyssean company, the noisy cave of Aeolus gradually place themselves in the mind of the reader, rapidly or less rapidly according as he is familiar or unfamiliar with Homer. These correspondences are part of Joyce's mediaevalism and are chiefly his own affair, a scaffold, a means of construction, justified by the result, and justifiable by it only. The result is a triumph in form, in balance, a main schema, with continuous interweaving and arabesque."[56] Pound does not here discount the Homeric parallels, but certainly downplays them: the parallels were a tool for composition, not interpretation, and nothing good (he suggests) will come of overestimating their importance for a reading of *Ulysses*.

For his part Joyce seems to have held both of these positions regarding his Homeric framework at different times. His frequently repeated advice to first-time readers (for instance his aunt Josephine Murray, and that most cooperative of critics Stuart Gilbert) was to sit down with both the *Odyssey* and Lamb's *Adventures of Ulysses* before attempting the novel. In February 1922 Joyce wrote to Harriet Shaw Weaver, "What can I say about the *Odyssey*? . . . It is curious that no critic has followed up Mr. Larbaud's clue on the parallelism of the two books. They think it is too good to be true" (*L* 1:200). It would still be another eighteen months before Eliot would "follow up Mr. Larbaud's clue"—and more specifically, Joyce's promptings—and make the Homeric parallels the best-known feature of *Ulysses*.

But as his career progressed, Joyce himself put less and less stock in the parallels; and by the time *Finnegans Wake* was nearing completion, his attitude toward the mythical method had changed dramatically. Ellmann relates the following story: "Joyce's attitude towards [Gilbert's] book gradually altered. Vladimir Nabokov recalled a conversation with him at dinner in the Léons' flat about 1937. Joyce said something disparaging about the use of mythology in modern literature. Nabokov replied in amazement, 'But you employed Homer!' 'A whim,' was Joyce's comment. 'But you collaborated with Gilbert,' Nabokov persisted. 'A terrible mistake,' said Joyce, 'an advertisement for the book. I regret it very much'" (*JJ* 616).[57] As Joyce came to see, whatever advantages there might be to employing the mythical method as a means of composition, using the Homeric parallels as a heuristic for criticism has its dangers. Too heavy a reliance on the parallel structure of *Ulysses* can result in the novel's being read as a cipher: criticism, even simple reading, degenerates into parallel-hunting.[58] Larbaud, in his talk at the *Ulysses* séance, warned his audience that "we are before a book which has a key. Where then is that key? It is, I venture to say, in the door, or rather on the cover. It is the title: *Ulysses*" (Deming 1:260). Two of the early studies of *Ulysses*, Paul Jordan Smith's *A Key to the "Ulysses" of James Joyce* and Rolf Loehrich's *The Secret of "Ulysses,"* similarly bear witness in their very titles to the often reductive legacy of the Larbaud-Gilbert reading.[59]

As Larbaud's lecture uneasily acknowledges, *Ulysses* as published has no Homeric titles appended to the episodes. It has become such a critical convention to cite chapters by their Homeric names that we have perhaps tended to forget it; but one of the last authorial decisions Joyce made regarding *Ulysses* was that the only clue to its Homeric "origins" allowed to stand would be its title. Larbaud, while trumpeting Joyce's use of the *Odyssey*, at the same time realized the difficulties it posed for readers: "Naturally, Joyce has traced for himself, and not for the reader, this minutely detailed scheme, these eighteen sub-divided panels, this close web. There is no explanatory heading or sub-heading. It is for us to decipher, if we care to take the trouble" (Deming 1:261).

In Larbaud's view, the Homeric scheme was primarily for Joyce's own use, and "on this web, or rather in the compartments thus prepared, Joyce has arranged his text" (Deming 1:261). And for Joyce, as perhaps for Eliot, the mythical method was a way of balancing chance and structure in his text.[60] Joyce recognized that writing is always a process of discovery; he told Arthur Power, "A book, in my opinion, should not be planned out beforehand, but as one writes it will form itself, subject, as I say, to the constant emotional promptings of one's personality" (*CJJ* 95). But while Joyce, like Merleau-Ponty, realized that "my own words take me by surprise and teach me what I think,"[61] he was at the same time constantly concerned that his work be carefully structured, whether that structure was intrinsic to the work or not—in Stevens's terms, whether structure was discovered within or imposed from without. In his first volume of fiction, *Dubliners,* Joyce felt the need to impose a kind of overarching structure on that most formless of all fictional genres, the short-story collection; hence more than a year after beginning the first of the stories he devised the classification "stories of my childhood," "stories of adolescence," "stories of mature life," and "stories of public life in Dublin," using those headings to give the semblance of a structure to a volume that of itself had no "organic form." Again, Eliot called the mythical method of *Ulysses* "a way of controlling, of ordering, of giving a shape and a significance to the immense panorama of futility and anarchy which is contemporary history" (Eliot 177); but much more importantly, the Homeric trelliswork was for Joyce a means of keeping the unpredictable process of discovery which is writing within manageable—if artificial—bounds.

The discipline the Homeric parallels imposed on Joyce served as well an altogether different purpose. Throughout his career, Joyce searched for—indeed, *created*—problems to overcome in his writing. I have maintained that composition was for Joyce a process of discovery, the uncertainty of which he often found frightening (and attempted to master in various ways—the mythical method being but the most obvious). At the same time, writing was for Joyce the act of overcoming obstacles; whether the obstacles were "natural" or "artificial"—even self-imposed—seems not to have mattered. Which is not to say that Joyce didn't "kick against the pricks"; his letters, especially, are full of railings against the conditions under which he had to work (iritis, poverty, family pressures, disputes with publishers, censorship, piracy). But, as Jim Dixon in Kingsley Amis's *Lucky Jim* puts it, "The reason why Prometheus couldn't get away from his vulture was that he was keen on it, and not the other way round."[62] John Cage, in a series of mesostics called "Composition in Retrospect,"[63] sets out his own protocol for composition, which seems to me very similar to one aspect of Joyce's (unarticulated) working method:[64]

aCt

In

acco Rd

with obstaCles

Using

theM

to find or define the proceSs

you're abouT to be involved in

the questions you'll Ask

if you doN't have enough time

to aCcomplish

what you havE in mind

conSider the work finished.[65]

This aspect of Joyce's mythical method—the Homeric parallels as a hurdle, rather than a scaffold—has not been explored in the criticism. Beckett, in his essay on *Finnegans Wake,* referred to the various mythic parallels employed in that text as "a structural convenience—*or inconvenience.*"[66] If Joyce did in fact claim, as Beckett told Ellmann, that he had discovered he could do anything with language he wanted (*JJ* 702), then new challenges had to be invented if writing was to continue. After the challenge of creating *Ulysses* in the ways he set out to do, Joyce again needed something new; early on in the composition of *Finnegans Wake,* he wrote to Harriet Shaw Weaver that its "construction is quite different from *Ulysses* where at least the ports of call were known beforehand" (*L* 1:204).

But in one of the earliest references to his "Work in Progress" in the letters, Joyce suggests to Weaver that his various structural devices—whatever their origin—were all essentially a means of self-discipline; Bloom's sexual sadomasochism found its answer in Joyce's textual masochism: "I made heaps of notes about it [the *Odyssey*] (supposedly) which I could not fit in. I was trying lately to sort these out according to a brand new system I have invented for the greater complication and torment of myself" (*L* 1:200). Joyce's tone here is obviously somewhat playful, yet the notion that his systems were invented for his "greater complication and torment" does suggest that Joyce suffered from what Yeats called "the fascination with what's difficult." For as Joyce himself admitted on several occasions, he was one of the least creative of our literature's "creative" artists; he asked Jacques Mercanton "Why should I regret my talent? I haven't any,"[67] and complained in a 1917 letter to Pound, for instance, "Unfortunately, I have very little imagination" (*L* 1:101). Beckett warns, in the opening of his piece in *Our Exagmination,* that "literary criticism is not book-keeping";[68] but for Joyce, perhaps to a greater degree than any other writer of this century, the creation of literature *was* akin to an elaborate sort of bookkeeping—or better, what accountants today call "creative bookkeeping." And as a consequence Joyce's mania for narrative structure may have simply been a result of making a virtue of necessity.

I have introduced the name of John Cage in order to discuss some of Joyce's structural predilections. While I believe that Cage, in retrospect, provides an interesting commentary on Joyce's working methods, it would be disingenuous to pretend that Joyce took any of these procedures so far as Cage did. Cage referred to his compositions written from the late forties or early fifties on as "nonintentional"; his goal (or one of them) in making music, or pictures, or texts was to free his art from his intentions. To this end he employed "chance operations," chiefly the *I Ching,* to make decisions for him about the work at hand; he came, he said, to see the process of creation as properly not concerned with making good decisions, but rather with asking good questions.

Joyce, in his way, was also a believer in the role of chance in the creation of the work of art; what Cage called chance, however, Joyce would have preferred to call luck. Joyce's superstitions are legendary—an inordinate fear, like those he ascribes to Stephen Dedalus, of "dogs, horses, firearms, the sea, thunderstorms, machinery, the country roads at night" (*P* 243); and these superstitions affected not only his personal life, but his work. Frank Budgen comments on the chance aspect of the composition—actually the data collection—of *Ulysses;* Joyce, he writes, "was always looking and listening for the necessary fact or word; and he was a great believer in his luck. What he needed would come to him"; similarly, Jacques Mercanton reports Joyce claiming that "Chance furnishes me what I need. I am like a man who stumbles along; my foot strikes something, I bend over, and it is exactly what I need."[69] The best-known story regarding Joyce's "chance operations" is the one Beckett told, and Ellmann relates, about the composition of *Finnegans Wake:* "Once or twice [Joyce] dictated a bit of *Finnegans Wake* to Beckett, though dictation did not work very well for him; in the middle of one such session there was a knock at the door which Beckett didn't hear. Joyce said, 'Come in,' and Beckett wrote it down. Afterwards he read back what he had written and Joyce said, 'What's that "Come in"?' 'Yes, you said that,' said Beckett. Joyce thought for a moment, then said, 'Let it stand.' He was quite willing to accept coincidence as his collaborator" (*JJ* 649). Stories like this one attest to the increasingly whimsical nature of Joyce's writing; as a symbol of this shift he brought Stephen Dedalus, the Romantic Artist with a capital *A*, back onstage at the beginning of *Ulysses*, only to upstage him with Leopold Bloom, the *bricoleur*—the inventive adman who solves his "aesthetic" problems with whatever materials are at hand. Bloom's work on the ad for Alexander Keyes, tea, wine, and spirit merchant, is a good case in point: Bloom takes the basic design for the ad (which he himself had not created) and, in response to his client's suggestion, will modify it to incorporate the symbol of Manx parliament by pirating an ad run in the Kilkenny paper.[70] Bloom has already realized in practical terms what Lyotard suggests, that "we are no longer at the stage of deploring the 'mechanical reproduction' of works; we know that industry does not mean the end of the arts, but their mutation."[71] The task of becoming a modern artist in "the age of mechanical reproduction" was not simply Stephen's task, as was argued in chapter 5, but Bloom's—and, by implication, Joyce's task, too.

But while Joyce recognized that the role of the artist in the twentieth century had changed dramatically from that lived out by his Romantic forebears—a lesson that Stephen (in *Ulysses*) has yet to learn—Cage went much further than Joyce would have wanted in erasing the artist from his art. A representative example of Cage's procedure is his *Etudes Australes* (1974) for piano. The *Etudes*, as Richard Kostelanetz points out in his liner notes for the Wergo recording, are a logical extension of the work Cage had been doing for many years: "Cage in the late forties continued to develop methods for minimizing his control over the aural results. For instance, he would sometimes choose his notes by first observing the miscellaneous imperfections such as holes, specks or discolorations, on a piece of paper and then intensifying them with his pen. A transparent sheet with music staves would then be placed over the marked paper, and Cage would trace the intensified marks onto the staves."[72] Composing in this manner, Cage called down upon himself an artificial, arbitrary, extrinsic framework within which to create.

In the *Etudes Australes* (as well as the *Etudes Boreales* and *Atlas Elipticalis*), Cage composed using a similar procedure. He describes the "inspiration" for the first of these works, *Atlas Elipticalis*, this way: "I had just accepted a commission from the Montreal Festival Society to write a piece for orchestra. As usual I didn't know what it would be, and I was sitting there wondering what form it would take. I had seen that the university [Wesleyan University, Middletown, Conn.] had a telescope; it was just up the hill. Before I knew it I was on my way to it. I asked them when I got there whether they had a library. They had a very good one. I browsed rather quickly. What I was looking for were points, points that were stars in the books that would become notes in my music."[73] In the *Atlas Australes,* Cage found those stars and thus had his notes. Kostelanetz details the remainder of the compositional process of *Australes:* "The title of *Etudes Australes* (1974) comes from *Atlas Australis,* a book of maps of stars as they can be seen from Australia. Cage first placed a transparent grid over these maps. By a complicated pro-cess involving decisions made with the aid of his favorite 64-choice Chinese chance manual, *I Ching,* Cage marked the locations of certain stars on the transparent paper. These were transferred to music staves arranged in four groups of four—an upper and lower clef for the pianist's right hand, and a second set of upper and lower clefs for the left hand."[74]

This, in concrete terms, is what Cage meant by acting "in accord with obstacles." Such a method acknowledges that all structure is finally arbitrary, whether it is the five lines and four spaces of the musical staff, or fourteen lines of iambic pentameter in a Shakespearean sonnet, or the phenomenological ordering of locodescriptive narrative (the predominant structure of *Ulysses,* of course), or the approximately eighteen episodes in Odysseus's wanderings, or the positioning of stars in the southern skies, or the random locations of wood chips in a sheet of poor-quality writing paper. To resurrect Stevens's distinction, all composition is for Cage the imposition rather than the discovery of order.

This belief, surely, is at the heart of Cage's achievement as an artist; Joyce was not far from this awareness himself, but such a discovery would have entailed an entire literary/critical paradigm shift that Joyce may at times have glimpsed, but never felt altogether comfortable with. Joyce, in 1922, was *not* a postmodern writer; the term had not been coined, the category didn't exist, and throwing one's lot in with the program of the modernists, as Joyce did, was perhaps the most avant-garde artistic gesture a creative writer could make. To suggest in the way I have here that Joyce's narrative structures do not have the importance that one part of him would have liked—and that Eliot so boldly proclaimed—is not to attempt to claim him as a postmodernist *avant la lettre;* it is rather—given the avenue for rereading modernism afforded by the work of Lyotard and others—to identify the spirit of a nascent postmodernism at work in the very heart of one of the monuments of literary modernism.

Thus while Joyce established his *Ulysses* schemata as a way to concentrate his energies and restrain somewhat his willfully indiscriminate pen, they did not finally work—a glance at the facsimile page proofs of an episode like "Aeolus" is perhaps the quickest way to establish this. The "perverse devil" of Joyce's literary conscience, his "holy ghost in the inkwell" that first goaded him during the writing of *Dubliners,* did not simply go into retirement once that chapter in the moral history of his country had been written. As Karen Lawrence acknowledges, as the writing of *Ulysses* progressed, "the presence of details becomes increasingly prominent in the text, as Joyce deliberately includes random details that lie outside the symbolic form he himself creates. These details resist recuperation as a part of the symbolic schema and thus dramatize the innate recalcitrance that materiality presents to the shaping imagination" (Lawrence 78). In *Ulysses,* the text consistently overflows its ostensible bounds; the style, in addition to being tightly controlled, as Joyce (in some moods) and many of his critics staunchly maintained, is at the same time wildly *extravagant*—in the strong etymological sense of that word of which Thoreau reminds us in *Walden.*[75]

Appropriately enough, it seems to have been Joyce's superstitions—his belief, specifically, that having the novel appear on his fortieth birthday would be a good omen—that finally convinced him to surrender the manuscript. Without that deadline pending, every time he received the "final" version of his novel from the printers Joyce had another go at it—a process of compositional accretion that in theory need have no end. Michael Groden describes Joyce as "a man always searching for a well-defined controlling order," but, he points out, "the episodes after 'Oxen of the Sun' often refused to remain within the ordering design he planned for them. These episodes, especially 'Circe' and 'Ithaca', took him much longer to write than he expected, and he found himself elaborating them far beyond his original intentions."[76] As we have seen, though, Joyce's stylistic prodigality in fact manifests itself long before "Oxen of the Sun"; it is evident at least as early in the compositional process as the "Wandering Rocks" episode, and textually in the rupture between the close of the "Hades" episode ("Thank you. How grand we are this morning!") and the opening of "Aeolus":

IN THE HEART OF THE HIBERIAN METROPOLIS

One might argue, however, that *Ulysses* went out of control long before either of these convenient markers: like Joyce's two-thousand-word "A Portrait of the Artist," which later became the 250-page *A Portrait of the Artist as a Young Man*, the *Dubliners* story "Ulysses" which, as Joyce wrote to Stanislaus in 1907, "never got any forrader than the title" (*L* 2:209), instead took on a life of its own, and as the novel *Ulysses* introduced the carnivalesque—the postmodern—note into modernist fiction.

7

JJ and the Carnivalesque Imagination

In his 1984 study *James Joyce*, Patrick Parrinder makes passing reference to the role in *Ulysses* and *Finnegans Wake* of what Mikhail Bakhtin has called the "carnivalesque." Bakhtin characterizes the carnivalesque this way: "Carnival discloses [certain] traits as the best preserved fragments of an immense, infinitely rich world. This permits us to use precisely the epithet 'carnivalesque' in that broad sense of the word. We interpret it not only as carnival per se in its limited form but also as the varied popular-festive life of the Middle Ages and the Renaissance; all the peculiarities of this life have been preserved in carnival, while the other forms have deteriorated and vanished" (*R* 218). Parrinder identifies the settings of both *Ulysses* and *Finnegans Wake* with "the institution of the carnival. Of Joyce's two major works, the first takes place on the day when its hero is cuckolded—traditionally an occasion for bawdiness and ridicule—while the second is a 'funferal' based on the Irish wake or funeral merrymaking. . . . The Irish wake, with its upside-down antidote to the gravity of mourning and bereavement, is the perfect symbol of Joyceian comedy."[1] *Finnegans Wake* is indeed, as its title hints, one large stylistic wake; "Life, he [HCE] said once . . . is a wake, livit or krikit" (*FW* 55). But much of the carnival atmosphere of the late episodes of *Ulysses* could equally be attributed to a wake—not a wake properly celebrated, like Tim Finnegan's, but paradoxically the emotionally impoverished wake of Paddy Dignam that proves insufficient to placate his restless spirit. That spirit—as it resurfaces, wreaking havoc on the finely worked surface of *Ulysses*—is the very embodiment of Joyce's postmodernism.

"Poor Dignam!" (*U* 57) is dead, but is not properly waked. In his book *Irish Wake Amusements*, Seán O Súilleabháin points out that in Irish legend "there is no lack of stories about those dead who returned to complain about the neglect in carrying out some traditional custom at the time of their decease";[2] and, true to form, Paddy Dignam "resurfaces" frequently during the remainder of the novel, and the life-affirming energy that should have been celebrated at his wake and at the pub after his burial instead irrupts through and disrupts the text. It is as if, his family and friends having been remiss in their duties, the text itself wakes Dignam; it is as if Dignam himself has come back to complain about the poverty of his interment. The absence of a wake (funeral merrymaking) in the first six episodes has cut a wake (furrow) through the final twelve. Memories of Dignam, the ghost of Dignam, haunt the last twelve episodes of *Ulysses*, periodically, unpredictably unsettling the post-"Hades" text. Dignam is gone, but his spirit, through carnivalesque quirks in the text, lives on.

Many critics have commented on the seemingly abrupt stylistic shift that occurs between the "Hades" and "Aeolus" episodes of *Ulysses*. Perhaps the most colorful response to this shift is Virginia Woolf's: "I have read 200 pages so far—not a third; & have been amused, stimulated, charmed interested by the first 2 or 3 chapters—to the end of the Cemetery scene; & then puzzled, bored, irritated, & disillusioned as by a queasy undergraduate scratching his pimples."[3] Joyce had to defend himself to even the most sympathetic of his early critics once he moved beyond the first six episodes. As noted earlier, Ezra Pound, on reading a typescript version of the "Sirens" episode, wrote Joyce: "you have once again gone 'down where the asparagus grows' and gone down as far as the lector most bloody benevolens can be expected to respire."[4] Even Harriet Shaw Weaver required reassurance of the soundness of Joyce's new method. Joyce responded with something like sympathy: "I understand that you may begin to regard the various styles of the episodes with dismay and prefer the initial style much as the wanderer did who longed for the rock of Ithaca" (*L* 1:129).

The "initial style" that Joyce refers to has the ascendancy in the first six episodes, if not absolute reign. Karen Lawrence has termed the style developed in these episodes the "narrative norm": "The symmetry of this second triad [of episodes] with the "Telemachiad" and the persistence of the same basic rules of narration encourage us to group the first six chapters together as providing the norm of the book" (Lawrence 49). Lawrence characterizes this norm as written in an "educated, precise voice associated with the artist figure," interspersed with interior monologue, and traces its source to the language of *A Portrait of the Artist as a Young Man* and "The Dead" (Lawrence 15). Joyce's name for this narrative voice, the "initial style," also brings to mind the narrative voice of Stephen the self-critical young artist of the "Proteus" episode, who recalls his project of writing books with initials for titles: "Books you were going to write with letters for titles. Have you read his F? O yes, but I prefer Q. Yes, but W is wonderful. O yes, W" (*U* 34). The "initial style" is the style of the opening episodes of *Ulysses;* it is also the preferred style of the would-be author of the books of initials, Stephen Dedalus, whose callow stylistic pretensions finally became unbearable for Joyce.

As work on *Ulysses* progressed, Joyce, as we have seen, grew tired of Stephen. Like Stephen's "person," Stephen's narrative voice had a shape that could not easily be changed. So after having narrated the "Telemachiad" through Stephen's consciousness, Joyce narrated the second triad of episodes through the mind of Bloom. Through free indirect discourse and Bloom's stream of consciousness, the narration of Bloom's first three episodes is colored by his verbal predilections, just as the narrative of the "Telemachiad" tends to take the shape of Stephen's language. For instance, the second paragraph of the "Calypso" episode begins in the "educated, precise voice" to which we have become accustomed through *A Portrait of the Artist as a Young Man* and the "Telemachiad" ("Mr. Leopold Bloom ate with relish the inner organs of beasts and fowls"), only to close on a decidedly Bloomian note: "Kidneys were in his mind as he moved about the kitchen softly, righting her breakfast things on the humpy tray. Gelid light and air were in the kitchen but out of doors gentle summer morning everywhere. Made him feel a bit peckish" (*U* 45). Surely the same hoard of words is not responsible for both "gelid" and "peckish"; a narrative consciousness is at work here that operates according to democratic, polyphonic principles.

In their principle of narration, if not the texture of their narratives, the first and second triads of episodes are largely of a piece. David Hayman characterizes their unity this way: "The first six chapters of *Ulysses* must be considered as a unit. They prepare the reader through dramatic exposition for the thematic concerns of the entire novel, through modifications in the techniques for the more radical style shifts of the later chapters, through the increasing use of the stream of consciousness for the phasing out of the conscious personal voice in the evening chapters."[5] These first six episodes, then, make up what Joyce called "the rock of Ithaca," and what Marilyn French has described as "the tonic or fundamental, Socrates' doorstep, home plate: it is the place we begin, the place that forms our expectations, the place we remember when we are away from it, and the place we end."[6]

If we accept for a moment the idea that *Ulysses* does have an "initial style," and that that style is at some point in the novel disrupted, the next logical step is to locate the site of that disruption. The answer most commonly given is that the reader first notices disruption of the "initial style" with the first headline of the "Aeolus" episode. Michael Groden puts it this way: "'In the Heart of the Hibernian Metropolis,' the opening words in the final version of 'Aeolus,' serve remarkably well to upset the expectations that *Ulysses* gradually promotes in the first six episodes. Despite its changes in style and its second beginning in the fourth episode, the book up to now has seemed unified in its balance between external description and interior monologue, and in its concentration on single characters, first Stephen Dedalus and then Leopold Bloom. 'Aeolus' stands apart from the six preceding episodes, and it boldly announces this fact."[7]

That the "Aeolus" episode stands apart from the first six is beyond dispute; as Lawrence puts it, "in 'Aeolus,' the book begins to advertise its own artifice" (Lawrence 58). The typography of the "Aeolus" episode immediately calls attention to the stylistic schism that has occurred. But a more subtle shift takes place earlier, in the narrative near the center of the "Hades" episode. French has pointed this out: "At the very end [*sic*] of Hades there are two breaks in decorum: the conversations among the other men that we are permitted to overhear when Bloom is absent. We realize instantly that the point of view resides not just with Stephen, nor with Stephen and Bloom, but somewhere else."[8] To illustrate this point, French cites the following text:

Martin Cunningham whispered:
–I was in mortal agony with you talking of suicide before Bloom.
–What? Mr Power whispered. How so?
–His father poisoned himself, Martin Cunningham whispered. Had the Queen's hotel in Ennis. You heard him say he was going to Clare. Anniversary.
–O God! Mr Power whispered. First I heard of it. Poisoned himself?
He glanced behind him to where a face with dark thinking eyes followed towards the cardinal's mausoleum. Speaking. (*U* 84)

About this incident, French remarks, "It is a brief passage, but there is no question that it is outside Bloom's perception. . . . The infelicitous repetition of 'whispered' and the final word, 'Speaking,' which refers to Bloom's occupation at the moment, emphasize the narrational position."[9]

This is, according to French, the first such troublesome narrative incident in the novel; others follow rapidly on its heels. Six pages later, we hear Martin Cunningham explain to Hynes that the purpose of Simon Dedalus's graveyard humor is "To cheer a fellow up. . . . It's pure good-

heartedness: damn the thing else" (*U* 88). In this phrasing, Cunningham's speech follows Bloom's unspoken thoughts of just a page earlier:
"Old rusty pumps: damn the thing else" (*U* 87). A glance at the synoptic text shows that while Bloom's phrase remains unchanged from the
first complete draft, Cunningham's comment to Hynes in that first draft
was "It's pure goodheartedness: nothing else."[10] It was not until the
second of five revisions of the episode that Joyce had Cunningham echo
Bloom's diction. If the echo were an inadvertent one, it's logical to assume that it would have been weeded out of, rather than woven into,
successive drafts of the passage. The echo makes even more sense when
we recall that the "old rusty pumps" to which Bloom refers are human
hearts, Joyce's "symbol" for the "Hades" episode. The text itself—rather
than any of its characters—evidences an associative logic here, a "memory," which sometimes determines the text even at the level of diction,
a memory which cannot be located in any of principals of the episode.
The narrative stance of the novel has shifted by the conclusion of the
"Hades" episode, as French has argued, and the evidence of the manuscripts makes clear that this shift was a considered narrative decision
on Joyce's part. What is splashed across the front page in the "Aeolus"
episode exists as an understated presence in the center of the "Hades"
episode: as French says, "the first real shocks—even on a first reading—occur in Hades."[11] The narration is no longer mediated by the
consciousness of Stephen, or of Bloom, or even both together—there
is a stranger among us, whom Max Halperen calls "The Uninvited
Guest."[12] Like that more widely celebrated gate-crasher M'Intosh, he
makes his mysterious entrance near the end of the "Hades" episode,
and the telling of the tale is never quite the same thereafter.

But wait a minute. Isn't this quest for the first disruption, on some
level, a shell game? Isn't the search for firsts, for revolutions, itself a
form of modernist inquiry? Lyotard, for one, thinks so: "In the same
way that modernity contains the promise of its overcoming, it is obliged
to mark, to date, the end of one period and the beginning of the next.
Since one is inaugurating an age reputed to be entirely new, it is right
to set the clock to the new time, to start it from zero again."[13] Attempting, as Lawrence, Hayman, French, and many others have done, to quar-
antine a portion of *Ulysses* that is pristine, guileless, straightforward in
its narrative strategies—indeed, dare I say it? *modernist*—is itself a profoundly modernist desire. What we discover, as we search for the inaugural moment of the postmodern stylistics of *Ulysses*, is a receding hori-
zon; from each new starting point, each new fault line that we discover,
we can look back and find yet another. Let me give just one example

and then abandon this quest, before it consumes us. In the opening pages of the novel, as Stephen comes down from the parapet and enters the "gloomy domed livingroom of the tower," we read this description of the atmosphere: "Two shafts of soft daylight fell across the flagged floor from the high barbicans: and at the meeting of their rays a cloud of coalsmoke and fumes of fried grease floated, turning" (*U* 10). In context, this is a fairly typical piece of third-person descriptive writing, unremarkable but for one striking image ("shafts of soft daylight") and one $10 word ("barbicans"); it sounds characteristic of what Lawrence calls the initial style, indeed quite similar to the sentence from page 8 that she uses to illustrate the style ("Woodshadows floated silently by through the morning peace from the stairhead seaward where he gazed").

But what are we to think when we run across these phrases again, seventeen pages later—and this time not in the third-person narration, but seemingly having migrated into Stephen's stream of consciousness? "The cold domed room of the tower waits," Stephen thinks as he walks upon the strand in "Proteus"; "Through the barbicans the shafts of light are moving ever, slowly ever as my feet are sinking, creeping duskward over the dial floor" (*U* 37). There are only two ways, I believe, to naturalize this echo. One is to say, quite simply, that this is bad writing; the phrases "shafts of light" and "barbicans" obviously struck Joyce as fine writing, so fine that he repeated them in chapter 3 without remembering that he had used them in chapter 1. Given the meticulousness of Joyce's method, however—the texts of both "Telemachus" and "Proteus" went through approximately eight stages of drafts and proofs—this explanation strikes me as implausible, if not impossible. The other explanation would be to say that Stephen was responsible for the language in what looked initially to be third-person narrative in the first episode; the "shafts of soft daylight" coming through the "high barbicans" in "Telemachus" is not, as we first assumed, third-person narrative, but rather pseudo-third-person narrative—free indirect discourse, or more specifically what I've called free indirect prose. The point of this little exercise—and there are many other such textual cruxes that we might examine, were we so inclined—is that the closer we look, the more difficult it becomes to find an initial style, a stylistically "safe," uncontaminated episode in the novel from which to judge Joyce's later stylistic experimentation. If the postmodern spirit lives within *Ulysses*, as I hope to have shown it does, none of its rooms are off limits: it has the run of the house.

Wherever precisely it begins, critics are almost unanimous in their understanding of the motivation for the stylistic upheaval that racks

Ulysses. The majority position is best summed up by Hayman, who writes that "In 'Aeolus,' the first chapter which Stephen and Bloom share, Joyce begins to undermine his narrative voice. The whimsical headlines assert a counter-nature to the objective persona, reminding us of the deliberate clowning of Sterne's *Tristram Shandy*, that early example of the self-shaping literary mind. Intrusive but not disruptive, these sardonic interjections break the rhythm of the chapter only to the degree that they usurp space within a temporally continuous context."[14]

All are in agreement that the stylistic aberrations of the "Hades" and "Aeolus" episodes "call into question," as Groden writes, "the relationship between the episodes' narrators and the characters, since their speaker is distinct from any of the characters or from the narrators";[15] individual critics do differ, however, in their assessment of the effect of these descriptions. French sees the textual "shocks" (such as the "Aeolus" episode's headlines) as a sign of healthy authorial self-awareness: "On the whole, the juxtapositions burlesque the subject matter. The gap between the headlines and the sections serves to mock man's grand ideas about himself, his elevated characterization of his trivial being and activities. . . . The author does not even spare his own novel: ONLY ONCE MORE THAT SOAP mocks the method of the book, its patient accumulation of seemingly insignificant details, and what is more, the headline is a lie—the soap does appear again later."[16] Lawrence, however, reads the headlines as "more disconcerting than helpful to the reader, for the spirit that motivates their creation seems arbitrary and capricious" (Lawrence 55).

Richer than either of these limited intepretations is Wolfgang Iser's description of the reader's response to the "Aeolus" episode's stylistic disturbances. Concerned, in Susan Sontag's phrase, with the "erotics of art," Iser considers *Ulysses*, and especially the "Aeolus" episode, to be one of those texts which have "stimulating moments that disturb and even provoke a certain nervousness in the reader."[17] Thus in his reading, the "gap" between what is promised in the headlines and what is delivered in the text gives the episode a "stimulating quality": "The macrostructure [headlines] of the chapter lends itself to this need for 'grouping,' though in a peculiar way. Heading and 'newspaper column' form the schema that incorporates the allusions and stylistic changes. The heading is an instruction as to what to expect. But the text which follows the caption . . . does not fulfill the expectation raised by the heading. . . . While the heading appears to gratify our basic need for grouping, this need is predominantly subverted by the text that follows."[18]

These hermeneutic gaps are not "disconcerting" in any pejorative sense; neither are they merely an attempt to "mock man's grand ideas about himself." They form, in the terminology of Roland Barthes, "the seam of the two edges, the interstice of bliss" (*PT* 13). One way of speaking of the stylistic shift that comes to a head near the close of the "Hades" episode is to describe *Ulysses* as a novel that gradually transforms itself from a "text of pleasure" into a "text of bliss": "Text of pleasure: the text that contents, fills, grants euphoria; the text that comes from culture and does not break with it, is linked to a comfortable practice of reading. Text of bliss: the text that imposes a state of loss, the text that discomforts (perhaps to the point of a certain boredom), unsettles the reader's historical, cultural, psychological assumptions, the consistency of his tastes, values, memories, brings to a crisis his relation with language" (*PT* 14).[19] That division in *Ulysses* between the "text of pleasure" and the "text of bliss" is a result of the fact that, as Lawrence puts it, *Ulysses* is "a book that changes its mind as it progresses and forces a corresponding change of mind in the reader": "When he wrote the first six chapters, Joyce did not yet fully realize the direction the second half of the novel would take. But his decision to leave the first chapters substantially intact was made after writing the entire novel"; "The opening section of the book was left as a kind of testimony to an older order, a norm for the reader at the same time as it is an anachronism in terms of the book as a whole" (Lawrence 6, 53). By leaving the "initial style" of the "Telemachiad" and the better part of the second triad of episodes intact, Joyce created yet another site of bliss. A stylistic gap exists not only between the headlines and text of the "Aeolus" episode (or within the text of any of the post-"Hades" episodes), but also between the narrative style of the early episodes of the novel and the anarchy of styles in the later episodes. With the hindsight gained through a reading of the final twelve episodes, even the first six episodes, that "testimony to an older order," become a text of bliss: the authorial self-consciousness that is so much in evidence in the later episodes helps to rescue the early episodes from the banality that Joyce has inscribed in "Aeolus," which Iser describes this way: "Now it does sometimes occur in this chapter that the expectations aroused by the headings are fulfilled. At such moments, the text seems banal, for when the reader has adjusted himself to the nonfulfillment of his expectations, he will view things differently when they are fulfilled. . . . If the text does fulfill the expectations aroused by the heading, no removing of gaps is required of the reader and he feels the 'letdown' of banality."[20] In the context of "Aeolus," we realize that such banality (what Barthes calls "the prattling text") is part of

Joyce's design for the episode; at times in "Aeolus," as in the entire "Ithaca" and "Eumaeus" episodes, "the prattle of the text is merely that foam of language which forms by the effect of a simple need of writing. . . . The writer of this text employs an unweaned language: imperative, automatic, unaffectionate, a minor disaster of the static . . ." (*PT* 4–5). In the "con-text of bliss," even the prattling text can become blissful: "thus the Biblical myth is reversed, the confusion of tongues is no longer a punishment, the subject gains access to bliss by the cohabitation of languages *working side by side:* the text of pleasure is a sanctioned Babel" (*PT* 3–4).

A good part of the reader's pleasure in the "Aeolus" episode results from just this juxtaposition of styles: Bloom's thoughts, Stephen's "artist's speech," bombastic public rhetoric, smug headlines. The three consecutive sections "SAD," "HIS NATIVE DORIC," and "WHAT WETHERUP SAID" contain a representative selection of the variety of voices in the "Aeolus" episode within the space of two pages (*U* 103–4). The *urtext* of this (arbitrarily delimited) section is "Doughy" Dan Dawson's plea for the reforestation of Ireland: "Or again if we but climb the serried mountain peaks, towering high on high, to bathe our souls, as 'twere, in the peerless panorama of Ireland's portfolio, unmatched, despite their wellpraised prototypes in other vaunted prize regions, for very beauty, of bosky grove and undulating plain and luscious pastureland of vernal green, steeped in the transcendent translucent glow of our mild mysterious Irish twilight . . ." (*U* 104).21 Dawson's speech provides the subtext for the scene in the *Evening Telegraph* office—the white noise against which all other speech is foregrounded—and Ned Lambert is never allowed to go on for very long with his recitation without strenuous protest from both Professor MacHugh and Simon Dedalus. United though the men are in their criticism of Dawson's overblown oratory, however, their criticisms differ greatly in tone. Professor MacHugh's comments betray a self-satisfied intellectual arrogance: "'Bombast!' the professor broke in testily. 'Enough of the inflated windbag!'"; "'The moon,' professor MacHugh said. 'He forgot Hamlet'" (*U* 104). MacHugh criticizes Dawson from the position of and in the language of a "bloody old pedagogue" (*U* 104). As a result, his own language is often dangerously close to the very bombast he criticizes:

–Is the editor to be seen? J. J. O' Molloy asked, looking towards the inner door.
–Very much so, professor MacHugh said. To be seen and heard. He's in his sanctum with Lenehan. (*U* 103)

In fact, some of the most pretentious of the episode's headlines seem to be mocking MacHugh's "high" style, especially his love of Latinate and other classical diction—"OMNIUM GATHERUM," "KYRIE ELEI-SON!" "O, HARP EOLIAN," and "ITALIA, MAGISTRA ARTIUM," for example. His penchant for witty remarks places him in a rather precarious position in this room full of ruthless critics of rhetoric, and yet, owing to the respect he enjoys among this company, his stale wit does not come in for criticism.

Simon Dedalus, for his part, answers Dawson's bombast with profanity and blasphemy:

> –Peaks, Ned Lambert went on, towering high on high, to bathe our souls, as it were . . .
> –Bathe his lips, Mr Dedalus said. Blessed and eternal God! Yes? Is he taking anything for it? . . .
> –O! Mr Dedalus cried, giving vent to a hopeless groan. Shite and onions! That'll do, Ned. Life is too short. (*U* 104)

Simon Dedalus's sacrilege is so habitual as to have become second nature; earlier, in the "Hades" episode, Bloom mulls over Dedalus's description of Father Coffey: "Burst sideways like a sheep in clover Dedalus says he will. With a belly on him like a poisoned pup. Most amusing expressions that man finds. Hhhn: burst sideways" (*U* 85). Even in the somber atmosphere of the "Hades" episode, Dedalus is unable to restrain his penchant for the scatological, referring to Crissie Goulding as "papa's little lump of dung" and describing the weather as "uncertain as a child's bottom" (*U* 73, 75). Throughout the "Aeolus" episode, his idiom, what the headlines of "Aeolus" dub "HIS NATIVE DORIC,"[22] is constantly knocking down all that is sacred, or that aspires to a high position:

> Mr Dedalus, staring from the empty fireplace at Ned Lambert's quizzing face, asked of it sourly:
> –Agonizing Christ, wouldn't it give you a heartburn on your arse? . . .
> –Come, Ned, Mr Dedalus said, putting on his hat. I must get a drink after that. (*U* 102, 104)

Bakhtin mentions this type of utterance, the "various genres of billingsgate: curses, oaths, popular blazons," as one manifestation of the carnivalesque, and remarks: "In Rabelais' time the so-called *jurons*, that is, profanities and oaths—were . . . colloquialisms. They were mostly concerned with sacred themes: 'the body of Christ,' 'the blood of Christ,' holy days, saints, and relics" (*R* 5, 188). Simon Dedalus's *jurons* are for the most part concerned with sacred themes as well, although a good number of them are of a "cloacal" rather than a sacrilegious nature. Myles Crawford, later in the episode, is caught up in this same grotesque spirit, and Bloom is his unfortunate victim:

> –Just this ad, Mr Bloom said, pushing through towards the steps, puffing, and taking the cutting from his pocket. I spoke with Mr Keyes just now. . . . But he practically promised he'd give the renewal. But he wants just a little puff. What will I tell him, Mr Crawford?
>
> K.M.A.
>
> –Will you tell him he can kiss my arse? Myles Crawford said throwing out his arm for emphasis. Tell him straight from the stable. . . .
>
> –Well, Mr Bloom said, his eyes returning, if I can get the design I suppose it's worth a short par. He'd give the ad, I think. I'll tell him. . . .
>
> K.M.R.I.A.
>
> –He can kiss my royal Irish arse, Myles Crawford cried loudly over his shoulder. Any time he likes, tell him. (*U* 120–1)

The profanity of Myles Crawford and Simon Dedalus is but a part of the larger movement of the carnivalesque in the "Aeolus" episode, which "builds its own world versus the official world, its own church versus the official church, its own state versus the official state" (*R* 88). Nothing sacred is allowed to stand in the episode, whether it be the bombastic inflated rhetoric of Dan Dawson ("What about that, Simon?" Ned Lambert asks. "How's that for high?" [*U* 102]) or the genuinely powerful oratory of John F. Taylor, as delivered by Professor MacHugh:

> –Israel is weak and few are her children: Egypt is an host and terrible are her arms. Vagrants and daylabourers are you called: the world trembles at our name.
>
> A dumb belch of hunger cleft his speech. He lifted his voice above it boldly.
>
> –But, ladies and gentlemen. . . . (*U* 117)

Bakhtin remarks that during carnival time, "pleasure is caused by degrading high literature. All that is high wearies in the long run. The more powerful and prolonged the domination of the high, the greater the pleasure caused by its uncrowning" (*R* 305). The "domination of the high" survives more or less intact through the first six episodes, but by the time we reach "Aeolus" the text will no longer brook any overbearing articulate voice—like Stephen's—or any pretense to eloquence whatsoever. Even those who are lucky enough to avoid the sharp tongues of Crawford and Dedalus and the "dumb belch" of a hungry orator are not able to avoid the criticism of the headlines themselves. Professor MacHugh, as we have seen, though he is off-limits to those present in the

Evening Telegraph office, is not able to dodge the criticism of the hoardings imbedded in the text.

To repeat Lawrence's remark, "in 'Aeolus,' the book begins to advertise its own artifice" (Lawrence 58). The function of the headlines as advertising copy is germane to the carnivalesque spirit of the episode. Bakhtin's comments on the discourse of advertising are equally pertinent to the headlines in "Aeolus": "Popular advertising is always ironic, always makes fun of itself to a certain extent. . . . The superlative is the prevailing tone; actually, all the adjectives used are in this mode. But it is, of course, no rhetorical tone; rather it is an ironically and maliciously exaggerated style" (*R* 160–61). The ironic, self-conscious tone of advertising copy is obviously well suited to the spirit of "Aeolus." For instance, the episode's announcement of Paddy Dignam's death is pretentious, and knows it: "WITH UNFEIGNED REGRET IT IS WE ANNOUNCE THE DISSOLUTION OF A MOST RESPECTED DUBLIN BURGESS" (*U* 98). At least three questions beg to be asked: Why does the headline feel it necessary to point out that its regret is "unfeigned"? Why the poetic inversion of normal syntax? And why the choice of the word "dissolution" for the death of an alcoholic? This headline is well aware of the irony of its message, and it seems to relish its role.

Of course, the advertising in "Aeolus" is not confined to the headlines. Bloom's business in the *Evening Telegraph* office is to try to produce a satisfactory ad for his client Mr. Keyes, and it is in this episode that for the first time "WE SEE THE CANVASSER AT WORK" (*U* 99).

Although the ad that Bloom creates for Keyes is not an especially memorable one (its central image having been suggested by the client himself), Bloom does recognize good advertising copy when he sees it: the jingle for Plumtree's Potted Meat goes through his mind several times during the day.

> *What is home without*
> *Plumtree's Potted Meat?*
> *Incomplete.*
> *With it an abode of bliss.* (*U* 61)

The Plumtree's jingle conforms to the formula of the *cris de Paris,* shouted by street hawkers during carnival in Rabelais's time: "The *cris* were loud advertisements called out by the Paris street vendors and composed according to a certain versified form; each cry had four lines offering and praising certain merchandise" (*R* 181). Bloom's own approach to advertising is more subtle, more complex and indirect, with less obvious designs on its audience. As a result, Bloom is never completely comfortable in the atmosphere of the *Evening Telegraph* office. This tension, the tension between two styles of advertising, is epitomized in Bloom's encounter with the newsboys near the episode's close:

> Mr. Bloom, breathless, caught in a whirl of wild newsboys near the offices of the *Irish Catholic* and *Dublin Penny Journal,* called:
>   –Mr. Crawford! A moment!
>   –*Telegraph!* Racing special!
>   –What is it? Myles Crawford said, falling back a pace.
>   A newsboy cried in Mr. Bloom's face:
>   –Terrible tragedy in Rathmines! A child bit by a bellows!
>   INTERVIEW WITH THE EDITOR
>   –Just this ad, Mr. Bloom said, pushing through towards the steps, puffing, and taking the cutting from his pocket. . . . (*U* 120)

The newsboy who shouts in Bloom's face seems almost to be taunting him with the outrageousness of the evening number's man-bites-dog headline. In comparison, Bloom's is indeed "just an ad."

The headlines' criticism (or mockery) of Professor MacHugh and Bloom is just one aspect of one of their more general functions—editorializing, which is often all but indistinguishable from mockery. The headline "SAD," for instance, is an editorial comment on the text that follows it, recounting the "painful case" of J. J. O'Molloy. Bloom silently muses on O'Molloy's failing fortunes: "Cleverest fellow at the junior bar he used to be. Decline, poor chap. That hectic flush spells finis for a man. Touch and go with him. What's in the wind, I wonder. Money worry. . . . Practice dwindling. A mighthavebeen. Losing heart. Gambling. Debts of honour. Reaping the whirlwind" (*U* 103). The word "sad" does not occur in Bloom's thoughts about O'Molloy, but he would certainly agree with the headline's one-word assessment of O'Molloy's "decline."

Not all of the headlines are constructed along these lines, however. Rather than constituting a homogenous "headline style," the headlines embody a rich and varied assortment of styles. The tone of the headlines varies from the synecdoche and metonymy of "THE WEARER OF THE CROWN" and "GENTLEMEN OF THE PRESS," to the straightforward informative tone of "WILLIAM BRAYDEN, ESQUIRE, OF OAKLANDS, SANDYMOUNT" and "NOTED CHURCHMAN AN OCCASIONAL CONTRIBUTOR," to the attention-seeking rhetorical flourishes of "O, HARP EOLIAN!" and "LINKS WITH BYGONE DAYS OF YORE," to the chatty familiarity of popular tabloids[23] in "WE SEE THE CANVASSER AT WORK" and "YOU CAN DO IT!" to the purely comic exuberance of the episode's final heading, "DIMINISHED DIGITS PROVE

TOO TITILLATING FOR FRISKY FRUMPS. ANNE WIMBLES, FLO WANGLES—YET CAN YOU BLAME THEM?"

What we find, then, is not only a stylistic gap between the headlines and the texts that follow them, but rich stylistic variety among the headlines themselves. Bakhtin calls this kind of variety "heteroglossia," and sees this "polyvocality" as the essence of the novel as a genre: "The novel can be defined as a diversity of social speech types (sometimes even diversity of languages) and a diversity of individual voices, artistically organized. The internal stratification of any single national language into social dialects, characteristic group behavior . . . is the indispensable prerequisite for the novel as a genre" (*DI* 262–63). In his work on Rabelais, Bakhtin further links this heterogeneity of styles to the language of the carnival: "The suspension of all hierarchical precedence during carnival time was of particular significance. . . . This led to the creation of special forms of marketplace speech and gesture, frank and free, permitting no distance between those who came in contact with each other and liberating from norms of etiquette and decency imposed at other times" (*R* 10). The concatenation of styles in the "Aeolus" episode, and indeed in all of the episodes from "Aeolus" through "Ithaca," is a stylistic manifestation of the carnivalesque.

The "Aeolus" episode is only the first episode to introduce an unmistakable note of carnival laughter, but in so doing, it sets the tone for the remainder of the book. Bakhtin describes the cathartic effect of laughter this way: "True ambivalent and universal laughter does not deny seriousness but purifies and completes it. Laughter purifies from dogmatism, from the intolerant and the petrified; it liberates from fanaticism and pedantry, from fear and intimidation, from didacticism, naivete and illusion, from the single meaning, the single level, from sentimentality" (*R* 122–23). Bakhtin claims that "carnival . . . was hostile to all that was immortalized and completed" (*R* 10), and the page proofs of the "Aeolus" episode with Joyce's emendations scratched all over them bear silent witness to the fact that this was Joyce's attitude toward his own work in his revisions. By the time he came to "recast" "Aeolus" late in 1921, Joyce had grown hostile to that "immortalized and completed" monument, the initial style, just as he had grown tired of Stephen, and for the same reason: it had a shape that couldn't be changed. But change it he did—in a guerrilla action, from the outside. Rather than change the voice of a character like Stephen—which, according to Joyce's lights, would have been artistic bad faith—Joyce allowed Stephen's voice, and his prose, to be relativized, to become just one line in a polyphonically orchestrated novel.

Joyce's insertion of the headlines into those late proofs is, as John Paul
Riquelme points out, "like Bloom's early conversation with Mr. Nan-
netti, the foreman, in which he converses by 'slipping his words deftly
into the pauses of the clanking.'"[24] Riquelme refers to this hypothetical
text-based agent of the headlines' insertion as "the teller." When discussing the textual motivation for the headlines, beside pointing to the
manuscript history of the episode and Joyce's decision to add the headlines, critics have been forced either to speak of a nameless and faceless
narrator or "teller" (Hayman, in his 1970 book "*Ulysses*": *The Mechanics
of Meaning*, introduced the influential concept of the Arranger) of the
episode who tags the short sections of the text with headlines, or else to
speak of the appearance of the headlines as an agentless "textual" operation, something that the text itself spontaneously generates.

Another possibility suggests itself, however. In a letter of 7 October
1921, Joyce tells Harriet Weaver: "*Eolus* is recast" (*L* 1:172). He uses fairly
traditional terms and images for the revision work he has done on the
other episodes he discusses in the letter: "Ithaca" he is "putting in order";
"Hades" and "Lotus-Eaters" are "amplified"; the other episodes, ex-
cluding the "Telemachia," are "retouched a good deal" (*L* 1:172). In this
context, "recast" is an unexpected choice, but it points to another possible source of the "Aeolus" headlines: Joyce "recast" the "Aeolus" episode by adding a member to the cast, one who controls the tone of the
episode. Halperen argues that we are to perceive a maker behind "Aeolus," not merely a collection of floating headlines: "We seem to have,
then, a series of headlines that interact with each other and, increasingly, with the characters of the episode—moving from the impersonality of the opening lines to a number of comments that take the form
of direct hits. And if we cannot speak of a narrator we can, I think, perceive a state of mind, an implied consciousness standing in for the author, one who is quite ambivalent about Dublin and its people and who,
ultimately, attempts to reject them."[25]

In reaction to the initial style, Joyce radically changed the shape of
the prose in the second half of the book. Many critics have described the
stylistic shift that sets in toward the end of the "Hades" episode; however, no one, to my knowledge, has made an especially compelling argument as to why this stylistic shift sets in, in such a flamboyant manner, at this particular juncture in the novel. One possible answer to this
question lies in the plot-level events of the "Hades" episode itself—
plot-level events that we may here elevate to the role of a textual mechanism. The main civic event of the episode—indeed, of the first six chapter of *Ulysses* —is the funeral of Paddy Dignam. We are first made aware

that Dignam is to be buried just a few pages into "Calypso," and the impending funeral casts a pall over Bloom's thoughts in the first few episodes in which he appears.

Contrary to Irish tradition, however, Paddy Dignam is not properly waked.[26] As Martin Cunningham says of the traditional funeral procession through the city of Dublin, "That's a fine old custom. . . . I am glad to see it has not died out" (*U* 73); in 1904, the Irish wake too was a living tradition, even if it had lost much of its ancient vitality. The wake, like the funeral procession itself, is one of those ancient Irish customs, utterly impractical, for which the eminently pragmatic Bloom has no use. His suggestion that the Dublin Corporation run municipal funeral trams from the quays to the cemetery gates "like they have in Milan, you know," draws Simon Dedalus's ire: "O, that be damned for a story" (*U* 81). Though reason is on Bloom's side, as he nearly convinces his listeners, the weight, the inertia of tradition is on theirs; as Stanislaus Joyce writes in *My Brother's Keeper*, "The dearest of all things in Ireland is the memory of the past."[27] As the gravediggers in Glasnevin Cemetery fling "heavy clods of clay in on the coffin," Bloom thinks: "Three days. Rather long to keep them in the summer. Just as well to get shut of them as soon as you're sure there's no" (*U* 91). In a practical sense, again, Bloom is right; especially if there is to be no wake, there is no real justification for keeping the corpse for three days before burial.

According to Rodney Owen, Dignam's funeral in the "Hades" episode is in its conception the "oldest" scene in *Ulysses*. The funeral of Matthew Kane, an acquaintance of the Joyce family, in July 1904 was the germ of what eventually became the "Hades," and to some extent "Aeolus" and "Cyclops," episodes of *Ulysses*. Owen writes: "My hypotheses about 'Ulysses' are that Joyce's idea was to write a story about Matthew Kane's funeral in July 1904, with the attendance there of a certain Mr. Alfred Hunter, perhaps the passing of Dublin statues and monuments on the way to the funeral, and a post-funeral scene in a pub where the mourners and citizens turn against Hunter, the main character."[28] Of course, the short story "Ulysses" grew into the novel *Ulysses*, and that funeral came to occupy but one short episode. But if Owen's hypotheses about the germ of "Ulysses" are correct, then Paddy Dignam's funeral did at one time during the novel's gestation play a very important part in the plot structure. "Hades" is, in some sense, at the very heart of *Ulysses*; Joyce's choice of the heart as the episode's symbol was not, perhaps, altogether capricious.

In the schema for *Ulysses* that he supplied Herbert Gorman, Joyce identifies Paddy Dignam with Odysseus's young companion Elpenor.

The parallel, though not often commented upon, is an illuminating one. At the close of the tenth book of the *Odyssey*, Odysseus rouses his crew from their swinish slumber in order to flee Circe's island:

> They were soon up, and ready at that word;
> but I was not to take my men unharmed
> from this place, even from this. Among them all
> the youngest was Elpênor—
> no mainstay in a fight nor very clever—
> and this one, having climbed on Kirkê's roof
> to taste the cool night, fell asleep with wine.
> Waked by our morning voices, and the tramp
> of men below, he started up, but missed
> his footing on the long steep backward ladder
> and fell that height headlong. The blow smashed
> the nape cord, and his ghost fled to the dark.[29]

Elpenor, like his Joycean counterpart Dignam, dies as a direct result of his drinking. But Elpenor's death resembles the death of *Finnegans Wake*'s hero even more closely than that of Dignam:

> The fall (bababadalgharaghtakamminarronnkonnbronntonnerronntuonnthunntrovarrhounawnskawntoohoohoordenenthurnuk!) of a once wallstraight oldparr is retaled early in bed and later on life down through all christian minstrelsy. The great fall of the offwall entailed at such short notice the pftjschute of Finnegan, erse solid man. . . .
>
> What then agentlike brought about that tragoady thundersday this municipal sin business? Our cubehouse still rocks as earwitness to the thunder of his arafatas. . . . all the uproar from all the aufroos . . . wan warning Phill filt tippling full. His howd feeled heavy, his hoddit did shake. (There was a wall of course in erection) Dimb! He stottered from the latter. Damb! he was dud. Dumb! Mastabatoom, mastabadtomm. . . .
> (*FW* 3, 5, 6)

Both men die of an inebriated faux pas from a ladder (as did Vico). Neither man, however, is content to stay down; as *Finnegans Wake* puts it, "Phall if you but will, rise you must" (*FW* 4). Finnegan comes back to life when whiskey is spilled on him during his wake—"Hohohoho, Mister Finn, you're going to be Mister Finnagain!" (*FW* 5). Elpenor, though he never comes back to life, does meet Odysseus again, as a shade, in Hades: "One shade came first—Elpênor, of our company, / who lay unburied still on the wide earth / as we had left him—dead in Kirkê's hall, / untouched, unmourned, when other cares compelled us. / Now when I saw him there I wept for pity."[30] The reason for Odysseus's sorrow is not merely that he has lost one of his crewmen; the narrator goes out of his way, in the earlier passage, to point out that Elpenor was neither courageous in battle, nor especially intelligent. Odysseus rather suffers from Stephen Dedalus's malaise, the "agenbite of inwit," over not having properly interred the dead Elpenor. Unhappy to have been left dead in Circe's den, Elpenor requests that Odysseus give his body a proper burial when he departs from the underworld:

> Son of great Laërtês,
> Odysseus, master mariner and soldier,
> bad luck shadowed me, and no kindly power;
> ignoble death I drank with so much wine.
> I slept on Kirkê's roof, then could not see
> the long steep backward ladder, coming down,
> and fell that height. My neck bone, buckled under,
> snapped, and my spirit found this well of dark.
> Now hear the grace I pray for . . .
> . . . .
> When you make sail
> and put these lodgings of dim Death behind,
> you will moor ship, I know, upon Aiaia Island;
> there, O my lord, remember me, I pray,
> do not abandon me unwept, unburied,
> to tempt the gods' wrath, while you sail for home;
> but fire my corpse, and all the gear I had,
> and build a cairn for me above the breakers—
> an unknown sailor's mark for men to come.
> Heap up the mound there, and implant upon it
> the oar I pulled in life with my companions.[31]

Odysseus's reply to Elpenor's request is immediate: "Unhappy spirit, / I promise you the barrow and the burial."[32] Elpenor requests of Odysseus not simply a burial, but something of a small memorial, a sort of "tomb of the unknown sailor." And to go along with his memorial, a memorial service; Elpenor desires an outpouring of sorrow over his death—a wake. Lovelace Bigge-Wither, in his "nearly literal" translation of the *Odyssey*, renders Elpenor's request this way: "Me not unwaked—unburied leave behind thee." The word translated "unwaked" or "unburied" is the Greek word *aklauton*, the negation of *klaio*, "to weep, lament, wail; often in Homer of any loud expression of pain or sorrow, especially for the dead."[33] That expression of sorrow in Irish is called the *caoine* (keen).

Like his Homeric counterpart, Paddy Dignam is ultimately unsatisfied with his post mortem treatment; his is, as Bloom comments, a "paltry funeral" (*U* 83). Odysseus's neglect of Elpenor's burial caused him and his crew a great deal of trouble; Odysseus was made by Circe to confront Elpenor's shade in Hades, and to make reparations for the wrong done to him. In much the same way, the ghost of Dignam comes back to haunt his Dublin acquaintances in the later episodes of *Ulysses*. Paddy first resurfaces just a few pages into the "Aeolus" episode, where his reentrance is, as we have seen, announced in a loud, ironic voice: "WITH UNFEIGNED REGRET IT IS WE ANNOUNCE THE DISSOLUTION OF A MOST RESPECTED DUBLIN BURGESS." Dignam next appears to Bloom in an especially carnivalesque manner—backwards: "He stayed in his walk to watch a typesetter neatly distributing type. Reads it backwards first. Quickly he does it. Must require some practice that. mangiD kcirtaP" (*U* 101).

Dignam's most impressive reappearance, however, does not come until the "Cyclops" episode. There, Alf Bergan is certain that he has just seen Dignam in Capel Street:

–How's Willy Murray those times, Alf?

–I don't know, says Alf. I saw him just now in Capel Street with Paddy Dignam. Only I was running after that. . . .

–You what? says Joe, throwing down the letters. With who?

–With Dignam, says Alf.

–Is it Paddy? says Joe.

–Yes, says Alf. Why?

–Don't you know he's dead? says Joe.

–Paddy Dignam dead! says Alf.

–Ay, says Joe.

–Sure I'm after seeing him not five minutes ago, says Alf, as plain as a pikestaff.

–Who's dead? says Bob Doran.

–You saw his ghost then, says Joe, God between us and harm.

–What? says Alf. Good Christ, only five. . . . What? . . . And Willy Murray with him, the two of them near whatdoyoucallhim's. . . . What? Dignam dead?

–What about Dignam? says Bob Doran. Who's talking about . . .?

–Dead! says Alf. He's no more dead than you are.

–Maybe so, says Joe. They took the liberty of burying him this morning anyhow.

–Paddy? says Alf.

–Ay, says Joe. He paid the debt of nature. God be merciful to him.

–Good Christ! says Alf.

Begob he was what you might call flabbergasted. (*U* 247)

As Professor MacHugh says of Bloom earlier, "The ghost walks" (*U* 102). The realistic explanation, of course, is that Alf Bergan, "running after that . . .," is mistaken in his identification. But Dignam's correspondence with Elpenor lends at least some credibility to Joe's explanation, that Alf "saw his ghost." The narrator proceeds to keen Dignam in his impression of best Celtic Revival style: "He is gone from mortal haunts: O'Dignam, sun of our morning. Fleet was his foot on the bracken: Patrick of the beamy brow. Wail, Banba, with your wind: and wail, O ocean, with your whirlwind" (*U* 248).

In the "Circe" episode, Dignam enjoys yet another resurrection. There, his manifestation is not frightening, but serves rather to support Bloom's alibi:

PADDY DIGNAM
(*in a hollow voice.*) It is true. It was my funeral. Doctor Finucane pronounced life extinct when I succumbed to the disease from natural causes. (*He lifts his mutilated ashen face moonwards and bays lugubriously.*)
BLOOM
(*in triumph.*) You hear?
PADDY DIGNAM
Bloom, I am Paddy Dignam's spirit. List, list, O list! (*U* 385)

The second half of *Ulysses* in one respect resembles a gothic novel: the spirit of Paddy Dignam is not at peace; disturbed, his ghost is condemned to wander about the novel in search of a final rest that never comes.

In book 12 of the *Odyssey*, Elpenor, having implored Odysseus, receives the burial he desires as soon as Odysseus and his crew reach the island of Aiaia:

When the young Dawn with finger tips of rose
made heaven bright, I sent shipmates to bring
Elpênor's body from the house of Kirkê.
We others cut down timber on the foreland,
on a high point, and built his pyre of logs,
then stood by weeping while the flame burnt through
corse and equipment.
                    Then we heaped his barrow,
lifting a gravestone on the mound, and fixed
his light but unwarped oar against the sky.
These were our rites in memory of him.[34]

Elpenor's corpse has now been properly mourned and buried, *requiescat in pace;* Paddy Dignam's Homeric counterpart provides us with an ancient model of the proper treatment of the dead.

The episode in *Ulysses* where death is most clearly the focus is, of course, "Hades." Like certain others, most notably "Cyclops," "Hades" is also an extremely tense episode; the funeral carriage containing Bloom, Simon Dedalus, Martin Cunningham, and Jack Power at times seems very cramped indeed. Although we later see further evidence of it in "Calypso" and "Lotus-Eaters," we first understand just how much an outsider Bloom is in Dublin society in "Hades." The friction that exists between Bloom and the others in the "Hades" episode is perhaps a genteel version of fighting that is traditionally part of Irish funerals:

> There is evidence to show that the relatives of the deceased looked forward to fighting at the funeral, and were very dissatisfied if none occurred. A story is told about the funeral of an old man in the northern part of Leinster. After a quiet, peaceful funeral, the mourners were about to leave the graveyard when the son of the dead man shouted:
> "This is a sad day, when my father is put into the clay, and not even one blow struck at his funeral!"
> As he ended his complaint, he delivered a blow at the man who happened to be nearest to him. In a few moments, fights were taking place all over the graveyard, each man taking on his neighbour. When the demands of the occasion had been met, the dead man's son called for a truce, and both he and everybody else went home satisfied.[35]

Rather than open fighting, the aggression in the "Hades" episode consists of thinly disguised antagonism, directed at Bloom by Simon Dedalus.

Perhaps the most vicious example of Simon's antagonism is his intentionally indelicate condemnation of Bloom's father's suicide. Mr. Power, seemingly unaware of Bloom's father's suicide, comments: "But the worst of all . . . is the man who takes his own life" (*U* 79). Martin Cunningham tries to frustrate this line of conversation, but Mr. Power, blissfully ignorant of Bloom's circumstances, continues on, and is joined by Simon Dedalus:

> –The greatest disgrace to have in the family, Mr Power added.
> –Temporary insanity, of course, Martin Cunningham said decisively. We must take the charitable view of it.
> –They say a man who does it is a coward, Mr Dedalus said.
> –It is not for us to judge, Martin Cunningham said. (*U* 79)

After this exchange, Bloom sits quietly, thinking about the good turn Cunningham has done him, or tried to do: "Sympathetic human man he is." But his thoughts move on from Cunningham to Simon Dedalus: "He looked away from me. He knows. Rattle his bones" (*U* 80). Bloom evidently believes that unlike Mr. Power, Simon Dedalus knows of his father's suicide, and is taking advantage of the situation to cause Bloom pain. Bloom at first prepares to make answer to Simon's accusation, but instead retreats into silence. His retaliation is purely mental: the phrase "rattle his bones," which Joyce added to Bloom's thoughts in a late draft, is from the burial song that has been running through Bloom's head throughout the episode: "Rattle his bones. Over the stones. Only a pauper. Nobody owns" (*U* 79).

As for Paddy Dignam, he has no son who will stand up for him at his funeral and demand that his father's death be taken notice of. When we encounter Paddy's son Patsy late in the day—and even his nickname seems to suggest that he is merely an effeminate, pale imitation of his father—he does not seem to have been strongly affected by his father's passing: "Opposite Ruggy O'Donohoe's Master Patrick Aloysius Dignam, pawing the pound and a half of Mangan's, late Fehrenbach's, porksteaks he had been sent for, went along warm Wicklow street dawdling. It was too blooming dull sitting in the parlour with Mrs Stoer and Mrs Quigley and Mrs MacDowell and the blind down and they all at their sniffles and sipping sups of the superior tawny sherry uncle Barney brought from Tunney's" (*U* 206).[36] Like Stephen, Patsy seems to be overly concerned with cutting an impressive figure while in mourning: "From the sidemirrors two mourning Masters Dignam gaped silently. . . . Master Dignam on his left turned as he turned. That's me in mourning. . . . He met other schoolboys. Do they notice I'm in mourning?" (*U* 206).

In a larger sense, two worldviews collide in "Hades": two different attitudes toward life and death, two different approaches to mourning. These two views, the English and the Celtic, are everywhere in conflict in the episode. Paddy Dignam, of good Irish stock, has died; tradition, the racial memory, demand that his body be waked and his spirit laid to rest. But through the influence of English tradition and Roman Catholicism, Irish funeral customs have survived into the twentieth century only in a greatly attenuated version.

The English approach to death is precisely the one that Patsy Dignam and Stephen Dedalus have adopted; or perhaps rather than actually having adopted its philosophy, they merely play the role that it dictates for the bereaved firstborn son. Stephen and Patsy mourn in 1903–4; the entire British Empire has just recently had a full-dress rehearsal of the proper way to mourn, with the death of Queen Victoria. Even in her life, of course, Victoria had done much to popularize mourning wear; in *Mourning Dress*, Lou Taylor explains that

The importance of the royal influence on Victorian mourning etiquette was supreme. In the class conscious, middle-class suburbs, two elements combined to produce such a desirable example that few could resist it. First, all the elaborate etiquette of family funerals derived from satisfactorily ancient royal usage. Secondly, following the sudden death by typhoid of Prince Albert in 1861, the much respected Queen wore mourning dress for the remaining forty years of her life. Her example was copied by many of her middle-class subjects. They might be shut out of high society but they could copy exactly the dress of the Queen herself, for families found themselves frequently going through mourning periods. It was Victoria, the middle-class ideal of Christian widowhood, who fanned the cult of mourning, spreading it to all classes of society during her lifetime. After Albert's death she shrouded herself in crape-covered black weeds all the rest of her life, the only difference in her dresses being in her waist measurement.[37]

But with Victoria's death, an entire empire mourned, or at least put on mourning. As John Morley writes, "The last great and universal demonstration of mourning happened when Queen Victoria died; even in Dublin, commented the *Lady's Pictorial*, its correspondent saw only two people not in black. Black was everywhere in London even the first day after her death; this speedy assumption was assisted by the fashionable ubiquity of black that season."[38]

The period of mourning following a death is a time of intense introspection, of societally sanctioned self-absorption, for the family of the deceased. Patsy Dignam seems to have been almost completely unaffected by the death of his father. A few short hours after the funeral, he is both physically and mentally miles away from the death, absorbed by the boxing advertisement he sees: "Myler Keogh, Dublin's pet lamb, will meet sergeantmajor Bennett, the Portobello bruiser, for a purse of fifty sovereigns. Gob, that'd be a good pucking match to see" (*U* 206). He even thinks about how he might con his mother out of the price of admission ("I could easy do a bunk on ma"). Stephen, on the other hand, becomes morbidly self-absorbed; he thinks of nothing during his period of mourning more than his own image, the figure he cuts while he "struts and frets." For instance, he refuses a pair of trousers offered by Mulligan strictly on the basis of their color:

–I have a lovely pair with a hair stripe, grey. You'll look spiffing in them. I'm not joking, Kinch. You look damn well when you're dressed.
–Thanks, Stephen said. I can't wear them if they are grey.
–He can't wear them, Buck Mulligan told his face in the mirror. Etiquette is etiquette. He kills his mother but he can't wear grey trousers. (*U* 5)

Stephen's mourning is almost purely a facade; his sorrow seems to be composed of public opinion and, as Mulligan calls it, "etiquette."

At certain points in the narrative, Stephen seems to be aware of his need to transcend the *ressentiment* that characterizes his present way of life. But he has no idea of how to effect this transformation; Mulligan's advice, "give up the moody brooding," may be both philosophically and psychologically sound, but it is not especially helpful. As Stephen begins to tell the "Parable of the Plums," Professor MacHugh interrupts him to inquire as to the location of Fumbally's Lane, the story's setting. Stephen answers MacHugh's inquiry, and then forces himself to continue: "On now. Dare it. Let there be life" (*U* 119). Stephen's silent fiat artfully alters the Creator's "Let there be light": the substitution is valid precisely because Stephen believes the greatest artistic creations to be affirmations of life. The story that Stephen goes on to tell, however, is not an affirmation of life; it is instead an indictment of the spiritual death of "Dear Dirty Dublin," a story with as much spleen as any in *Dubliners*. This forging of the uncreated conscience of his race is a necessary stage in Stephen's artistic development, but at some point he must move beyond this purely negative criticism toward some sort of affirmation. At some point, Stephen must declare himself free of all that death, as he had grandiloquently done at the close of *A Portrait*: "Free. Soulfree and fancyfree. Let the dead bury the dead. Ay. And let the dead marry the dead" (*P* 248). The "young artist" has become quite adept at creating *Dubliners*-style parables of paralysis and sterility; but if his artistic vision is ever to mature fully, Stephen must learn to look beyond death, look through death to life.

If Stephen the "autobiographical" character remains mired in *ressentiment* throughout the course of this novel, his creator has, in creating *Ulysses*, clearly moved beyond his character's fixation. Stanislaus points this out in a diary entry, although he does not appear to understand fully the significance of what he writes: "Jim told me that he is going to expand his story 'Ulysses' into a short book and make a Dublin 'Peer Gynt' of it. . . . I suggested that he should make a comedy of it, but he won't" (*JJ* 265). The joke, of course, is that a Dublin *Peer Gynt* could not be anything but a comedy, in the earliest sense of the word (Greek *komos*, "merrymaking, revel"). As such, it will do what Stephen cannot: "The world is destroyed," Bakhtin writes, "so that it may be regenerated and renewed. While dying it gives birth. The relative nature of all that exists is always gay; it is the joy of change" (*R* 48).

It is this ability to view life as "the joy of change" that Bloom shows in abundance. Bloom's healthy acceptance of death stands in refreshing contrast to Stephen's "moody brooding." As Parrinder writes, Bloom's "commitment to 'warm fullblooded life' is reached in defiance of the failures in his own life and, in particular, it is a rejection of suicide. He has come to terms with his father's suicide with the help of his generalized view of the human condition. The fantasy of repeating his father's act is briefly present in 'Sirens.' . . . But Bloom is content with his annual pilgrimage to his father's grave and his daytime thoughts, unlike Stephen's, are not dominated by his bereavement."[39] Bloom's healthy acceptance of death, however, is largely overshadowed in the "Hades" episode by the prevailing English attitude toward death. All of the episode's principals, including Bloom, are concerned to keep an eye to the proprieties. In choosing his funeral clothing, Bloom follows the same code as Stephen; he considers that his light-colored suit would be cooler for this warm June day, but realizes that he must out of respect to the Dignam family wear the black: "Be a warm day I fancy. Specially in these black clothes feel it more. Black conducts, reflects, (refracts is it?), the heat. But I couldn't go in that light suit. Make a picnic of it" (*U* 46–47). Bloom's practical mind realizes that on a warm day the light-colored suit would be a better choice; at the same time, Bloom, one of the novel's most compassionate characters, in no way wishes to offend the Dignam family.

Beneath this thin veneer of civility, however, an altogether different spirit is trying to break loose in the "Hades" episode. While listening to the Burial of the Dead service, Bloom catches himself humming under his breath: "The ree the ra the ree the ra the roo. Lord, I mustn't lilt here" (*U* 86). Jokes are constantly breaking out amongst the members of the funeral party, momentarily destroying the high seriousness of the occasion. Martin Cunningham warns, "We had better look a little serious" (*U* 78), and yet he along with everyone else realizes that there is nothing truly disrespectful about this graveyard humor. For despite the "grave" deportment dictated by the English way of death, a native Irish carnivalesque spirit strains to breath through. This spirit, as I have suggested earlier, is the spirit that animates the Irish tradition of the wake. The wake is an objective correlative of the "yes" to life, the affirmation of life toward which Stephen inchoately gropes, the playfulness which the text of *Ulysses*, after Paddy Dignam goes unwaked, enacts.

Parrinder states that the wake is the perfect symbol of Joycean comedy; it is also the Irish carnivalesque event par excellence. In *Rabelais and His World*, Bakhtin does allude briefly to funeral merrymaking as a species of the carnivalesque: "Eating and drinking were also the main features of the commemoration of the dead. When honoring patrons and benefactors buried in the church, the clergy organized banquets and drank to their memory the so-called *'poculum charitatis'* or *'charitas vini.'* A record of Kvedlinburg Abbey openly states that the clergy's banquet feeds and pleases the dead: *plenius inde recreantur mortui.* The Spanish Dominicans drank to the memory of their deceased patrons, toasting them with the typical ambivalent words *viva el muerto.* In these examples the gaiety and laughter have the character of a banquet and are combined with the images of death and birth (renewal of life) in the complex unity of the material bodily lower stratum" (*R* 79–80). At the end of *Irish Wake Amusements,* O Súilleabháin makes the same connection between the wake and carnival: "I think that it is possible to make a connection and comparison between wake-games and associated amusements, on the one hand, and what went on at the great fairs (at Teltown, for example) which were held at certain places in ancient Ireland, on the other. Professor D. A. Binchy, in his article about The Fair of Tailtiu and the Feast of Tara, says: 'From several statements in the Laws (e.g. Crith Gablach 500 f., etc.) it is clear that the king of every tribe was bound to convene an *óenach* [funeral games] at regular intervals. The site of the fair was normally an ancient burial ground: indeed the tradition reflected in many poems and sagas that the *óenach* originated in the funeral games held for kings and heroes may have a kernel of truth.'"[40]

For reasons I will discuss below, the twentieth-century descendant of the wake is often an anemic imitation of the traditional form; the wake's animating spirit, however, is a festive one: "Moments of death and revival, of change and renewal always led to a festive perception of the world" (*R* 9). The traditional Irish wake, in its games and set pieces, gave both outlet and form to this festive spirit: "Feasting, drinking, and the use of snuff were usual, wherever the occasion suited. So too, storytelling, riddling, verse-making and . . . many games . . . were popular. . . . [Our forefathers] went to the wakes to enjoy themselves; and old people have told me that in the old days the wake of an old person was a far merrier and more enjoyable occasion than even a wedding."[41] John Dunton, an English nobleman who visited Ireland at the close of the seventeenth century, fills out the details this way:

> After night fall the corpse was carried forth without any shouting or noise into a Great Barn. . . . About midnight, most of the company being then gathered that was expected to come, great platters of boiled flesh were brought into the barn and abundance of bread, all made in fine white cakes of wheat flour. I do not here mean small cakes like our saffron ones or biscuits, but of size as large as a sieve and near three inches thick, portions of which with flesh was [*sic*] distributed to every one of the people,

and great tubs of drink . . . with which they filled themselves so that all night they kept an intolerable belching, though I did not hear one make a crack at the other end, so odious is this among them and so little is the other taken notice of. . . . And now came tobacco and pipes, and sneezing, and of a sudden I had such a representation of hell as Don Que Vevodo himself never saw. . . . The elder sort of sat sneezing or belching, whilst a lusty young fellow snatches a kercher (that is the wreath of linen wherewith the women's heads are covered) from her head, and tied it about his hat as a distinguishing mark of his office among them. Then as captain or master of misrule he selected a band of about a dozen young fellows who hauled out so many women of the younger sort for their mates; and by these were the rudest, most unpolished and barbarous sorts of sports used that ever were seen, especially in such a place where such an object of mortality lay; to which not one that I saw showed the least regard.[42]

We know from other contemporary reports as well that the English, from the time of their first acquaintance with the Irish, found the wake an abomination; and if he has not made it abundantly apparent already through his editorializing, Dunton goes on to close his narrative with undisguised condemnation: "In short, such was the unexpressible rudeness I saw there, that I know not whether I had not as soon suffer a dead friend to be disfigured by rats, as expose him to such unaccountable barbarity; and if any stranger were to make a judgment of the other customs of the Irish by this one of waking their dead, he might justly reckon them among the rudest and most beastly people in the world."[43] The English and Irish funeral customs are wholly incompatible; this, as I have suggested earlier, is one of the reasons for the subterranean tensions the reader feels in the "Hades" episode. The English tradition implicitly encourages, while not explicitly valorizing, a posture of "moody brooding" in the "bereaved"; the wake tradition encourages a larger, almost cosmic view of the death, a perspective that helps the "bereaved" to transcend the limitations of narrow egotism. The bereaved are the focus of attention at an English funeral; at an Irish wake, the focus is the deceased: as O Súilleabháin suggests, "The great occasion was in honour of the deceased alone, and he was the one and only guest. We can more easily understand, if we remember this viewpoint, why cards were put into the hands of the corpse, or a pipe into his mouth, or why, on some occasions, the dead was taken out on the floor to join in the dance."[44]

The wake in the Joyce corpus which most fully embodies this carnivalesque spirit is, of course, Finnegan's. While in one sense the entire book is a wake, the most condensed wake "scene" occurs just a few pages from the opening "riverrun":

> Shize? I should shee! Macool, Macool, orra whyi deed ye diie? of a trying thirstay mournin? Sobs they sighdid at Fillagain's chrissormiss wake, all the hoolivans of the nation, prostrated in their consternation and their duodisimally profusive plethora of ululation. There was plumbs and grumes and cheriffs and citherers and raiders and cinemen too. And the all gianed in with the shoutmost shoviality. Agog and magog and the round of them agrog. To the continuation of that celebration until Hanand-hunigan's extermination! Some in kinkin corass, more, kankan keening. Belling him up and filling him down. He's stiff but he's steady is Priam Olim! 'Twas he was the dacent gaylabouring youth. Sharpen his pillows-cone, tap up his bier! E'erawhere in this whorl would ye hear sich a din again? With their deepbrow fundigs and the dusty fidelios. They laid him brawdawn alanglast bed. With a bockalips of finisky fore his feet. And a barrowload of guenesis hoer his head. Tee the tootal of the fluid hang the twoddle of the fuddled, O! (*FW* 6)

Inspired by the description in the Irish American ballad, Finnegan's wake is a far more festive occasion than urban Irish wakes had become by the twentieth century.

Joyce's first treatment of funeral rites and the rites of passage from life to death is the rather halfhearted wake given Father Flynn in "The Sisters." As the story opens, Father Flynn is already dead, and the second half of the story takes place in the parlor downstairs from the corpse. Nannie and Eliza hold a very tame sort of wake for their deceased brother—the guests partake of sherry and cream crackers (much like the "festivities" Patsy Dignam opts to forgo). Rather than a festive, carnivalesque celebration, Father Flynn's "wake" is thick with tension:

> No one spoke: we all gazed at the empty fireplace.
> My aunt waited until Eliza sighed and then said:
> –Ah, well, he's gone to a better world.
> Eliza sighed again and bowed her head in assent. My aunt fingered the stem of her wine-glass before sipping a little.
> –Did he . . . peacefully? she asked.
> –O, quite peacefully, ma'am, said Eliza. You couldn't tell when the breath went out of him. He had a beautiful death, God be praised. (*D* 15)

The obvious explanation for the relative solemnity of Father Flynn's wake is that a Dionysian celebration would not have been thought proper for an Irish Catholic priest. Despite some of the claims of the Irish Cath-

olic Church down through the centuries, the wake is *not* in its conception a Christian institution, and the Church's pronouncements against the
Irish wake have been continuous since at least the seventeenth century,
and probably much earlier. O Súilleabháin notes that "The lively, merry,
boisterous wakes of former years have almost totally disappeared; only
their memory remains. New ideas, new ways of thinking and, above all,
the influence of the Church have all been involved in their ending. The
more or less continual barrage of episcopal condemnation of abuses
slowly, but surely, achieved its purpose."[45] As any reader of Joyce knows,
the Irish are an intensely religious people, in form if not always in substance. What I have to this point been calling the English attitude toward death is very strong in the Church as well. Both the British and
the Irish Catholic Church found the wake in some way threatening;
when a people no longer fears death, those who seek to tame it have lost
a very significant part of their control. O Súilleabháin goes on to cite
some of the many Church condemnations of the "pagan" Irish wake:

> We also condemn and reprobate, in the strongest terms, all unnatural
> screams and shrieks, and fictitious, tuneful cries and elegies, at wakes,
> together with the savage custom of howling and bawling at funerals, rather
> to join, at the proper times, during the night and morning of the wake,
> with other pious persons, in fervent prayer, for the soul of the deceased:
> to comfort those that are in affliction, and in the interim also to meditate
> seriously on death, or otherwise to observe a becoming silence; shewing
> in their whole deportment a most edifying and sober gravity—which
> should always appear in every Christian on so awful an occasion, where
> the real image of death lies before his eyes.

> Since the original purpose of wakes was that the soul of the deceased
> might be helped by the prayers of those who attended, it is evident that
> this purpose is being defeated when immodest games are carried on, which
> suppress the memory of Death in the minds of those present.

> At every wake, some good book concerning Death or Hell or Judgment
> or Heaven should be read.

> They [the clergy] must point out to the parishioners that the playing of
> lewd games at wakes, where Death should rather be pondered on, is syn-
> onymous with turning their backs on their Faith.[46]

Clearly, the Church's view of wakes was such as to rule out a true "funferal" for Father Flynn. For carnival laughter is anarchic; "In the world
of carnival the awareness of the people's immortality is combined with
the realization that established authority and truth are relative" (*R* 256).

Joyce's fullest attempt at describing an urban late-nineteenth/early-twentieth-century wake is Stephen's sister Isabel's wake in *Stephen Hero*. Isabel's wake, while it remains in the background of the episode, is still a more thorough rendering than the death and rites of the Rev. James Flynn. In *Stephen Hero*, Stephen's sister Isabel dies, and the vigil at the Daedalus house is described in some detail: "Isabel's death was the occasion of bringing to the house many of Mrs. Daedalus' relatives. They knocked a little timidly at the hall-door and though they were very retiring in manner their host convicted them—the females, at least—privately of making a cunning use of their eyes. The males he received in the long empty drawingroom in which an early fire had been lit. During the two nights of the girl's wake a big company assembled in the drawingroom: they did not smoke but they drank and told stories. The morning after the table looked like a marine-stores so crowded was it with empty bottles, black and green" (*SH* 166). Because *Stephen Hero* remained unpublished at the time of the writing of *Ulysses*, Joyce felt free to cannibalize that material for his new novel, and the "Hades" episode borrows broadly from Isabel's funeral. The most significant difference, of course, is that Isabel has the wake that Paddy never does. Although Isabel's wake is a relatively solemn affair (she was after all only a young girl, taken in the prime of life), there are hints, as in the "Hades" episode of *Ulysses*, of a more festive spirit trying to break loose. Mr. Daedalus, greeting the women at the door, accuses them of "making a cunning use of their eyes." They have come to the door knocking a little timidly, and Mr. Daedalus seems determined from the start to relieve some of the tension that everyone associated with the wake feels. As time passes, stories are told, and, more important, much alcohol is consumed. The collection of beer bottles on the table the next morning is in some sense symbolic of the two spirits present at the wake: the black bottles of death and mourning and the green bottles of life and regeneration.

Alcohol is an important ingredient in Isabel's wake and continues to be important after her funeral. A second major difference between the interments of Isabel and Paddy is that after Isabel's burial, the funeral party stop for a drink:

> The mourning party . . . got into the carriages and drove back along the Glasnevin road. At Dunphy's corner the carriage drew up behind the carriages of other funerals. In the bar Mr. Wilkinson stood the party the first drink: the drivers of the carriages were called in and they stood by the door in a clump and rubbed their coat-sleeves across their bony battered-looking faces until they were asked to name their drink. They all chose

pints and indeed their own bodily tenements were not unlike hardly used
pewter measures. The mourners drank small specials for the most part.
Stephen, when asked what he would drink, answered at once:
—A pint. (*SH* 168)

The drinks paid for by Mr. Wilkinson are but the "first drinks" of the afternoon, and if, as is the Irish custom, each of the men in the funeral
party stands the group a drink, the mourners will not be leaving Dunphy's soon.

In the "Hades" episode of *Ulysses*, drinks, although anticipated, are
not forthcoming. "First round Dunphy's," Simon Dedalus says as the
funeral carriage approaches the pub on the way to the cemetery (*U* 81);
it is difficult, if not impossible, to determine in this context whether
"round" is meant as a description of their carriage's course ("'Dunphy's,'
Mr. Power announced as the carriage turned right"), or rather refers to
a round of drinks to follow the interment. But if Simon is referring to
drinks after the funeral, those drinks are never imbibed—or if drunk,
they're drunk offstage. No scene of postfuneral drinking is narrated in
Ulysses. Both Bloom and Simon Dedalus appear in the newspaper office
in the next episode, not having "passed round the consolation," as Bloom
had expected they would do: "Dunphy's corner," Bloom thinks as they
drive by. "Mourning coaches drawn up, drowning their grief. A pause
by the wayside. Tiptop position for a pub. Expect we'll pull up here on
the way back to drink his health. Pass round the consolation. Elixir of
life" (*U* 81). Drinking to Paddy's "health," as Bloom puts it, would have
been a bit belated; but the benefits of funeral drinking, as Bloom goes
on to articulate, are not for the dead, but for the living. The drinking is
consolation for the living; drinking to the memory of the dead, drinking the *"charitas vini,"* is, like the wake, a defiant assertion of life in the
face of death. Bloom's concluding phrase, "elixir of life," is nearly a literal translation of the Irish for whiskey, *uisce beathadh* (English: "usque-
baugh," literally "water of life"), which, as Robert Adams remarks, "has
been known to raise Irishmen from the dead."[47] Raise the dead is precisely what whiskey does in the ballad from which Joyce's last novel
takes its name:

> One morning Tim was rather full,
>   His head felt heavy which made him shake,
> He fell from the ladder and broke his skull,
>   So they carried him home his corpse to wake.
> . . . .
> Then Mickey Malone raised his head,

> When a noggin of whiskey flew at him,
> It missed and falling on the bed,
> The liquor scattered over Tim;
> Bedad he revives, see how he rises,
> And Timothy rising from the bed,
> Says, "Whirl your liquor round like blazes,
> Thanam o'n dhoul, do ye think I'm dead?" (*JJ* 543–44).

As Adams points out, "The whole question of drink, which bulked so large as a social issue in Ireland around the turn of the century, is crucially if ambiguously related to the events of the chapter. Paddy Dignam is dead of drink after having lost his job because of drink; prudent Molly says the last word on the social drinking that leads inevitably to this end: 'and they call that friendship killing and then burying one another.' Richie Goulding has clearly set his foot on the same path. But Joyce also represents a heroic dimension in Irish drinking—it is a kind of tribal communion, a celebration of the revival of a buried god."[48] In Irish folklore, whiskey has the power to raise the dead; but Bloom is interested not so much in drink's mythical powers, the "creamy dreamy" (*U* 225), as in "warm fullblooded life" (*U* 94). If the "elixir of life" has any value, if there is "a heroic dimension" to becoming "usquebauched" (*FW* 319), it is that the living may have life, and have it abundantly.

But as Adams indicates, there is of course a darker side to all this drinking. At Isabel's wake and after her burial drinking serves as a release for tension and as an act of communion, as do the tamer sherry and cream crackers at Paddy Dignam's and Father Flynn's wakes. But alcohol also kills. It has killed Paddy Dignam, as Bloom realizes: "Blazing face: redhot. Too much John Barleycorn. Cure for a red nose. Drink like the devil till it turns adelite. A lot of money he spent colouring it" (*U* 79). It looks as if, in time, it may kill Richie Goulding as well; some would argue that it killed Joyce. But there does seem to be something "heroic" about such a death, about going "proud, open-eyed and laughing to the tomb." Bakhtin speaks of the "gay diseases" gout and syphilis, "the result of overindulgence in food, drink, and sexual intercourse" (*R* 161); surely alcoholism would qualify as one of these "gay diseases."

Bloom's last phrase while looking at Paddy, "A lot of money he spent in colouring it [his nose]," brings out another important aspect of the wake—its extravagance. O Súilleabháin points out that the family of the deceased was almost expected to go into debt for the wake: "The cost of providing the means for such celebrations at wakes and funerals must have fallen heavily on the relatives of the deceased. Indeed, many contemporary commentators (mainly foreigners) on this aspect of death customs stated that many a family became impoverished on account of it."[49] But even this impoverishment has a place in the strange economy of the wake; by depleting their stores, the family of the deceased show their faith in the social network, which will not let them starve. Georges Bataille explains it this way: "Society is essentially based on the weakness of the individuals for which its own strength compensates. In a sense it is that which the individual is not—it is bound to the primacy of the future. Yet it cannot deny the present: that remains an element about which no definite decision is reached. This is where festivity comes in. During feasts, sacrifice constitutes the significant moment: it concentrates the attention on the expenditure of resources for the sake of the present moment—the expenditure of those very resources which care for the morrow should warn us to preserve."[50]

The extravagance associated with the wake serves to affirm the present moment. It is also a profoundly communal gesture; it is at once a celebration of community and a gesture of surrender to the flux of life. This, according to Bakhtin, is the essence of the "festive": "The feast is always essentially related to time, either to the recurrence of an event in the natural (cosmic) cycle, or to biological or historical timeliness. Moreover, through all the stages of historic development feasts were linked to moments of crisis, of breaking points in the cycle of nature or in the life of society and man" (R 9). The death of the head of the household is of course one of these "moments of crisis" in the life of society. The wake, then, functions as a rite of passage in the life of the individual and of the family, both nuclear (the Dignams) and extended (friends, relatives, Sandymount society). But the funeral and wake are unique among rites of passage, for in all other rites the "guest of honor" is an active participant; here the deceased is obviously present but does not play an active part, his death rather functioning to reaffirm the links amongst family members and between the family and society. By exhausting their resources on the wake, the family at once invites society to join in the festival and puts itself in a (financially) vulnerable position, trusting its future to the beneficence of society. At the moment of death one is most poignantly alone; and yet that death then serves as a spur to community, for the funeral rites are always a communal act. Thus, when Bloom sees "M'Intosh" at the graveside, he thinks: "Now who is that lankylooking galoot over there in the macintosh? Now who is he I'd like to know? Now I'd give a trifle to know who he is. Always someone turns up you never dreamt of. A fellow could live on his lonesome all his life. Yes, he could. Still he'd have to get someone to sod him after he died though he could dig his own grave. We all do. Only man buries. No, ants too" (*U* 90). Dignam tragically has dug his own grave, and has had to "get someone to sod him." To the degree that his "sodding" unites society, his death is sacrificial and "not in vain."

Wake not only functions as an (absent) structural center in the "Hades" episode; the linguistic sign "wake" goes through various permutations throughout the text of *Ulysses*, unsettling the text wherever it appears. In the title of his last novel Joyce played with the multiple meanings of the word "wake" by leaving "Finnegans" without an apostrophe; and it is perhaps not too fanciful to suppose that the multiple meanings of "wake" were in his mind at some level as early as the composition of *Ulysses*. In an essay on *Finnegans Wake*, Stephen Heath explores the various meanings of "wake": "The focus of the writing of *Finnegans Wake* between night and day is given in the 'wake' of the title: between the wake of death and the wake of life (the wideawake language), the wake of the perpetual tracing of forms, as one speaks of the 'wake' of a ship, and disturbance, division, difference traced over the surface of the sea. This wake is that described by Derrida as *différance*, 'the movement by which language, or any other code, any system of reference in general becomes "historically" constituted as a fabric of differences.'"[51] Only once in *Ulysses* does the word *wake* occur where it undoubtedly refers to funeral merrymaking. A few pages into the "Hades" episode, Bloom thinks of Tweedy, the crown solicitor for Waterford, who has had a "Terrible comedown, poor wretch! Kicked about like snuff at a wake" (*U* 77). The phrase is a second-draft addition, and looks it; it seems to have the same ontological status/function as the added reference to wind in the "Aeolus" episode, or the river names in "Anna Livia Plurabelle"— thematic ornamentation, "excessive form," rather than being germane to the matter of the episode or to Bloom's state of consciousness. But its occurrence does introduce the idea of the wake to an episode that otherwise would contain no mention of it, despite its comic deployment of the suppressed wake's energies.

This, then, is the illicit Joyce of postmodernism. With world enough and time, I would move on here to a consideration of the larger implications—political as well as aesthetic—of Joyce's nascent postmodernity; I am to some degree comforted by the fact that so many recent studies have investigated the politics of Joyce's styles and textual practices.[52] Style is never innocent. Lest we should forget, Mikhail Bakhtin's work serves to remind us that stylistic experimentation, in any but the worst sort of dilettante, is always coterminous with an ideological position; in Joyce's case, as with all carnivalesque writers, that stance was anti-authoritarian and antidogmatic. Bakhtin called this responsibility for one's art "answerability"; in "Art and Answerability," he writes: "For as much as I have experienced and understood in art, I must answer with my life, so that what I have experienced and understood in art does not remain without effect in life."[53] The anarchic and irreverent stylistic upheavals that mark the last twenty years of Joyce's career are about as close to overt political involvement as this quiet and humane man ever got. Given the sometimes ugly political legacy bequeathed by the modernists (one thinks of Pound, Lewis, Yeats . . .), Joyce's "doctrinaire" refusal to side with any political movement or regime must be seen as the natural result of the gay relativity of his late work.[54] Speaking of the modernist "episteme," Hassan notes that "the Authority of Modernism—artistic, cultural, personal—rests on intense, elitist, self-generated orders in times of crisis, of which the Hemingway Code is perhaps the starkest exemplar, and Eliot's Tradition or Yeats's Ceremony is a more devious kind. Such elitist orders, perhaps the last of the world's Eleusinian mysteries, may no longer have a place amongst us, threatened as we are, at the same instant, by extermination and totalitarianism" (Hassan 45). This is perhaps the most compelling reason of all to reread modernism through postmodern glasses: to bring to the dock the works of our modernity and to try to discover wherein lies their freedom—to discover within the works of the modernists themselves the antidote to their sometimes "authoritative discourse." When we do look, we will find that it is, in many cases, there; our postmodern glosses might then help us to confer on the great works of modernism an altogether different legacy.

Afterword: On Ignoring *Finnegans Wake*

Ulysses towers over the rest of Joyce's writings, and in comparison to its noble originality and unique lucidity of thought and style the unfortunate *Finnegans Wake* is nothing but a formless and dull mass of phony folklore, a cold pudding of a book, a persistent snore in the next room, most aggravating to the insomniac I am. . . . *Finnegans Wake*'s façade disguises a very conventional and drab tenement house, and only the infrequent snatches of heavenly intonations redeem it from utter insipidity. I know I am going to be excommunicated for this pronouncement.

—Vladimir Nabokov

Finnegans Wake is, of course, the one book that is considered by nearly all of Joyce's commentators to be a postmodern text: "a monstrous prophecy of our postmodernity," Ihab Hassan calls it, "a monstrous prophecy that we have begun to discover (thanks to many deep readers) but have not yet decided how to heed" (Hassan 115, 99). For the writer of a book on Joyce and postmodernism, then, this final chapter should be a cakewalk; and yet, as my chapter title suggests, it's a text I've largely ignored. The growing body of critical writing on *Finnegans Wake* testifies to the continuing fascination it has exercised over a number of contemporary continental theoreticians, including Michel Butor, Hélène Cixous, Jacques Derrida, Umberto Eco, Julia Kristeva, Jacques Lacan, Philippe Sollers, and others; Hassan would appear to be right when he suggests that "all good structuralists [and, apparently, poststructuralists] go to *Finnegans Wake* on their way to heaven" (Hassan 107).[1] Surely, the *Wake*'s stock has been extraordinarily strong for the past twenty-five years within the Joyce community as well; beginning with Norman O. Brown's *Closing Time* (1973), a minimum reading list would include Ihab Hassan's *Paracriticisms: Seven Speculations for the Times* (1975), Margot Norris's *The Decentered Universe of "Finnegans Wake"* (1976), John Bishop's *Joyce's Book of the Dark* (1986), David Hayman's *The "Wake" in Transit* (1990), Kimberly J. Devlin's *Wandering and Return in "Finnegans Wake"* (1991), and the five installments of John Cage's *Writing through Finnegans Wake* (1976–81).

If ever there was a book written for the postmodern moment, it would seem to be *Finnegans Wake*. Indeed, one begins to suspect that had Joyce not written *Finnegans Wake*, contemporary literary theory would have had to invent it: for in its willfully overdetermined structure and self-conscious Babel of languages, poststructural theory finds the ideal proof-text for every aspect of postmodern *écriture*. As Margot Norris puts it: "Although James Joyce's *Finnegans Wake* is generally credited with the invention of postmodernism . . . one could argue that it is the other way around: that postmodern theory rescued *Finnegans Wake* from its marginalization by New Criticism and endowed it with a rationale for canonization. By transforming all of the *Wake*'s resistances to critical domestication—its unintelligibility, its neologismical language, its logo-poetic self-referentiality—into the marks of metaphysical invention, post-modern criticism made *Finnegans Wake* the spearhead of a literature of philosophically revolutionary potential."[2] Norris's argument here, how-ever, isn't that *Finnegans Wake* doesn't deserve its place of honor in the pantheon of postmodern literature; rather, she argues that in writing about the *Wake* we've privileged a Derridean notion of textuality at the cost of effacing the text's engagement with modern European history, an oversight Norris begins in her essay to correct.

But in the face of such formidable opposition, I want to suggest here—briefly—that the *Wake*'s stylistic upheaval is, paradoxically enough, a less revolutionary stylistics than that which Joyce produced in *Ulysses*. For in spite of its surface compliance with an outside structuring device (the Homeric parallels), *Ulysses* merely obeys the letter of the law; it is a spiritually lawless text, concerned with getting out from under the tyr-anny imposed by a unitary voice or style. *Finnegans Wake* on the other hand, while obviously breaking sharply with traditional notions of char-acter, plot, narrative, and even the stylistic practices of Joyce's earlier texts, establishes its own law outside the received law once it has bro-ken free—becomes a law unto itself. *Finnegans Wake*, though one may never be quite *comfortable* reading it, does get noticeably easier the fur-ther one reads; its "initial style" is also its final style. The protean *Ulys-ses* is never the same text long enough for one to grow accustomed to its manifold strategies. *Ulysses* is a guerrilla text, constantly shifting the grounds of its narrative experiments; *Finnegans Wake* is an outlaw all right, but remains consistent within itself in a way that *Ulysses* does not care to.[3] *Finnegans Wake* makes *us* laugh, and laugh at ourselves; but we do not see the text laughing at itself to the extent we do in *Ulysses*. *Finnegans Wake* does violence to the word, the phrase, the sentence; *Ulysses* explodes the very notion of the Book.[4] This seeming regression may be explicable within the framework of Lyotard's analysis of modernism and postmodernism; *Ulysses* would be the postmodern work which clears a space for the untimely modernism of *Finnegans Wake*.

In the superlanguage of *Finnegans Wake* Joyce attempts to overcome the inherent limitations of any national language, or any dialect, or any sociolect, as Bakhtin would call them. To Stefan Zweig, Joyce insisted, "I'd like a language which is above all languages, a language to which all will do service" (*JJ* 397). But Bakhtin, Barthes, and Lyotard would all find such a gesture utopian. Even the Joyce who drafted *Stephen Hero* would seem not to endorse such a project; in this book's opening chapter I discussed briefly the irony with which Stephen Daedalus's pretensions to intellectual "vivisection," plain scientific ideas in plain words, were treated. In effect, the linguistic project of *Finnegans Wake* betrays the wisdom that the author of *Stephen Hero* showed when he ironically exposed the naivete of Stephen Daedalus, who wanted a precise, scientific language that would not distort the world of experience; in *Finnegans Wake* Joyce seems instead to want an expressionistic, synthetic language that will not distort that world. Christopher Butler has written of Joyce's texts generally that "stylistic diversity enshrines an essentially relativist attitude towards the 'truthful' depiction of reality";[5] Joyce's Babel-busting stance in the *Wake*, however, would seem to violate that relativistic awareness.

While disliking the *Wake* cuts me off from a rather august group of admirers—among them some very smart critics who are also good friends—I'm not exactly all alone out here. Unfortunately, though, I think most of the early resistance to *Finnegans Wake* was reactionary rather than principled, and examples of criticism hostile to *Dubliners, A Portrait*, and *Ulysses* could be adduced with equal ease. Two examples come to mind, however, of readers who most certainly *should* have been sympathetic to Joyce's final project but, try as they might, couldn't warm up to *Finnegans Wake*. One is Joyce's brother Stanislaus. The complete record of their disagreement over the value of *Finnegans Wake* is recorded in just one letter from volume 3 of the *Letters;* in order to create the proper atmosphere, let me quote just the "tasty bits" from that 7 August 1924 letter to James, written by Stanislaus after having read an early installment of the *Wake* ("Mamalujo") in the *Transatlantic Review:*

I have received one instalment of your yet unnamed novel in the Transatlantic Review. I don't know whether the drivelling rigmarole about half
a tall hat and ladies' modern toilet chambers (practically the only things
I understand in this nightmare production) is written with the deliberate
intention of pulling the reader's leg or not. . . . Or perhaps—a sadder sup-
position—it is the beginning of softening of the brain. The first instalment faintly suggests the Book of the Four Masters and a kind of Biddy
in Blunderland and a satire on the supposed matriarchal system. It has
certain characteristics of a beginning of something, is nebulous, chaotic
but contains certain elements. That is absolutely all I can make of it. But!
It is unspeakably wearisome. Gorman's book on you practically proclaims
your work as the last word in modern literature. It may be the last in another sense, the witless wandering of literature before its final extinction.
Not that I imagine that literature will ever die as long as men speak and
write. But they may cease to read or at least to read such things. I for one
would not read more than a paragraph of it, if I did not know you. . . .

    If literature is to develop along the lines of your latest work it will cer-
tainly become, as Shakespeare hinted centuries ago, much ado about nothing. Ford in an article you sent me suggests that the whole thing is to be
taken as a nonsense rhythm and that the reader should abandon himself
to the sway of it. I am sure, though the article seems to have your approval, that he is talking through his half a tall hat. In any case I refuse to
allow myself to be whirled round in the mad dance by a literary dervish.
(L 3:102–3)

Clearly, there's more than simple literary criticism going on here; Stanislaus and James had experienced something of a rift, and at least part
of the venom vented here is personal, not professional. It is true, as well,
that this is an early reaction; it is, however—perhaps not insignificantly—
Stanislaus' only comment on *Finnegans Wake* preserved in the *Letters*.
When Joyce attempted to present him with a copy of *Finnegans Wake*
when it was published in 1939, Stanislaus refused it; in *My Brother's
Keeper*, written during World War II, his brother's final novel is almost
completely ignored.[6]

    I suppose the line in this letter that most haunts me is the last line in
the first paragraph I've quoted: "I for one would not read more than a
paragraph of it, if I did not know you." Hugh Kenner has written that
without *Ulysses*, *Dubliners* would be just another book, long since forgotten; I think this is even more true of *Finnegans Wake* than of *Dubliners* or *A Portrait*. As Stanislaus suggests, *Finnegans Wake* may be a novel
that rides on the coattails of its elder siblings—sort of the Billy Carter
or Roger Clinton of modern literature. In a note to chapter 1 I mused a
bit about how our preconceptions affect the way we approach Joyce's

texts; there, I talked about how allowing Joyce the benefit of the doubt results in our reading *A Portrait* as an ironic text, in the way that Kenner has. The same thing, on a much larger scale, is I believe at work in the reception of *Finnegans Wake;* and by the time the *Wake* was published, after appearing "in progress" for almost fifteen years, Joyce had put quite a literary-critical/promotional machinery in place for the volume, including but certainly not limited to the Festschrift he organized in 1929—ten years before the novel was published!—*Our Exagmination Round His Factification for Incamination of Work in Progress.* Stanislaus hints at this in the second paragraph I've quoted, in which he refers to Ford Madox Ford's article which suggests a strategy for reading *Work in Progress*—an article mailed to him by his brother, and which he suspects bears his brother's seal of approval.

The second notable early snub came from Ezra Pound. Pound, of course, had expressed reservations about some of the wilder episodes of *Ulysses* (as had Stanislaus), but ultimately came around to Joyce's way of seeing things; about *Finnegans Wake,* though, he never did. His first written response (to MS pages of *Finnegans Wake*), a letter of 15 November 1926 (and thus following hard on the heels of Stanislaus' rebuff), looks like this:

> Ms. arrived this A.M. All I can do is to wish you every possible success.
>
> I will have another go at it, but up to present I make nothing of it whatever. Nothing so far as I make out, nothing short of divine vision or a new cure for the clapp can possibly be worth all the circumambient peripherization.
>
> Doubtless there are patient souls, who will wade through anything for the sake of the possible joke . . . but . . . having no inkling whether the purpose of the author is to amuse or instruct . . . in somma. . . .
>
> Up to the present I have found diversion in the Tristan and Iseult paragraphs that you read years ago . . . mais apart ça. . . . And in any case I don't see what which has to do with where. . . . Undsoweiter. (*L* 3:146; ellipses in original)

Though he and Joyce largely stayed on good terms, Pound's opinion of *Finnegans Wake* never really improved; in a piece for the *New Review* (1931), Pound tried to make light of their differences of opinion: "I thoroughly approve of Mr. Joyce making experiments; he is at liberty to dine in restaurants I dislike; no man could write two 'Ulysses,' one after the other. . . . I respect Mr. Joyce's integrity as an author in that he has not taken the easy path. I never had any respect for his common sense or for his intelligence. I mean general intelligence, apart from his gifts as a writer."[7] As time wore on, however, Pound lost his patience; in 1934, he

wrote in the *New English Weekly,* "Joyce's mind has been deprived of
Joyce's eyesight for too long. You cannot say it is closed altogether, but
Joyce knows very little of life as it has been in the large since he finished
'Ulysses.' He has sat within the grove of his thought, he has mumbled
things to himself, he has heard his voice on the phonograph and thought
of sound, sound, mumble, murmur."[8] So it was not merely prejudiced
Joyce detractors who decried *Finnegans Wake,* but in fact some of his life-
long supporters. William Faulkner's epitaph for the *Wake* is perhaps my
favorite: "James Joyce was one of the great men of my time. He was
electrocuted by the divine fire. . . . He was probably—might have been
the greatest, but he was electrocuted. He had more talent than he could
control."[9]

What we need now, however, is not mere ad hominem attack, nor the
possibly jealous attacks of other writers, but a principled, intelligent,
resistant reading of *Finnegans Wake.* What we need, perhaps, is what
Carl Jung (in *"Ulysses:* A Monologue," which Calvin Bedient calls a "great,
greatly resisting, finally grateful essay on *Ulysses"*)[10] did for *Ulysses:*
critical writing that respects *Finnegans Wake* enough to take it seriously,
while respecting Joyce enough to face squarely the fact that not all of his
experiments were successes. It was a possibility that Joyce himself was
not afraid to countenance, though the novel cost him seventeen difficult
and painful years; "It is I who could draw up the best indictment against
my work," he said for example to Jacques Mercanton. "Isn't it arbitrary
to pretend to express the nocturnal life by means of conscious work, or
through children's games?"[11] If there's one obvious area in which Joyce
studies has thus far refused to postmodernize itself, it is this: that very
few, if any, commentators on Joyce's work are willing to resist the powerful influence of Joyce's promotional apparatuses and reputation. One
important element of a postmodern reassessment of Joyce, or any of the
larger-than-life figures of British and American literary modernism, must
be a willingness to point out Joyce's failures as well as his much-her-
alded successes—to cry out when the emperor has no clothes. To disagree with Beckett when he suggests that in Joyce's work "there isn't a
syllable that's superfluous"—that in his work Joyce was "tending toward omniscience and omnipotence as an artist."[12] Or with Anthony
Burgess when, parroting Beckett, he claims that *"Finnegans Wake* is one
of the few books of the world that totally resists cutting. Despite its
bulk, it contains not one word too many, and there is the danger that to
pull at a single thread will unravel the entire fabric."[13] Joyce is not God;
rather, he is a "poor dogsbody," fallible like the rest of us, and his texts
preserve a record of his failings as well as his triumphs. The time has

long since past for us to acknowledge that simple fact. If Joyce is as good as we say he is, he'll come out of it all right.

Nabokov, only half kidding, suggests (in this chapter's epigraph) that he'll be ostracized for his dissenting views on the importance of *Finnegans Wake*, and I share something of his apprehension. And I believe that the metaphor he chooses to convey his fear—that of excommunication from the Church—is especially apt. Look, for a moment, at these statements, taken from the early pages of three different studies of *Finnegans Wake*, which together span almost a quarter century of *Finnegans Wake* criticism:

> On first looking into Joyce's *Wake*—long ago when, as *Work in Progress*, it was coming out in the magazine *transition*—I too was dismayed; for I had expected another *Ulysses*. It was not until the fable of the Ondt and the Gracehoper appeared that I found the thing readable; and not until the publication of the *Wake* in 1939 that I found it good.

> Learning to read *Finnegans Wake* changed the way I read. I suspect that is the situation for other readers of the *Wake* as well. I never had been comfortable distinguishing literal from figural, what made sense from what did not, and *Finnegans Wake* reinforced that reluctance. It showed me the roots of coherence in incoherence, and of incoherence in coherence; it washed the literal so thoroughly in the figurative and the figurative in the literal that neither has come out "clean" again.

> It was becoming inevitable that I would attempt FW and I felt that since first looking at it I had been conserving my psychological assets in anticipation of the task. I made a new start in the summer. My technique was slightly fanatical. I was so anxious to capture the undistorted experience that on reaching page 29, where the first chapter ends, I tied a thread round all the remaining pages to prevent my accidentally looking ahead. Every few months there would be a solemn undoing of the thread: I would read a new chapter and then tie up the remaining ones. It took two and a half years to reach the end of FW.[14]

The authors of these testimonials are, respectively, William York Tindall, Susan Shaw Sailer, and Roland McHugh; many other commentators on *Finnegans Wake* have made similar statements, in a similar tone, and I certainly don't mean to single out these three texts for my skepticism. But these passages do have at least two characteristics in common which should command our attention here. The first is their similarity to traditional narratives of religious conversion. Those who write about *Finnegans Wake* seem to feel compelled to give us their testimony; for once they stood unbelieving outside the fold, before experiencing the novel in its full power—something of an epiphany, I suppose. They have been the unworthy recipients of *Finnegans Wake*'s amazing grace: "I once was lost, / But now am found, / Was blind but now I see." McHugh's entire small book is cast as the spiritual autobiography of a *Finnegans Wake* reader, ending, like the spiritual biography of Stephen Dedalus, with an ambivalently apostate gesture: "The longer you neglect Joyce's works, the more satisfying they eventually become. So for the present I'm giving *Finnegans Wake* a rest."[15]

The second salient feature of most writing on *Finnegans Wake* that these excerpts are meant to suggest is an unshakable belief in the novel's unique status in the canon of world literature. Thus reading *Finnegans Wake* is not, we are to understand, like reading any other book; indeed, understanding of "the *Wake*." And as a pseudosacred text, *Finnegans Wake* requires a specialized vocabulary, as well. The novel is not consistently referred to as *Finnegans Wake*—a manageable enough title, one would have thought—but is regularly called "the *Wake*" or, as in McHugh's book, simply "FW." It has accrued its own adjective ("Wakean"), and is said to be written in its own language ("Wakese"); it apparently requires its own citation format (*FW* 3.20), as if it were a sacred text, or an epic poem—or, one darkly suspects, as if the writer doubted his reader's willingness to read through an entire page in search of the passage in question.[16] Over the years, *Finnegans Wake* has garnered two periodicals to itself: *A Wake Newslitter* and *A Finnegans Wake Circular*. As the first (now defunct) periodical's title suggests, critics are fond of appropriating *Finnegans Wake*'s neologisms into the titles of their work—including, though not restricted to, *Finnegans Wake* alternatives for *Ulysses* ("miraculous sindbook," "ulyssesly unreadable blue book of Eccles," etc.). And throughout its devotees' narratives—both in the stories they tell, and in the language in which they choose to tell them—we are told that this is not a book to be attempted home alone.

Finnegans Wake is a conceptual novel, in the way that Cage's is conceptual music; as such, it suffers from the occupational hazard of conceptual art: it's more interesting as a concept than as art. I am a great admirer of John Cage, and yet I admit I'd rather read Cage on the idea behind the *Etudes Australes* and *Boreales* than listen to them; and I'd rather read Joyce's letters and reported comments on *Finnegans Wake*—and the responses that *Finnegans Wake* has occasioned in lively thinkers like Hugh Kenner, Bernard Benstock, Margot Norris, Umberto Eco, John Bishop, John Cage, Jacques Derrida, Derek Attridge, and so on—than read *Finnegans Wake* itself. Maybe I'm alone in this; but the remarks of

Stanislaus Joyce, Ezra Pound, William Faulkner and Vladimir Nabokov—along with many, many other well-known denunciations of *Finnegans Wake* that I've not bothered to rehearse here—suggest I'm not.

Finally, I believe the reason that *Finnegans Wake* is, for most of us, a less satisfactory text than *Ulysses*, is this: *Finnegans Wake* is industrial-strength postmodern stylistics; it's 99 and 44/100 percent pure. But in writing, that's not finally a very fulfilling blend. Postmodern stylistics derives a great deal of its pizzazz precisely from its brushing up against more staid language; it must interact dynamically, dialogically, with the language of the fathers, the language of the culture, rather than settling statically into a hermetic language of its own. In chapter 2, I mentioned briefly Kristeva's idea of limit texts: the notion that modernism and postmodernism exist not as alternatives (modern/postmodern), but as the two ends of a continuum of writing (modern→postmodern). If the instructions for assembling a tricycle stand at one pole, the stylistic anarchy of *Finnegans Wake* is nearly at the other; or as Yeats's Michael Robartes says in another context, "there's no human life at the full or the dark."[17] All texts of bliss—hell, even texts of pleasure—live in between the sterile poles of pure modernism and postmodernism.

To quote Barthes for the last time: "There are those who want a text (an art, a painting) without a shadow, without the 'dominant ideology'; but this is to want a text without fecundity, without productivity, a sterile text (see the myth of the Woman without a Shadow). The text needs its shadow: this shadow is *a bit* of ideology, *a bit* of representation, *a bit* of subject: ghosts, pockets, traces, necessary clouds: subversion must produce its own chiaroscuro" (*PT* 32). This is the problem with *Finnegans Wake*, as with a good deal of 1960s–1970s American metafiction: they're all text, no shadow; all postmodernism, no modernism. Such texts fulfill a sort of taxonomic function; *Finnegans Wake* itself has become a kind of museum exhibit of postmodern stylistics, a touchstone for the purity of those postmodern texts that live in the shade. But it's those shady texts, finally, that we hanker after.

Notes

Bibliography

Index

Notes

Preface

1. Leo Bersani, "Against *Ulysses*," *Raritan* 8, no. 2 (Fall 1988): 1–32.

Chapter 1. The Illicit Joyce of Postmodernism

1. In *The Pound Era,* Hugh Kenner writes of "any *Irish Homestead* reader's knowledge that no boat sails from Dublin to Buenos Aires. That boat from the North Wall is bound for Liverpool, and given Frank's show of easy prosperity we may wonder what will happen to Eveline there" ([Berkeley and Los Angeles: Univ. of California Press, 1971], 37). For an intelligent response to Kenner's various readings of "Eveline," see Sidney Feshbach, "'Fallen on His Feet in Buenos Ayres' (*D* 39): Frank in 'Eveline,'" *James Joyce Quarterly* 20 (1983): 223–27.

2. We might recall, as well, that Stephen's break with his mother, and Mother Church, comes over his refusal to perform his "easter duty" (*P* 239).

3. Eveline's situation, and her tortured question, would have been especially resonant for Joyce, of course, since on the night of 9 October 1904 Nora had followed him (at a respectable distance) onto a boat docked at the Dublin quays and into exile in Paris, never looking back.

4. These last two queries are chapter titles from Richard Ellmann's *"Ulysses" on the Liffey* (New York: Oxford Univ. Press, 1972), 23–26, 159–76.

5. I find this whole issue far more troubling that space here will allow me to explore. Let me give a salient example, which will come up again with a vengeance in chapter 5: How do we know that Joyce looks askance at Stephen's pride? The plurality of readings of the novel over the past twenty-five years or so agree that Stephen is the object of authorial irony. I personally agree with Hugh Kenner's reading of Stephen and the textual clues that are meant to tip us off to Stephen's preciousness; but let's face it, it's a *very* ingenious reading (see, for instance, Kenner's *Ulysses* [London: Allen & Unwin, 1982], 6–8). If the narrative is subtly undercutting Stephen's pretensions to grandeur, as Kenner and others maintain, why did it take readers more than fifty years to recognize the fact? I do believe that Joyce criticizes Stephen; I think our initial sympathy with him, and with his artistic project, is precisely the kind of "reader trap" I'll

talk about in chapter 4. What troubles me, I suppose, is whether we would ever have arrived at such clever readings, which exculpate Joyce from having written a callow novel, if we didn't start our inquiry with the presupposition that Joyce didn't write callow novels. Our reasoning follows this pseudosyllogistic outline: I admire Joyce's writing; I therefore approach a work like *A Portrait* with admiration, and if the work disappoints on some level—doesn't jibe with my sense of "the Joycean"—I assume the work to be ironic. "Joyce is better/ knows better than this," I reassure myself; "his portrait of Stephen must be ironic." Joyce must *know* that Stephen is precious; and if we look carefully at the language, we can *see* that he knows. This happens in criticism of *Ulysses*, as well; if Bloom gets some bit of physics wrong, we seem never to entertain the possibility that Joyce, and not only Bloom, might have made an error.

As I will argue in the afterword, I suspect that much the same mechanism is at work in the reception of *Finnegans Wake*. Joyce wrote it; Joyce is a genius, and can't have made a seventeen-year-long error (besides, "A man of genius makes no mistakes," as we've all learned from Stephen/Joyce. "His errors are volitional and are the portals of discovery" [*U* 156]); therefore, *Finnegans Wake* is a work of genius, a masterpiece. We must somehow get past this kind of thinking—that Joyce is, in Beckett's words, approaching omniscience and omnipotence as a writer—if we're to form a just estimation of his real genius.

6. Kevin J. H. Dettmar, ed., *Rereading the New: A Backward Glance at Modernism* (Ann Arbor: Univ. of Michigan Press, 1992), 14–15.

7. Laurie Anderson, "Language Is a Virus," *Home of the Brave*, Warner Bros. 9 25400-2; see also *United States* (New York: Harper & Row, 1984), n.p.

8. Donald Marshall, foreword to Stephen Melville, *Philosophy beside Itself* (Minneapolis: Univ. of Minnesota Press, 1986), xvi. I owe this reference to Eloise Knowlton; her essay "Fending off the Object: Criticism, Postcriticism, and the Joycean," in Dettmar, *Rereading the New*, investigates the phenomenon of "writing like a modernist" in far greater detail than I am able here.

9. Benjamin Lee Whorf, *Language, Thought, and Reality: Selected Writings of Benjamin Lee Whorf*, ed. John B. Carroll (Cambridge: M.I.T. Press, 1956), 214.

10. See Kevin J. H. Dettmar, "Selling *Ulysses*," *James Joyce Quarterly*, vol. 30, no. 4/vol. 31, no. 1 (Summer/Fall 1993): 795–812.

11. Derek Attridge and Daniel Ferrer, eds., *Post-Structuralist Joyce: Essays from the French* (Cambridge: Cambridge Univ. Press, 1984), 7.

12. Richard Rorty, *Philosophy and the Mirror of Nature* (Princeton: Princeton Univ. Press, 1979), 377.

13. Kevin J. H. Dettmar, "If Guinness Is as Cheap as Milk," rev. of Albert Wachtel, *The Cracked Lookingglass: James Joyce and the Nightmare of History*, *James Joyce Literary Supplement*, Fall 1992, 4.

14. Richard Eder, rev. of David Lehmann, *Signs of the Times*, *Los Angeles Times*, 14 Feb. 1991.

15. Gilles Deleuze and Claire Parnet, *Dialogues*, trans. Hugh Tomlinson and Barbara Habberjam (New York: Columbia Univ. Press, 1987), 16.

16. Dana Polan, Translator's Introduction, in Gilles Deleuze and Félix Guattari, *Kafka: Toward a Minor Literature*, trans. Polan (Minneapolis: Univ. of Minnesota Press, 1986), xxiv.

Chapter 2. Theorizing Postmodern Stylistics

1. Jack Solomon, *The Signs of Our Time: The Secret Meanings of Everyday Things* (1988; New York: Harper & Row, 1990), 211.

2. See, for instance, Morton P. Levitt's essay "The Invention of Postmodernism: A Critical Fable," in Dettmar, *Rereading the New*, 87–96.

3. Jean-François Lyotard, "Rules and Paradoxes and Svelte Appendix," trans. Brian Massumi, *Cultural Critique* 5 (Winter 1986–87): 209. See also "Note on the Meaning of 'Post-,'" in *The Postmodern Explained: Correspondence, 1982–1985*, ed. Julian Pefanis and Morgan Thomas, trans. Don Barry et al. (Minneapolis: Univ. of Minnesota Press, 1993), 75–80. Elsewhere, Lyotard has confessed, "I have myself used the term 'postmodern.' It was a slightly provocative way of placing (or displacing) into the limelight the debate about knowledge" ("Rewriting Modernity," in *The Inhuman: Reflections on Time*, trans. Geoffrey Bennington and Rachel Bowlby [Stanford: Stanford Univ. Press, 1991], 34).

4. Hassan xi; Thomas Docherty, ed., *Postmodernism: A Reader* (New York: Columbia Univ. Press, 1993), 1.

5. See Brian McHale, *Postmodernist Fiction* (New York: Methuen, 1987), 3–11.

6. Although McHale would not himself, I expect, accept this description of his work, since he makes much of the distinction between the "epistemological dominant" of modernism and the "ontological dominant" of postmodernism. Clearly, no critical work can be purely one or the other—perhaps it would be fair to say that McHale's study is governed by an "inductive dominant," mine by a "deductive dominant." In the sequel to *Postmodernist Fiction*, McHale implicitly modifies his earlier methodology: "The choice of one construct over the other . . . can only be made *strategically*, that is, in the light of the kind of work which, it is hoped, the construct could accomplish. By 'work' here I mean the generation of new insights, new connections and groupings, interesting problems and hypotheses, and so on. And this is the main criterion not only in the case of the competing constructions of modernism, but in literary periodization generally" (*Constructing Postmodernism* [London and New York: Routledge, 1992], 57–58).

7. See especially McHale's brief coda, "The Sense of Joyce's Endings," 233–35. His more recent essay on *Ulysses*, collected in *Constructing Postmodernism* (42–58), makes an argument more consonant with mine.

8. Linda Hutcheon, *A Poetics of Postmodernism: History, Theory, Fiction* (New York: Routledge, 1988), 88.

9. Jerome Klinkowitz is simply wrong to claim that *moderne* is the French word for "postmodernism" (*Rosenberg/Barthes/Hassan: The Postmodern Habit of Thought* [Athens: Univ. of Georgia Press, 1988], 76); but, as I will explore, the French

word *postmoderne* didn't exist until Lyotard imported it from English just months before Barthes's death. In spite of my quibble with his terminology, Klinkowitz's chapter on Barthes is the best short treatment to date of Barthes's postmodernity.

10. Like Lyotard in his early writings, Barthes also regularly distinguished between "classic" and "modern" texts, meaning by the latter what we would now call "postmodern" texts; for more on this problem of terminological slippage, see my discussion of Lyotard below.

11. Of critical studies that have appeared to date, only Mary Bittner Wiseman's *The Ecstasies of Roland Barthes* (Critics of the Twentieth Century Series [London: Routledge, 1989]) makes the connection between Barthes's writing and postmodernism. Wiseman writes that Barthes's experiments necessitate "the re-drawing of conceptual boundaries that follows upon the experiences of bliss or madness, Barthes's two ecstasies. The first ecstasy inaugurates a poststructuralism, the second a postmodernism" (xiv). Wiseman explores Barthes's "postmodern conception of the self or human subject" (2), and calls his "Inaugural Lecture, Collège de France" "a quiet manifesto of postmodernism" (15), but does not explore the stylistic contours of Barthes's postmodernism.

12. Roland Barthes, "Inaugural Lecture, Collège de France," trans. Richard Howard, in *A Barthes Reader*, ed. Susan Sontag (New York: Hill & Wang, 1982), 457.

13. Unfortunately, Barthes would later use "literature" as a term of praise, rather than disparagement: "In order to escape the subjection and power of language," he declares in his "Inaugural Lecture, Collège de France," "the only remaining alternative is, if I may say so, to cheat with speech, to cheat speech. This salutary trickery, this evasion, this grand imposture which allows us to understand speech *outside the bounds of power,* in the splendor of a permanent revolution of language, I for one call *literature*" (462).

14. In this last phrase I play on the title of Henry Sussman's book, *Afterimages of Modernity: Structure and Indifference in Twentieth-Century Literature* (Baltimore and London: Johns Hopkins Univ. Press, 1990).

Barthes meditates at some length on the stakes of his terminology in *The Pleasure of the Text:* "Is pleasure only a minor bliss? Is bliss nothing but extreme pleasure? Is pleasure only a weakened, conformist bliss—a bliss deflected through a pattern of conciliations? Is bliss merely a brutal, immediate (without mediation) pleasure? On the answer (yes or no) depends the way in which we shall write the history of our modernity. For if I say that between pleasure and bliss there is only a difference of degree, I am also saying that the history is a pacified one: the text of bliss is merely the logical, organic, historical development of the text of pleasure; the avant-garde is never anything but the progressive, emancipated form of past culture: today emerges from yesterday, Robbe-Grillet is already in Flaubert, Sollers in Rabelais, all of Nicolas de Stael in two square centimeters of Cézanne. But if I believe on the contrary that pleasure and bliss are parallel forces, that they cannot meet, and that between them there is more than a struggle: an *incommunication*, then I must certainly believe that history, our history, is not peaceable and perhaps not even intelligent, that the text of bliss always rises out of it like a scandal (an irregularity), that it is always the trace of a cut, of an assertion (and not a flowering)" (*PT* 20).

15. Wiseman, *Ecstasies of Roland Barthes*, 86.

16. Stephen quotes Whitman, "Song of Myself," section 51, ll. 6–7. In *Walt Whitman: The Complete Poems*, ed. Francis Murphy (New York: Penguin, 1975).

17. Roland Barthes, *Roland Barthes*, trans. Richard Howard (New York: Hill & Wang, 1977), 112.

18. Barthes, "Inaugural Lecture," 469.

19. Hence Randy Malamud's confident (and, I believe, mistaken) description of Joyce as a modernist stylist in as recent a book as his *The Language of Modernism* (Ann Arbor: UMI Research Press, 1989), 131–79.

20. The writing of realism depends upon a view of language that Jacques Derrida has called "white mythology." See "White Mythology: Metaphor in the Text of Philosophy," in *Margins of Philosophy*, trans. Alan Bass (Chicago: Univ. of Chicago Press, 1982), 207–71.

21. Barthes, "Inaugural Lecture," 462.

22. By which Barthes means that which we would now call the postmodern.

23. Israel Shenker, "Moody Man of Letters," in *Samuel Beckett: The Critical Heritage*, ed. Lawrence Graver and Raymond Federman (London: Routledge & Kegan Paul, 1979), 148.

24. Roland Barthes, *Critical Essays*, trans. Richard Howard (Evanston, Ill.: Northwestern Univ. Press, 1972), 144, 147.

25. Barthes, "Inaugural Lecture," 464.

26. Julia Kristeva, *Desire in Language: A Semiotic Approach to Literature and Art*, ed. Leon S. Roudiez, trans. Thomas Gora, Alice Jardine, and Leon S. Roudiez (New York: Columbia Univ. Press, 1980), 78.

27. Barthes, *Roland Barthes*, 179–80.

28. Although the Rabelais book wasn't published until 1965, it was written as a doctoral thesis in the 1930s.

29. Katerina Clark and Michael Holquist, *Mikhail Bakhtin* (Cambridge: Harvard Univ. Press, 1984), 317.

30. Ibid., 276.

31. Ibid., 80.

32. Kristeva, *Desire in Language*, 65.

33. Bakhtin's singling out of Byron here has important implications, I think, for the way we read *A Portrait*; since Joyce took his earlier self as the Byronic hero of that novel, it was never fully "novelized"—Stephen's voice drowns out all competing voices, resulting not in a dialogue, but rather in a self-important monologue. We will consider *A Portrait* in greater detail in chapter 5.

34. "In this book Joyce has arrived at a very singular and perhaps unique literary distinction: the distinction of having, not in a negative but a very positive sense, no style at all. I mean that every sentence Mr. Joyce writes is peculiarly

and absolutely his own; that his work is not a pastiche; but that nevertheless, it has none of the marks by which a 'style' may be distinguished" (T. S. Eliot, "Contemporary English Prose," *Vanity Fair* 20, no. 5 [July 1923], 51).

35. Claude Lévi-Strauss, *The Savage Mind* (Chicago: Univ. of Chicago Press, 1966), 17, 19.

36. Kristeva, *Desire in Language,* 65–66.

37. Again one is reminded of Eliot, this time the Eliot of "Tradition and the Individual Talent": "What happens when a new work of art is created is something that happens simultaneously to all the works of art which preceded it. The existing monuments form an ideal order among themselves, which is modified by the introduction of the new (the really new) work of art among them. The existing order is complete before the new work arrives; for order to persist after the supervention of novelty, the *whole* existing order must be, if ever so slightly, altered; and so the relations, proportions, values of each work of art toward the whole are readjusted; and this is conformity between the old and the new" (Eliot 38–39).

38. In this light, the etymology of "carnival" is rather ironic: from the medieval Latin *carnevale,* "removal of flesh." The English word *carnival,* then, works via carnivalesque logic: carnival (especially *mardi gras*) anticipates the "removal of flesh" with a full-bodied *celebration* of the flesh.

39. Friedrich Nietzsche, *The Birth of Tragedy and The Case of Wagner,* trans. Walter Kaufmann (New York: Viking, 1967), 40.

40. Jean-François Lyotard, *Driftworks,* ed. Roger McKeon (New York: Semiotext(e), 1984), 83.

41. Ibid., 26–27.

42. Julia Kristeva, *Revolution in Poetic Language,* trans. Margaret Waller (New York: Columbia Univ. Press, 1984), 81.

43. Lyotard, *Driftworks,* 28–29.

44. Kristeva, *Revolution,* 223.

45. Richard Pearce seems to have something like this in mind when he coins the term "body-text"; see his discussion in *The Politics of Narration: James Joyce, William Faulkner and Virginia Woolf* (New Brunswick: Rutgers Univ. Press, 1991), 50–55.

46. Kristeva, *Revolution,* 225.

47. This is perhaps Lyotard's best-known definition of postmodernism: "Simplifying to the extreme, I define *postmodern* as incredulity toward metanarratives. This incredulity is undoubtedly a product of progress in the sciences: but that progress in turn presupposes it. To the obsolescence of the metanarrative apparatus of legitimation corresponds, most notably, the crisis of metaphysical philosophy and of the university institution which in the past relied on it. The narrative function is losing its functors, its great hero, its great dangers, its great voyages, its great goal. It is being dispersed in clouds of narrative language elements—narrative, but also denotative, prescriptive, descriptive, and so on" (*PC* xxiv).

48. Lyotard's language here is very close to that of Samuel Beckett in the *Three Dialogues* with Georges Duthuit. Beckett describes the painting of Tal Coat as

"Total object, complete with missing parts, instead of partial object" (Samuel Beckett, *Disjecta: Miscellaneous Writings and a Dramatic Fragment*, ed. Ruby Cohn [London: John Calder, 1983], 138).

49. While not using the categories "modern" and "postmodern," Beckett was making this same distinction almost forty years ago in the *Three Dialogues*. The first two painters under discussion, Tal Coat and André Masson, are "modernists," "thrusting towards a more adequate expression of natural experience"; the third of the painters under discussion, Bram van Velde, is postmodern, creating an art that turns from the achievements of "the tradition" "in disgust," "weary of its puny exploits, weary of pretending to be able, of being able, of doing a little better the same old thing, of going a little further along a dreary road"—an art "unresentful of its insuperable indigence and too proud for the farce of giving and receiving" (Beckett, *Disjecta,* 138, 139, 141).

50. Julia Kristeva also focuses on the antifascist nature of postmodern writing in her one essay to date devoted to the subject; see "Postmodernism?" *Bucknell Review* 25, no. 2 (1980), 136–41.

51. Lyotard, *Driftworks*, 79.

52. The cyclic nature of modernism/postmodernism is implicit in Barthes's work as well, although he does not go as far as Lyotard, who maintains not only that modernism makes postmodernism possible, but that each postmodernism clears the ground for a new modernism.

53. Lyotard, *The Inhuman*, 25.

54. Ibid.

55. Ihab Hassan, *The Dismemberment of Orpheus: Toward a Postmodern Literature*, 2d ed. (Madison: Univ. of Wisconsin Press, 1982), 139.

56. Gilles Deleuze, "Intellectuals and Power," in Michel Foucault, *Language, Counter-Memory, Practice*, ed. Donald F. Bouchard, trans. Donald F. Bouchard and Sherry Simon (Ithaca: Cornell Univ. Press, 1977), 208.

57. Leon S. Roudiez, Introduction, in Kristeva, *Revolution*, 10.

58. Reviewing *Ulysses* in 1923, John Middleton Murry remarked precisely this quality: "The curse of nimiety, of too-muchness, hangs over it as a whole" (John Middleton Murry, review of *Ulysses, Nation & Athenæum*, 22 April 1922 [Deming 1:197]).

59. I have written about this antimetaphorical thrust in Beckett's fiction; see "The Figure in Beckett's Carpet: *Molloy* and the Assault on Metaphor," in *Rethinking Beckett: A Collection of Critical Essays*, ed. Lance St. John Butler and Robin J. Davis (Basingstoke: Macmillan; New York: St. Martin's, 1990), 68–88.

60. These examples belong to Roudiez; see his introduction to Kristeva, *Revolution*, 5.

Chapter 3. From Interpretation to "Intrepidation": "The Sisters"

1. This is, even by 1904 standards, a rather meager payment; Mr. Philip Beaufoy received "payment at the rate of one guinea a column"—a total of three

pounds, thirteen and six—for his *Tit-Bits* piece, "Matcham's Masterstroke" (*U* 56).

2. Marvin Magalaner and Richard M. Kain, *Joyce: The Man, the Work, the Reputation* (New York: New York Univ. Press, 1956), 54.

3. Michael Groden et al., eds., *The James Joyce Archive*, 63 vols. (New York: Garland, 1978), 4:3.

4. Joyce managed to overcome the indignity of this juxtaposition by using Cantrell & Cochrane's in *Ulysses*, where Leopold Bloom reads their ad: "Mr. Bloom stood at the corner, his eyes wandering over the multicoloured hoardings. Cantrell and Cochrane's Ginger Ale (Aromatic), Clery's Summer Sale" (*U* 62). Later, witnessing the mass at All Hallows, he thinks again of the ginger ale as a substitute for the communion wine: "Wine. Makes it more aristocratic than for example if he drank what they are used to Guinness's porter or some temperance beverage Wheatley's Dublin hop bitters or Cantrell and Cochrane's ginger ale (aromatic)" (*U* 67). And finally, in the "Sirens" episode, Miss Douce turns herself "with grace of alacrity towards the mirror gilt Cantrell and Cochrane's" (*U* 215).

5. Groden et al., *James Joyce Archive*, 4:3, 3a.

6. Ellmann writes, for instance, that during their first late-night meeting during the summer of 1902, Joyce "complained [to Æ] that Yeats had gone over to the rabblement" (*JJ* 99).

7. Jean-Michel Rabaté has also employed the vocabulary of this letter to talk of the animating principle of *Dubliners:* "For Joyce . . . coming to terms with the peculiar otherness that literature keeps in store meant a uniquely idiosyncratic combination of 'ghost' and 'imp' in the act of writing. . . . Are they fighting, ink versus pen, good angel versus evil genie, holy and perverse spirits playing out again the drama of yes and no, or are they united in a wholesale denunciation of Dublin? To try to answer this question will be my first step in this reading of Joyce's perverse strategies, a step which will take us to *Dubliners*" (Jean-Michel Rabaté, *James Joyce: Authorized Reader* [Baltimore and London: Johns Hopkins Univ. Press, 1991], 19).

8. Florence L. Walzl, *"Dubliners,"* in *A Companion to Joyce Studies*, ed. Zack Bowen and James F. Carens (Westport, Conn: Greenwood Press, 1984), 161. Cf. Joyce's letter to Harriet Shaw Weaver, 8 November 1916: "Mr Norman, editor of the *Irish Homestead* (Dublin), agreed to take stories from me but after the second story he told me that his readers had complained" (*L* 1:98).

9. Joyce seems to have known he had already worn out his welcome at the *Homestead;* he writes to Stanislaus in the letter that accompanied the manuscript of "Hallow Eve": "I send you the fourth story of 'Dubliners'—'Hallow Eve'—which I want you to offer at once to the Editor of the Irish Homestead. Perhaps they are annoyed with me and won't honour me by printing any more" (*L* 2:77).

10. William Gass, *In the Heart of the Heart of the Country* (Boston: Godine, 1981), xxvii. A comparison of the manuscript, serial, and *Dubliners* versions of "The

Sisters" points to the increasing complexity and indirection of the prose, among other differences.

11. John Gordon calls attention to the almost ritualistic, incantatory quality of this opening sentence: "Like most of the protagonists of *Dubliners*, he [the boy of "The Sisters"] has done some reading—evidently of Poe or some imitator—and becomes familiar with iconography of exotic menace. The first sentence, with its ominous fairy-tale 'third stroke,' reflects a habit of looking for mystery in one's impressions" (John Gordon, *James Joyce's Metamorphoses* [Dublin: Gill & Macmillan, 1981], 16).

12. William York Tindall, *A Reader's Guide to James Joyce* (New York: Farrar, Straus and Giroux, 1959), 17.

13. Quoted in William York Tindall, *Samuel Beckett* (New York: Columbia Univ. Press, 1964), 7.

14. The narrator's (ab)use of the narrative structure and conventions of the detective story is not a new discovery. Hugh Kenner nearly made this claim thirty years ago, writing that "the detective story remains a two-dimensional parody of the Joycean short story" (Hugh Kenner, *Dublin's Joyce* (Bloomington: Indiana Univ. Press, 1956), 176); more recently and more pertinently, Suzanne Ferguson has mapped out some of the "structural and thematic analogues" between *Dubliners* and detective stories. Her argument runs that detective fiction is "a genre that exhibits a number of features remarkably like those of the *Dubliners* stories: the pattern of quest for hidden meaning; combined fascination with and horror at the surface disorder of contemporary urban experience; the suppression or deletion of 'normal' narrative sequence and substitution of 'clues' to these suppressed elements; the coalescence of the disparate clues in a moment of discovery or epiphany; and the reader's active involvement in assimilating the clues and interpreting them, coming to understand along with the protagonist the whole of the hitherto veiled truth of the situation." Near the beginning of her essay Ferguson cites Francis Nevins on the function of the detective—"the central ritual of detective fiction is the process whereby the inexplicable, the absurd, the nightmarish are fused by the power of human intelligence into a rationally harmonious mosaic"—and argues that this is the way that *Dubliners* works (Suzanne Ferguson, "A Sherlook at *Dubliners*: Structural and Thematic Analogues in Detective Stories and the Modern Short Story," *James Joyce Quarterly* 16 [1978–79], 112, 111). Although the characters are not able to "solve" the mysteries presented them, Ferguson writes, we as readers are.

Ferguson's reading points out quite forcefully that there are finally far more than two detectives in "The Sisters"—for both readers and critics of the story quite automatically cast themselves in that role. But in assuming that we as readers and critics will be more successful than Joyce's detectives-in-the-text—an assumption certainly not supported by the accumulated critical commentary on the story—Ferguson finally misses the point.

15. Mr. James Duffy is another of these peculiar "cases"; in his tale, the most

obviously "detective" of all of the *Dubliners* stories, the dénouement relies on our noticing that he has discharged the role of detective very badly. Duffy is a detective manqué—a defective detective—as the narrator of "The Sisters" seems poised to become. As we will explore in chapter 4, his "deduction" about Mrs. Sinico's death is self-serving and just plain wrong.

16. John Cawelti, *Adventure, Mystery, and Romance: Formula Stories as Art and Popular Culture* (Chicago: Univ. of Chicago Press, 1976), 83.

17. G. K. Chesterton, *The Defendant* (London: Dent, 1901), 119.

18. Cawelti, *Adventure, Mystery, and Romance*, 96.

19. Dennis Porter, *The Pursuit of Crime: Art and Ideology in Detective Fiction* (New Haven: Yale Univ. Press, 1981), 216.

20. Sir Arthur Conan Doyle, *Adventures of Sherlock Holmes* (New York: Harper & Row, 1930), 56. Joyce would seem to allude to this passage in the following sentence from *Finnegans Wake*: "The boxes, if I may break the subject gently, are worth about fourpence pourbox but I am inventing a more patent process, foolproof and pryperfect (I should like to ask that Shedlock Homes person who is out for removing the roofs of our criminal classics by what *deductio ad domunum* he hopes *de tacto* to detect anything unless he happens of himself, *movibile tectu*, to have a slade off) after which they can be reduced to a fragment of their true crust by even the youngest of Margees if she will plase to be seated and smile if I please" (*FW* 165–66).

21. Michael Holquist, "Whodunit and Other Questions: Metaphysical Detective Stories in Post-War Fiction," *New Literary History* 3 (1971): 141.

22. In proffering this explanation the boy of course assumes that we, like him, are detectives; and, as we will investigate later, he is surely right, although it is a habit of mind the story—indeed the volume—is intended to break us of.

23. Denis Donoghue, *The Arts without Mystery* (Boston: Little, Brown, 1983), 12.

24. R. B. Kershner's is now the standard treatment of Joyce's use of popular literature; see *Joyce, Bakhtin, and Popular Literature: Chronicles of Disorder* (Chapel Hill: Univ. of North Carolina Press, 1989). See also Michael Seidel's lucid discussion of Joyce and popular fictions of exile in *Exile and the Narrative Imagination* (New Haven: Yale Univ. Press, 1986), 71–104.

25. William W. Stowe, "From Semiotics to Hermeneutics: Modes of Detection in Doyle and Chandler," in *The Poetics of Murder: Detective Fiction and Literary Theory*, ed. Glenn W. Most and William W. Stowe (San Diego: Harcourt Brace Jovanovich, 1983), 41.

26. William V. Spanos, *Repetitions: The Postmodern Occasion in Literature and Culture* (Baton Rouge: Louisiana State Univ. Press, 1987), 26.

27. Samuel Beckett, *Molloy*, in *Three Novels: Molloy, Malone Dies, The Unnamable* (New York: Grove, 1958), 113.

28. Ibid., 137. This verbal echo of the sisters' pronouncement over the body of Father Flynn would, of course, not have escaped Beckett.

29. Ibid., 176.

30. Doyle, *Adventures of Sherlock Holmes*, 104.

31. Cawelti, *Adventure, Mystery, and Romance*, 26.

32. Spanos, *Repetitions*, 48. Michael Holquist pinpoints the essential difference between the traditional and "metaphysical" detective story in rather similar terms: "The metaphysical detective story does not have the narcotizing effect of its progenitor; instead of familiarity, it gives strangeness, a strangeness which more often than not is the result of jumbling the well known patterns of classical detective stories. Instead of reassuring, they disturb" (Holquist, "Whodunit and Other Questions," 155).

33. Lewis Carroll, *The Annotated Alice*, ed. Martin Gardner (New York: New American Library, 1960), 95, 97.

34. Ibid., 95n.

35. Hélène Cixous, "Joyce: The (R)use of Writing," in *Post-Structuralist Joyce*, ed. Derek Attridge and Daniel Ferrer (Cambridge: Cambridge Univ. Press, 1984), 20.

36. Ibid., 20.

37. Ibid., 21.

38. Porter, *Pursuit of Crime*, 227.

39. Tindall, *Reader's Guide to James Joyce*, 13.

40. In Amanda Cross's *The James Joyce Murders*, the titles of all the *Dubliners* stories serve as punning titles for the chapters of her mystery, which centers on the theft of the manuscript of the apocryphal sixteenth *Dubliners* story, "Ulysses," based on Mr. Alfred H. Hunter's day in Dublin. "Conventional" Joyce criticism, of course, says that sixteenth story was never written—Joyce in a letter to his brother says it "never got any forrader than the title" (*L* 2:209)—but instead was metamorphosed into the novel *Ulysses*. Bartholomew Gill has recently brought out another murder mystery grounded in Joyce's fiction, *The Death of a Joyce Scholar*, which playfully reanimates the terrain of *Ulysses*.

41. In this context, Marjorie Nicolson's early (1927) remarks on the strange spell detective fiction casts over academics sounds somewhat ironic; according to Porter, she "finds that detective novels appeal to academics because they afford an escape not from life, as is usually assumed, but from literature. And by literature she meant particularly the contemporary avant-garde novel of early modernism, Joyce and company" (Porter, *Pursuit of Crime*, 223–24).

42. Porter, *Pursuit of Crime*, 226.

43. William Shakespeare, *All's Well That Ends Well*, II.iii.1–6.

44. Frank O'Connor, *The Lonely Voice: A Study of the Short Story* (Cleveland: World Publishing, 1963), 114. While never having written specifically on "The Sisters," John Cage does adopt this basic posture in his reading of all of Joyce's work, as reflected for instance in these remarks on *Finnegans Wake*: "I had the notion when I was asked to write for the Walker Art Center in the series on 'The Meanings of Modernism,' to write a text against the 'march of understanding,' and to make clear the virtues of remaining ignorant in the face of art. [Professor Louis] Mink says that it is no longer possible to take this naïve attitude, that enough is known about *Finnegans Wake* to make it imperative to know more

and, ultimately, to destroy it. I work at . . . keeping it mysterious. Instead of understanding it, I would like, if I can, to help keep the work of Joyce mysterious" (John Cage, *Conversing with Cage*, ed. Richard Kostelanetz (New York: Limelight Editions, 1988), 136–37).

45. Porter, *Pursuit of Crime*, 225.

46. Beckett, *Molloy*, 165.

47. The strange dynamics of Father Flynn's "wake" will be examined in greater detail in chapter 7.

48. The standard text on the confinement of the mentally ill from the sixteenth century is, of course, Michel Foucault's *Madness and Civilization: A History of Insanity in the Age of Reason*, trans. Richard Howard (New York: Vintage, 1973).

49. Synge's *The Shadow of the Glen*, in the dialogue between the Tramp and Nora Burke, provides a good example of this traditional suspicion of the newly dead.

50. Sigmund Freud, "Thoughts for the Times on War and Death," in *The Standard Edition of the Complete Psychological Works of Sigmund Freud*, ed. James Strachey, vol. 14 (1914–16) (London: Hogarth Press, 1957), 293–94.

51. R. D. Laing, *The Politics of Experience* (New York: Pantheon, 1967), 121. I am aware that Laing's reputation is not currently as high as it once was, in spite of the embroidering of his ideas by Deleuze and Guattari in their influential *Anti-Oedipus* and *A Thousand Plateaus;* nevertheless, in spite of his sometimes "over the top" rhetoric and overly broad claims, I believe that Laing is onto something fundamental about the social function of mental illness, and that his insights do help us to recognize an important aspect of what is happening/being done to Father Flynn. In *Anti-Oedipus,* Deleuze and Guattari describe schizophrenia as "not an illness, not a 'breakdown' but a 'breakthrough,' however distressing and adventurous: breaking through the wall or the limit separating us from desiring-production, causing the flows of desire to circulate. Laing's importance lies in the fact that, starting from certain intuitions that remained ambiguous in Jaspers, he was able to indicate the incredible scope of this voyage" (Gilles Deleuze and Félix Guattari, *Anti-Oedipus: Capitalism and Schizophrenia,* trans. Robert Hurley, Mark Seem, and Helen R. Lane [Minneapolis: Univ. of Minnesota Press, 1983], 362).

52. C. H. Peake, *James Joyce: The Citizen and the Artist* (Stanford: Stanford Univ. Press, 1977), 15.

53. Hayden White, "Foucault Decoded: Notes from Underground," in *Tropics of Discourse: Essays in Cultural Criticism* (Baltimore and London: Johns Hopkins Univ. Press, 1978), 246.

54. Laing, *Politics of Experience*, 115.

55. Ibid., 120.

56. Cawelti, *Adventure, Mystery, and Romance*, 80.

57. Thus, the sisters are in effect both criminals and police—the corrupt law enforcement system encountered so often in the hard-boiled detective novel.

Finnegans Wake, in one of its telling transmutations, refers to them as the "petty constable Sistersen," "the parochial watch" (*FW* 186). My reading, I believe, mediates between the two opposed readings of the story offered by Vicki Mahaffey: "The elusive target of 'The Sisters' is not the sisters, but habit, and particularly the comfortable habit of evaluation" (*Reauthorizing Joyce* [Cambridge: Cambridge Univ. Press, 1988], 31).

58. Stefano Tani, *The Doomed Detective: The Contribution of the Detective Novel to Postmodern American and Italian Fiction* (Carbondale: Southern Illinois Univ. Press, 1984), 76.

59. Susan Sontag, *Against Interpretation* (New York: Farrar, Straus & Giroux, 1966), 7.

60. Jacques Derrida, "Structure, Sign, and Play in the Discourse of the Human Sciences," in *Writing and Difference,* trans. Alan Bass (Chicago: Univ. of Chicago Press, 1978), 292.

61. Ibid.

62. David I. Grossvogel, *Mystery and Its Fictions: From Oedipus to Agatha Christie* (Baltimore and London: Johns Hopkins Univ. Press, 1979), 40.

63. *PT* 14. Dennis Porter, using the terminology of the earlier Barthes, writes that the traditional detective story is "the model of the readable *(lisible)* text" (Porter, *Pursuit of Crime,* 83).

64. Grossvogel, *Mystery and Its Fictions,* 40.

65. Ibid., 254.

Chapter 4. The *Dubliners* Epiphony: (Mis)Reading the Book of Ourselves

1. Hugh Kenner, *The Mechanic Muse* (New York: Oxford Univ. Press, 1987), 77.

2. Edward Brandabur, *A Scrupulous Meanness: A Study of Joyce's Early Work* (Urbana: Univ. of Illinois Press, 1971), 42.

3. Colin MacCabe, *James Joyce and the Revolution of the Word* (New York: Harper & Row, 1979), 34.

4. Phillip Herring, *Joyce's Uncertainty Principle* (Princeton: Princeton Univ. Press, 1987), 10.

5. Clive Hart uses this term in rather a different sense in his discussion of the "Wandering Rocks" episode in Clive Hart and David Hayman, eds., *James Joyce's "Ulysses": Critical Essays* (Berkeley and Los Angeles: Univ. of California Press, 1974).

6. Homer Obed Brown, *James Joyce's Early Fiction: The Biography of a Form* (Cleveland: Case Western Reserve Univ. Press, 1972), 40.

7. Ibid., 48.

8. Tindall, *Reader's Guide to James Joyce,* 15.

9. Garry M. Leonard, *Reading "Dubliners" Again: A Lacanian Perspective* (Syracuse: Syracuse Univ. Press, 1993), 203, 204.

10. Herring, *Joyce's Uncertainty Principle,* 28. I certainly do not mean to suggest that a careful reading of the popular literature with which Joyce litters his

texts, such as Brandy Kershner has performed in *Joyce, Bakhtin, and Popular Literature,* is without value. But Kershner is quite clear about what the value of such a source study is; the titles are not symbols or clues that will magically unlock the mysterious texture of the stories.

11. Cage, *Conversing with Cage,* 208.

12. William Empson, "The Theme of *Ulysses,*" *Kenyon Review* 18 (Winter 1956): 36.

13. MacCabe, *James Joyce and the Revolution of the Word,* 29.

14. Beckett, *Molloy,* 91.

15. Zack Bowen, "Joyce and the Epiphany Concept: A New Approach," *Journal of Modern Literature* 9 (1981–82): 106–7.

16. Donald T. Torchiana, *Backgrounds for Joyce's "Dubliners"* (Boston: Allen & Unwin, 1986), 18.

17. "Liturgy of S. Chrysostom," in *Liturgies Eastern and Western,* ed. F. E. Brightman, 2 vols. (Oxford: Oxford Univ. Press, 1896), 1:375.

18. Although since Vatican II (1962–65), an epiclesis has been added to the canon of the Roman Catholic Mass.

19. Thus, clearly, I read this letter rather differently than does Richard Ellmann, who comments that while living in Trieste Joyce "often went to the Greek Orthodox Church to compare its ritual, which he considered amateurish, with the Roman" (*JJ* 195).

Furthermore, in the Orthodox service the elements of the Eucharist are hidden, but the priest at intervals rends the veil and reveals himself. Joyce's description of the Mass was of course written long before the memorable words he put into the mouth of Stephen Dedalus, in which Stephen likens the artist to the God of creation, who remains "within or behind or beyond or above his handiwork, invisible, refined out of existence, indifferent, paring his fingernails" (*P* 215). Joyce's fascination with the Greek priest who reveals himself, rather than the Roman priest who conceals himself, suggests a certain distance from Stephen's artist-creator fantasy that I'd like to explore further in chapter 5.

20. Stanislaus Joyce, *My Brother's Keeper,* ed. Richard Ellmann (London: Faber, 1958), 116.

21. While critics have expended considerable time and ink puzzling over exactly what Joyce meant by "a style of scrupulous meanness," the fact is that we will never know with any certainty. In the face of that uncertainty, I am inclined to believe that "scrupulous meanness" refers to the surface stylistic poverty of most of the volume's narrative—the most noticeable characteristic for *Dubliners*'s first generation of readers. For example, Gerald Gould, writing in the *New Statesman:* "He has plenty of humour, but it is always the humour of the fact, not of the comment. He dares to let people speak for themselves with the awkward meticulousness, the persistent incompetent repetition, of actual human intercourse. If you have never realised before how direly our daily conversation needs editing, you will realise it from Mr. Joyce's pages. One very powerful

story, called 'Grace,' consists chiefly of lengthy talk so banal, so true to life, that one can scarcely endure it—though one can still less leave off reading it" (Deming 1:63). Or, more pithily, Ezra Pound: "I can lay down a good piece of French writing and pick up a piece of writing by Mr. Joyce without feeling as if my head were being stuffed through a cushion" (Deming 1:66).

22. MacCabe, *James Joyce and the Revolution of the Word*, 28.

23. Morris Beja, "One Good Look at Themselves: Epiphanies in *Dubliners*, " in *Work in Progress: Joyce Centenary Essays*, ed. Richard F. Peterson, Alan M. Cohn, and Edmund L. Epstein (Carbondale: Southern Illinois Univ. Press, 1983), 3.

24. Scholes and Litz write in their edition of *Dubliners* that "critics have applied the notion of epiphany to that moment in a *Dubliners* story when some sort of revelation takes place. . . . 'Epiphany' thus comes to mean a moment of revelation or insight such as usually climaxes a *Dubliners* story" (D 255).

25. *D*, 254. Stanislaus Joyce seems to have had only this second type of epiphany in mind in his well-known description of the epiphanies: "Another experimental form which his literary urge took . . . consisted in the noting of what he called 'epiphanies'—manifestations or revelations. Jim always had a contempt for secrecy, and these notes were in the beginning ironical observations of slips, and little errors and gestures—mere straws in the wind—by which people betrayed the very things they were most careful to conceal" (S. Joyce, *My Brother's Keeper*, 134).

26. Tindall suggests that this pairing of epiphanies is Joyce's usual procedure in *Dubliners:* "In most of these stories, there are two epiphanies, similar but not identical: one for the reader, the other for the hero or victim" (Tindall, *Reader' Guide to James Joyce*, 28).

27. This is the epiphany Stephen records there:

The Young Lady—(drawling discretely) . . . O, yes . . . I was . . . at the . . . cha . . . pel . . .

The Young Gentleman—(inaudibly) . . . I . . . (again inaudibly) . . . I . . .

The Young Lady—(softly) . . . O . . . but you're . . . ve . . . ry . . . wick . . . ed . . . (*SH* 211)

28. Bowen, "Joyce and the Epiphany Concept," 107.

29. Virginia Woolf, *To the Lighthouse* (New York: Harcourt, Brace, World, 1955), 310.

30. Wayne Booth, *The Rhetoric of Fiction*, 2d ed. (Chicago: Univ. of Chicago Press, 1983), 335–36.

31. Hugh Kenner, *Ulysses* (London: Allen & Unwin, 1982), 6.

32. See Hugh Kenner, *Joyce's Voices* (Berkeley and Los Angeles: Univ. of California Press, 1978). I'm the first to admit that Kenner's ear for Joyce's voices is better than anyone's in the business; my objection is to his predilection needlessly to coin new terms for time-honored phenomena. What he calls the Uncle Charles Principle—suggesting, along the way, that Joyce created it—differs in no way from the *style indirect libre* that Flaubert was exploiting in the mid-nineteenth century.

33. Beja, "One Good Look at Themselves," 10, 9.

34. Bowen, "Joyce and the Epiphany Concept," 106.

35. Sir Walter Scott, *The Abbot* (Philadelphia: J. B. Lippincott, 1887), 14–15.

36. In a letter to R. W. D. Rouse, 30 December 1934 (Ezra Pound, *Selected Letters, 1907–1941*, ed. D. D. Paige [New York: New Directions, 1971], 263).

37. Setting aside "The Sisters," about which critics are almost evenly divided, only five of the stories are consistently understood as closing with the protagonist's epiphany—"An Encounter," "Araby," "A Little Cloud," "A Painful Case," and "The Dead." These are also, perhaps not coincidentally, all stories which critics have identified as especially autobiographical. For those who find epiphany in these endings, this fact no doubt suggests that Joyce wished to work out his own salvation through these autobiographical characters, and through them assert his superiority to the rest of the Dubliners; I would instead argue that critics' identification of these characters with their author has colored their readings, and that we hesitate to criticize the boy in "Araby," or Gabriel, because to damn them would seem to be to damn their creator as well.

38. Though the instances are too numerous to discuss in any detail here, Joyce systematically undermines the traditional symbolic equation of the mirror with self-awareness throughout *Dubliners*. Two representative examples, from "The Boarding House": at the story's close, Polly Mooney looks into her mirror but doesn't see herself; she simply touches up her mask: "Polly sat for a little time on the side of the bed, crying. Then she dried her eyes and went over to the looking-glass. She dipped the end of the towel in the water-jug and refreshed her eyes with the cool water. She looked at herself in profile and readjusted a hairpin above her ear" (*D* 68). So too Mrs. Mooney: "Nearly the half-hour! She stood up and surveyed herself in the pier-glass. The decisive expression of her great florid face satisfied her . . . "(*D* 65). Vicki Mahaffey has examined Joyce's use of this topos in *Ulysses;* see *Reauthorizing Joyce,* 104–14.

39. Herring, *Joyce's Uncertainty Principle,* 24–25.

40. Gérard Genette, *Narrative Discourse: An Essay in Method,* trans. Jane E. Lewin (Ithaca: Cornell Univ. Press, 1980), 174.

41. While critics are fond of citing Duffy's odd habit, none seems to have noticed that the sentence following this one is a perfect example of that habit: "He never gave alms to beggars and walked firmly, carrying a stout hazel." That the narrative itself so closely conforms to Duffy's own compositional predilections lends further credence to the idea that he is, in some sense, the author of this "adventureless tale," or at least the unacknowledged shaper of its style.

42. Bowen, "Joyce and the Epiphany Concept," 107.

43. T. S. Eliot, "A Message to the Fish," in *James Joyce: Two Decades of Criticism,* ed. Seon Givens (New York: Vanguard, 1963), 468.

44. "Lush" seems to have been a term of abuse for Joyce. Ellmann tells the story of Joyce's hearing some of Lawrence's *Lady Chatterley's Lover* read aloud: "Joyce asked Stuart Gilbert to read him some pages from it. He listened carefully, then pronounced only one word: 'Lush '" (*JJ* 615n).

45. Bowen, "Joyce and the Epiphany Concept," 109–10.

46. Kenner, *Ulysses*, 7.

47. Bowen, "Joyce and the Epiphany Concept," 110.

48. Margot Norris reports that her students inevitably come to class having "figured out" that "clay" equals "death"—"as though this constituted some sort of punch line, some sort of illumination that makes sense of an otherwise meaningless joke" (Margot Norris, *Joyce's Web: The Social Unraveling of Modernism* [Austin: Univ. of Texas Press, 1992], 121). My reading of "Clay"—indeed, all of *Dubliners*—is indebted in more ways than citation can indicate to Norris's discussion; her chapter on "Clay" painstakingly elaborates the mechanics of Maria's "desirous edition" of the text of "Clay," and should be consulted in its entirety for the light it sheds not only on "Clay," but on the dynamics of narrative desire that informs all of *Dubliners*.

49. Tindall, *Reader's Guide to James Joyce*, 4–5. As I have noted above, Tindall's claim that self-realization constitutes the climax of "most" of *Dubliners's* stories is an exaggeration, since only six of the fifteen stories have been read as ending in the protagonist's self-realization with any consistency.

50. Beja, "One Good Look at Themselves," 9, 13.

51. Bowen, "Joyce and the Epiphany Concept," 107.

52. Jane P. Tompkins, ed., *Reader-Response Criticism: From Formalism to Post-Structuralism* (Baltimore and London: Johns Hopkins Univ. Press, 1980), ix.

53. Norris, although more honest than most, herself falls into this trap, making it clear that she has not been seduced: "'Clay' is a 'deceptively' simple little story by design: its narrative self-deception attempts, and fails, to mislead the reader" (Norris, *Joyce's Web*, 120).

54. Tindall, *Reader's Guide to James Joyce*, 31.

55. Norris, *Joyce's Web*, 123.

56. Ibid., 125.

57. Thus in this instance I disagree completely with the position Kenner puts forth in *The Mechanic Muse*. Using the analogy of the Dublin Corporation men who are paid to "watch holes"—presumably so that no one will fall into them—Kenner writes: "No other body of fiction so resembles a city in necessitating such guides and such watchmen. Nor does any other body of fiction so resemble a city in containing such holes into which the naive may fall, or such loose stones over which they may stumble" (82). My argument, again, is that we're meant to stumble, to tumble—indeed, it's good for us; Kenner, one of the best of Joyce's "guides and watchmen," cannot seem to appreciate this point.

58. Norris, *Joyce's Web*, 120.

59. Leonard, *Reading "Dubliners" Again*, 6.

60. Kathy Acker, "Devoured by Myths: An Interview with Sylvère Lotringer," in *Hannibal Lecter, My Father* (New York: Semiotext(e), 1991), 15.

61. Jonathan Swift, *A Tale of a Tub with Other Early Works 1696–1707*, ed. Herbert Davis (Oxford: Blackwell, 1965), 140.

Chapter 5. Dedalus, ~~Dead Alas!~~ Dead At Last

1. There is an interesting parallel between Barthes's constantly evolving nomenclature and Lyotard's shift from the terms classic/modern to modern/postmodern. Perhaps it has to do with the fact that "postmodern writing" was "discovered," and came to be generally acknowledged, during the evolution of their ideas. In Lyotard's case, it seems likely that he came upon the term "postmodern" during the gestation of his own ideas about texts, perhaps through the writing of Ihab Hassan; skeptics suggest that he was drawn to the term because of its aura of hip Americanness.

2. Joseph Buttigieg's reading notwithstanding. I think his criticism of the way that the Joyce industry has reified the terms of the text is exactly right; but once he has cleared the ground in this way, I don't think he goes on to construct a very convincing postmodern reading of the book. See *A Portrait of the Artist in Different Perspective* (Columbus: Ohio State Univ. Press, 1987).

3. See Booth, *Rhetoric of Fiction*.

4. T. E. Hulme, "Romanticism and Classicism," in *Speculations: Essays on Humanism and the Philosophy of Art*, ed. Herbert Read (New York: Harcourt, Brace, 1936), 116.

5. Ibid., 118.

6. Percy Bysshe Shelley, *The Complete Poetical Works of Percy Bysshe Shelley*, ed. Roger Ingpen and Walter E. Peck, 10 vols. (New York: Gordian Press, 1965), 7:117. Robert Spoo has recently examined Joyce's debt to Shelley and the "Defence of Poetry" specifically, and to Romantic aesthetics more generally; see *James Joyce and the Language of History: Dedalus's Nightmare* (New York: Oxford Univ. Press, 1994), 57–65. For an exemplary discussion of Stephen's reading of Shelley—a reading seemingly oblivious to the contradictions and self-critique in Shelley's (and Byron's) various pronouncements and poses—see Mahaffey, *Reauthorizing Joyce*, 86–94.

7. The best treatment of Rimbaud's influence on Joyce is Phillip Herring's "Joyce and Rimbaud: An Introductory Essay," in *James Joyce: An International Perspective*, ed. Suheil Badi Bushrui and Bernard Benstock (Gerrards Cross, Eng.: Colin Smythe, 1982), 170–89.

8. Translation mine. In Verlaine's French: «Grand, bien bâti, presque athlétique, au visage parfaitement ovale d'ange en exil, avec des cheveux chatain-clair mal en order et des yeux d'un bleu pâle inquiétant.»

9. In *Stephen Hero*, Joyce describes Stephen Daedelus in almost identical fashion: "His coarse brownish hair was combed high off his forehead but there was little order in its arrangement. A girl might or might not have called him handsome: the face was regular in feature and its pose was almost softened into beauty by a small feminine mouth. In a general survey of the face the eyes were not prominent: they were small light blue eyes which checked advances. They were quite fresh and fearless but in spite of this the face was to a certain extent the face of a debauchee" (*SH* 23).

10. Arthur Rimbaud to Georges Izambard, 13 May 1871, in *Rimbaud: Complete Works, Selected Letters*, trans. Wallace Fowlie (Chicago: Univ. of Chicago Press, 1966), 307.

11. As Cranly puts it to Stephen: "You need not look upon yourself as driven away if you do not wish to go or as a heretic or an outlaw" (*P* 245).

12. The note is reproduced as Plate VII in Ellmann's *James Joyce*.

13. Ellmann uses this expression from *Finnegans Wake* (*FW* 535) to describe Joyce's first drama.

14. The possessive pronoun here, used almost casually by Joyce in a letter to Stanislaus, should not be overlooked. Joyce went so far as to say to Adolph Hoffmeister that "In the first story in *Dubliners*, I wrote that the word 'paralysis' filled *me* with horror and fear, as though it designated something evil and sinful" (Willard Potts, ed., *Portraits of the Artist in Exile: Recollections of James Joyce by Europeans* [San Diego: Harcourt Brace Jovanovich, 1986], 132; emphasis added).

15. The nine hundred manuscript pages cover only about one half of the sixty-three-chapter book that Joyce had planned.

16. Frank Budgen, *James Joyce and the Making of "Ulysses"* (Bloomington: Indiana Univ. Press, 1960), 105.

17. Louis Gillet suggests that after completing *Finnegans Wake*, "in his mind was rising the idea for a new poem whose fundamental theme would be the murmur of the sea" (Potts *Portraits of the Artist in Exile*, 203).

18. Declan Kiberd has written a thorough critique of the notions of military and sexual heroics in Joyce's texts; see "The Vulgarity of Heroics: Joyce's *Ulysses*," in Bushrui and Benstock, in *James Joyce: An International Perspective*, 156–68.

19. Pearce, *Politics of Narration*, 56.

20. The classic discussion of this technique is Kenner's chapter "The Uncle Charles Principle," in *Joyce's Voices*, 15–38.

21. I realize that by saying this I'm flying in the face of Brandy Kershner's impressive analysis of *A Portrait* as a dialogic novel. I'm fundamentally in agreement with Kershner, in the sense that (as his exhaustive primary research shows) Joyce wove Stephen's consciousness from an impressive number of noncanonical "popular" literary texts; Kershner argues that "Bakhtin stresses that the formulation of the self is a linguistic process; consciousness, for him, is a matter of self-articulation in an inner monologue that depends upon and responds to the surrounding environment of speech" (19). My sense, though, is that all those texts are just grist to Stephen's mill: the pulp novels that he ingests become the pulp of recycled writing paper, so that while Stephen writes the book of himself on paper which is a tissue of earlier writings, he effectively, willfully effaces them. In June 1928 Joyce wrote to Valéry Larbaud, then engaged in the French translation of *Ulysses*, and encouraged him to give up marking all of Stephen's unattributed quotations in the text with inverted commas: "when the words half quoted are from an obscure writer p.e. 'orient and immortal wheat' (from Thomas Traherne) what does it help a French reader to see ' ' there. He will

know early in the book that S.D.'s mind is full like everyone else's of borrowed words" (L 1:263). Stephen's artistic method through the end of A Portrait is primarily plagiarism; were he to acknowledge his sources, perhaps, or to allow them to sing their own songs in their own voices, we might with justice call the novel dialogic. But Stephen is not yet ready to affirm, with Barthes (in "The Death of the Author"), that "The text is a tissue of quotations drawn from innumerable centres of culture" (IMT 146). In other words, A Portrait should, in theory, be dialogic: but it's not; Stephen prevents it from unfolding in that manner. To call the text "dialogic" seems to me to strain the term beyond usefulness. For Kershner's dialogic analysis, see Joyce, Bakhtin, and Popular Literature, esp. 151–65. Similarly, Richard Pearce argues that a monologic novel is one in which "the voice of the author dominates" (50), and that's clearly not the case with A Portrait; yet if we consider Stephen's voice the voice of an author—presumably similar to the authorial voice of the young Joyce, before he "found his voice(s)"—the novel can be seen as monologic in this specialized sense. For Pearce's argument, see The Politics of Narration, 1–23, 50–55. For a reading that suggests that Stephen is indeed ready to "deessentialize the author function," see Patrick McGee, Paperspace: Style as Ideology in Joyce's "Ulysses" (Lincoln: Univ. of Nebraska Press, 1988), 39–47.

Bloom, on the other hand—in Jennifer Wicke's apt description—"is a collocation of outside languages, the vanishing point of private language. A primary constructor of this interior flow is, demonstrably, advertising language, its imagery and desire. Ads locate and fix 'Bloom,' rather than the other way around" (Advertising Fictions: Literature, Advertising, and Social Reading [New York: Columbia Univ. Press, 1988], 140).

22. According to Stanislaus, in My Brother's Keeper, this was for Joyce a term of mild disdain.

23. Dorrit Cohn, Transparent Minds: Narrative Modes for Presenting Consciousness in Fiction (Princeton: Princeton Univ. Press, 1978), 33.

24. A similar struggle, between the high calling of art and the carnivalesque impulse to undermine it, animates the recent work of the Dublin band U2 (on the albums Achtung Baby and Zooropa). If the analogy is at all useful, think of Bono, the preening and posing chanteur, as Stephen Dedalus, and the Edge as the deconstructive, self-critical James Joyce. An album like The Joshua Tree (1987) is Romantic/High Modernist; Zooropa (1993), an uncomfortable admixture of modernism and postmodernism, like A Portrait. The overwhelming presence of Bono, like Joyce's focus on Stephen, finally prevents either Achtung Baby or Zooropa from becoming wholly postmodern.

25. Jean-François Lyotard, "Gift of Organs," trans. Richard Lockwood, in Driftworks, 89.

26. Arthur Symons, The Symbolist Movement in Literature (1899; 2d ed., New York: E. P. Dutton, 1908), 8–9.

27. Michael Groden, for example, writes: "Joyce originally planned to carry Stephen's story far beyond his departure from Dublin. For one thing, the sur-

viving university section in *Stephen Hero* ends with chapter 25, whereas Joyce conceived sixty-three chapters in all. More specific evidence comes from Joyce's early notes (from Pola in late 1904), where there is a reference to 'Dr. Doherty and the Holy City.' Doherty, who was eventually renamed Buck Mulligan and used in *Ulysses*, appears in a fragmentary postuniversity scene set in a Martello tower. Joyce wrote out this scene much later than 1904, in fact, long after *Stephen Hero* Hero was abandoned . . . but it represents part of his original plan. The fragment, which Gabler dates around 1912 to 1913, indicates that even this late in the composition of *A Portrait*, Joyce planned to include incidents beyond Stephen's departure for Paris. . . . Eventually, he reworked the tower scene for the opening episode of *Ulysses*" ("Textual and Publishing History," in *A Companion to Joyce Studies*, ed. Zack Bowen and James F. Carens [Westport, Conn: Greenwood Press, 1984], 86). See also A. Walton Litz, *The Art of James Joyce: Method and Design in "Ulysses" and "Finnegans Wake,"* rev. ed. (Oxford: Oxford Univ. Press, 1964), 137; Robert Scholes and Richard M. Kain, eds., *The Workshop of Daedalus: James Joyce and the Raw Materials for "A Portrait of the Artist as a Young Man"* (Evanston: Northwestern Univ. Press, 1965), 106; and Hans Walter Gabler, "Joyce's Text in Progress," in *The Cambridge Companion to James Joyce* , ed. Derek Attridge (Cambridge: Cambridge Univ. Press, 1990), 221.

28. Though this point was not immediately clear to all readers: "Another American 'critic' who wanted to interview me (I declined) told me he had read the book with great interest but that he could not understand why Bloom came into it. I explained to him why and he [was] surprised and disappointed for he thought Stephen was *Ulysses*" (*L* 1:184).

29. *Pound/Joyce* , ed. Forrest Read (New York: New Directions, 1967), 148.

30. Ibid., 158. To be fair, Pound did eventually come around; in a 22 November 1918 letter, he wrote Joyce that "Bloom is a great man, and you have almightily answered the critics who asked me whether having made Stephen, more or less autobiography, you could ever go on and create a second character. 'Second character is the test' etc. etc., jab jab jobber jabble" (ibid., 145). In an essay published in May 1918, he had written, "*Bloom* answers the query that people made after the Portrait. Joyce has created his second character. He has moved from autobiography to the creation of the complementary figure. Bloom on life, death, resurrection, immortality. Bloom and the Venus de Milo. Bloom brings life into the book. All Bloom is vital" (Ezra Pound, *Literary Essays of Ezra Pound* , ed. T. S. Eliot [New York: New Directions, 1968], 416).

31. Budgen, *James Joyce and the Making of "Ulysses,"* 105.

32. Budgen's account casts doubt on whether the proper reading of the telegram should be "Nother dying," as Gabler has edited it, or instead "Mother," as all previous editions had had it. Budgen, recollecting Joyce's reading aloud of the "Proteus" episode from the pages of the *Little Review*, renders it "Mother," without comment (Budgen, *James Joyce and the Making of "Ulysses,"* 51). Gabler defends his reading this way: "Joyce wrote 'Nother' in the draft manuscript Buffalo V.A.3. and the Rosenbach fair copy. Darantière's compositors set 'Mother'

in the first *(placard)* proofs, and Joyce changed back to 'Nother.' An officious hand reintroduced 'Mother' in the final proofs after Joyce had last seen them" (Hans Walter Gabler, "Stephen in Paris," *James Joyce Quarterly* 17 [1980]: 311).

33. Freud, *Standard Edition,* 16:276.

34. Ibid., 14:243.

35. William Butler Yeats, "September 1913," in *W. B. Yeats: The Poems,* ed. Richard J. Finneran (New York: Macmillan, 1983), 108.

36. I will mention the Barthes essay below; the Foucault piece is "What is an Author?" in *Language, Counter-Memory, Practice* , ed. Donald F. Bouchard, trans. Donald F. Bouchard and Sherry Simon (Ithaca: Cornell Univ. Press, 1977), 113–38.

37. Joyce visited Shelley's grave while living in Rome in 1907.

38. Cage, *Conversing with Cage,* 211–12.

39. Rabaté, *James Joyce: Authorized Reader,* 3.

40. Walter Benjamin, "The Work of Art in the Age of Mechanical Reproduction," in *Illuminations,* ed. Hannah Arendt, trans. Harry Zohn (New York: Schocken, 1969), 231–32.

41. Fernand Léger, "The Esthetics of the Machine: Manufactured Objects, Artisans and Artists," *Little Review* 9, no. 4 (Autumn/Winter 1923–24), 57.

42. Walter Benjamin, "The Author as Producer," in *Reflections: Essays, Aphorisms, Autobiographical Writings,* ed. Peter Demetz, trans. Edmund Jephcott (New York: Harcourt Brace Jovanovich, 1978), 225.

43. *Irish Homestead,* 16 January 1904, 1.

44. Keith Williams, *The English Newspaper: An Illustrated History to 1900* (London: Springwood Books, 1977), 72.

45. Until recently, I had assumed that Joyce had cooked up a rather implausible subject for Deasy's writing here. Then I read this letter in the *Irish Homestead,* on the subject of spraying potatoes:

Dear Sir,

I observe in your last issue a letter on this subject from my friend, Mr. Vernon Cochrane, in which he invites me to give my opinion of the quality of a parcel of potatoes which he handed to me one afternoon in November last. I had them cooked same evening for dinner in Victoria Hotel, Sligo, and mine host and all his guests who partook of them declared that they had tasted nothing so good from the 1903 crop. Whether this excellence was due entirely to spraying I cannot say. Perhaps variety had something to do with it, and a suitable change of seed. Moreover, the soil and climate are ideal. Early maturity has a great influence on quality in a season like last, and to this end I am persuaded that a great gain would accrue to Ireland from the sprouting before planting of late varieties.

Yours faithfully,

M. G. Wallace.

Terreglestown, Dumphries

January 6th, 1904. (*Irish Homestead,* 9 January 1904, 33)

46. In much of Kenner's writing, but especially *The Mechanic Muse*, 5–15, 63–82.

47. Wicke, *Advertising Fictions*, 157.

48. Tindall suggests that Mulligan's word "snotgreen" may owe something to Rimbaud's "Le bateau ivre" (*Reader's Guide to James Joyce*, 139); Joseph Prescott argues that "History is a nightmare" derives from Laforgue's *Mélanges posthumes* ("Notes on Joyce's *Ulysses*," *MLQ* 13 [1952]: 149–62); Stephen's epigram about "the cracked lookingglass of a servant" is just one of the many echoes of Wilde; Swinburne is, of course, referred to by name; Stephen's mental review of his books of epiphanies, "One feels as if one . . . ," is mock Pater (especially the "Pico" section of *The Renaissance*); the phrase "the faunal noon" depends upon Mallarmé's *L'après-midi d'une faue*.

49. Jean-François Lyotard, "Representation, Presentation, Unpresentable," in *The Inhuman*, 124.

50. Additionally, as Hugh Kenner discusses, Gabler's emendation of the reading text of *Ulysses*—specifically, his restoration of thirty-eight exclamation marks to Mulligan's speech in the "Telemachus" episode—demonstrates that Joyce "meant to show Buck Mulligan exclaiming like a hearty fellow in 1900's fiction" (*Mechanic Muse*, 74).

51. Mahaffey, *Reauthorizing Joyce*, 59.

52. Friedrich Nietzsche, *On the Genealogy of Morals and Ecce Homo*, ed. Walter Kaufmann, trans. Kaufmann and R. J. Hollingdale (New York: Random House, 1967), 46.

53. This phrase, while taken from Joyce's essay on Mangan (*CW* 83), resurfaces in a couple of places in the fiction: "Thus the spirit of man makes a continual affirmation" (*SH* 80); "Bloom dissented tacitly from Stephen's views on the eternal affirmation of the spirit of man in literature" (*U* 544).

54. Friedrich Nietzsche, *Twilight of the Idols and The Anti-Christ*, trans. R. J. Hollingdale (New York: Penguin, 1968), 103.

55. Max Scheler, *Ressentiment*, ed. Lewis A. Coser, trans. William W. Holdheim (New York: Free Press, 1961), 45–46.

56. Gilles Deleuze, *Nietzsche and Philosophy*, trans. Hugh Tomlinson (New York: Columbia Univ. Press, 1983), 117–18.

Chapter 6. Toward a Nonmodernist *Ulysses*

1. The details of the following account of the history of Euclidean and non-Euclidean geometry, about which I claim no expertise, I owe to Douglas R. Hofstadter's *Gödel, Escher, Bach: An Eternal Golden Braid* (New York: Vintage, 1979); Philip J. Davis and Reuben Hersh, *The Mathematical Experience* (Boston: Houghton Mifflin, 1981); and the *Encyclopedia Britannica* article "Non-Euclidean Geometry" (*The New Encyclopedia Britannica*, 15th ed.).

2. The first four Euclidean postulates are as follows:

   1. A straight line segment can be drawn joining any two points.

2. Any straight line segment can be extended indefinitely in a straight line.
3. Given any straight line segment, a circle can be drawn having the segment as radius and one end point as center.
4. All right angles are congruent.
But the fifth postulate is a good bit more unwieldy:
5. If two lines are drawn which intersect a third in such a way that the sum of the inner angles on one side is less than two right angles, then the two lines inevitably must intersect each other on that side if extended far enough. (Hofstadter, *Gödel*, 90)

3. Ibid., 91.

4. Davis and Hersh, *Mathematical Experience*, 219.

5. Hofstadter, *Gödel*, 90–91.

6. Ibid.

7. Davis and Hersh, *Mathematical Experience*, 221.

8. Buttigieg, *Portrait of the Artist in Different Perspective*, 17. In the last sentence, Buttigieg quotes William V. Spanos in "Modern Literary Criticism and the Spatialization of Time: An Existential Critique," *Journal of Aesthetics and Art Criticism* 29 (1970): 97.

9. Clive Bell, *Art* (New York: Frederick A. Stokes, [1913]), 8.

10. Pound, *Literary Essays*, 11.

11. Ezra Pound, *Selected Prose, 1909–1965,* ed. William Cookson (New York: New Directions, 1973), 374.

12. Yvor Winters, *In Defense of Reason* (New York: W. Morrow, 1947), 61–62.

13. John Crowe Ransom, *Beating the Bushes: Selected Essays, 1941–1970* (New York: New Directions, 1972), 38–39.

14. For an intelligent, though wholly credulous, reading of Joyce's use of expressive form in *Ulysses*, see Umberto Eco, *The Aesthetics of Chaosmos: The Middle Ages of James Joyce*, trans. Ellen Esrock (Cambridge: Harvard Univ. Press, 1989), 35–38.

15. *Pound/Joyce*, 157. Pound was, in better moods, a good deal more sympathetic to Joyce's project; in his "Paris Letter" (June 1922), Pound writes: "James (H[enry].) speaks with his own so beautiful voice, even sometimes when his creations should be using *their* own; Joyce speaks if not with the tongue of men and angels, at least with a many-tongued and multiple language, of small boys, street preachers, of genteel and ungenteel, of bowsers and undertakers, of Gertie McDowell and Mr. Deasey [sic]" (*Pound/Joyce*, 196).

16. McGee, *Paperspace*, 71.

17. Indeed, Gilbert states in his preface, with refreshing candor: "It should be mentioned that in the course of writing this Study I read it out to Joyce, chapter by chapter, and that, though he allowed me the greatest latitude in the presentation of the facts and indeed encouraged me to treat the subject on whatever lines were most congenial to me, it contains nothing (with the exception of Chapter V, written for this new edition) to which he did not give his full approbation; indeed there are several passages which I directly owe to him" (Stuart Gilbert, *James Joyce's "Ulysses": A Study* [1930; New York: Vintage Books, 1952], viii).

18. Litz, *Art of James Joyce*, 44. Litz acknowledges having taken the term "expressive form" from Winters.

19. Michael Groden, *"Ulysses" in Progress* (Princeton: Princeton Univ. Press, 1977), 152, 157.

20. Ibid., 17.

21. Joyce's official biographer, Herbert Gorman, takes a much more romantic view of the subject: "*Exiles* completed [c. April 1915], he returned to *Ulysses*. The idea was clear in his mind and so was the variegated yet unified technique through which he intended to present it" (Herbert Gorman, *James Joyce* [New York: Rinehart, 1948], 227). The manuscript research of Litz and Groden, I believe, effectively disproves Gorman's assertion.

22. *Pound/Joyce*, 157.

23. Patrick Parrinder, *James Joyce* (Cambridge: Cambridge Univ. Press, 1984), 163.

24. Pound, *Selected Prose*, 42.

25. Ezra Pound, "Vortex: Pound," in *Blast*, ed. Windham Lewis (London: John Lane, 1914), 154.

26. Ferdinand de Saussure, *Course in General Linguistics*, ed. Charles Bally and Albert Sechetray, trans. Ray Harris (LaSalle, Ind.: Open Court, 1986), 68, 69. Hugh Kenner has invoked the name of Saussure in passing in a discussion of "The Mooske and the Gripes"; see "Approaches to the Artist as a Young Language Teacher," in *¡Viva Vivas!: Essays in Honor of Eliseo Vivas on the Occasion of His Seventy-Fifth Birthday, July 13, 1976*, ed. Henry Regnery (Indianapolis: Liberty Press, 1976), 335–36.

27. Litz, *Art of James Joyce*, 46, 47.

28. Unless, of course, we open up the category of modern literature to the discourse of advertising, as Jennifer Wicke has so brilliantly done in *Advertising Fictions*.

29. Gilbert, *James Joyce's "Ulysses,"* 179.

30. Litz, *Art of James Joyce*, 49.

31. Mahaffey, *Reauthorizing Joyce*, 142–43.

32. Litz, *Art of James Joyce*, 44. Richard Ellmann refers to this incident to illustrate essentially the same point as Litz (*JJ* 551).

33. Joyce uses the same pun, this time in a purely verbal (rather than multimedia) form, in *Ulysses*; in the "Aeolus" episode, J. J. O'Molloy warns Myles Crawford, a native of Cork, "your Cork legs are running away with you" (*U* 114). The pun here involves an allusion to an Ulster ballad, "The Runaway Cork Leg," in which "cork" is the oak bark, not the Munster city. See Don Gifford, *"Ulysses" Annotated: Notes for James Joyce's "Ulysses,"* with Robert J. Seidman, 2d ed. (Berkeley and Los Angeles: Univ. of California Press, 1988), 144.

34. See Gregory Ulmer, "The Puncept in Grammatology," in *On Puns: The Foundation of Letters*, ed. Jonathan Culler (Oxford: Blackwell, 1988), 164–89. Derek Attridge has done the best work specifically on Joyce's punning; see his "Unpacking the Portmanteau, or Who's Afraid of *Finnegans Wake?"* in *On Puns,*

140–55; a longer version of this essay appears in his *Peculiar Language: Literature as Difference from the Renaissance to James Joyce* (Ithaca: Cornell Univ. Press, 1988), 188–209.

35. Gilbert, *James Joyce's "Ulysses,"* 192.

36. Ibid., 193; Peake, *James Joyce: The Citizen and the Artist,* 188.

37. Litz, *Art of James Joyce,* 51.

38. Thus, C. H. Peake is surely wrong to suggest that Joyce was fond of the technique "because of its indirectness and its capacity to give a subtle colouring to an episode" (*James Joyce: The Citizen and the Artist,* 188). The same sort of linguistic play in "Aeolus" is organized around the word *key(e)s;* the chapter contains too many keys altogether. Kathy Acker has playfully pointed this out in *My Death My Life by Pier Paolo Passolini,* where she juxtaposes a metonymically organized still-life description of the table in front of her with Joyce's intentionally symbolically overloaded descriptions in "Aeolus"; indeed, she pirates/plagiarizes about fifteen lines from the chapter (7:21–7, 141–51) having to do with keys, the House of Keys, Alexander Keyes, and, implicitly, the interpretive keys that such symbols provide. See Acker, *My Death My Life by Pier Paolo Passolini* (New York: Grove, 1988), 201–2. For a reading complementary in many ways to my own, see Henry Sussman, *Afterimages of Modernity,* 35–39.

Patrick McGee makes a similar argument about "Lotus Eaters," pointing out that "there are flowers everywhere resonating with the names Flower and Bloom and proliferating beyond the control or consciousness of any individual character" (McGee, *Paperspace,* 29).

39. Peake, *James Joyce: The Citizen and the Artist,* 189–90.

40. Groden, *"Ulysses" in Progress,* 93.

41. Gilbert, *James Joyce's "Ulysses,"* viii.

42. The definitions of these terms, unless otherwise indicated, are taken from Richard Lanham's *Handlist of Rhetorical Terms,* 2d ed. (Berkeley and Los Angeles: Univ. of California Press, 1991).

43. Gilbert, *James Joyce's "Ulysses,"* 242.

44. Alexander Pope, *Pastoral Poetry and "An Essay on Criticism,"* in *The Poems of Alexander Pope,* 6 vols. (New Haven: Yale Univ. Press, 1961), 1:281–82. Pope states his theory discursively in a 25 November 1710 letter: "It is not enough that nothing offends the Ear, that the Verse be (as the French call it) Coulante but a good Poet will adapt the very Sounds, as well as Words, to the Things he treats of. So that there is (if one may express it so) a Style of Sound: As in describing a gliding stream the Numbers shou'd run easy & flowing, in describing a rough Torrent or Deluge, sonorous & swelling, & so of the rest. This is evident ev'ry where in Homer and Virgill, and no where else that I know of to any observable degree" (Pope, *Pastoral Poetry,* 281n).

45. Pound, *Literary Essays,* 25.

46. Peake, *James Joyce: The Citizen and the Artist,* 223.

47. Bloom thinks about this phrase earlier in the episode: "Chamber music. Could make a kind of pun on that. It is a kind of music I often thought when

she. Acoustics that is. Tinkling. Empty vessels make most noise. Because the acoustics, the resonance changes according as the weight of the water is equal to the law of falling water. Like those rhapsodies of Liszt's, Hungarian, gip- syeyed. Pearls. Drops. Rain. Diddleiddle addleaddle ooddleooddle. Hissss. Now. Maybe now. Before" (*U* 232). As Bloom's associational thinking nicely suggests, the sound of anything can be thought musical, and the sound of Molly's tin- kling urine is, in some sense, not so far removed from a Liszt rhapsody or a Handel suite—all species of water music.

48. Joseph Frank's influential "Spatial Form in Modern Literature" (*Critiques and Essays in Criticism, 1920–1948*, ed. Robert W. Stallman [New York: Ronald Press, 1949]) for instance, insists on the spatial nature of *Ulysses;* but while he is careful to build his case using citations from the modernist writers themselves, Frank was already (1945) citing not Joyce (as he had cited Pound, Eliot, Proust, and Flaubert) in support of a spatial reading of *Ulysses,* but instead Joyce's crit- ics—Stuart Gilbert and Harry Levin—as well as Stephen Dedalus. In essence, Frank is able to justify his spatial reading of *Ulysses* only by conflating Joyce's poetics with Flaubert's, and Stephen's.

49. Perry Meisel, *The Myth of the Modern: A Study of British Literature and Crit- icism after 1850* (New Haven: Yale Univ. Press, 1987), 144; I have sometimes thought that the essay should have been titled "*Ulysses* and the Myth of Order." For an intelligent discussion of Eliot's early response to Joyce's writing, see Stan- ley Sultan's "*Ulysses,*" "*The Waste Land,*" *and Modernism: A Jubilee Study* (Port Washington, N.Y.: Kennikat Press, 1977).

50. Eliot 175; *Letters of T. S. Eliot 1898–1922,* ed. Valerie Eliot (San Diego: Har- court, Brace, Jovanovich, 1988), 1:455.

51. *Random House Dictionary of the English Language,* 2d ed., unabridged (New York: Random House, 1987), s.v. *discover.*

52. Wallace Stevens, *The Collected Poems* (New York: Vintage-Random House, 1954), 403–4.

53. John Middleton Murry, review, *Nation* and *Athenaeum,* 22 April 1922 (Dem- ing 1:196).

54. Gilbert, *James Joyce's "Ulysses,"* ix.

55. T. S. Eliot, "The Frontiers of Criticism," in *On Poetry and Poets* (New York: Farrar, Straus and Cudahy, 1957), 121.

56. *Pound/Joyce,* 197.

57. Joyce also came to regret having given a copy of the *Ulysses* schema to an- other of his sympathetic critics, Valéry Larbaud: he did so, he wrote to Weaver, "in order to help him confuse the audience a little more. I ought not to have done so" (*JJ* 519).

58. At its worst, an awareness of the Homeric parallels can lead to an almost paranoid style of reading. If readers are conditioned to look for a general sym- bolic scheme in a text, the odds are quite good they'll find it—especially "good" readers like us. The power of suggestion, especially in regard to pattern recog- nition, it quite strong; finally, nearly any text can be read as a cryptogram, and

the more challenging the writing, the more it resists our habitual ways of reading, the more plausible the allegorical interpretation becomes for readers. Even *Alice in Wonderland* has been variously read as a religious, political, and proto-Freudian allegory.

Harry Levin and Charles Shattuck, two otherwise percipient critics of modern literature, fell into this trap. Their essay "First Flight to Ithaca" (in *James Joyce: Two Decades of Criticism*, ed. Seon Givens [New York: Vanguard, 1948], 47–94) details the Homeric parallels which, they claim, undergird Joyce's *first* work of fiction, *Dubliners.* That essay has been almost uniformly ridiculed in Joyce circles; and yet it does stand as a graphic reminder of just how powerful an influence an interpretive framework can exert over our readings. I think it's unlikely that Joyce used the Homeric parallels to construct the *Dubliners* stories; but if Levin and Shattuck—and many others after them—have seen them, then they are, in some sense, "there": such is the power of heuristic devices like the mythical method. And Joyce, though he would doubtless be surprised by Levin and Shattuck's "discovery," would, I think, be pleased.

59. In his lectures to literature students on *Ulysses,* Vladimir Nabokov went so far as to call Joyce's schemata "tongue-in-cheek," and Gilbert "a bore": "I must especially warn against seeing in Leopold Bloom's humdrum wanderings and minor adventures on a summer day in Dublin a close parody of the *Odyssey,* with the adman Bloom acting the part of Odysseus, otherwise Ulysses, man of many devices, and Bloom's adulterous wife representing chaste Penelope while Stephen Dedalus is given the part of Telemachus. That there is a very vague and very general Homeric echo of the theme of wanderings in Bloom's case is obvious, as the title of the novel suggests, and there are a number of classical allusions among the many other allusions in the course of the book; but it would be a complete waste of time to look for close parallels in every character and every scene of the book. There is nothing more tedious than a protracted and sustained allegory based on a well-worn myth; and after the work had appeared in parts, Joyce promptly deleted the pseudo-Homeric titles of his chapters when he saw what scholarly and pseudoscholarly bores were up to. Another thing. One bore, a man named Stuart Gilbert, misled by a tongue-in-cheek list compiled by Joyce himself, found in every chapter the domination of one particular organ—the ear, the eye, the stomach, etc.—but we shall ignore that dull nonsense too. All art is in a sense symbolic; but we say 'stop, thief' to the critic who deliberately transforms an artist's subtle symbol into a pedant's stale allegory—a thousand and one nights into a convention of Shriners." Vladimir Nabokov, *Lectures on Literature,* ed. Fredson Bowers (New York: Harcourt, Brace, Jovanovich, 1980), 287–88.

60. Derek Attridge puts it this way: "It's the rich systematizations of *Ulysses* and *Finnegans Wake,* their ordered heterogeneity and multiplicitous coherence, that render their meanings forever unsystematizable—because of the inevitable outbreaks of coincidence that defy all predictability and programming. Joyce's own ambiguous attitude towards the structural frameworks of these

texts . . . merely confirm the texts' own ironic play with their ordering principles, whether Homeric comparisons or Viconian cycles. Monuments they may be, but they are also, and in the same gesture, comic dismantlings of the urge, so prominent around Joyce, to monumentalize." Derek Attridge, "The Postmodernity of Joyce: Chance, Coincidence, and the Reader," in *Joyce Studies Annual 1995*, ed. Thomas F. Staley (Austin: Univ. of Texas Press, 1995), 14.

61. Quoted in Derrida, "Force and Signification," in *Writing and Difference*, 11.

62. Kingsley Amis, *Lucky Jim* (New York: Penguin, 1954), 129.

63. The mesostics are built around the words Method, Structure, Intention, Discipline, Notation, Indeterminacy, Interpenetration, Imitation, Devotion, and Circumstances.

64. Cage's mesostics are also, in a sense, the reductio ad absurdum of the notion of expressive form; they substitute the *name* of an object and make it the focus of visual/typographic mimesis—which is, in fact, the essence of Joyce's expressive form in the Anna Livia Plurabelle section of *Finnegans Wake*, where Joyce worked the *names* of hundreds of rivers into the text.

65. John Cage, *X: Writings '79–'82* (Middletown: Wesleyan Univ. Press, 1983), 149.

66. Samuel Beckett et al., *Our Exagmination Round His Factification for Incamination of Work in Progress*, (1929; 2d ed., New York: New Directions, 1962), 7; emphasis added.

67. Jacques Mercanton, "The Hours of James Joyce," in *Portraits of the Artist in Exile*, ed. Potts, 213.

68. Beckett et al., *Our Exagmination*, 4.

69. Budgen, *James Joyce and the Making of Ulysses*, 171; Jacques Mercanton, "The Hours of James Joyce," in Potts, *Portraits of the Artist in Exile*, 213.

70. As Jennifer Wicke writes, "Bloom receives the signals that the culture is sending out, and he makes his own mix of them" (*Advertising Fictions*, 129). For a fuller treatment of the Alexander Keyes ad, see Wicke, *Advertising Fictions*, 145–47.

71. Jean-François Lyotard, "Representation, Presentation, Unpresentable," in *The Inhuman*, 124.

72. Richard Kostelanetz, jacket notes for John Cage, *Etudes Australes for Piano (Complete)* (Wergo 60152/55).

73. John Cage, jacket notes for *Etudes Australes and Ryoanji* (New York: Mode 1/2).

74. Kostelanetz, jacket notes, *Etudes Australes for Piano*. Cage elsewhere narrates how he came upon these maps: "In 1964 I went around the world with the Cunningham Dance Company. When we came to Prague we were paid but were told that the money we received had no value except in Prague. I used what I was given to buy books about mushrooms and maps of the stars. *Atlas Elipticalis* maps the great circle around the Sun, *Atlas Australis* the southern sky, *Borealis* the northern" (Cage, jacket notes, *Etudes Australes and Ryoanji*).

75. In his review, Middleton Murry wrote that "*Ulysses* has form, a subtle form, but the form is not strong enough to resist overloading, not sufficient to prevent Mr. Joyce from being the victim of his own anarchy" (Deming 1:197).

76. Groden, "*Ulysses*" *in Progress*, 52. Kenner points out, for instance, that "34 percent of the Ithaca episode" "was actually written on the margins of proof-sheets," demonstrating that "the sight of the printer's artifact, its text extricated at last from his own execrable handwriting and his typists' irregular transcriptions, tended to prompt his most expansive flights" (*Mechanic Muse*, 74).

Chapter 7: JJ and the Carnivalesque Imagination

1. Parrinder, *James Joyce*, 6–7.

2. Seán O Súilleabháin, *Irish Wake Amusements*, trans. O Súilleabháin (Cork: Mercier Press, 1967), 173.

3. Virginia Woolf, *The Diary of Virginia Woolf*, ed. Anne Olivier Bell (San Diego: Harcourt Brace Jovanovich, 1978), 2:188–89.

4. *Pound/Joyce*, 157.

5. David Hayman, "*Ulysses*": *The Mechanics of Meaning* (Englewood Cliffs: Prentice-Hall, 1970), 78–79.

6. Marilyn French, *The Book as World: James Joyce's "Ulysses"* (Cambridge: Harvard Univ. Press, 1976), 54.

7. Groden, "*Ulysses*" *in Progress*, 66.

8. French, *Book as World*, 13–14.

9. Ibid., 56–57.

10. James Joyce, *Ulysses: A Critical and Synoptic Edition*, ed. Hans Walter Gabler et al. (New York and London: Garland, 1984), 1:218.

11. French, *Book as World*, 56.

12. See Max Halperen, "The Uninvited Guest in James Joyce's 'Aeolus,'" in *A Fair Day in the Affections: Literary Essays in Honor of Robert B. White, Jr.*, ed. Jack D. Durant and M. Thomas Hester (Raleigh: Winston Press, 1980), 187–96.

13. Lyotard, "Rewriting Modernity," in *The Inhuman*, 25–26.

14. Hayman, "*Ulysses*": *The Mechanics of Meaning*, 80.

15. Groden, "*Ulysses*" *in Progress*, 32.

16. French, *Book as World*, 99, 101.

17. Wolfgang Iser, "Indeterminacy and the Reader's Response in Prose Fiction," in *Aspects of Narrative: Select Papers from the English Institute*, ed. J. Hillis Miller (New York: Columbia Univ. Press, 1971), 2.

18. Ibid., 35–36.

19. Carl Jung, for one, was bored by *Ulysses*, and made no bones about it: "Joyce bores me to tears, but it is a vicious dangerous boredom such as not even the worst banality could induce. It is the boredom of nature, the bleak whistling of the wind over the crags of the Hebrides, sunrise and sunset over the wastes of the Sahara, the roar of the sea—real Wagnerian 'programme music' as Curtius rightly says, and yet eternal repetition" (C. G. Jung, "*Ulysses*: A Mono-

logue," in *The Spirit in Man, Art, and Nature,* trans. R. F. C. Hull, Bollingen Series XX [New York: Pantheon Books-Random House, 1966], 114).

20. Iser, "Indeterminacy and the Reader's Response," 37.

21. I have silently spliced together discrete bits of this speech as it's read by Ned Lambert. The surviving fragment of Joyce's first poem, "Et Tu, Healy," suggests that Joyce himself had more than just an objective understanding of such bombast:

> My cot, alas, that dear old shady home
> Where oft in youthful sport I played
> Upon thy verdant grassy fields all day
> Lingered for a moment in thy bosom's shade.
>
> His quaint-perched aerie on the crags of time
> Where the rude din of this . . .
> Can trouble him no more.

James Joyce, *Poems and Shorter Writings,* ed. Richard Ellmann, A. Walton Litz, and John Whittier-Ferguson (London: Faber, 1991), 71.

22. One of the more helpful corrections in the text of the "Aeolus" episode in Gabler's edition is the movement of this headline from before Professor Mac-Hugh's comment, "'The moon,' professor MacHugh said . . . ," to after it (*U* 104). In the 1961 Random House edition, there is a possible ambiguity as to whether "HIS NATIVE DORIC" refers to Professor MacHugh's idiom or Simon Dedalus'; in the new text there can be no question. The redundancy of "native doric," however, remains—bombast in the headlines as well as in the text.

23. It is interesting to note the changing popular image of the press that is evidenced in the word "tabloid." The first *OED* entry glosses it as "a term registered on 14 March, 1884, by Mssrs. Burroughs, Wellcome and Co., as a trademark applied to chemical substances used in medicine and pharmacy prepared by them." It came to be used figuratively to mean "the compressed or concentrated form" of a drug, and was first metaphorically applied to the popular press in 1901: "He advocated tabloid journalism." This first twentieth-century use of the word indicates a general public desire for a more concentrated, easier-to-swallow journalism, "the allembracing give us this day our daily press" (*U* 528).

24. John Paul Riquelme, *Teller and Tale in Joyce's Fiction: Oscillating Perspectives* (Baltimore and London: Johns Hopkins Univ. Press, 1983), 191.

25. Halperen, "Uninvited Guest," 191.

26. Riana O'Dwyer has written on Joyce's use, during the writing of *Finnegans Wake,* of French sociologist Stefan Czarnowski's study *Le culte des héros et ses conditions sociales: Saint Patrice, héros national de l'Irlande,* which touches on Irish wake and burial customs. See O'Dwyer, "Czarnowski and *Finnegans Wake:* A Study of the Cult of the Hero," *James Joyce Quarterly* 17, no. 3 (Spring 1980): 285–89.

27. S. Joyce, *My Brother's Keeper,* 46.

28. Rodney Wilson Owen, *James Joyce and the Beginnings of "Ulysses"* (Ann Arbor: UMI Research Press, 1983), 8.

29. Homer, *The Odyssey*, trans. Robert Fitzgerald (Garden City, N.Y.: Anchor-Doubleday, 1963), 182.

30. Ibid., 186.

31. Ibid., 187.

32. Ibid.

33. Henry George Liddell, *A Greek-English Lexicon* (Oxford: Clarendon, 1966).

34. Homer, *Odyssey*, 209.

35. O Súilleabháin, *Irish Wake Amusements*, 72.

36. Patsy's demeanor is reminiscent of the behavior of the narrator of "The Sisters," after he's read the card announcing the father's death: "I walked away slowly along the sunny side of the street, reading all the theatrical advertisements in the shop-windows as I went. I found it strange that neither I nor the day seemed in a mourning mood and I felt even annoyed at discovering in myself a sensation of freedom as if I had been freed from something by his death" (*D* 12).

37. Lou Taylor, *Mourning Dress: A Costume and Social History* (London: George Allen and Unwin, 1983), 122.

38. John Morley, *Death, Heaven, and the Victorians* (Pittsburgh: Univ. of Pittsburgh Press, 1978), 77.

39. Parrinder, *James Joyce*, 148–49.

40. O Súilleabháin, *Irish Wake Amusements*, 173–74.

41. Ibid., 162.

42. Quoted in Deward MacLysaght, *Irish Life in the Seventeenth Century* (Oxford: Blackwell, 1950), 349–50.

43. Ibid., 350–51.

44. O Súilleabháin, *Irish Wake Amusements*, 172.

45. Ibid., 164.

46. Ibid., 140, 149, 152, 153.

47. Robert M. Adams, "Hades," in *James Joyce's "Ulysses": Critical Essays*, ed. Clive Hart and David Hayman (Berkeley and Los Angeles: Univ. of California Press, 1974), 110.

48. Ibid., 110–11n.

49. O Súilleabháin, *Irish Wake Amusements*, 23.

50. Georges Bataille, *Literature and Evil*, trans. Alastair Hamilton (London: Calder and Boyars, 1973), 38.

51. Stephen Heath, "Ambiviolences," in *Post-Structuralist Joyce*, ed. Derek Attridge and Daniel Ferrer (Cambridge: Cambridge Univ. Press, 1984), 52.

52. Though the number of these studies is growing quite large, I am thinking primarily of Patrick McGee, *Paperspace: Style as Ideology in Joyce's "Ulysses"*; Dominic Manganiello, *Joyce's Politics* (London: Routledge & Kegan Paul, 1980); Suzette Henke, *James Joyce and the Politics of Desire* (New York: Routledge, 1990); Cheryl Herr, *Joyce's Anatomy of Culture* (Urbana: Univ. of Illinois Press, 1986);

Stephen Watt, *Joyce, O'Casey, and the Irish Popular Theater* (Syracuse: Syracuse Univ. Press, 1991); Seamus Deane, *Celtic Revivals: Essays in Modern Irish Literature, 1880–1980* (London: Faber and Faber, 1985); and David Lloyd, *Anomalous States: Irish Writing and the Post-Colonial Moment* (Durham: Duke Univ. Press, 1993).

53. Quoted in Clark and Holquist, *Mikhail Bakhtin*, 56.

54. The most intelligent recent discussion of the authoritarian politics of modernism in general is Michael North's *The Political Aesthetic of Eliot, Yeats, and Pound* (Cambridge: Cambridge Univ. Press, 1991).

Afterword. On Ignoring *Finnegans Wake*

1. For a thorough discussion of the French critical reception of Joyce's texts in general, and *Finnegans Wake* in particular, see Geert Lernout, *The French Joyce* (Ann Arbor: Univ. of Michigan Press, 1990). See also Alan Roughey, *James Joyce and Critical Theory: An Introduction* (Ann Arbor: Univ. of Michigan Press, 1991).

2. Margot Norris, "The Postmodernization of *Finnegans Wake* Reconsidered," in Dettmar, *Rereading the New*, 343.

3. In the first installment of his *Writing through "Finnegans Wake"* John Cage, a great admirer of *Finnegans Wake*, puts it this way: "Due to N. O. Brown's remark that syntax is the arrangement of the army, and Thoreau's that when he heard a sentence he heard feet marching, I became devoted to nonsyntactical 'demilitarized' language. I spent well over a year writing *Empty Words*, a transition from a language without sentences (having only phrases, words, syllables, and letters) to a 'language' having only letters and silence (music). This led me to want to learn something about the ancient Chinese language and to read *Finnegans Wake*. But when in this spirit I picked up the book, Joyce seemed to me to have kept the old structures ('sintalks') in which he put the new words he had made" (*Writing through "Finnegans Wake,"* *James Joyce Quarterly* 15, special supplement [1978]: n.p.).

4. Lyotard: "in Joyce, it is the identity of writing which is the victim of an excess of the book *(au trop de livre)* or of literature" (*PC* 80). Vicki Mahaffey, though she esteems *Finnegans Wake* more highly than I do, touches on this same point: "Joyce's resistance to the unnatural stabilization of language and of value . . . becomes increasingly more specific as he moves his primary focus to an individual in *Portrait*, to narrative style in *Ulysses*, and finally to individual words and letters in *Finnegans Wake*" (*Reauthorizing Joyce*, 4).

5. Christopher Butler, "Joyce, Modernism, and Post-Modernism," in *The Cambridge Companion to James Joyce*, ed. Derek Attridge (Cambridge: Cambridge Univ. Press, 1990), 261.

6. Richard Ellmann, introduction, in S. Joyce, *My Brother's Keeper*, 24.

7. Ezra Pound, "After Election," in *Pound/Joyce*, 239.

8. Ezra Pound, "E. E. Cummings Alive," in *Pound/Joyce*, 256.

9. William Faulkner, *Faulkner in the University: Class Conferences at the Univer-*

sity of Virginia 1957–1958, ed. Frederick L. Gwynn and Joseph L. Blotner (Charlottesville: Univ. of Virginia Press, 1959), 280.

10. Calvin Bedient, "Modernism and the End of Beauty," in Dettmar, *Rereading the New,* 105.

11. Quoted in Potts, *Portraits of the Artist in Exile,* 213.

12. Quoted in Shenker, "Moody Man of Letters," 148.

13. Anthony Burgess, foreword to *A Shorter "Finnegans Wake"* (New York: Viking, 1968), vii.

14. Tindall, *Reader's Guide to "Finnegans Wake,"* 24; Susan Shaw Sailer, *On the Void of to Be: Incoherence and Trope in "Finnegans Wake"* (Ann Arbor: Univ. of Michigan Press, 1993), 3; Roland McHugh, *The "Finnegans Wake" Experience* (Berkeley and Los Angeles: Univ. of California Press, 1981), 25.

15. McHugh, *"Finnegans Wake" Experience,* 110.

16. To date, all English-language versions of *Finnegans Wake* share a common pagination; thus line numbers aren't necessary, as they would be in *Paradise Lost,* to help readers locate a passage in different editions of the text. And, we might note, line numbers are used as a matter of course in the criticism of this text which is itself printed without line numbers; some recent criticism of *Ulysses,* using the Gabler edition, has adopted a system of chapter and line-number citations, though the Gabler *Ulysses* is printed with line numbers.

17. Yeats, "The Phases of the Moon," in *W. B. Yeats: The Poems,* 164.

Bibliography

Acker, Kathy. "Devoured by Myths: An Interview with Sylvère Lotringer." In *Hannibal Lecter, My Father*, 1–24. New York: Semiotext(e), 1991.

Acker, Kathy. *My Death My Life by Pier Paolo Passolini*. New York: Grove, 1988.

Adams, Robert M. "Hades." In *James Joyce's "Ulysses": Critical Essays*, edited by Clive Hart and David Hayman, 91–114. Berkeley and Los Angeles: University of California Press, 1974.

Amis, Kingsley. *Lucky Jim*. New York: Penguin, 1954.

Anderson, Laurie. *Home of the Brave*. Warner Bros. 9 25400-2.

Anderson, Laurie. *United States*, New York: Harper & Row, 1984.

Attridge, Derek. *Peculiar Language: Literature as Difference from the Renaissance to James Joyce*. Ithaca: Cornell University Press, 1988.

Attridge, Derek. "The Postmodernity of Joyce: Chance, Coincidence, and the Reader." In *Joyce Studies Annual 1995*, edited by Thomas Staley, 10–18. Austin: University of Texas Press, 1995.

Attridge, Derek. "Unpacking the Portmanteau, or Who's Afraid of *Finnegans Wake?*" In *On Puns: The Foundation of Letters*, edited by Jonathan Culler, 140–55. Oxford: Blackwell, 1988.

Attridge, Derek, and Daniel Ferrer, eds. *Post-Structuralist Joyce: Essays from the French*. Cambridge: Cambridge University Press, 1984.

Bakhtin, Mikhail. *The Dialogic Imagination: Four Essays*. Edited by Michael Holquist. Translated by Caryl Emerson and Michael Holquist. Austin: University of Texas Press, 1981.

Bakhtin, Mikhail. *Problems of Dostoevsky's Poetics*. Edited and translated by Caryl Emerson. Minneapolis: University of Minnesota Press, 1984.

Bakhtin, Mikhail. *Rabelais and His World*. Translated by Hélène Iwolsky. Bloomington: Indiana University Press, 1984.

Barthes, Roland. *Critical Essays*. Translated by Richard Howard. Evanston, Ill.: Northwestern University Press, 1972.

Barthes, Roland. *Image, Music, Text*. Translated Stephen Heath. New York: Farrar, Straus & Giroux, 1977.

Barthes, Roland. "Inaugural Lecture, Collège de France." Translated by Richard Howard. In *A Barthes Reader*, edited by Susan Sontag, 457–78. New York: Hill & Wang, 1982.

Barthes, Roland. *The Pleasure of the Text.* Translated by Richard Miller. New York: Farrar, Straus & Giroux, 1975.

Barthes, Roland. *Roland Barthes.* Translated by Richard Howard. New York: Hill & Wang, 1977.

Barthes, Roland. *The Rustle of Language.* Translated by Richard Howard. New York: Hill & Wang, 1986.

Barthes, Roland. *S/Z.* Translated by Richard Miller. New York: Hill & Wang, 1974.

Barthes, Roland. *Writing Degree Zero.* Translated by Annette Lavers and Colin Smith. New York: Hill & Wang, 1967.

Bataille, Georges. *Literature and Evil.* Translated by Alastair Hamilton. London: Calder and Boyars, 1973.

Beckett, Samuel. *Disjecta: Miscellaneous Writings and a Dramatic Fragment.* Edited by Ruby Cohn. London: John Calder, 1983.

Beckett, Samuel. *Molloy.* In *Three Novels: Molloy, Malone Dies, The Unnamable,* 7–176. New York: Grove, 1958.

Beckett, Samuel, et al. *Our Exagmination Round His Factification for Incamination of Work in Progress.* 2d ed. New York: New Directions, 1962.

Bedient, Calvin. "Modernism and the End of Beauty." In *Rereading the New: A Backward Glance at Modernism,* edited by Kevin J. H. Dettmar, 99–115. Ann Arbor: University of Michigan Press, 1992.

Beja, Morris. "One Good Look at Themselves: Epiphanies in *Dubliners.*" In *Work in Progress: Joyce Centenary Essays,* edited by Richard F. Peterson, Alan M. Cohn, and Edmund L. Epstein, 3–14. Carbondale: Southern Illinois University Press, 1983.

Bell, Clive. *Art.* New York: Frederick A. Stokes, [1913].

Benjamin, Walter. "The Author as Producer." In *Reflections: Essays, Aphorisms, Autobiographical Writings,* edited by Peter Demetz, translated by Edmund Jephcott, 220–38. New York: Harcourt Brace Jovanovich, 1978.

Benjamin, Walter. "The Work of Art in the Age of Mechanical Reproduction." In *Illuminations,* edited by Hannah Arendt, translated by Harry Zohn, 217–51. New York: Schocken, 1969.

Bersani, Leo. "Against *Ulysses.*" *Raritan* 8, no. 2 (Fall 1988): 1–32.

Bishop, John. *Joyce's Book of the Dark: "Finnegans Wake."* Madison: University of Wisconsin Press, 1986.

Booth, Wayne C. *The Rhetoric of Fiction.* 2d ed. Chicago: University of Chicago Press, 1983.

Bowen, Zack. "Joyce and the Epiphany Concept: A New Approach." *Journal of Modern Literature* 9 (1981–82): 106–7.

Brandabur, Edward. *A Scrupulous Meanness: A Study of Joyce's Early Work.* Urbana: University of Illinois Press, 1971.

Brown, Homer Obed. *James Joyce's Early Fiction: The Biography of a Form.* Cleveland: Case Western Reserve University Press, 1972.

Brown, Norman O. *Closing Time.* New York: Random House, 1973.

Budgen, Frank. *James Joyce and the Making of "Ulysses."* Bloomington: Indiana University Press, 1960.

Burgess, Anthony, ed. *A Shorter "Finnegans Wake."* New York: Viking, 1968.

Bushrui, Suheil Badi, and Bernard Benstock, eds. *James Joyce: An International Perspective.* Gerrards Cross: Colin Smythe, 1982.

Butler, Christopher. "Joyce, Modernism, and Post-Modernism." In *The Cambridge Companion to James Joyce,* edited by Derek Attridge, 259–82. Cambridge: Cambridge University Press, 1990.

Buttigieg, Joseph. *A Portrait of the Artist in Different Perspective.* Columbus: Ohio State University Press, 1987.

Cage, John. *Conversing with Cage.* Edited by Richard Kostelanetz. New York: Limelight Editions, 1988.

Cage, John. Liner notes to *Etudes Australes and Ryoanji.* New York: Mode ½, n.d.

Cage, John. *Writing through "Finnegans Wake." James Joyce Quarterly* 15, special supplement (1978): n.p.

Cage, John. *X: Writings 79–82.* Middletown, Conn: Wesleyan University Press, 1983.

Carroll, Lewis. *The Annotated Alice.* Edited by Martin Gardner. New York: New American Library, 1960.

Cage, John. "Writing for the Fourth Time through *Finnegans Wake,*" 1–49. In *X: Writings '79–'82.* Middletown, Conn: Wesleyan University Press, 1983.

Cage, John. "Writing for the Second Time through *Finnegans Wake,*" 133–76. In *Empty Words: Writings '73–'79.* Middletown, Conn: Wesleyan University Press, 1979.

Cawelti, John. *Adventure, Mystery, and Romance: Formula Stories as Art and Popular Culture.* Chicago: University of Chicago Press, 1976.

Chesterton, G. K. *The Defendant.* London: Dent, 1901.

Cixous, Hélène. "Joyce: The (R)use of Writing." In *Post-Structuralist Joyce,* edited by Derek Attridge and Daniel Ferrer, 15–30. Cambridge: Cambridge University Press, 1984.

Clark, Katerina, and Michael Holquist. *Mikhail Bakhtin.* Cambridge: Harvard University Press, 1984.

Cohn, Dorrit. *Transparent Minds: Narrative Modes for Presenting Consciousness in Fiction.* Princeton: Princeton University Press, 1978.

Davis, Philip J., and Reuben Hersh. *The Mathematical Experience.* Boston: Houghton Mifflin, 1981.

Deane, Seamus. *Celtic Revivals: Essays in Modern Irish Literature, 1880–1980.* London: Faber and Faber, 1985.

Deleuze, Gilles. "Intellectuals and Power." In Michel Foucault, *Language, Counter-Memory, Practice: Selected Essays and Interviews,* edited by Donald F. Bouchard, translated by Donald F. Bouchard and Sherry Simon, 205–17. Ithaca: Cornell University Press, 1977.

Deleuze, Gilles. *Nietzsche and Philosophy.* Translated by Hugh Tomlinson. New York: Columbia University Press, 1983.

Deleuze, Gilles, and Félix Guattari. *Anti-Oedipus: Capitalism and Schizophrenia.* Translated by Robert Hurley, Mark Seem, and Helen R. Lane. Minneapolis: University of Minnesota Press, 1983.

Deleuze, Gilles, and Claire Parnet. *Dialogues.* Translated by Hugh Tomlinson and Barbara Habberjam. New York: Columbia University Press, 1987.

Deming, Robert H., ed. *James Joyce: The Critical Heritage.* 2 vols. New York: Barnes & Noble, 1970.

Derrida, Jacques. "White Mythology: Metaphor in the Text of Philosophy." In *Margins of Philosophy,* translated by Alan Bass, 207–71. Chicago: University of Chicago Press, 1982.

Derrida, Jacques. *Writing and Difference.* Translated by Alan Bass. Chicago: University of Chicago Press, 1978.

Dettmar, Kevin J. H. "The Figure in Beckett's Carpet: *Molloy* and the Assault on Metaphor." In *Rethinking Beckett: A Collection of Critical Essays,* edited by Lance St. John Butler and Robin J. Davis, 68–88. Basingstoke: Macmillan; New York: St. Martin's, 1990.

Dettmar, Kevin J. H. "If Guinness Is as Cheap as Milk." Review of Albert Wachtel, *The Cracked Lookingglass: James Joyce and the Nightmare of History. James Joyce Literary Supplement* (Fall 1992): 4.

Dettmar, Kevin J. H. "Selling *Ulysses.*" *James Joyce Quarterly* 30, no. 4/31, no. 1 (Summer/Fall 1993):795–812.

Dettmar, Kevin J. H., ed. *Rereading the New: A Backward Glance at Modernism.* Ann Arbor: University of Michigan Press, 1992.

Devlin, Kimberly J. *Wandering and Return in "Finnegans Wake": An Integrative Approach to Joyce's Fictions.* Princeton: Princeton University Press, 1991.

Docherty, Thomas, ed. *Postmodernism: A Reader.* New York: Columbia University Press, 1993.

Donoghue, Denis. *The Arts without Mystery.* Boston: Little, Brown, 1983.

Doyle, Sir Arthur Conan. *Adventures of Sherlock Holmes.* New York: Harper & Row, 1930.

Eco, Umberto. *The Aesthetics of Chaosmos: The Middle Ages of James Joyce.* Translated from the Italian by Ellen Esrock. Cambridge: Harvard University Press, 1989.

Eder, Richard. Review of David Lehmann, *Signs of the Times. Los Angeles Times,* 14 February 1991.

Eliot, T. S. "Contemporary English Prose." *Vanity Fair* 20, no. 5 (July 1923): 51, 98.

Eliot, T. S. "The Frontiers of Criticism." In *On Poetry and Poets.* New York: Farrar, Straus and Cudahy, 1957.

Eliot, T. S. *Letters of T. S. Eliot, 1898–1922.* Edited by Valerie Eliot. San Diego: Harcourt Brace Jovanovich, 1988.

Eliot, T. S. "A Message to the Fish." In *James Joyce: Two Decades of Criticism,* edited by Seon Givens, 468–71. New York: Vanguard, 1963.

Eliot, T. S. *Selected Prose of T. S. Eliot.* Edited by Frank Kermode. New York: Harcourt Brace Jovanovich, 1975.

Ellmann, Richard. *James Joyce*. Rev. ed. New York: Oxford University Press, 1982.

Ellmann, Richard. *"Ulysses" on the Liffey*. New York: Oxford University Press, 1972.

Empson, William. "The Theme of *Ulysses*." *Kenyon Review* 18 (Winter 1956): 26–52.

Faulkner, William. *Faulkner in the University: Class Conferences at the University of Virginia 1957–1958*. Edited by Frederick L. Gwynn and Joseph L. Blotner. Charlottesville: University of Virginia Press, 1959.

Ferguson, Suzanne. "A Sherlook at *Dubliners*: Structural and Thematic Analogues in Detective Stories and the Modern Short Story." *James Joyce Quarterly* 16 (1978–79): 111–21.

Feshbach, Sidney. "'Fallen on His Feet in Buenos Ayres' (*D* 39): Frank in 'Eveline.'" *James Joyce Quarterly* 20(1983): 223–27.

Foucault, Michel. *Madness and Civilization: A History of Insanity in the Age of Reason*. Translated by Richard Howard. New York: Vintage, 1973.

Foucault, Michel. *The Order of Things: An Archaeology of the Human Sciences*. New York: Vintage-Random House, 1970.

Foucault, Michel. "What Is an Author?" In *Language, Counter-Memory, Practice*, edited by Donald F. Bouchard, translated by Donald F. Bouchard and Sherry Simon, 113–38. Ithaca: Cornell University Press, 1977.

Frank, Joseph. "Spatial Form in Modern Literature." In *Critiques and Essays in Criticism, 1920–1948*, edited by Robert W. Stallman, 315–28. New York: Ronald Press, 1949.

French, Marilyn. *The Book as World: James Joyce's "Ulysses."* Cambridge: Harvard University Press, 1976.

Freud, Sigmund. *The Standard Edition of the Complete Psychological Works of Sigmund Freud*. Edited by James Strachey. 26 vols. London: Hogarth Press, 1953–74.

Gabler, Hans Walter. "Joyce's Text in Progress." In *The Cambridge Companion to James Joyce*, edited by Derek Attridge, 213–36. Cambridge: Cambridge University Press, 1990.

Gabler, Hans Walter. "Stephen in Paris." *James Joyce Quarterly* 17 (1980): 306–11.

Gass, William. *In the Heart of the Heart of the Country*. Boston: Godine, 1981.

Genette, Gérard. *Narrative Discourse: An Essay in Method*. Translated by Jane E. Lewin. Ithaca: Cornell University Press, 1980.

Gifford, Don, with Robert J. Seidman. *"Ulysses" Annotated: Notes for James Joyce's "Ulysses."* 2d ed. Berkeley and Los Angeles: University of California Press, 1988.

Gilbert, Stuart. *James Joyce's "Ulysses": A Study*. 1930. New York: Vintage Books, 1952.

Gordon, John. *James Joyce's Metamorphoses*. Dublin: Gill & Macmillan, 1981.

Gorman, Herbert. *James Joyce*. New York: Rinehart, 1948.

Groden, Michael. "Textual and Publishing History." In *A Companion to Joyce*

Studies, edited by Zack Bowen and James F. Carens, 71–128. Westport, Conn.: Greenwood Press, 1984.

Groden, Michael. *"Ulysses" in Progress.* Princeton: Princeton University Press, 1977.

Groden, Michael, et al., eds. *The James Joyce Archive.* 63 vols. New York: Garland, 1978.

Grossvogel, David I. "Agatha Christie: Containment of the Unknown." In *Mystery and Its Fictions: From Oedipus to Agatha Christie.* Baltimore and London: Johns Hopkins University Press, 1979.

Halperen, Max. "The Uninvited Guest in James Joyce's 'Aeolus.'" In *A Fair Day in the Affections: Literary Essays in Honor of Robert B. White, Jr.,* edited by Jack D. Durant and M. Thomas Hester, 187–96. Raleigh: Winston Press, 1980.

Hart, Clive. "Wandering Rocks." In *James Joyce's "Ulysses": Critical Essays,* edited by Clive Hart and David Hayman, 181–216. Berkeley and Los Angeles: University of California Press, 1974.

Hassan, Ihab. *The Dismemberment of Orpheus: Toward a Postmodern Literature.* 2d ed. Madison: University of Wisconsin Press, 1982.

Hassan, Ihab. *Paracriticisms: Seven Speculations for the Times.* Urbana: University of Illinois Press, 1975.

Hassan, Ihab. *The Postmodern Turn: Essays in Postmodern Theory and Culture.* Columbus: Ohio State University Press, 1987.

Hayman, David. *"Ulysses": The Mechanics of Meaning.* Englewood Cliffs: Prentice-Hall, 1970.

Hayman, David. *The "Wake" in Transit.* Ithaca: Cornell University Press, 1990.

Heath, Stephen. "Ambiviolences." In *Post-Structuralist Joyce,* edited by Derek Attridge and Daniel Ferrer, 31–68. Cambridge: Cambridge University Press, 1984.

Henke, Suzette. *James Joyce and the Politics of Desire.* New York: Routledge, 1990.

Herr, Cheryl. *Joyce's Anatomy of Culture.* Urbana: University of Illinois Press, 1986.

Herring, Phillip. "Joyce and Rimbaud: An Introductory Essay." In *James Joyce: An International Perspective,* edited by Suheil Badi Bushrui and Bernard Benstock, 170–89. Gerrards Cross: Colin Smythe, 1982.

Herring, Phillip. *Joyce's Uncertainty Principle.* Princeton: Princeton University Press, 1987.

Hofstadter, Douglas R. *Gödel, Escher, Bach: An Eternal Golden Braid.* New York: Vintage, 1979.

Holquist, Michael. "Whodunit and Other Questions: Metaphysical Detective Stories in Post-War Fiction." *New Literary History* 3 (1971): 150–74.

Homer. *The Odyssey.* Translated by Robert Fitzgerald. Garden City, N.Y.: Doubleday, 1961.

Hulme, T. E. "Romanticism and Classicism." In *Speculations: Essays on Humanism and the Philosophy of Art,* edited by Herbert Read, 111–40. New York: Harcourt, Brace, 1936.

Hutcheon, Linda. *A Poetics of Postmodernism: History, Theory, Fiction.* New York: Routledge, 1988.

Irish Homestead (Dublin, Ireland), 16 January 1904.

Iser, Wolfgang. "Indeterminacy and the Reader's Response in Prose Fiction." In *Aspects of Narrative: Select Papers from the English Institute,* edited by J. Hillis Miller, 1–45. New York: Columbia University Press, 1971.

Joyce, James. *The Critical Writings of James Joyce.* Edited by Ellsworth Mason and Richard Ellmann. New York: Viking, 1959.

Joyce, James. *Dubliners: Text, Criticism, and Notes.* Edited by Robert Scholes and A. Walton Litz. New York: Penguin, 1976.

Joyce, James. *Finnegans Wake.* New York: Viking, 1939.

Joyce, James. *Letters.* Vol. 1 edited by Stuart Gilbert, vols. 2 and 3 edited by Richard Ellmann. New York: Viking, 1966.

Joyce, James. *Poems and Shorter Writings.* Edited by Richard Ellmann, A. Walton Litz, and John Whittier-Ferguson. London: Faber, 1991.

Joyce, James. *A Portrait of the Artist as a Young Man: Text, Criticism, and Notes.* Edited by Chester G. Anderson. New York: Penguin, 1968.

Joyce, James. *Stephen Hero.* Edited by John J. Slocum and Herbert Cahoon. 2d ed. New York: New Directions, 1963.

Joyce, James. *Ulysses.* Edited by Hans Walter Gabler et al. New York: Random House, 1986.

Joyce, James. *Ulysses: A Critical and Synoptic Edition.* Edited by Hans Walter Gabler et al. 3 vols. New York and London: Garland, 1984.

Joyce, Stanislaus. *My Brother's Keeper.* Edited by Richard Ellmann. London: Faber, 1958.

Jung, C. G. "*Ulysses:* A Monologue." In *The Spirit in Man, Art, and Nature,* translated by R. F. C. Hull. Bollingen Series XX, 109–32. New York: Pantheon Books-Random House, 1966.

Kenner, Hugh. "Approaches to the Artist as a Young Language Teacher." In *¡Viva Vivas!: Essays in Honor of Eliseo Vivas on the Occasion of his Seventy-Fifth Birthday, July 13, 1976,* edited by Henry Regnery, 331–53. Indianapolis: Liberty Press, 1976.

Kenner, Hugh. *Dublin's Joyce.* Bloomington: Indiana University Press, 1956.

Kenner, Hugh. *Joyce's Voices.* Berkeley and Los Angeles: University of California Press, 1978.

Kenner, Hugh. *The Mechanic Muse.* New York: Oxford, 1987.

Kenner, Hugh. *The Pound Era.* Berkeley and Los Angeles: University of California Press, 1971.

Kenner, Hugh. *Ulysses.* London: Allen & Unwin, 1982.

Kershner, R. B. *Joyce, Bakhtin, and Popular Literature: Chronicles of Disorder.* Chapel Hill: University of North Carolina Press, 1989.

Kiberd, Declan. "The Vulgarity of Heroics: Joyce's *Ulysses.*" In *James Joyce: An International Perspective,* edited by Suheil Badi Bushrui and Bernard Benstock, 156–68. Gerrards Cross: Colin Smythe, 1982.

Klinkowitz, Jerome. *Rosenberg/Barthes/Hassan: The Postmodern Habit of Thought.* Athens: University of Georgia Press, 1988.

Knowlton, Eloise. "Fending off the Object: Criticism, Postcriticism, and the Joycean." In *Rereading the New: A Backward Glance at Modernism,* edited by Kevin J. H. Dettmar, 27–39. Ann Arbor: University of Michigan Press, 1992.

Kostelanetz, Richard. Jacket notes for John Cage, *Etudes Australes for Piano Complete,* n.p. Wergo 60152/55.

Kristeva, Julia. *Desire in Language: A Semiotic Approach to Literature and Art.* Edited by Leon S. Roudiez. Translated by Thomas Gora, Alice Jardine, and Leon S. Roudiez. New York: Columbia University Press, 1980.

Kristeva, Julia. "Postmodernism?" *Bucknell Review* 25, no. 2 (1980): 136–41.

Kristeva, Julia. *Revolution in Poetic Language.* Translated by Margaret Waller. New York: Columbia University Press, 1984.

Kristeva, Julia. *Σημειωτικὴ: Recherches pour une sémanalyse.* Paris: Éditions du Seuil, 1969.

Laing, R. D. *The Politics of Experience.* New York: Pantheon, 1967.

Lanham, Richard. *Handlist of Rhetorical Terms.* 2d ed. Berkeley and Los Angeles: University of California Press, 1991.

Lawrence, Karen. *The Odyssey of Style in "Ulysses."* Princeton: Princeton University Press, 1981.

Léger, Fernand. "The Esthetics of the Machine: Manufactured Objects, Artisans and Artists." *Little Review* 9, no. 3 (Spring 1923) no. 4 (Autumn/Winter 1923–24): 45–49, 55–58.

Leonard, Garry M. *Reading "Dubliners" Again: A Lacanian Perspective.* Syracuse: Syracuse University Press, 1993.

Lernout, Geert. *The French Joyce.* Ann Arbor: University of Michigan Press, 1990.

Lévi-Strauss, Claude. *The Savage Mind.* Chicago: University of Chicago Press, 1966.

Levin, Harry, and Charles Shattuck. "First Flight to Ithaca." In *James Joyce: Two Decades of Criticism,* edited by Seon Givens, 47–94. New York: Vanguard, 1948.

Levitt, Morton P. "The Invention of Postmodernism: A Critical Fable." In *Rereading the New: A Backward Glance at Modernism,* edited by Kevin J. H. Dettmar, 87–96. Ann Arbor: University of Michigan Press, 1992.

Liddell, Henry George. *A Greek-English Lexicon.* Oxford: Clarendon, 1966.

"Liturgy of S. Chrysostom." In *Liturgies Eastern and Western,* edited by F. E. Brightman, 1:353–99. 2 vols. Oxford: Oxford University Press, 1896.

Litz, A. Walton. *The Art of James Joyce: Method and Design in "Ulysses" and "Finnegans Wake."* Rev. ed. Oxford: Oxford University Press, 1964.

Lloyd, David. *Anomalous States: Irish Writing and the Post-Colonial Moment.* Durham: Duke University Press, 1993.

Lyotard, Jean-François. *Driftworks.* Edited by Roger McKeon. New York: Semiotext(e), 1984.

Lyotard, Jean-François. *The Inhuman: Reflections on Time.* Translated by Geoffrey Bennington and Rachel Bowlby. Stanford: Stanford University Press, 1991.

Lyotard, Jean-François. *The Postmodern Condition: A Report on Knowledge.* Translated by Geoff Bennington and Brian Massumi. Minneapolis: University of Minnesota Press, 1984.

Lyotard, Jean-François. *The Postmodern Explained: Correspondence, 1982–1985.* Edited by Julian Pefanis and Morgan Thomas. Translated by Don Barry et al. Minneapolis: University of Minnesota Press, 1993.

Lyotard, Jean-François. "Rules and Paradoxes and Svelte Appendix." Translated by Brian Massumi. *Cultural Critique* 5 (Winter 1986–87): 209–19.

Lyotard, Jean-François, and Jean-Loup Thébaud. *Just Gaming.* Translated by Wlad Godzich. Minneapolis: University of Minnesota Press, 1985.

MacCabe, Colin. *James Joyce and the Revolution of the Word.* New York: Harper & Row, 1979.

McGee, Patrick. *Paperspace: Style as Ideology in Joyce's "Ulysses."* Lincoln: University of Nebraska Press, 1988.

McHale, Brian. *Constructing Postmodernism.* London and New York: Routledge, 1992.

McHale, Brian. *Postmodernist Fiction.* London and New York: Methuen, 1987.

McHugh, Roland. *The "Finnegans Wake" Experience.* Berkeley and Los Angeles: University of California Press, 1981.

MacLysaght, Deward. *Irish Life in the Seventeenth Century.* Oxford: Blackwell, 1950.

Magalaner, Marvin, and Richard M. Kain. *Joyce: The Man, the Work, the Reputation.* New York: New York University Press, 1956.

Mahaffey, Vicki. *Reauthorizing Joyce.* Cambridge: Cambridge University Press, 1988.

Malamud, Randy. *The Language of Modernism.* Ann Arbor: UMI Research Press, 1989.

Manganiello, Dominic. *Joyce's Politics.* London: Routledge & Kegan Paul, 1980.

Marshall, Donald. Foreword to Stephen Melville, *Philosophy Beside Itself,* xi–xxiv. Minneapolis: University of Minnesota Press, 1986.

Meisel, Perry. *The Myth of the Modern: A Study of British Literature and Criticism after 1850.* New Haven: Yale University Press, 1987.

Morley, John. *Death, Heaven, and the Victorians.* Pittsburgh: University of Pittsburgh Press, 1978.

Nabokov, Vladimir. *Lectures on Literature.* Edited by Fredson Bowers. New York: Harcourt Brace Jovanovich, 1980.

Nabokov, Vladimir. *Strong Opinions.* New York: McGraw-Hill, 1973.

The New Encyclopedia Britannica, 15th ed.

Nietzsche, Friedrich. *The Birth of Tragedy and The Case of Wagner.* Translated by Walter Kaufmann. New York: Viking, 1967.

Nietzsche, Friedrich. *On the Genealogy of Morals and Ecce Homo.* Edited by Walter Kaufmann. Translated by Walter Kaufmann and R. J. Hollingdale. New York: Random House, 1967.

Nietzsche, Friedrich. *Twilight of the Idols and The Anti-Christ.* Translated by R. J. Hollingdale. New York: Penguin, 1968.

Norris, Margot. *The Decentered Universe of "Finnegans Wake."* Baltimore and London: Johns Hopkins University Press, 1976.

Norris, Margot. *Joyce's Web: The Social Unraveling of Modernism.* Austin: University of Texas Press, 1992.

Norris, Margot. "The Postmodernization of *Finnegans Wake* Reconsidered." In *Rereading the New: A Backward Glance at Modernism,* ed. Kevin J. H. Dettmar, 343–62. Ann Arbor: University of Michigan Press, 1992.

North, Michael. *The Political Aesthetic of Yeats, Eliot, and Pound.* Cambridge: Cambridge University Press, 1991.

O Súilleabháin, Seán. *Irish Wake Amusements.* Translated by O Súilleabháin. Cork: Mercier Press, 1967.

O'Connor, Frank. *The Lonely Voice: A Study of the Short Story.* Cleveland: World Publishing, 1963.

O'Dwyer, Riana. "Czarnowski and *Finnegans Wake* : A Study of the Cult of the Hero." *James Joyce Quarterly* 17, no. 3 (Spring 1980): 281–91.

Owen, Rodney Wilson. *James Joyce and the Beginnings of "Ulysses."* Ann Arbor: UMI Research Press, 1983.

Oxford English Dictionary. 2d ed. Oxford: Oxford University Press, 1989.

Parrinder, Patrick. *James Joyce.* Cambridge: Cambridge University Press, 1984.

Peake, C. H. *James Joyce: The Citizen and the Artist.* Stanford: Stanford University Press, 1977.

Pearce, Richard. *The Politics of Narration: James Joyce, William Faulkner, and Virginia Woolf.* New Brunswick: Rutgers University Press, 1991.

Polan, Dana. Translator's introduction to Gilles Deleuze and Félix Guattari, *Kafka: Toward a Minor Literature,* translated by Dana Polan, xxii–xxix. Minneapolis: University of Minnesota Press, 1986.

Pope, Alexander. *Pastoral Poetry and "An Essay on Criticism."* In *The Poems of Alexander Pope,* edited by E. Audra and Aubrey Williams. 6 vols. New Haven: Yale University Press, 1961.

Porter, Dennis. *The Pursuit of Crime: Art and Ideology in Detective Fiction.* New Haven: Yale University Press, 1981.

Potts, Willard, ed. *Portraits of the Artist in Exile: Recollections of James Joyce by Europeans.* San Diego: Harcourt Brace Jovanovich, 1986.

Pound, Ezra. *The Cantos of Ezra Pound.* New York: New Directions, 1970.

Pound, Ezra. *Literary Essays of Ezra Pound.* Edited by T. S. Eliot. New York: New Directions, 1968.

Pound, Ezra. *Selected Letters, 1907–1941.* Edited by D. D. Paige. New York: New Directions, 1971.

Pound, Ezra. *Selected Prose, 1909–1965.* Edited by William Cookson. New York: New Directions, 1973.

Pound, Ezra. "Vortex: Pound." In *Blast*, edited by Wyndham Lewis, 153–54. London: John Lane, 1914.

Pound/Joyce. Edited by Forrest Read. New York: New Directions, 1967.

Power, Arthur. *Conversations with James Joyce*. Edited by Clive Hart. London: Millington, 1974.

Prescott, Joseph. "Notes on Joyce's *Ulysses*." *MLQ* 13 (1952): 149–62.

Rabaté, Jean-Michel. *James Joyce: Authorized Reader*. Baltimore and London: Johns Hopkins University Press, 1991.

Random House Dictionary of the English Language. 2d ed., unabridged. New York: Random House, 1987.

Ransom, John Crowe. *Beating the Bushes: Selected Essays, 1941–1970*. New York: New Directions, 1972.

Rimbaud, Arthur. *Rimbaud: Complete Works, Selected Letters*. Translated by Wallace Fowlie. Chicago: University of Chicago Press, 1966.

Riquelme, John Paul. *Teller and Tale in Joyce's Fiction: Oscillating Perspectives*. Baltimore and London: Johns Hopkins University Press, 1983.

Rorty, Richard. *Philosophy and the Mirror of Nature*. Princeton: Princeton University Press, 1979.

Roughey, Alan. *James Joyce and Critical Theory: An Introduction*. Ann Arbor: University of Michigan Press, 1991.

Sailer, Susan Shaw. *On the Void of to Be: Incoherence and Trope in "Finnegans Wake."* Ann Arbor: University of Michigan Press, 1993.

Saussure, Ferdinand de. *Course in General Linguistics*. Edited by Charles Bally and Albert Sechetray. Translated by Ray Harris. La Salle, Ind.: Open Court, 1986.

Scheler, Max. *Ressentiment*. Edited by Lewis A. Coser. Translated by William W. Holdheim. New York: Free Press, 1961.

Scholes, Robert, and Richard M. Kain, eds. *The Workshop of Daedalus: James Joyce and the Raw Materials for "A Portrait of the Artist as a Young Man."* Evanston: Northwestern University Press, 1965.

Scott, Sir Walter. *The Abbot*. Philadelphia: J. B. Lippincott, 1887.

Seidel, Michael. *Exile and the Narrative Imagination*. New Haven: Yale University Press, 1986.

Shakespeare, William. *All's Well That Ends Well*. Edited by G. K. Hunter. London: Methuen, 1959.

Shelley, Percy Bysshe. *The Complete Poetical Works of Percy Bysshe Shelley*. Edited by Roger Ingpen and Walter E. Peck. 10 vols. New York: Gordian Press, 1965.

Shenker, Israel. "Moody Man of Letters." In *Samuel Beckett: The Critical Heritage*, edited by Lawrence Graver and Raymond Federman, 146–49. London: Routledge & Kegan Paul, 1979.

Solomon, Jack. *The Signs of Our Time: The Secret Meanings of Everyday Things*. New York: Harper & Row, 1990.

Sontag, Susan. *Against Interpretation*. New York: Farrar, Straus & Giroux, 1966.

Spanos, William V. "Modern Literary Criticism and the Spatialization of Time: An Existential Critique." *Journal of Aesthetics and Art Criticism* 29 (1970): 87–104.

Spanos, William V. *Repetitions: The Postmodern Occasion in Literature and Culture*. Baton Rouge: Louisiana State University Press, 1987.

Spoo, Robert. *James Joyce and the Language of History: Dedalus's Nightmare*. New York: Oxford University Press, 1994.

Stevens, Wallace. *The Collected Poems*. New York: Vintage-Random House, 1954.

Stowe, William W. "From Semiotics to Hermeneutics: Modes of Detection in Doyle and Chandler." In *The Poetics of Murder: Detective Fiction and Literary Theory*, edited by Glenn W. Most and William W. Stowe, 367–83. San Diego: Harcourt Brace Jovanovich, 1983.

Sultan, Stanley. *"Ulysses," "The Waste Land," and Modernism: A Jubilee Study*. Port Washington, N.Y.: Kennikat Press, 1977.

Sussman, Henry. *Afterimages of Modernity: Structure and Indifference in Twentieth-Century Literature*. Baltimore and London: Johns Hopkins University Press, 1990.

Swift, Jonathan. *A Tale of a Tub with Other Early Works, 1696–1707*. Edited by Herbert Davis. Oxford: Blackwell, 1965.

Symons, Arthur. *The Symbolist Movement in Literature*. 1899. 2d ed. New York: E. P. Dutton, 1908.

Tani, Stefano. *The Doomed Detective: The Contribution of the Detective Novel to Postmodern American and Italian Fiction*. Carbondale: Southern Illinois University Press, 1984.

Taylor, Lou. *Mourning Dress: A Costume and Social History*. London: George Allen and Unwin, 1983.

Tindall, William York. *A Reader's Guide to "Finnegans Wake."* London: Thames and Hudson, 1969.

Tindall, William York. *A Reader's Guide to James Joyce*. New York: Farrar, Straus & Giroux, 1959.

Tindall, William York. *Samuel Beckett*. New York: Columbia University Press, 1964.

Tompkins, Jane P., ed. *Reader-Response Criticism: From Formalism to Post-Structuralism*. Baltimore and London: Johns Hopkins University Press, 1980.

Torchiana, Donald T. *Backgrounds for Joyce's "Dubliners."* Boston: Allen & Unwin, 1986.

Ulmer, Gregory. "The Puncept in Grammatology." In *On Puns: The Foundation of Letters*, edited by Jonathan Culler, 164–89. Oxford: Blackwell, 1988.

Verlaine, Paul. *Les poètes maudits: Tristan Corbière, Arthur Rimbaud, Stéphane Mallarmé*. 1884. Paris: H. Champion, 1979.

Wallace, M. G. Letter to the Editor. *Irish Homestead*, 9 January 1904, 33.

Walzl, Florence L. "*Dubliners*." In *A Companion to Joyce Studies*, edited by Zack Bowen and James F. Carens, 157–228. Westport, Conn.: Greenwood Press, 1984.

Watt, Stephen. *Joyce, O'Casey, and the Irish Popular Theater.* Syracuse: Syracuse University Press, 1991.

White, Hayden. *Tropics of Discourse: Essays in Cultural Criticism.* Baltimore and London: Johns Hopkins University Press, 1978.

Whitman, Walt. "Song of Myself." In *Walt Whitman: The Complete Poems,* edited by Francis Murphy, 63–124. New York: Penguin, 1975.

Whorf, Benjamin Lee. *Language, Thought, and Reality: Selected Writings of Benjamin Lee Whorf.* Edited and introduced by John B. Carroll. Foreword by Stuart Chase. Cambridge: M.I.T. Press, 1956.

Wicke, Jennifer. *Advertising Fictions: Literature, Advertising, and Social Reading.* New York: Columbia University Press, 1988.

Williams, Keith. *The English Newspaper: An Illustrated History to 1900.* London: Springwood Books, 1977.

Winters, Yvor. *In Defense of Reason.* New York: W. Morrow & Co., 1947.

Wiseman, Mary Bittner. *The Ecstasies of Roland Barthes.* Critics of the Twentieth Century Series. London: Routledge, 1989.

Woolf, Virginia. *The Diary of Virginia Woolf.* Edited by Anne Olivier Bell, assisted by Andrew McNeillie. 5 vols. San Diego: Harcourt Brace Jovanovich, 1977–84.

Woolf, Virginia. *To the Lighthouse.* New York: Harcourt, Brace, World, 1955.

Yeats, William Butler. *W. B. Yeats: The Poems.* Edited by Richard J. Finneran. New York: Macmillan, 1983.

Index